FRENCH GRAMMAR

Second Edition

FRENCH GRAMMAR

A Complete Reference Guide

DANIEL J. CALVEZ

McGraw-Hill

New York Chicago San Francisco Lisbon London Madrid Mexico City
Milan New Delhi San Juan Seoul Singapore Sydney Toronto

The McGraw·Hill Companies

1 2 3 4 5 6 7 8 9 0 VLP/VLP 3 2 1 0 9 8 7 6 5 4

ISBN 0-07-144498-X

McGraw-Hill books are available at special quantity discounts to use as premiums and sales promotions, or for use in corporate training programs. For more information, please write to the Director of Special Sales, Professional Publishing, McGraw-Hill, Two Penn Plaza, New York, NY 10121-2298. Or contact your local bookstore.

This book is printed on acid-free paper.

Preface

Designed for use by students of French at all levels, including self-learners, *French Grammar: A Complete Reference Guide* contains all of the structures presented in beginning books, along with additional details, exceptions, tables, and helpful lists. Written to meet the practical needs of all learners, *French Grammar* serves as an essential guide to writing and speaking correct French.

In this book, grammatical terminology is clearly defined. In this way, no one should be in doubt as to what, for example, a relative pronoun or a reflexive verb might be.

Grammar points are concisely, but fully explained. The agreement of adjectives and the uses of tenses, articles, and pronouns—to mention only a few of the topics covered—are treated in more detail than would be necessary in an English grammar book, where certain points are taken for granted. For example, the French verb system may seem overwhelming to some English-speaking learners: confusion may arise from the abundance of persons, tenses, moods, irregular verbs, and so forth. This text simplifies the presentation of verbs by organizing stems and endings into a practical, easy-to-use system, rather than by simply providing a list of the tenses of all irregular verbs.

French Grammar is divided into units dealing with specific grammatical structures: nouns, verbs, adjectives, pronouns, and so on. Units present specific forms and tables that conveniently summarize topics, such as the prepositions required in infinitive constructions (§§ 278C), prepositions used with place names (§§ 170), conjunctions requiring the subjunctive (§§ 174), conjunctions requiring the indicative (§§ 179), adverbs ending in ***-ment*** (§§ 196), negative expressions (§§ 203), adverbs of time (§§ 224), adverbs of place (§§ 237), irregular verbs (§§ 258), and many more (see Lists and Tables in the Index).

Readers will notice that some section headings are in English and others in French. This occurs because certain structures common in one language may not exist in the other. Moreover, certain terms commonly used by language specialists are not familiar to most learners. The section headings are thus designed to make this book easy to use and result directly from teaching experience and the desire to help students answer their questions.

Units are not arranged sequentially by difficulty since this book is not written as a course textbook, but rather as a grammar reference for quick, convenient learning. As such, its usefulness is not limited to a course, but extends to years of French study both in and outside the classroom.

The exercises provide basic practice in the handling of grammatical difficulties. With the models provided, they will also serve as expanded examples for every facet of the grammar spectrum presented in the book.

With its comparative approach and emphasis on the differences between French and English, *French Grammar* is the key to overcoming learners' misunderstandings and difficulties with the French language.

Contents

FRENCH GRAMMAR

ARTICLES

1. French articles.

The French articles are as follows:

	definite	indefinite	partitive
masculine singular	le (l')	un	du (de l')
feminine singular	la (l')	une	de la (de l')
masc. and fem. plural	les	des	des

Contractions: when the prepositions ***de*** or ***à*** precede the articles ***le*** or ***les***, contractions must be made in the following manner:

de le	→	du
de les	→	des
à le	→	au
à les	→	aux

Nous parlons du concert des Beatles.
We are talking about the concert of the Beatles.
Ils pensent aux grandes vacances. Nous allons au restaurant.
They are thinking about summer vacation. We are going to a restaurant.

No contraction is made with ***la*** or ***l'***, nor when ***le*** or ***les*** is a personal pronoun.

La vie de l'homme. La fin de la guerre.
Man's life. The end of the war.
Essayez de les arrêter. Nous venons de le rencontrer.
Try to stop them. We have just run into him.

2. Definite articles (use).

The definite article must be used before a noun in the following cases:

A. In a general sense, or to indicate that one wants to consider a whole category, species, group, etc., particularly if the preceding verb is ***aimer, préférer, détester, adorer,*** or one that expresses appreciation.

J'aime le pain de seigle.
I like rye bread.

Les hommes sont mortels.
Men are mortal.

Il déteste le foie de veau.
He hates calves' liver.

Les vieux adorent souvent les animaux.
Old people often love animals.

B. With names of languages, school subjects, sports, the elements in chemistry, all things unique in nature (singular) or designating a category, a group, a species.

J'apprends le français, la chimie et les maths (ma matière principale).
I am learning French, chemistry and math (my main subject).

Le mercure, le charbon, l'eau, l'air.
Mercury, coal, water, air.

La lune, le soleil, les étoiles, les arbres, les animaux, les invertébrés.
The moon, the sun, the stars, trees, animals, invertebrates.

C. With names of countries, states, provinces, continents, oceans, mountains, plains, rivers, etc., but not with names of cities, unless the article is an integral part of the name.

La France, l'Europe, la Californie, la Normandie, l'Atlantique, le Danube, les Alpes, le Sahara, Le Havre, La Nouvelle-Orléans.
France, Europe, California, Normandy, the Atlantic ocean, the Danube, the Alps, the Sahara, Le Havre, New Orleans.

D. With abstract nouns used in a general sense.

La blancheur, la charité, la peur, l'orgueil, l'ordre, le courage, l'imagination, l'intuition.
Whiteness, charity, fear, pride, order, courage, imagination, intuition.

E. With a name preceded by a title, with a title alone, and if the title follows ***monsieur*** or ***madame*** (except when the person is being addressed directly), and when an article is an integral part of the name.

Bonjour docteur Dupont, avez-vous vu le docteur Dubois ou le professeur Le Hir?
Good morning, Dr. Dupont, have you seen Dr. Dubois or professor Le Hir?

Monsieur le directeur. Messieurs les jurés.
Mister director. Gentlemen of the jury.

Le roi a écouté les comtes, les ducs et les princes.
The king listened to the counts, dukes, and princes.

Monsieur, madame, mademoiselle, and M^e (Maître, a lawyer's title) never have an article when they are followed by a family name. Their abbreviated forms ***M.***, ***Mme, Mlle,*** and ***M^e*** are used in narratives, whereas the full forms are used in dialogues, as well as in mailing addresses.

M. Chartier s'est rendu chez Me Renoir.
Mr. Chartier went to Mr. Renoir's (office). (narrative)

Mais voilà monsieur Chartier, avec mademoiselle Dubois!
Look, there goes Mr. Chartier, with Miss Dubois! (dialogue)

Bonjour, monsieur. Merci, madame. Au revoir, Maître.
Good morning, sir. Thank you, ma'am. Good bye, sir (to an attorney, for example).

but: Pierrot, regarde le monsieur!
Peter, look at the gentleman!

F. With a quantity, or an item to be purchased, to indicate "price per."

15 francs la livre. 30 francs le kilo. 6 francs la douzaine.
15 francs a pound. 30 francs a kilo. 6 francs a dozen.

5 francs les dix. 50 francs la place, l'entrée, le billet.
5 francs for ten. 50 francs a seat, to enter, a ticket.

753 francs l'aller (simple); l'aller et retour.
753 francs one way; for a return ticket.

G. In the expressions . . . (miles, km, etc.) per hour, . . . (dollars, francs, etc.) an hour.

Ils roulent souvent à 80 miles à l'heure.
They often drive at 80 miles an hour.

Il ne gagne que 4 dollars de l'heure.
He only makes 4 dollars an hour.

H. With parts of the body and articles of clothing instead of a regular possessive adjective (§§55, 56) Possession must be clear from the beginning of the sentence (as with reflexive verbs, or when object personal pronouns are present), and the situation described must be of an ordinary nature.

Je me lave les mains. Vous lui lavez les mains.
I wash my hands. You wash his (her) hands.

Il se tenait debout, les mains dans les poches, le chapeau sur la tête.
There he stood, his hands in his pockets, his hat on his head.

Elle a les yeux bleus et les cheveux blonds, mais ses sourcils sont noirs.
She has blue eyes and blond hair, but her eyebrows are black.

If the situation described is not of an ordinary nature, or if the part of the body or article of clothing in the sentence or in the clause is the subject of the verb, a possessive should be used.

Son nez était très long.
Her (his) nose was very long.

L'acrobate a mis ses jambes autour de son cou.
The acrobat placed his legs around his neck.

I. With days of the week, parts of the day, and time expressions in general, to indicate "every," or to convey an idea of repeated, regular, or habitual occurrence. Note that the English prepositions are not expressed in French; the definite article is sufficient to convey their meaning.

Le matin nous lisons, l'après-midi nous faisons du ski, le soir nous dansons, et la nuit nous dormons.
In the morning we read, in the afternoon we ski, in the evening we dance, and at night we sleep.

Autrefois, les écoliers avaient congé le jeudi (les jeudis).
Formerly, school children had the day off on Thursdays.

Les soirs d'hiver, nous faisions des veillées.
On winter evenings, we had late gatherings by the fire.

L'été, nous allons à la mer.
In the summer, we go to the beach.

J. With superlatives. (The article may be replaced by a possessive adjective.)

Le plus grand bâtiment du monde. Mon meilleur ami.
The largest building in the world. My best friend.

La catastrophe la plus effroyable du siècle.
The most frightful catastrophe of the century.

K. With dates.

Le 29 septembre 1987. Le jeudi 12 mars. Mardi, le 30 avril. (Comma: the date is an afterthought.)
September 29, 1987. Thursday March 12. Tuesday April 30.

Nous arriverons le premier mai.
We'll arrive on May first.

L. With infinitives and adjectives used as nouns. See §8C.

Le rire est le propre de l'homme.
Laughter is proper to man alone.

Le boire, le manger, le dîner, le souper . . .
Drinking, eating, dinner, supper . . .

L'essentiel est que . . .
The essential thing is that . . .

Le comique de l'histoire . . .
The comic thing (aspect, factor) of the story . . .

3. Definite articles (do not use).

The definite article should not be used in the following cases:

A. With a title, alone or followed by a family name, in direct address.

Bonjour, docteur Richard. Merci, docteur.
Good morning, Dr. Richard. Thank you, doctor.

Comment allez-vous, madame Dumas? Et vous, mademoiselle?
How are you, Mrs. Dumas? And you, Miss?

NOTE: ***Monsieur, madame, mademoiselle, docteur***, etc., are frequently used without a family name. It is also common to combine two titles (the second with a definite article) as in ***monsieur le curé, monsieur le maire, madame la présidente, monsieur le ministre***, etc.

B. With days of the week to indicate "next" or "last". The adjectives ***prochain*** (*next*) and ***dernier*** (*last*) may be added for clarity, but are unnecessary.

Les examens commenceront samedi (prochain).
Exams will begin (this, next) Saturday.

Nous avons vu Paul jeudi (dernier).
We saw Paul last Thursday.

C. With unmodified names of cities, unless the name contains an article.

Je travaille à Paris, mais j'habite au Mans.
I work in Paris but I live in Le Mans.

Nous revenons de San Francisco, et nous sommes passés par La Nouvelle-Orléans.
We are back from San Francisco, and we passed (flew, drove, etc.) through New Orleans.

but: J'irai visiter la vieille Rome, la Rome des gladiateurs.
I'll visit the ancient Rome, the Rome of the gladiators.

D. After the preposition ***en*** except in the following expressions:

en l'air	in the air, up there
en l'absence de	in the absence of . . .
en l'an	in the year . . .
en l'honneur de	in honor of . . .

Il est en France. Il voyage en auto. Il est en vacances. En présence du juge.
He is in France. He travels by car. He is on vacation. In the presence of the judge.

E. After ***avec*** (and abstract noun) and after ***sans*** (and abstract or concrete noun).

Une soupe sans sel. Du café sans sucre mais avec du lait.
A soup without salt. Coffee without sugar but with cream.

Il est sorti sans manteau.
He went out without a coat on.

Il a agi avec sagesse mais sans imagination.
He acted wisely but without imagination.

Certains vont à leurs cours sans encre ni papier.
Some go to their classes without paper or pen (lit.: without ink or paper).

Voulez-vous votre bouquet avec ou sans ruban?
Will you have your bouquet with or without a ribbon?

F. After the preposition ***de*** in the following cases:

1) When ***de*** means *from*, before the name of a city or a country whose name is feminine, unless an article is part of the name.

Je reviens de New York. Je reviens de France.
I am returning from New York. I am returning from France.

De La Rochelle au Havre il y a bien 400 km.
From La Rochelle to Le Havre it's a good 400 km.

2) When ***de*** precedes the direct object of an absolute negation (compare §4 and see §5B)

Ils n'ont pas de pain. Ils n'ont que des gâteaux.
They don't have any bread. All they have is pastries.

Il n'y a plus de morale!
Morality no longer exists!

Les jeunes ne boivent jamais d'alcool.
Young people never drink any alcohol.

but: Ce ne sont pas des mûres, ce sont des framboises.
These are not blackberries, they are raspberries. (***être*** cannot have a direct object)

but: Je ne regarde pas des diapositives, je regarde des photos.
I am not looking at slides, I am looking at prints. (The negation is not absolute; I am looking at something.)

3) When ***de*** is part of an expression of quantity (except with ***bien*** : *a lot of*, and ***la plupart*** : *most*).

Beaucoup de pommes. Peu d'argent. Trop de loisirs.
Lots of apples. Little money. Too much free time.

Nous avons assez de temps pour faire un peu de travail.
We have enough time to do a little work.

Bien des gens voudraient vivre heureux.
Many people would like to live happy lives.

La plupart du temps il ne fait rien.
Most of the time he does nothing.

4) When ***de*** is a preposition required by the preceding verb or verbal expression, and the object of the preposition is presented in an undetermined sense.

Nous parlons de politique et de gastronomie.
We are talking of politics and gastronomy.

J'ai besoin de repos. J'ai envie de musique et de coca.
I need rest. I feel like (. . .) music and Coke.

Nous manquons de vin et nous nous contentons d'eau.
We are out of wine and we have to be satisfied with water.

but: J'ai besoin du livre que je t'avais prêté.
I need the book that I had lent you.

5) When ***de*** is an adjectival (modifying a noun) or adverbial (modifying a verb, an adjective) phrase.

Une classe de français. Elle pleure de joie.
A French class. She is crying for joy.

Coupable de meurtre. Entouré d'eau. Bordé d'arbres.
Guilty of murder. Surrounded by water. Lined with trees.

G. After ***à*** followed by an undetermined name of city.

Je vais à Paris. Nous habitons à New York.
I am going to Paris. We live in New York.
but: Nous allons au Paris des artistes.
We are going to the Paris of the artists.

H. In the following ***à*** and ***avoir*** idiomatic expressions:

à bicyclette	on bicycle
à bonne fin (mener)	(to bring) to a successful end
à bras ouverts	with open arms
à bras raccourcis	with might and main
à cheval	on horseback
à coup sûr	for certain
à dos de . . .	on . . . back (animal other than horse)
à fond	in depth, completely
à genoux	on (one's) knees
à merveille	marvelously
à mort	to death
à peine	hardly
à perpétuité (condamnation)	forever (punishment)
à pied	on foot
à rebours	the wrong way (manner)
à reculons	backwards
à table	at, to the table
à tâtons	groping, feeling one's way
à temps	in time
à terre	on the ground
à tort	wrongly
à tort et à travers	at random, erratically
à tort ou à raison	rightly or wrongly
à toute vitesse	at full speed
à vie (condamnation)	for life (punishment)
à volonté	at will
goutte à goutte	drop by drop
pas à pas	step by step, slowly

Only people or animals can be used as subject of ***avoir*** in the following expressions:

avoir beau (and infinitive)	to . . . in vain; to strive to . . . as (he) might, . . .
avoir besoin de	to need
avoir bon goût	to have good taste
avoir bonne mémoire	to remember well, rightly
avoir chaud	to be warm
avoir conscience	to be conscious, aware
avoir confiance en	to trust, have confidence in

avoir envie de	to feel like (having something)
avoir faim	to be hungry
avoir foi en	to have faith in
avoir froid	to be cold
avoir hâte de	to be in a hurry to
avoir honte de	to be ashamed to, of
avoir horreur de	to hate, loathe
avoir mal à	to have a . . . ache, sore . . .
en avoir marre de . . . (pop.)	to be tired of, fed up with . . .
avoir peur de	to be afraid, scared to
avoir pitié de	to pity, feel for
avoir raison de	to be right, wise, correct (in...)
en avoir ras le bol de . . . (pop.)	to be fed up with . . .
avoir soif	to be thirsty
avoir sommeil	to be sleepy
avoir soin de	to be careful to, take care of
avoir souvenance de	to remember
avoir tendance à	to be prone to, inclined to
avoir tort (de)	to be wrong, ill-advised
but:	
avoir un faible pour	to have a soft (weak) spot for

The noun contained in the preceding expressions may be modified, in which case a determiner (article or other) may be used. Compare the following examples:

J'ai envie de partir. J'ai une envie irrésistible de m'en aller.
I feel like leaving. I have an irresistible urge to leave.

Elle a peur. Elle a une peur bleue.
She is scared. She has a "terrible" fear.

The expression may also be modified with certain adverbs—see §§204 and 212.

4. *Indefinite articles (use).*

Use the indefinite article generally as in English. Use the indefinite article also before a predicate noun if the French expression ***c'est (ce sont)*** precedes. This is valid even if in English the predicate is an adjective (see §286).

C'est un Français. Ce sont des Français.
He is French. They are French.

C'est un musulman. C'est une socialiste.
He is a Moslem. She is a socialist.

C'est une pharmacienne. Ce sont des étudiants.
She is a pharmacist. They are students.

but: Il est étudiant. Elle est démocrate. Ils sont baptistes.
He is a student. She is a democrat. They are Baptist.

An indefinite article should also be used before the direct object of a negative verb if the negation is not absolute, in other words if the sentence deals with *types* or *categories* instead of mere *existence* (compare §3F2), or if the negative expression is *ne . . . que*.

Tu as une voiture, toi, mais moi, je n'ai qu'une bicyclette.
You have a car, but *I* have a bicycle only.

Je ne regarde pas un film, je regarde une émission de sport.
I am not watching a movie, I'm watching a sports program. (A program is being watched. The negation is not absolute.)

NOTE: The best way to make this kind of statement is by using the emphatic phrase ***c'est (ce sont)*** or its negative form ***ce n'est pas (ce ne sont pas)***, in any appropriate tense.

Ce n'est pas un film que je regarde, c'est une émission de sport.
I am not watching a movie, I am watching a sports program.

5. *Indefinite articles (do not use).*

The indefinite article should not be used in the following cases:

A. With predicate nouns and adjectives used to indicate profession, nationality, religion, political affiliation, title. (***c'est*** as mentioned in §4 above cannot be used in this case.)

Il est médecin. Elle est italienne. Ils sont catholiques.
He is a doctor. She is Italian. They are Catholic.

Elle est professeur. Elles sont socialistes.
She is a professor. They are socialist.

B. In negative sentences, if the negation is absolute (compare with §4 above and see §3F2 and §3F4). The indefinite article should then be replaced by ***de*** or ***d'*** before the direct object of the negative verb. Note that in the case of a verb requiring ***de***, nothing else has to be added.

J'ai une voiture. Je n'ai pas de voiture. Je n'ai qu'une vieille voiture.
I have a car. I don't have a car. I have only an old car.

Je parle de monuments historiques. Je ne parle pas de frivolités.
I am talking about historical monuments. I am not talking about frivolities.

Nous avons besoin d'aide. Nous n'avons pas besoin de critique.
We need (some) help. We don't need (any) criticism.

Elle a envie de langoustines. Elle n'a pas envie d'huîtres.
She feels like having shrimp. She doesn't feel like having oysters.

NOTE: ***C'est*** cannot have a direct object; therefore its negative form ***ce n'est pas*** must be followed by a full article (see note in §4 above).

Ce n'est pas de l'eau, c'est de la limonade.
This is not water, it is Sprite (or 7Up).

Ce n'est pas une Cadillac, c'est une Ferrari.
It is not a Cadillac, it is a Ferrari.

C. With nouns in apposition.

Louis XIV, roi de France, a fait bâtir Versailles.
Louis XIV, king of France, had Versailles built.

Son père, célèbre psychiatre, lui avait dit . . .
His father, a famous psychiatrist, had said to him . . .

Elle le regardait fixement, chose qu'il détestait.
She stared at him, a thing that he hated.

NOTE: An article—generally a definite article—may be used with a noun in apposition when the information provided is offered as a reminder of what everyone is supposed to know but might have forgotten.

Voltaire, le célèbre philosophe du dix-huitième siècle, vivait près de la Suisse.
Voltaire, the famous eighteenth century philosopher, lived near Switzerland.

6. Partitive articles (use).

The partitive article should be used in the following cases:

A. To translate *some* or *any* with singular or plural nouns, whenever none of the exceptions given in §7 below exists.

Je veux du pain. Je veux aussi des pommes.
I want (some) bread. I also want (some) apples.

Voulez-vous du lait? Prendrez-vous du sucre?
Do you want some milk? Will you take some sugar?

Avez-vous des questions?
Do you have any questions?

Est-ce qu'il a des parents dans cette ville?
Does he have any relatives in this city?

B. To determine a noun in French, when the meaning sought is indefinite or partitive. This excludes sentences in which the noun is a direct object of a verb of liking or disliking such as ***aimer, adorer, préférer, détester,***, or in which the noun is viewed in a general sense. It includes, however, sentences in which the noun is the direct object of a verb like ***avoir, manger, boire, vouloir, prendre***, etc.

J'ai de l'argent. Avez-vous de la monnaie? Montrez du courage et de l'imagination. Vous aurez de la chance.
I have (some) money. Have you got (any) change? Show courage and imagination. You will have luck.

Je veux du chocolat. Je vais prendre du vin blanc.
I want (some) chocolate. I'll have (some) white wine.

but: J'aime l'argent! Je hais la pauvreté! Je préfère l'ordre au désordre.
I love money! I hate poverty! I prefer order to disorder.

7. *Partitive articles (do not use).*

All forms of the partitive article must be reduced to ***de (d')*** alone in the following cases:

A. Before the direct object of a negative verb if the negation is absolute, which excludes ***ne . . . que*** (see also §5B).

Elle ne veut pas d'enfants. Il n'a pas d'imagination.
She does not want (any) children. He has no imagination.

Nous n'avons pas de billets pour le match. Nous n'avons pas de chance.
We don't have (any) tickets for the game. We do not have any luck.

but: Nous n'avons que des ennuis, que de la malchance!
We only have misfortunes! All we have is bad luck!

NOTE: An infinitive construction in the negative follows the same rule, even though the infinitive itself is not constructed negatively:

Je ne vais pas manger de viande ni boire d'alcool ce soir.
I won't eat meat nor drink alcohol tonight.

B. Before an adjective preceding a plural noun.

J'ai de beaux livres et de magnifiques aquarelles.
I have beautiful books and magnificent watercolors.

NOTE: If the adjective and the noun are so closely associated that they cannot be separated without causing a change in the meaning of the group, the group is treated as a simple noun and the rule does not apply.

Des jeunes filles.
Girls (an age group beyond childhood and before adulthood).

Des petits pois.
English peas.

C. After an expression of quantity, or a verb or verb phrase always constructed with ***de***.

J'ai acheté beaucoup de cadeaux et il me reste peu d'argent.
I bought lots of presents and I have little money left.

J'ai besoin d'aide. J'ai envie de caramels mous.
I need help. I feel like having soft caramels.

Ils se sont contentés de fruits.
They were satisfied with fruit.

Une poignée de dollars. Une quinzaine de jours.
A fistful of dollars. About two weeks.

Des milliers de personnes.
Thousands of people.

but: Dix ans. Vingt personnes. Cent dollars.
Ten years. Twenty people. One hundred dollars.

NOTE: Some expressions of quantity are exceptions. ***Plusieurs*** (*several*) and ***quelques*** (*some, a few*) immediately precede the nouns they determine. ***La plupart*** (*most, the majority*) and ***bien*** (*lots*) both require *de* and a *definite article*.

Plusieurs livres. Quelques dollars de plus.
Several books. A few dollars more.

La plupart des Américains ont deux voitures.
Most Americans have two cars.

Bien des jeunes se croient très malins.
Lots of youngsters think they are very smart.

NOUNS

8. Nouns and gender.

Nouns, also called substantives, are either masculine or feminine. Masculine is the gender of male beings, feminine that of female beings. There is no neuter in French.

A. Nouns representing animals generally designate the species or the category rather than the sex of the animal. Some categories are represented by a masculine noun, others by a feminine one.

Mon chien s'appelle Médor. Il est beau, n'est-ce pas?
My dog's name is Fido. He (she) is beautiful, isn't he (she)?

Ton chat. Une souris. Un canard. Une mouche. Un mouton. Une grenouille.
Your cat. A mouse. A duck. A fly. A sheep. A frog.

As in English, the sex of animals is frequently indicated by quite different male and female names, and offspring by other names (in the masculine) not identifying sex.

CATEGORY	MALE	FEMALE	OFFSPRING
chat cat	**matou** tomcat	**chatte** cat	**chaton, petit chat** kitten
chien dog	**chien** dog	**chienne** bitch	**chiot, petit chien** puppy
vache cow	**taureau** bull	**vache, génisse** cow, heifer	**veau** calf
cheval horse	**étalon** stallion	**jument, pouliche** mare, young mare	**poulain** foal
mouton sheep	**bélier** ram	**brebis** ewe	**agneau** lamb
cochon, porc pig, swine, hog	**verrat** boar	**truie** sow	**petit cochon, porcelet** piglet
poule, poulet chicken	**coq** rooster	**poule** hen	**poussin** chick
canard duck	**canard** duck	**cane** duck	**caneton** duckling
oie goose	**jars** gander	**oie** goose	**oison** gosling
dinde turkey	**dindon** tom turkey	**dinde** hen turkey	**dindonneau** poult

There are broader names that include several categories of animals:

Le bétail. La volaille. (Les animaux de) la basse-cour.
Cattle. Poultry. (All the animals raised in the farmyard.)

As a rule, these collective nouns must still be considered grammatically singular and thus command singular verb endings. On the other hand, English collective names of animals such as sheep, deer, fish, etc., which are grammatically singular but yet command plural verb forms, have corresponding French names that can be singular or plural in form as needed. See also §10.

Les poissons sautent. Quatorze moutons. Deux chevreuils.
Fish are jumping. Fourteen sheep. Two deer.

B. Nouns representing things also are either masculine or feminine. The only way to determine their gender is by memorization, or by observation of their ending when these are frequently used suffixes. As an extremely general rule, the mute E ending indicates feminine. The consonants and the vowels A, I, O, U as endings indicate masculine. However, the number of exceptions is such that it is necessary either to observe more than a single letter ending, or to recognize a suffix (see §9).

C. Many nouns representing concepts, abstractions, or generalizations are actually adjectives, infinitives, participles, or adverbs that were turned into nouns by simple addition of an article in front of them. All these words used substantively are masculine.

le boire	drinking	**le manger**	eating
le rire	laughter	**le coucher**	going to bed
le lever	getting up	**le toucher**	touch
le savoir	knowledge	**le devoir**	duty
le beau	beauty, what's beautiful	**le bon**	what is good
l'essentiel	what is essential	**le mauvais**	what is
le bien	the good (moral)	**le mal**	evil, what's bad, wrong
le doux	what is soft, sweet	**l'amer**	what is bitter
le sucré	what is sweet	**le possible**	what is possible
le comique	what is comical	**le sérieux**	what is serious
le tragique	what is tragic	**le dramatique**	what is dramatic
le pathétique	pathos	**le déjà vu**	what has been seen before
le passé	the past	**l'avenir**	what's to come, the future
le faux	what is false, wrong	**le vrai**	what is true
le réel	what is real	**l'irréel**	what is unreal

Several of these nouns may be accompanied by an idea of degree or quantity, thus allowing the use of such expressions as ***beaucoup de, peu de, trop de***, etc., and the use of a partitive article as a determiner. In such contexts, these abstract words take on a concrete meaning, with the sense of "measurable amount, certain quantity, discernable element of," etc.

Il y a du vrai dans ce qu'elle dit.
There is some truth in what she is saying.

Il y a du bon et du mauvais dans ce rapport.
There is some good and some bad in this report.

NOTE: Some substantives of this type may have a masculine form and a feminine form:

Le pratique.
What is practical, the practical aspect.

La pratique.
Practice, hands-on experience.

D. Adjectives and participles may also be used substantively to designate persons or things with the given characteristics. The gender and number are then determined by that of the person or thing in question. Adjectives of nationality used substantively must begin with a capital letter.

Un ancien combattant. Une rescapée. Des figurants. Des pauvres.
A veteran. A rescued woman. Some extras. Some poor people.

Un vieux. Une vieille. Les vieux. Un Américain. Une Mexicaine. Des Japonaises.
An old man. An old woman. Old folks. An American man. A Mexican woman. Some Japanese women.

Un fiancé. Une fiancée. Les nouveaux-mariés. Une blessée.
An engaged man. An engaged woman. The newlyweds. An injured woman.

9. Endings and suffixes.

The following is a short list of the endings and suffixes that are generally masculine (on the left) or feminine (on the right), with some of the common exceptions. Memorization, practice, and a good dictionary are essential on the subject of gender.

MASCULINE

-asme
-age except: ***image*** image; ***page*** page(of book); ***rage*** rabies, rage
-ème except ***crème***
-ement
-eur except abstract nouns
-gramme
-graphe
-isme
-logue
-mètre
-oir
-pode
-scaphe
-scope

FEMININE

-ade except ***jade***
-ance
-ée except:
athée atheist
lycée French H.S.
mausolée mausoleum
pygmée pygmy
scarabée beetle
trophée trophy
-ence
-eur except concrete nouns and persons
-euse
-ise
-lle except
vermicelle vermicelli
polichinelle (see dict.)
-nne
-ose

-té except abstract nouns	**-sse**	
	-tte	
	-trice	
	-tion except ***bastion***	
	-son (after vowel) except:	
	bison	buffalo
	blason	coat of arms
	blouson	jacket
	diapason	tuning fork
	poison	poison
	tison	fire brand
	vison	mink
	-sion	
	-té except concrete nouns	
	-ude	
	-tié	
	-ure except:	
	augure	augur, omen
	mercure	mercury
	murmure	murmur, whisper
	all chemistry terms in **-ure**	
	-oire except:	
	accessoire	accessory
	auditoire	audience
	interrogatoire	questioning
	ivoire	ivory
	laboratoire	laboratory
	mémoire	research paper
	observatoire	observatory
	promontoire	promontory
	réfectoire	dining hall
	répertoire	repertory
	territoire	territory

This listing is neither exhaustive nor absolute. It is essential, however, that the gender of all nouns be ascertained, since correct French grammar requires agreement of adjectives, pronouns, participles, determiners, etc., with the noun.

10. Number.

A noun (or pronoun) must be either singular or plural. The plural is generally marked by adding an **s** to the singular form. However, if the singular form of the noun ends in **s**, **x**, or **z**, nothing is added for the plural.

French family names do not add **s** in the plural.

Les Dupont. Les Bonard. Les Jones.
The Duponts. The Bonards. The Joneses.

A. Some nouns exist only in the singular. Many are the same in English and represent concepts and abstractions (see list in §8B). Others are singular in one language and plural in the other. Among these are the following:

ENGLISH	NORMAL MEANING	SPECIAL MEANING
advice	**des conseils**	**un conseil** (one piece of advice)
business	**les affaires**	**une affaire** (one deal, a bargain)
ethics		**la morale, l'éthique** (code)
fish	**des poissons** (several) **du poisson** (to eat)	**un poisson**
fruit	**des fruits**	**un fruit**
furniture	**des meubles** **le mobilier** (collective: "movable" property)	**un meuble** (a piece of furniture)
hair	**des cheveux** **des poils**	**un cheveu** (one strand) **un poil** (other than on human head) le poil (animal's coat)
hundred	(see §48)	
manners	**les mœurs** (habits)	**la conduite** (behavior)
mathematics	**les mathématiques**	
morals	**les mœurs** (habits)	**la morale** (code)
news	**des nouvelles** **les informations** (TV or radio newscast)	**une nouvelle** (one news item)
pair	**2, 3 , etc., paires de**	**une paire de**
people	**des gens** (general) **des personnes**	(no singular) **une personne** **du monde** (: "company"; "a crowd")
peoples	**des peuples**	**un peuple** (nation, ethnic group)
physics		**la physique**
politics		**la politique**
progress	**des progrès**	**un progrès** (one instance of progression) **du progrès** ("some" advance) **le progrès** (the concept, in general terms)
statistics	**des statistiques** (data)	**la statistique** (the science)
thousand	(see §48)	

B. Collective words are singular words representing groups or categories. They normally command singular agreement in French: agreement of the verb, of the adjective, of the pronoun, etc. Note that a given collective singular word may be replaced by a plural expression when the idea of individuality must take precedence over the collective idea.

COLLECTIVE WORD ENGLISH	COLLECTIVE WORD FRENCH	INDIVIDUAL EXPRESSION: MEMBER OF . . . (PLURAL (REPLACES COLLECTIVE WORD)
the Administration	**le Cabinet**	**ministre, secrétaire**
the Air Force	**l'armée de l'air**	**un soldat, un officier,** **un appelé** (draftee)

the Army	**l'armée** (f.)	**un soldat, un officier, un appelé** (draftee), **un militaire**
the Assembly	**l'Assemblée** (f.)	**membre de l'Assemblée**
clergy	**le clergé**	**membre du clergé**
Congress	**le Congrès**	**un membre du Congrès**
couple	**ménage** (m.) **couple** (m.) **foyer** (m.)	**le mari, l'homme, le conjoint, la femme, la conjointe l'époux, l'épouse**
crew	**équipage** (m.)	**membre de l'équipage**
faculty	**faculté** (f.)	**membre de la faculté, professeur**
family	**famille** (f.)	**membre de la famille, parent,** etc.
government	**le gouvernement** (m.)	**membre du gouvernement, ministre, officiel, haut fonctionnaire,** etc.
	l'administration (the whole machine of government, down to desk clerks)	**un fonctionnaire, un employé de l'administration**
the House	**la Chambre**	**un député** (representative)
jury	**jury** (m.)	**un juré, un membre du jury**
the military	**l'armée**	**les militaires (un militaire** means "a soldier in uniform")
the Navy	**la marine**	**marin, officier, un appelé** (draftee)
the personnel	**le personnel**	**un employé, une employée**
police	**la police** (f.)	**policier, gendarme agent de police**
the Senate	**le Sénat**	**sénateur, membre du Sénat**
staff (plant workers)	**le personnel**	**un employé, une employée**
staff (household)	**le service le personnel**	**un domestique, un serviteur une servante, une bonne (à tout faire), une domestique**
team	**équipe** (f.)	**membre de l'équipe, co-équipier, joueur, participant**

La police est venue. Les agents ont arrêté le type.
The police came. The policemen arrested the guy.

NOTE: The practice of using a plural pronoun ("they") to recall a singular collective noun is an allowable rhetorical process (syllepse), but generally avoided in written French.

C. Some nouns are used only in the plural. Among them are:

alentours (m.)	surrounding area
annales (f.)	annals
archives (f.)	archives
armoiries (f.)	coat of arms
arrhes (f.)	down payment, deposit
assises (f.) **(cour d'—)**	criminal court
bestiaux (m.)	head(s) of cattle
décombres (m.)	ruins, debris
dépens (m.)	expense, (court) cost
échecs (m.)	chess

entrailles (f.)	entrails, womb
environs (m.)	surrounding area, neighborhood
fiançailles (f.)	engagement (to be married)
frais (m.)	cost, expenses
funérailles (f.)	funeral ceremony
mémoires (m. pl.)	memoirs
menottes (f.)	handcuffs
mœurs (f.)	morals, customs of a society
obsèques (f.)	funeral ceremony
pourparlers (m.)	talks (leading to treaty)
vivres (m.)	food, food reserves

D. Finally, some nouns exist with one meaning in the singular and another in the plural.

un ciseau (a chisel)	**des ciseaux** (scissors)
une lunette (spy glass)	**des lunettes** (glasses, spectacles

11. Irregular plurals.

Several nouns have irregular plurals. Among them are:

aïeul	**aïeux**	ancestors
bonhomme	**bonshommes**	guys, "buddies"
ciel	**cieux**	heavens
	ciels	skies
gentilhomme	**gentilshommes**	gentlemen
madame	**mesdames**	ladies
mademoiselle	**mesdemoiselles**	young ladies
monsieur	**messieurs**	gentlemen
œil	**yeux**	eyes

Bœuf, ***œuf*** and ***os*** form their plural regularly, but with a change in pronunciation: the vowels become closed vowels, and the final consonants are silenced.

Singular nouns with endings in **-al, -ail, -au, -eu** and **-ou**, form categories with irregular plural endings.

A. **-al** changes to **-aux**

Un cheval, des chevaux. Un général, des généraux. Un canal, des canaux. Un mal, des maux.
One horse, horses. A general, generals. A canal, canals. An evil, evils.

NOTE: The following are exceptions and simply add **s** for the plural:

aval	downstream; guarantee, endorsement
bal	dance, ball
cal	(a) callous
carnaval	carnival

chacal	jackal
festival	festival
pal	stake (for impalement)
récital	recital
régal	feast, treat, great meal

B. **-ail** merely adds **s** for the plural. The following seven nouns, however, change **-ail** to **-aux**:

bail	lease
corail	coral
émail	enamel
soupirail	vent hole
travail	work, job
vantail	leaf of folding door
vitrail	stained glass window

C. **-au** and **-eu** endings add **x** in the plural, except the following, which add **s**:

bleu	blue; blue work clothes; freshman, new recruit, rookie
pneu	tire
landau	baby carriage

D. **-ou** endings have a regular plural in **s**, except the following, which add **x**:

bijou	jewel
caillou	stone, rock
chou	cabbage
genou	knee
hibou	owl
joujou	toy (childish term)
pou	louse

12. Plural of compound nouns.

In compound nouns, only nouns and adjectives may take the mark of the plural.

Des grands-parents. Des cache-nez.
Grandparents. Scarves.

A noun preceded by a preposition within a compound noun generally remains invariable.

Des chefs-d'œuvre. Des hors-d'œuvre.
Masterpieces. Appetizers, hors-d'œuvres.

Meaning may determine the agreement of the parts in a compound noun:

Un essuie-mains.
A hand towel (for hands).

Des gratte-ciel.
Skyscrapers (only one sky).

NOTE: Despite the French spelling reform of 1991 and the optional spelling authorized by it for many compound nouns, a good dictionary remains essential on this subject.

ADJECTIVES

13. Gender and number.

An adjective must agree in gender and number with the noun or pronoun it refers to. The feminine is formed by adding **e** to the masculine, except if the masculine already ends in **e**.
The plural is formed by adding **s** to the singular (masculine or feminine). If the masculine singular form already ends in **s** or in **x**, the masculine plural is the same.

14. Feminine endings with spelling modification.

The following list shows masculine endings of adjectives and their corresponding feminine endings, where the feminine formation involves some additional spelling modification.

MASCULINE	FEMININE	EXAMPLE
-eau	**-elle**	**nouveau / nouvelle**
-er	**-ère**	**épicier / épicière**
-et	**-ette**	**muet / muette**
-eur	**-eure, -euse**	**meilleur / meilleure** **moqueur / moqueuse**
-eux	**-euse**	**ennuyeux / ennuyeuse**
-f	**-ve**	**veuf / veuve // juif / juive**
-gu	**-guë**	**ambigu / ambiguë**
-ic	**-ique**	**public / publique**
-l	**-lle, -le**	**gentil / gentille // civil / civile**
-n	**-ne, -nne**	**fin / fine // italien / italienne**
-teur	**-teuse, -trice**	**menteur / menteuse** **moteur / motrice**
-x	**-se, -ce, -sse**	**heureux / heureuse // doux / douce** **faux / fausse**

15. Irregular feminine.

The following adjectives have a totally irregular feminine form that cannot be derived from the above rules:

MASCULINE	FEMININE	MEANING
béni	**bénie, bénite**	blessed
bénin	**bénigne**	benign

blanc	**blanche**	white
coi (rare)	**coite** (rare)	still, snug
complet	**complète**	complete
concret	**concrète**	concrete
discret	**discrète**	discreet
favori	**favorite**	favorite
frais	**fraîche**	fresh, cool
franc	**franche**	frank
franc	**franque**	Frank, Frankish
fou	**folle**	crazy
grec	**grecque**	Greek
long	**longue**	long
malin	**maligne**	sly; malignant
mou	**molle**	soft
rigolo (fam.)	**rigolote**	funny
sec	**sèche**	dry
secret	**secrète**	secret
tiers	**tierce**	third
vieux	**vieille**	old

NOTE: Adjectives of nationality do not begin with a capital letter, but nouns do.

16. Plural endings.

The following rules govern the formation of the plural of adjectives:

A. The adjectives with a masculine singular ending in **-ou** simply add **s** for the masculine plural. The feminine of such adjectives is usually irregular (see §15 above), and the feminine plural is formed by adding **s**, according to the general rule of formation of the plural (§13).

Un caramel mou. Des caramels mous.
One soft caramel. Soft caramels.

Un monde fou. Ils sont fous, ces gens-là!
A maddening crowd. Those people are crazy!

B. The adjectives with a masculine singular ending in **-eau** add **x** for the masculine plural. The feminine of such adjectives always ends in **-eau** in the singular, and the feminine plural is formed by adding **s**, according to the general rule (§13).

Un nouveau programme. De nouveaux programmes.
A new program. New programs.

C. The adjectives with a masculine singular ending in **-al** change that ending to **-aux** in the masculine plural, except for the following, which simply add **s**:

bancal	lame, shaky
fatal	fatal
final	final
glacial	ice cold

idéal	ideal
jovial	jovial
natal	native
naval	naval

Un conte moral. Des contes moraux.
A moral story. Moral stories.

The feminine plural of such adjectives is formed by adding **s** to the feminine singular (§13).

17. Agreement of adjectives.

The general rule of agreement as stated in §13 is that an adjective must agree with the noun or pronoun it refers to. The mechanics of agreement, the formation of the regular as well as irregular masculine, feminine, singular, and plural, were presented in §14, §15, and §16. The following paragraphs will present the exceptions to the general rules of agreement of adjectives.

18. Irregular agreement of simple adjectives.

A. The following nouns are invariable when used as adjectives of color:

café au lait	color of coffee with cream
carmin	carmine
cerise	cherry red
chocolat	chocolate
framboise	raspberry red
marron	brown, chestnut
noisette	hazelnut
olive	olive green
orange	orange
prune	prune, purple red

Des chandails orange.
Orange sweaters.

The following agree when used as adjectives, as do all adjectives of color.

écarlate	scarlet
fauve	tawny
mauve	mauve
pourpre	purple
rose	pink

Des chemises roses. Des bonbons rouges. Trois tulipes noires et deux bleues.
Pink shirts. Red candies. Three black tulips and two blue ones.

B. The following adjectives are invariable if placed before the noun they refer to, but agree with the noun if they are placed after it:

attendu	considering
ci-inclus	enclosed, herein
ci-joint	enclosed
(y) compris	included, including
demi	half
excepté	excepted, not counting, save
nu	naked, bare
passé	passed, past
supposé	supposing
vu	considering

Il était nu-pieds. Il avait la tête nue.
He was barefoot. He was bare-headed.

Une demi-heure. Deux heures et demie. Minuit et demi.
Half an hour. Half past two (or: two and a half hours). Half past midnight ("minuit" is masculine).

C. Adjectives used as adverbs are invariable, except ***grand, tout***, and ***frais*** (see §197 and its note; §43, notes 2, 3).

Ces robes coûtent cher. Elle s'est arrêtée net.
These dresses cost a lot. She stopped abruptly.

D. The adjective ***possible*** is invariable when it is used with ***le plus, le moins, le mieux***.

Lisez le plus de livres possible.
Read as many books as possible.

but: Donnez tous les détails possibles.
Give all possible details.

E. The adjective ***grand*** used as the first term of a compound noun agrees only in the masculine plural, and remains invariable otherwise.

Un grand-père. Des grands-pères. Je n'ai pas vu grand-chose.
A grandfather. Grandfathers. I didn't see much.

Ma grand-mère. Mes deux grand-mères (or: grands-mères).
My grandmother. Both my grandmothers.

19. Irregular agreement of compound adjectives.

A. When a compound adjective is made of two nouns, adjectives, or past participles, both agree in gender and number, except if the compound adjective is one of color, in which case each part is invariable (C, below).

Des remarques aigres-douces.
Bitter-sweet remarks.

Des robes bleu-ciel.
Sky-blue dresses.

B. When the first word of a compound adjective is an adverb, an adjective used as an adverb, or a preposition, only the second term agrees, provided that it is a noun, an adjective, or a participle.

Des signes avant-coureurs.
Warning signs. Tell-tale signs (preceding an event).

C. Two adjectives, nouns, or participles combined in a compound to indicate one color remain invariable.

Des murs bleu-vert.
Blue-green walls.

However an agreement may have to be made within the compound adjective itself between the (two) terms used:

Une abondance de bruns terre-brûlée.
An abundance of burnt-earth browns (**brûlée** agrees with **terre**).

20. Position of adjectives.

The rules of position of French adjectives are far less precise than those concerning English adjectives. Instead of being a handicap to the language, this fact is an advantage in that it allows the writer of French to make use of various possibilities for effects of style.

The following are the basic principles governing the position of adjectives:

A. Participles, adjectives of color, and descriptive adjectives (shape, nationality, origin, religion, office, etc.) follow the noun they refer to.

Une voiture rouge. Une ville moderne. Un pays civilisé.
A red car. A modern city. A civilized country.

B. The following short, common adjectives precede the noun they refer to. If they are placed after the noun, they take on an emphatic value.

autre	other
beau	beautiful
bon	good, right
court	short
gentil	nice, kind
grand	tall, large
gros	big, large, thick
jeune	young
joli	pretty
long	long
mauvais	bad, wrong

méchant	bad, mean
nouveau	new (but not **neuf**)
petit	small, little
vieux	old

Un jeune homme. Un homme jeune.
A young man. A (grown) man who is still young looking.

C. The following adjectives of appreciation regularly follow the noun they refer to, but placed before the noun, they take on a more personal, more subjective meaning.

célèbre	famous
énorme	enormous
excellent	excellent
fameux	famous
formidable	tremendous
magnifique	magnificent
terrible	terrible, terrific, terrifying
triste	sad

Ils ont reçu des nouvelles tristes.
They received sad news. (mere mention of the fact)

Ils ont reçu de tristes nouvelles.
They received sad news. (subjective: I share their sadness)

D. The following adjectives change meaning according to their position in relation to the noun they refer to. This is also the rule with many other adjectives, which have or suggest a figurative meaning when they precede and a literal meaning when they follow. The rule is not absolute and should be used with caution. Emphasis may be achieved by changing the place of the adjective in relation to the noun, and sometimes a change of position may be required for reasons of euphony.

FRENCH ADJECTIVE	PRECEDING THE NOUN	FOLLOWING THE NOUN
amer	bitter, painful	bitter (taste)
ancien	former	old, ancient
brave	kind, good	courageous
certain	certain, some	sure
cher	dear	expensive
dernier	the last, final	last occurred
différent	various	different
grand	great	tall
maigre	meager, poor	lean, skinny
même	same	very
pauvre	unfortunate	poor (financially)
propre	own, personal	clean, proper

Le même jour. Le jour même.
The same day. That very day.

E. When two or more adjectives describe the same noun, each one has its position as prescribed by the rules above.

Une belle voiture rouge.
A beautiful red car.

But if the two (or more) adjectives normally should both precede or both follow the nouns, several possibilities exist.

1) They may be connected by ***et*** and placed both after the noun.

Une voiture petite et jolie.
A car that is small and pretty. (emphasis due to displacement)

2) For three or more adjectives, commas are used; the last two may be connected by ***et***.

Une belle, jeune et riche héritière.
A pretty, young, and rich heiress.

3) They may be placed in juxtaposition (i.e. no connecting word, no comma) only if the adjectifs concerned can all precede or all follow the noun by virtue of the principles given above.

Une jolie petite voiture.
A pretty little car.

Une magnifique nouvelle petite voiture.
A magnificent new little car (newly created).

but: Une très jolie petite voiture neuve.
A very pretty new little car (newly bought).

4) Some descriptive adjectives that are considered a regular characteristic of the noun may be placed before the noun, but adjectives of color and participles may not.

Une étroite planche fendue servait de passerelle.
A narrow, cracked board served as a small bridge.

Un riche banquier. Un cruel tyran.
A rich banker. A cruel tyrant.

but: Le Prince Charmant.
The Prince Charming.

5) It is wise to avoid an accumulation of pure adjectives with the same noun, a procedure that can result in awkward or heavy style. One or the other of the adjectives desired may be turned into a prepositional modifier or into a relative clause instead.

Une jeune et riche héritière d'une grande beauté.
A young and rich heiress of great beauty.

Une jeune héritière qui était belle et riche.
A young heiress who was rich and pretty.

Another way of avoiding a heavy accumulation is to introduce an adverb to modify one or the other of the adjectives desired.

C'était une riche héritière, très jeune et extrêmement belle.
She was a rich heiress, very young and extremely beautiful.

21. Notes on adjectives.

A. The position of each adjective in relation to the next is the same in French as in English. The more essential are placed closer to the noun.

Une voiture (1) de sport (2) décapotable (3) blanche.
A white (3) convertible (2) sports (1) car.

B. An English noun can easily be used as an adjective simply by being placed before another noun. This is not possible in French. An adjectival construction—a prepositional phrase, a relative clause—must be used. This French construction applies also to the translation of many English past participles, present participles, and participle imitations.

Une voiture de sport.
A sports car.

Une côte de porc.
A pork chop.

Un verre à champagne. Un verre de champagne.
A champagne glass. A glass of champagne.

Un mouchoir à carreaux.
A checkered handkerchief.

Un plafond à poutres de chêne.
An oak-beamed ceiling.

Une fenêtre à (or: aux) vitres en losange.
A diamond-paned window.

C. On occasion, a full relative clause may be necessary to render the English adjectival construction.

Un remède qui vient d'être découvert.
A newly-discovered remedy.

Un Américain qui craint Dieu et qui paie ses impôts.
A God-fearing, tax-paying American.

Un Américain qui a du sang dans les veines.
A red-blooded American.

There are also situations in which the adjectives being used belong in the domain of the idiomatic: these should then be translated not in terms of the vocabulary contained in the expressions, but in terms of the *concept* being expressed and with the *imagery* current or acceptable in the target language.

Un poltron. Un couard. Un trouillard (fam.).
A coward. A low-down, yellow-bellied coward.

Un cow-boy à la gachette facile.
A trigger-happy cowboy.

22. *Comparative of adjectives.*

The comparative is formed by placing before the adjective serving to make the comparison one of the following adverbs:

plus	*more, . . .-er*
moins	*less*
aussi	*as*
si, aussi	*(not) so, (not) as*

The second term of a comparison is introduced by ***que***.

Paul est plus grand que Pierre.
Paul is taller than Peter.

Paul est aussi grand que Jean.
Paul is as tall as John.

Paul n'est pas aussi grand que moi.
Paul is not as tall as I.

Paul est moins grand que moi.
Paul is less tall than I.

The word *than* and the word *as*, used to introduce the second term of a comparison, should be expressed as ***que*** in French, whether the second term is a noun, a pronoun, or a whole clause. If the second term is a number (including ***un*** and fractions) or a quantity, ***que*** should then be replaced by ***de***.

Paul a moins de dix dollars sur lui.
Paul has more than ten dollars with him.

Paul a perdu plus de la moitié de son argent.
Paul lost more than half of his money.

See irregular comparatives in §23 below; also §209.

23. *Superlative of adjectives.*

The superlative of adjectives is formed by placing immediately before the adjective in question one of the following expressions:

le plus	*the most, the . . .-est*
le moins	*the least*

The English word *in* following a superlative is always expressed as ***de*** (not ***dans***).

NOTE: This is the case also whenever *in* begins a prepositional phrase referring to a noun. ***Dans*** should be used for *in* only when the phrase refers to a verb.

Paul est le plus grand garçon de la famille.
Paul is the tallest boy in the family.

Jeanne est la fille la plus intelligente de la classe.
Jeanne is the most intelligent girl in the class.

but: Il a trouvé trois vieilles pièces dans un tiroir.
He found three old coins in a drawer.

but: Il n'aime pas travailler le matin parce qu'il se couche à deux heures du matin.
He does not like to work in the morning because he goes to bed at two a.m. (two in the morning).

Note that in the second example the article in *the most* has to agree with the noun referred to: ***la plus***. Note also that the article is repeated when the superlative adjective follows the noun.

The superlative of an adjective preceding the noun may use a possessive adjective instead of an article.

C'est mon plus cher désir, mon désir le plus cher.
It is my greatest, my deepest desire.

Some adjectives have irregular comparative and superlative forms:

NORMAL	COMPARATIVE	SUPERLATIVE
bon good	**meilleur** better	**le meilleur** the best
mauvais bad	**pire** **plus mauvais** worse	**le pire** **le plus mauvais** the worst
petit small	**moindre** **plus petit** smaller, slighter	**le moindre** **le plus petit** the smallest, the slightest

The irregular forms of ***mauvais*** and ***petit*** are used only with certain words in ready-made expressions accepted by usage.

Il n'a pas compris? Tant pis pour lui.
He hasn't understood? Too bad (for him).

Cela va de mal en pis.
It's going worse and worse (from bad to worse).

Il n'a pas la moindre idée de ce qui se passe.
He doesn't have the slightest idea about what's going on.

(For comparative and superlative of adverbs, see §§209-210)

24. Prepositions after adjectives.

When an adjective or a participle is used as a predicate of the subject following the verb ***être***, it frequently requires a certain preposition to introduce its infinitive modifier (see §278D). The preposition is generally the same if the modifier is a noun (see examples of use of individual English prepositions in §§107-166).

Il est humain de se tromper.
It is human to make mistakes.

Les hommes sont faciles à duper.
Men are easy to deceive.

Nous sommes pressés de rentrer.
We are in a hurry to go back home.

DEMONSTRATIVE ADJECTIVES

25. *Forms.*

The demonstrative adjective, as all adjectives, must agree in gender and number with the noun it determines. The forms of the demonstrative adjectives are:

	singular	**plural**
masculine	ce (cet)	ces
feminine	cette	ces

The alternate masculine singular form ***cet*** is to be used when the next word begins with a vowel sound.

The forms of the demonstrative adjective may be stressed when needed, to make the difference between *this, these* and *that, those*, to show proximity or distance (in space or time). This is done by adding the invariable adverbial particles ***-ci*** (for proximity) and ***-là*** (for distance) to the noun.

Ce livre-ci. Ces voitures-là. Cet homme-là. Cette photo-ci.
This book. These cars. That man. This picture.

26. *Use of demonstrative adjectives.*

The unstressed forms of the demonstrative adjective should be used in most cases, indifferently, for *this, that, these, those.* There are, however, certain established expressions of time that should not be changed.

PROXIMITY

ce matin	this morning
cet après-midi	this afternoon
ce soir	tonight, this evening
cette nuit	tonight (late), with present or future
—	last night (late), with past tense
	(last night referring to evening: **hier soir**)
cette semaine	this week
ce mois-ci	this month
cette année	this year
ces jours-ci	in a few days (near future)
—	one of these days (general present)
—	a few days ago (near past)
en ce moment(-ci)	at this time, right now

DISTANCE

ce matin-là	that morning
cet après-midi-là	that afternoon
ce soir-là	that evening
cette nuit-là	that night
ce jour-là	that day
cette semaine-là	that week
ce mois-là	that month
cette année-là	that year
à cette époque-là	at that time (very distant)
en ce temps-là	at that time (very distant)
à ce moment(-là)	at that time (moment, instant)

The stressed forms should be used only when contrast, opposition, difference, selection, proximity or distance need to be emphasized. This is especially true if two terms to be contrasted, opposed, etc., are present in the same sentence.

Regardez cette maison.
Look at that (this) house.

Je vais prendre ce plat-ci.
I'll have this dish.

Achète ce livre-ci plutôt que ce canard-là.
Buy this book rather than that worthless newspaper.

27. Notes on demonstrative adjectives

A. *This, that, these, those* are also demonstrative pronouns (see §57, §58).

B. *This* and *that* are sometimes used as adverbs of degree or intensity before adjectives or other adverbs. Notice the various corresponding French expressions used to render them in the following examples:

Il était gros comme ci (comme ça)!
He was this fat (that fat). (with a hand gesture)

Ah, c'est vraiment si loin que ça (cela)?
Ah, it is really that far?

Il ne s'est pas si mal débrouillé. Pas si mal que ça (cela).
He didn't handle it that badly. Not that bad.

Elle n'a pas perdu tant que ça d'argent (tant d'argent que ça).
She didn't lose that much money.

—Elle est si folle qu'on l'a enfermée. —A ce point?
—She is so crazy that they locked her up. —That crazy (bad, much)?

C. The stressed form of the demonstrative adjective with the adverbial particle ***-là*** may be used derogatorily to convey scorn, anger, etc.

Qu'est-ce que c'est que ce travail-là!
What kind of work is that!

D. *That* is also a relative pronoun (see §§95-103) and a subordinating conjunction (see §§171-194).

Je reconnais la voiture qu'il conduisait.
I recognize the car that he was driving.
Je sais qu'ils doivent arriver demain.
I know that they are to arrive tomorrow.

INDEFINITE ADJECTIVES

28. Forms.

The indefinite adjective, as any other adjective, must agree in gender and number with the noun it refers to. The following list shows the various forms of the indefinite adjectives. The parentheses indicate the forms that are seldom used. Each adjective is explained in detail in a subsequent paragraph.

singular		plural	
masculine	**feminine**	**masculine**	**feminine**
aucun	aucune	(aucuns)	(aucunes)
autre	autre	autres	autres
certain	certaine	certains	certaines
chaque	chaque		
différent	différente	différents	différentes
divers	divers	divers	diverses
maint	mainte	maints	maintes
même	même	mêmes	mêmes
nul	nulle	(nuls)	(nulles)
		plusieurs	plusieurs
quel	quelle	quels	quelles
quelconque	quelconque	quelconques	quelconques
quelque	quelque	quelques	quelques
tel	telle	tels	telles
tout	toute	tous	toutes

29. Note on the use of indefinite adjectives.

Several of the indefinite adjectives listed above function as determiners in the same way as articles do. They must then precede the noun "in lieu" of regular articles or other determiners.

Aucun repos. Certains dossiers. Chaque candidate.
No rest. Certain files. Each (female) candidate.

Différents personnages. Nul besoin d'ajouter que . . . . Plusieurs cas.
Different characters. No need to add that . . . . Several cases.
Tel père. Divers articles. Maintes fois. Toute réponse.
This or that father. Various articles. Many a time. Any (and all) answer.

Some of these determining indefinites may be preceded by a definite article, a possessive adjective, or a demonstrative adjective, thus losing some of their indefinite character.

Je lui ai rendu les quelques dollars que je lui avais empruntés.
I gave him back the few dollars that I had borrowed from him.
C'est la première fois qu'un tel film a été présenté.
It is the first time that such a movie was shown.
J'ai lu les divers articles que le professeur nous avait dit de lire pour aujourd'hui.
I read the various articles that the professor had assigned us for this class.

Many of the indefinite adjectives listed in §28 are also indefinite pronouns (see §59).

30. Aucun.

Aucun is both an indefinite pronoun and an indefinite adjective. For ***aucun*** as a pronoun, see §62.

As an adjective, it always precedes the noun it refers to except in a few existing fixed or idiomatic phrases. ***Aucun*** is used in the plural only with the few nouns that have no singular (see §10).

Aucun has two meanings or uses:

A. It has a negative meaning when it is used in connection with ***ne*** preceding the verb. ***Aucun*** may be alone as a correlative of ***ne***, or it may be accompanied by other negative words, except ***pas***.

Aucun homme n'est immortel. Je n'ai aucun regret.
No man is immortal. I have no regret(s); I don't have any regret(s)
Il ne finit jamais aucun travail pour personne.
He never completes any job for anyone.

B. ***Aucun*** has a positive meaning in a subordinate clause dependent on a negative verb or dependent on a verb that expresses inquiring, doubt, or restriction. It has a positive meaning also when it is used as part of the second member of a comparative construction. Note that the word *any* in that context could be replaced by *a single*, *one single*, or *any single*.

Cette comédie est plus intéressante qu'aucun film récent.
This comedy is more interesting than any recent movie.
Je ne pense pas qu'aucun roman soit meilleur.
I don't think that any novel can be better.
Peut-on accepter son jugement sans qu'aucune objection soit soulevée?
Can one accept his judgment without any objection being raised?

31. Autre.

Autre may have several meanings depending on the way in which it is used.

A. ***Autre*** immediately preceding a noun and following an appropriate determiner means "other."

Une autre fois. L'autre jour. Cet autre problème.
Another time. The other day. This (that) other problem.

Since ***autre*** is an adjective that precedes the noun, its plural use causes the indefinite article to be reduced from ***des*** to ***d'*** (see §5D).

D'autres amis sont venus nous voir.
Other friends came to see us.

Since ***autre*** begins with a vowel, the alternate forms of the demonstrative and possessive adjectives must be used when appropriate.

Essayez cet autre stylo. Il s'agit de mon autre cousine.
Try out this other pen. I'm talking about my other cousin.

Fais voir ton autre main! Son autre sœur est en Europe.
Show me your other hand! His (her) other sister is in Europe.

B. ***Autre*** is sometimes placed after ***nous*** or ***vous***., or after the verb ***être*** as a predicate of the subject. It has then the less indefinite meaning of "different", "not the same kind", "a category apart".

Ce livre-ci est intéressant, mais celui-là est tout autre.
This book is interesting, but that one is quite different.

Nous autres, Américains, nous buvons du Coca-Cola. Eux, non.
We Americans (as for us Americans, we) drink Coca-Cola. As for them, they don't.

C. ***Autre*** is found in association with ***un*** in several reciprocal expressions: ***l'un et l'autre*** . . . ("both . . ."), ***l'un ou l'autre*** . . . ("either . . ."), ***ni l'un ni l'autre*** . . . ("neither . . ."). These expressions precede nouns and may be in any gender or number.

L'une et l'autre clefs sont bonnes.
Both keys are good.

Choisissez les uns ou les autres échantillons.
Choose either group of samples.

Je n'accepte ni les unes ni les autres conditions.
I accept neither set of conditions.

Used with a subject noun, ***l'un et l'autre*** commands a plural verb, but ***l'un ou l'autre*** and ***ni l'un ni l'autre*** command singular verbs except if the form is obviously plural (***les uns ou les autres***).

Ni l'une ni l'autre idée ne me plaît.
Neither idea satisfies me.

The expressions containing ***l'un*** and ***l'autre*** are not too frequent in adjective form and may be replaced by ***les deux***.

Les deux idées me plaisent. Aucune des deux idées ne me plaît. Choisissez l'un des deux échantillons.
I like both ideas. I like neither idea. Choose one of the two samples.

Autre part is an adverbial expression meaning *"elsewhere," "somewhere else."* For *nowhere, somewhere, anywhere,* see §§37, 41, and 240.
D'autre part is a phrase meaning *on the other hand.*

For the forms of the indefinite pronoun, see §63.

32. Certain.

Certain directly precedes the noun it refers to. It is rarely used in the singular without an indefinite article, but it is used in the plural in lieu of one (see §29).

Un certain monsieur Dupont. Certaines limites sont nécessaires.
One Mr. Dupont. Certain limits are necessary.
Certains candidats sont très populaires, d'autres (le sont) moins.
Certain (some) candidates are very popular, others (are) less (so).

When ***certain*** follows a noun, it no longer has an indefinite value (see §20), but takes on the meaning of "sure," "assured."

Un succès certain. Des victoires certaines.
A sure success. Assured victories.

33. Chaque.

Chaque is always singular and always precedes the noun it refers to. ***Chaque*** translates both *each* and *every* when the idea to be conveyed is one of individuality. But when an idea of plurality is sought, the word *every* may be better rendered by a form of ***tout***, another indefinite adjective (see §43).

Chaque jour. Tous les matins. Chaque semaine. Tous les ans. Chaque année.
Each morning. Every morning. Each week. Every year. Each year.
Chaque semaine. Tous les huit jours. Toutes les semaines. À chaque minute.
Each week. Every week. Every week. (At) each minute.
Toutes les deux heures. Tous les dix centimètres. Tous les deux mois.
Every two hours. Every ten centimeters. Every other month. (***Chaque*** cannot be used before a number.)

34. Différent, divers.

Like several other indefinite adjectives, these two generally precede the noun. They have then a clearly indefinite value and function as determiners of plural nouns, with the meaning of "various," "several," "sundry," etc.

Différents problèmes, diverses solutions.
Various problems, various solutions.

Différents is used to insist on the fact that the items described are not alike.

Les différentes attitudes des candidats.
The various (constrasting) attitudes of the candidates.

Les divers plats d'un menu.
The various (several) dishes in a meal.

This meaning of ***différents*** is even stronger when it is placed after the noun, where it takes on a more descriptive value and can be used in the singular as well as in the plural.

Une solution différente. Des coiffures différentes.
A different solution. Different hairdos.

Divers may also be used after the noun. Its meaning stresses the variety or multiplicity of the items in question ("varied," "multiple," etc.).

Des occupations diverses. Des faits divers.
Varied occupations (of all types). Facts of all kinds.

There is also a type of newspaper report dealing with miscellaneous events, hence the singular ***un fait divers***, one item of such news.

35. Maint.

Maint is an expression of quantity that should be used only in formal composition. It corresponds to the English expression "many a."

Maintes fois.
Many a time. Oftentimes.

In informal French or where the style is less elevated, ***maint*** should be replaced by ***de nombreux (de nombreuses), bien des, plus d'un (plus d'une)***. See also §§204, 215, 216.

De nombreuses fois. Plus d'une fois. Bien des fois.
Many times. More than once. Lots of times.

De nombreux réfugiés se pressaient vers les bateaux.
Many refugees hurried toward the boats.

36. *Même.*

Même means "same" when it precedes the noun it refers to.

Nous faisons toujours les mêmes exercices.
We always do the same exercises.

C'est la même chose. Il est né le même jour que moi.
It's the same (thing). He was born the same day as I.

When it directly follows the noun or pronoun, ***même*** means "very," "self." It must agree with the noun or pronoun also in that position.

Il est parti le matin de Paris et il est arrivé à San Francisco le soir même.
He left Paris in the morning and he arrived in San Francisco that very night.

Elles l'ont fait elles-mêmes.
They did it themselves.

Note that when ***même*** follows a personal pronoun, a hyphen must be used to connect the two.
Même may also be an adverb meaning "even:" (§201). The adverbial expression *the same* is rendered by a prepositional phrase: ***de la même manière, de la même façon***.

Il traite tout le monde de la même manière.
He treats everyone the same.

See also §20D.

37. *Nul.*

Nul precedes the noun it refers to. It is used mostly in the singular, the plural being rare and reserved for nouns that have no singular form (see §10). ***Nul*** must be used in correlation with the particle ***ne*** as the second part of a negative construction. ***Ne*** precedes the verb of the clause.

Nul homme n'est immortel.
No man is immortal.

Nulle part is an adverbial expression meaning "nowhere," "not . . . anywhere." See also §§31, 41, and 240 for ***autre part*** (*elsewhere*), ***quelque part*** (*somewhere, anywhere*), and ***ailleurs*** (*anywhere else*). *From nowhere* is expressed in phrases such as ***on ne sait d'où, Dieu sait d'où, comme par enchantement***.

On ne pouvait la trouver nulle part.
She could not be found anywhere. She was nowhere to be found.

Des insectes énormes apparurent on ne sait d'où.
Enormous insects appeared from nowhere.

Nul is also a regular descriptive adjective that can be used as a predicate complement. It then means *null, void.* "null," "void." It is used colloquially to mean "worthless" or "good for nothing."

Votre contrat est nul. Elle est nulle en math.
Your contract is null (void, worthless). She is no good in math.

Nul is also an indefinite pronoun (§67).

38. Plusieurs.

Plusieurs exists only in the plural. It precedes the noun it refers to, and it has only one form for both the masculine and the feminine.

Nous avons le choix entre plusieurs solutions valables.
We have a choice between several good solutions.

Plusieurs is also an indefinite pronoun (§70). See also §29.

39. Quel.

Quel the indefinite adjective must be distinguished from ***quel*** the interrogative adjective or exclamatory adjective (§§44-46).

As an indefinite adjective, ***quel*** must directly precede the conjunction ***que***, followed by a verb in the subjunctive (see §174, whatever). The verb is always ***être***, sometimes contained in infinitive constructions with ***pouvoir***, ***devoir***, etc. ***Quel*** is in the position of a predicate adjective, and as such, it must agree with the subject of the verb. If the subject of the verb is *not* a personal pronoun, the subject and verb must be inverted. But if the subject of the verb *is* a personal pronoun, no inversion should be made.

Quels que soient leurs désirs, . . .
Whatever their desires may be, . . .

Quels qu'ils soient, quelle que puisse être leur forme . . .
Whatever they are, whatever their shape may be . . .

Ils ont promis de me soutenir, quelles que soient les suites de ma décision.
They promised to back me up, no matter what the consequences of my decision might be.

40. Quelconque.

Quelconque always follows the noun it refers to and must agree with it only by adding a final ***s*** in the plural . Its primary meaning is that of "any," "just any," in the sense of average, no matter what kind.

Prenez une décision quelconque.
Make just any decision (but do make one).

By context or by tone, ***quelconque*** may take on a derogatory meaning, especially so if it is modified by an adverb of degree or intensity (***très, trop,*** etc.) or associated with a negation.

Ce poème est très quelconque (plutôt quelconque).
This poem is very ordinary (rather poor).
Ce restaurant n'est pas un endroit quelconque.
This restaurant is not your ordinary spot (not just any sort of place).

The indefinite pronoun corresponding to ***quelconque*** is ***quiconque*** (§74).

41. Quelque.

Quelque has several uses and meanings that must be distinguished.

A. ***Quelque*** may be used as an indefinite determiner meaning "some," "a little," "a few," "an indefinite amount of," etc. It must then precede the noun and agree with it. It is clearly more indicative of a quantity than the indefinite article ***des*** or the partitive articles ***du, de la, des***.

Cela prendra quelque temps et quelque argent.
This will take some time and require some (a little) money.
Il me faut quelques volontaires.
I need a few volunteers.

B. Used before a number, ***quelque*** is invariable and means "about," "approximately," "around," "some."

Il y a quelque cent ans, un scandale eut lieu.
Some one hundred years ago, a scandal broke out.
Il leur faudra quelque 15 heures pour aller de Paris à Rome.
It will take them around 15 hours to go from Paris to Rome.

C. ***Quelque*** may be used in correlation with the conjunction ***que*** preceding a verb in the subjunctive mood. It then means "whatever," "whichever," "no matter what (or which)" (compare with ***quel*** in §39 above). ***Quelque*** in that construction must precede the noun it refers to (and its other modifiers, if any) and agree with it, and the verb of the clause must be in the subjunctive mood.

Quelques vues que vous ayez sur la question, . . .
No matter which views you have on the question, . . .

D. ***Quelque*** may also be used as an adverb in a construction similar to the one described in C above. It must then directly precede the *adjective* or *adverb* (not a noun) it modifies, remain invariable, and be correlated with the conjunction ***que*** followed by a verb in the subjunctive. In addition, if the subject of the verb is ***not*** a personal pronoun, the subject and the verb must be inverted.

Ils ne sont pas heureux, quelque riches qu'ils soient.
They are not happy, however rich they are.

Quelque pénible que soit votre situation de famille, je tiens à vous rappeler que vous n'avez que deux jours de congé.
However painful your family situation may be, I must remind you that you have only two days off.

NOTE: The use of ***quelque*** in correlation with ***que*** and a verb in the subjunctive mood is a heavy construction. It should be reserved for very formal style. In less formal writing, independent clauses with the appropriate adverbs of concession (***cependant, néanmoins, pourtant***) should be used.

Votre situation de famille est peut-être pénible. Néanmoins je tiens à vous rappeler que vous n'avez que deux jours de congé.
Your family situation may be painful. Nevertheless I must remind you that you have only two days off.

Quelque part is an adverbial expression meaning *somewhere*. For *elsewhere, nowhere,* and *anywhere*, see §31 (***autre***), §37 (***nul***), and §240 (***ailleurs***).

The indefinite pronouns corresponding to ***quelque*** are ***quelqu'un*** (*someone*) and ***quelque chose*** (*something*). See §§71-72.

42. Tel.

Tel may be used in several ways.

A. It may be used without any explicit correlation. It simply modifies a noun and can do so in three different constructions.

1) ***Tel*** may directly precede the noun and be used in lieu of an article (see §29). It then has a strong indefinite value.

Tel jour, à telle heure, à tel endroit.
On such (or such) a day, at such a time, in such a place.

2) ***Tel***, still directly placed before the noun, may itself be preceded by ***un, une, de*** (but not ***des***, see §7B). Its value is then less indefinite in that one can sense that it is being used as a substitute for a more specific adjective such as ***pareil, semblable***, etc., or for a comparative construction showing equality. ***Tel*** is then an exclamatory word equivalent to ***quel*** (see §46D).

Il a fait preuve d'un tel courage! Quel courage il a montré!
He showed such courage! What courage he showed!

Je n'ai jamais vu un tel manque de bonne foi, un tel hypocrite!
I have never seen such lack of good faith, such a hypocrite!

Si vous avez encore de tels résultats la prochaine fois, vous échouerez.
If you still get such results next time, you will fail.

De telles choses ne se disent pas.
Such things are not said.

Des choses pareilles (semblables) ne se font pas.
Such things are not done.

3) ***Tel*** may be placed before the verb ***être*** and be a predicate complement of the inverted subject.

Telles étaient ses raisons. Telle est ma décision. Tels furent les faits.
Such were his reasons. Such is my decision (that's my decision). Such were the facts (those were the facts).

B. ***Tel*** may be placed after the noun if it is followed by the conjunction ***que*** and the second term of a comparison.

J'admire un homme tel que Ghandi.
I admire a man such as Ghandi.

C. The second term of the comparison may be a complete clause (introduced by *as* or *that* in English).

Je vois bien la scène telle que vous l'avez décrite.
I can visualize the scene such as you described it.
Leur nombre était tel qu'aucun ennemi n'en sortit vivant.
Their number was such (so great) that no enemy survived.

D. ***Tel*** is used in a few idiomatic expressions:

tel quel	as is, such as it is
en tant que tel	as such
tel et tel	this and that
tel ou tel	this or that
tel est pris qui croyait prendre	the one is deceived who thought of deceiving
tel père, tel fils	like father, like son

Tel is also an indefinite pronoun (§76).

43. *Tout.*

Tout may be used in several constructions.

A. To make a broad generalization, it is used with a noun in the singular. No article, demonstrative adjective, or possessive adjective may modify the same noun.

Tout homme est mortel. Tout étudiant peut entrer gratuitement.
Every man is mortal. Every (any, all) student may enter without paying.

NOTE: The use of singular ***tout*** is restricted to generalizations that have almost an absolute or a universal character, and should not be attempted for limited generalizations where a plural would be more appropriate.

Tout citoyen français est sujet aux lois de la France.
All French citizens are subject to the laws of France.

Tous les Français boivent du vin.
All French people drink wine.

B. The concept of entirety or wholeness is rendered by ***tout*** or ***toute*** directly preceding a singular article, demonstrative adjective or pronoun, possessive adjective or pronoun.

Toute la terre. Tout le monde.
The whole world (Earth). Everybody, everyone.

Toute une journée. Toute sa maison a brûlé. Toute cette semaine.
A whole (entire) day. His entire house burned down. This whole week (all week long).

Toute la mienne. Tout le sien. Tout celui-là. Toute celle que vous avez écrite.
All mine. All his. All of that one (that whole one). All of the one (that) you wrote.

C. The concept of plurality is rendered by placing ***tous*** or ***toutes*** directly before a plural definite or indefinite article, possessive adjective or pronoun, or demonstrative adjective or pronoun, but after a stressed personal pronoun.

Tous les étudiants sont invités. Tous les hommes sont frères.
All the students are invited. All men are brothers.

Toutes mes amies. Tous ceux-là. Tous les miens. Tous ceux qui le veulent.
All my (girl) friends. All those. All mine. All those who so desire.

Nous tous, nous toutes. Vous tous, vous toutes. Eux tous. Elles toutes.
All of us (masc. and fem.). All of you (masc. and fem.). All of them (masc.). All of them (fem.).

NOTES:

1) ***Tout*** may be made to refer to a noun or pronoun (subject or object) through a verb. ***Tout*** must then be placed after the verb in a simple tense, and between the auxiliary and the past participle in a compound tense. The ***s*** of ***tous*** is strongly pronounced when ***tous*** comes ***after*** the noun or pronoun it refers to.

Les enfants dorment tous. Les feuilles sont toutes tombées.
The children are all asleep. The leaves have all fallen.

Ces livres? Il les a tous lus. Mes photos? Je les ai toutes rangées.
These books? He read them all. My pictures? I put them all up.

Ils sont tous partis. Vous êtes toutes punies.
They are all gone (all of them have left). You (girls) are all punished (all of you are punished).

2) ***Tout*** may be an adverb meaning ***completely, entirely***. As an adverb, it is invariable. However, when it immediately precedes an adjective beginning in a consonant or an aspirate H, it may take a feminine ending (singular or plural), provided that the adjective itself agrees with a feminine noun or pronoun.

La petite fille était toute triste. Le petit garçon était tout triste.
The little girl was very sad. The little boy was very sad.

Notice that in the feminine plural, this may create ambiguity:

Les petites filles étaient toutes tristes.
The little girls were very sad.
All the little girls were very sad (see note 1, above).

but: Les petits garçons étaient tout tristes.
The little boys were very sad.

Les petits garçons étaient tou*s* tristes ("s" is pronounced).
All the little boys were sad.

3) As an adverb, ***tout*** may also be used in correlation with the conjunction ***que*** followed by a verb in the indicative mood. ***Tout*** then means "however" and may take a feminine ending as explained in note 2, above (see also §219).

Toutes riches qu'elles sont, elles ne sont pas heureuses.
However rich they are, they are not happy (no matter how rich they are . . .; rich as they are . . .)

4) ***Tout*** is also an indefinite pronoun (§77).

INTERROGATIVE ADJECTIVES

44. Forms.

The forms of the interrogative adjective are as follows:

	singular	**plural**
masculine	quel	quels
feminine	quelle	quelles

The exclamatory adjective has the same forms (see §46D).

45. Uses.

The interrogative adjective may be used in the following ways:

A. Directly before a noun. If the noun modified by ***quel*** is the subject of the verb, the construction of the sentence is the same as in English.

Quelle question était la plus difficile?
Which question was the most difficult?

If the noun modified by ***quel*** is *not* the subject of the verb, the subject and verb must be inverted. The inversion is simple when the subject is a personal pronoun.

Quel livre lisez-vous en ce moment?
What book are you reading presently?

The inversion may be simple or complex if the subject is a noun or a pronoun other than personal. A complex inversion may be necessary in order to avoid ambiguity.

Ma fille étudie la médecine. Quelles études fait la vôtre (la vôtre fait-elle)?
My daughter is studying medicine. What is yours majoring in?
La mienne prépare un diplôme d'ingénieur.
Mine is majoring in engineering.
Quel animal poursuit le chat?
Which animal do cats chase? (: mouse)
Which animal chases cats? (: dog)

but with complex inversion:

Quel animal le chat poursuit-il?
Which animal do cats chase?

B. Directly before the verb ***être***. ***Quel*** is thus in a predicative position. ***Être*** is followed by the noun or pronoun subject.

Quel est ce livre? Quels sont vos ordres? Quelle a été sa réaction?
What book is this? What are your orders? What was his (her) reaction?

C. With the interrogative expressions ***est-ce qui*** (subject) or ***est-ce que*** (object) placed after the noun modified by ***quel*** (and its other modifiers, if any). No inversion is to be made in this case.

Quel livre est-ce que vous lisez? Quel problème est-ce qui vous tracasse?
What book are you reading? What problem troubles you?

Quels nouveaux modèles de voitures françaises connaissez-vous?
What new models of French cars do you know?

Constructions with ***est-ce que*** and particularly ***est-ce qui*** may be awkward and should be restricted to very informal language.

46. Notes.

A. Applied to persons, ***quel***, by comparison with ***qui*** (see §§78-81), asks for more than a name or mere identity. It asks for quality (profession, occupation, function, etc.) and may express "what kind of," "what is the role of," etc.

Quel est cet homme?—C'est le concierge.
What man is this? —He is the custodian.

Qui est cette femme? —C'est madame Ledoux.
Who is this woman? —That's Mrs. Ledoux.

B. ***Quel*** may be used in indirect questions. In such sentences, no inversion is made when the subject is a personal pronoun. Inversion is allowed if the subject is a noun or a pronoun other than personal, or if it is needed for reasons of clarity or style, such as when the subject has long modifiers.

Je veux savoir quels livres vous avez achetés.
I want to know what books you bought.

L'enfant se demande quel cadeau a reçu son frère et quel cadeau recevra celui dont c'est l'anniversaire.
The child is wondering what present his brother has received and which present the boy whose birthday it is will get.

C. ***Quel*** is also an indefinite adjective that can be used in correlation with the conjunction ***que*** followed by a verb in the subjunctive (see §39, §174).

Quelles que soient vos excuses, votre action est impardonnable.
Whatever your excuses, your action is unforgivable.

D. ***Quel*** is also an exclamatory adjective. It may be used in exclamations with or without a complete sentence. No article may be used between ***quel*** and the noun.

Quel malheur! Quels artistes!
What a misfortune! What artists!

Quelle nuit nous avons passée!
What a night we spent!

E. When ***quel*** modifies the direct object of a verb in a compound tense, the past participle must agree with that direct object in gender and number, since it precedes (see §§272-273).

Quelles valises ont-ils emportées?
Which suitcases did they take?

Quelle honteuse défaite ont subie les filles de l'équipe adverse!
What a shameful defeat the girls of the opposite team have experienced!

NUMBERS

47. Cardinal numbers.

The cardinal numbers are as follows:

1	un
2	deux
3	trois
4	quatre
5	cinq
6	six
7	sept
8	huit
9	neuf
10	dix
11	onze
12	douze
13	treize
14	quatorze
15	quinze
16	seize
17	dix-sept
18	dix-huit
19	dix-neuf
20	vingt
21	vingt et un
22	vingt-deux
23	vingt-trois, etc.
30	trente
31	trente et un
32	trente-deux, etc.
40	quarante
41	quarante et un
42	quarante-deux, etc.
50	cinquante
51	cinquante et un
52	cinquante-deux,. etc.
60	soixante
62	soixante-deux, etc.
69	soixante-neuf
70	soixante-dix (see note, below)
71	soixante et onze
72	soixante-douze
73	soixante-treize, etc.
79	soixante-dix-neuf
80	quatre-vingts
81	quatre-vingt-un
82	quatre-vingt-deux, etc.
89	quatre-vingt-neuf
90	quatre-vingt-dix
91	quatre-vingt-onze
92	quatre-vingt-douze
93	quatre-vingt-treize
94	quatre-vingt-quatorze, etc.
97	quatre-vingt-dix-sept
98	quatre-vingt-dix-huit
99	quatre-vingt-dix-neuf

100	cent
101	cent un
102	cent deux, etc.
110	cent dix
111	cent onze, etc.
199	cent quatre-vingt-dix-neuf
200	deux cents
201	deux cent un, etc.
300	trois cents
301	trois cent un, etc.
399	trois cent quatre-vingt-dix-neuf
400	quatre cents
500	cinq cents
612	six cent douze
775	sept cent soixante-quinze
800	huit cents
925	neuf cent vingt-cinq
999	neuf cent quatre-vingt-dix-neuf
1000	mille
1001	mille un
1002	mille deux, etc.
1010	mille dix
1011	mille onze, etc.
1099	mille quatre-vingt-dix-neuf
1100	mille cent
1200	mille deux cents

1350	mille trois cent cinquante	10.000	dix mille
1972	mille neuf cent soixante-douze	11.000	onze mille
2000	deux mille	12.500	douze mille cinq cents
3000	trois mille, etc.	100.000	cent mille
9000	neuf mille	500.000	cinq cent mille

The following are not adjectives. They are nouns and as such must be preceded by a determiner (another number) even at the level of the single unit. They also require the use of the preposition ***de*** before a following noun.

1.000.000	un million
2.000.000	deux millions
100.000.000	cent millions
1.000.000.000	un milliard
10.000.000.000	dix milliards
1.000.000.000.000	un billion

NOTES: 1) In Belguim and Switzerland, the numbers between 70 and 99 are not the same as in France. 70 is *septante*, 80 is *octante* in Belgium, *huitante* in Switzerland, and 90 is *nonante* (*neuvante* in some areas of Switzerland).

2) As a result of the spelling reform of 1991, the use of a hyphen in compound numbers above one hundred should be tolerated.

48. Notes on cardinal numbers.

Numbers are called cardinal numeral adjectives if they indicate a quantity, and ordinal numeral adjectives if they indicate ranking (see §50). Numbers from 17 through 99 must be written with hyphens except where ***et*** is used.

A. Cardinal numbers are invariable. However, ***vingt*** and ***cent*** add "s" when they are preceded by a number higher than one, if they end the figure.

Quatre-vingts. Trois cents. Quatre-vingt-trois. Trois cent cinquante.
Eighty. Three hundred. Eighty-three. Three hundred fifty.

Cent quatre-vingt-cinq est un nombre impair. Cent est un nombre pair.
One hundred twenty-five is an odd number. One hundred is an even number.

B. The expressions "hundreds of" and "thousands of" cannot be expressed with ***cent*** and ***mille***. These must be replaced by the nouns ***centaine*** and ***millier*** respectively.

Des centaines de spectateurs. Quelques milliers d'auditeurs. Des milliers d'insectes.
Hundreds of spectators. A few thousand listeners. Thousands of insects.

Million, milliard, and ***billion***, as well as ***millier*** and all the nouns created from numbers by adding to them the suffix ***-aine*** (see C, below), must be preceded by ***un, une,*** or an appropriate determiner in the singular (compare with ***cent*** and ***mille***). They must also add ***s*** in the plural. And the preposition ***de*** must be added after them to introduce the noun (see §7C), unless the figure is not rounded to those numbers.

Huit millions d'habitants. Quarante milliards de francs. Des billions d'étoiles.
Eight million inhabitants. Forty billion francs. Trillions of stars.

Trois millions cinq cent mille personnes.
Three million five hundred thousand people.

C. The suffix ***-aine*** may be added to the following numbers only, to form feminine nouns of quantity:

8	**une huitaine**
9	**une neuvaine**
10	**une dizaine**
12	**une douzaine**
15	**une quinzaine**
20	**une vingtaine**
30	**une trentaine**
40	**une quarantaine**
50	**une cinquantaine**
60	**une soixantaine**
100	**une centaine**

In the singular, the above nouns mean "about," "approximately." But when they are multiplied by another number, they take on a more precise meaning of "units or groups comprising exactly," like *dozen* in English. ***Neuvaine*** has limited usage: it is a Roman Catholic nine-day period of devotion.

Il n'y avait qu'une dizaine de personnes à la soirée.
There were only about ten persons at the party.

Il y a cinq dizaines de feuilles dans ce paquet.
There are five times ten sheets in this package.

Une huitaine and ***une quinzaine*** are frequently used with the word ***jour*** to indicate "about a week" and "about two weeks."

Nous devons rester à Paris une quinzaine de jours.
We are to stay in Paris for a couple of weeks.

Revenez me voir sous huitaine.
Come back to see me before a week has passed.

To translate an approximation with numbers other than those listed above, use ***environ, à peu près, dans les, près de,*** etc., before the number or after the noun multiplied.

Environ soixante-dix ans. Soixante-dix ans environ. Dans les soixante-dix ans. À peu près soixante-dix ans.
About seventy years (more or less).

Près de soixante-dix ans.
Almost seventy years (not quite).

D. ***Huit*** and ***quinze*** are frequently used with the word ***jour*** to indicate one week and two weeks, respectively. The noun ***semaine*** may also be used, of course, but not the numbers seven or fourteen with the word ***jours***.

Je vous reverrai dans huit ou quinze jours.
I'll see you again in a week or two.

Huit and ***quinze*** are also used with the preposition ***en*** to indicate "a week from," "two weeks from," respectively.

La réunion est reportée au 15, jeudi en huit.
The meeting is postponed until the 15th, Thursday week (a week from this Thursday).

E. The decimal system has been in use in France since the revolution of 1789. A decimal is marked with a comma, pronounced "virgule." A fraction of a single unit is written with a zero before the comma (pronounced "zéro virgule" for "point").

3,14	**0,5 mm**	**27,75 F**	**2,20 dollars**
3.14	.5 mm	27.75 francs	$ 2.20

Thousands, millions, billions are frequently marked with a period, but modern editors prefer a blank space.

10.542.690 habitants. 10 542 690 habitants.
10,542,690 inhabitants. A population of 10,542,690.

Time is normally given within two 12-hour periods. To specify *a.m.* or *p.m.*, the expressions ***du matin*** (morning), ***de l'après-midi*** (afternoon, till four or five o'clock), and ***du soir*** (after four or five o'clock) may be used.
Transportation schedules and official public events are given with reference to the 24-hour clock.

Je me suis couché à une heure et demie (1h30) du matin.
I went to bed at one thirty (1:30) a.m.

10h du soir. 0h45 (zéro heure quarante-cinq, or: minuit quarante-cinq). 3h de l'après-midi.
10:00 p.m.. 0:45 (45 minutes after or past midnight). 3:00 p.m..

NOTE: When the phrases *in the morning, in the afternoon, in the evening,* or *at night* are used adverbially, the English prepositions should not be translated. See §21.

49. *Uses of cardinal numbers.*

Cardinal numbers are to be used in dates and titles, except for the number 1, which is to be replaced by ***premier*** (see §§50-52).

Le 10 (dix) avril. Le 21 (vingt et un) mars. Le 1er (premier) mai.
April 10. March 21. Mai 1.

Louis XIV (quatorze). François 1er (premier).
Louis the Fourteenth. Francis the First.

A date contains no comma and no capital letter in French, but a definite article is necessary.

Le 13 mai 1972. Le vendredi 13 juin 1969.
May 13, 1972. Friday June 13, 1969.

The numerator in a fraction is also a cardinal number.

6/8 (six huitièmes).
Six-eighths.

For the case of numbers contained in prepositional phrases, see the chapter on prepositions.

50. Ordinal numbers.

The ordinal numbers are formed in French by adding the suffix ***-ième*** to the cardinal numbers, with the following observations and examples:

- If the cardinal number ends in *e*, this letter must be dropped before the suffix ***-ième*** is added: ***quatre, quatrième. Treize, treizième.***
- The number 5 adds ***-uième***: ***cinq, cinquième.***
- The number 9 changes *f* to *v* before the suffix ***-ième: neuf, neuvième.***
- The number 1 has an irregular formation, but only if it is not part of a larger number:

un	***premier, première***
vingt et un	***vingt et unième***
cent un	***cent unième***

- Compound numbers from 17 through 99 must be written with hyphens except where ***et*** is used.

first	1st	premier, première	1er, 1ère
second	2nd	second or deuxième	2e
third	3rd	troisième	3e
fourth	4th	quatrième	4e
fifth	5th	cinquième	5e
sixth	6th	sixième	6e
seventh	7th	septième	7e
eighth	8th	huitième	8e
ninth	9th	neuvième	9e
tenth	10th	dixième	10e
eleventh	11th	onzième	11e
twelfth	12th	douzième	12e

etc.			
seventeenth	17th	dix-septième	17e
eighteenth	18th	dix-huitième	18e
nineteenth	19th	dix-neuvième	19e
twentieth	20th	vingtième	20e
twenty-first	21st	vingt et unième	21e
twenty-second	22nd	vingt-deuxième	22e
twenty-third	23rd	vingt-troisième	23e
thirty-first	31st	trente et unième	31e
seventy-first	71st	soixante et onzième	71e
eighty-first	81st	quatre-vingt-unième	81e
ninety-first	91st	quatre-vingt-onzième	91e
one hundredth	100th	centième	100e
one hundred and first	101st	cent unième	101e
one thousandth	1000th	millième	1000e
one millionth	1,000,000th	millionnième	1.000.000e
etc.			

51. Notes on ordinal numbers.

A. Ordinal numbers must agree in gender and in number with the noun they refer to. The singular form is the same for the masculine and the feminine, except for ***premier, première*** and ***second, seconde***. The plural is formed by adding ***s*** to the singular.

Les premiers pas d'un enfant. Les premières places du théâtre sont plus chères que les secondes.
The first steps of a child. The first-row seats at the theater are more expensive than the second-row ones.

B. *First, second, third,* etc., used in listings or enumerations, must be understood as firtsly, secondly, thirdly, etc., and expressed as ***premièrement, deuxièmement, troisièmement,*** etc., or replaced by an appropriate adverbial expression such as ***en premier lieu, en second lieu,*** or ***d'abord, ensuite,*** etc.

52. Uses.

Only ***premier*** is used in dates and titles, and only for the number 1. For the rest, cardinal numbers must be used.

Le 1er (premier) mai. Le premier de l'an.
May first. The first of the year.

Le 21 (vingt et un) juin. Le 31 (trente et un) décembre.
June 21. December 31.

Ordinal numbers are used for the denominator in fractions. However, for the most common ones, alternate words are prefered:

Un demi. Un tiers. Un quart. Un cinquième.
One-half. One-third. One-fourth (quarter). One-fifth.

Une demi baguette. Une moitié de bâtard.
Half a baguette. Half of a loaf.

Un litre et demi de lait et une livre et demie de lentilles.
One and a half liters (quarts) of milk and one and a half pounds of lentils.

Deux tiers. Trois quarts. Quatre septièmes.
Two-thirds. Three-fourths. Four-sevenths.

See agreement of ***demi*** in §18B.

French usage requires a definite article before the numerator of a fraction, when the item being fractioned is well defined by the context. When the numerator is the unit 1, the article is placed directly before the denominator.

Le dixième de la population n'a pas voté.
One-tenth of the population did not vote.

Elle a vendu les deux tiers de ses biens.
She sold two-thirds of her assets.

Les trois quarts du temps, il pleut chez nous.
Most of the time (3/4 of the time), it rains where we live.

POSSESSIVE ADJECTIVES

53. Forms.

The possessive adjective has the following forms:

possessor	**object possessed**			
	singular		**plural**	
person	**masculine**	**feminine**	**masculine**	**feminine**
1st singular	mon	ma*	mes	mes
2nd singular	ton	ta*	tes	tes
3rd singular	son	sa*	ses	ses
1st plural	notre	notre	nos	nos
2nd plural	votre	votre	vos	vos
3rd plural	leur	leur	leurs	leurs

****Ma, ta, sa*** are used only when the *next word* begins with a consonant or with an aspirate H. If the next word begins with a vowel or a mute H, the masculine forms ***mon, ton, son*** should be used to avoid a hiatus (except with ***huit, huitième, onze, onzième***).

Ma voiture. Mon autre voiture. Mon auto. Ma belle auto.
My car. My other car. My car. My beautiful car.

Ton université. Ta nouvelle université.
Your university. Your new university.

Son ami. Son amie. Sa première amie. Son ancienne amie.
His (her) friend. His (her) friend. His (her) first friend. His (her) former friend.

54. Use of possessive adjectives.

The possessive adjectives, like all adjectives, must agree in gender and number with the noun they modify (the object possessed, not the possessor).

Son père et sa mère. Son frère et sa sœur.
His father and his mother. His brother and his sister.
Her father and her mother. Her brother and her sister.

NOTES: 1) The possessive adjectives should be repeated with each item in a series or a list.

On lui avait volé sa montre, son portefeuille, son briquet, ses clés, et jusqu'à ses lunettes.
They had robbed him of his watch, his wallet, his cigarette lighter, his keys, and even his glasses.

Mon frère et ma sœur. Mes frères et mes sœurs.
My brother and sister. My brothers and sisters.

2) After the word ***chacun*** (*each, all*) referring to a third person plural (any plural noun or pronoun except ***nous*** and ***vous***), possession may be indicated either by ***son, sa, ses*** (emphasis on the word ***chacun***) or by ***leur, leurs*** (emphasis on the third person plural in question).

Les étudiants avaient chacun son livre. Les étudiants avaient chacun leur livre.
All the students had each their own book.

But if the word ***chacun*** refers to ***nous*** or ***vous***, the possessive must be ***notre, nos*** or ***votre, vos***, respectively.

Nous avons chacun notre livre et nos cahiers.
We each have our own book and notebooks.

55. Possessive adjectives (do not use).

The following differences should be noted in the use of the possessive adjectives in English and in French:

A. Do not use possessive adjectives in French with parts of the body or clothing if the context clearly shows who the owner is. This is particularly the case when a reflexive or reciprocal pronoun, or an indirect object personal pronoun, precedes the verb. The possessive adjective should then be replaced by a definite article (see list of idiomatic expressions in §56).

Il se lave les mains. Sa mère lui lave les mains.
He washes his hands. His (her) mother washes his (her) hands.

Je lui ai lavé la tête.
I washed his (her) head (i.e. I gave him (her) a reprimand).

This rule is not absolute. Emphasis or precision can be obtained by using the possessive adjective. But using a possessive adjective together with a reflexive, reciprocal, or indirect object personal pronoun in the same clause would be repetitive.

B. The plural is not so frequent in French as it is in English after possessive adjectives. French prefers to use the singular when the context or the situation indicates that only one object possessed by each possessor is considered.

Tous les étudiants ont levé la main.
All the students raised their hands. (each student raises only one hand)
When the plural is used, it is to emphasize the number or the variety.

C. If the possessive adjective precedes a *gerund*, the whole group is usually replaced in French by a clause in the subjunctive (see §270C). However, if the English gerund can be rendered by an existing French noun, the possessive adjective remains.

Leur interminable bavardage m'énerve. Je suis irrité qu'ils parlent sans arrêt.
I am irritated by their endless talking.

Cela me rend fou qu'ils bavardent sans arrêt!
Their endless babbling drives me crazy!

Cela vous dérange-t-il que je fume?
Do you mind my smoking?

56. *Idiomatic expressions.*

The following expressions show examples of French idiomatic use of the definite article in preference to the possessive adjective. They also show examples of the idiomatic use of parts of the body in proverbial expressions.

Avoir la main lourde.
To be strict, heavy-handed (lit. to have a heavy hand)

Avoir la main légère.
To be lenient, easy (lit. to have a light hand)

Serrer la main à quelqu'un.
To shake hands with someone.

Nous nous sommes serré la main.
We shook hands.

Je lui ai serré la main.
I shook his (her) hand.

Se mettre le doigt dans l'œil.
To fool oneself. To have unrealistic expectations (lit. to put one's finger into one's eye).

Avoir le compas dans l'œil.
To have a good sense of perspective, measurement (lit. to have a compass in one's eye).

À l'œil.
Free, without paying, at no charge.

Ouvrir l'œil.
To be on the watch. To keep an eye open.

Ne dormir que d'un œil.
To sleep very lightly. To pretend to sleep in order to observe without arousing suspicion (lit. to sleep with only one eye).

Coûter les yeux de la tête.
To cost an arm and a leg.

Dormir sur ses deux oreilles.
To sleep very soundly, without care or worry (lit. to sleep on both ears).

Casser les oreilles à quelqu'un.
To annoy somebody by being too noisy (lit. break, split someone's ears).

À vue de nez.
At a rough estimate.

Cela lui met l'eau à la bouche. Il en a l'eau à la bouche.
That makes his mouth water.

Tomber de tout son long.
To fall flat on the ground (lit. to fall one's full length).

S'arracher les cheveux.
To get mad, wild, desperate about something (lit. to pull one's hair off).

En avoir le souffle coupé.
To be dumbfounded, breathtaken (by some event).

En perdre son latin. Y perdre son latin.
To be completely lost in or because of something (lit. to lose or forget one's latin because of, in something).

Hausser les épaules.
To shrug one's shoulders.

Faire son malin, son intéressant.
To show off (in reproach by adults to children).

S'en mordre les doigts.
To regret something sorely (lit. to bite one's fingers for it).

Casser les pieds à quelqu'un.
To bother someone. To be a pain in someone's neck.

Mettre (remettre) les pieds quelque part.
To set foot (again) somewhere.

Se casser la tête à faire quelque chose.
To work too hard at, worry too much about doing something.

Se gratter la tête.
To scratch one's head. To be puzzled.

Se creuser la tête.
To think very hard (lit. to hollow out one's head).

Avoir quelque chose en tête.
To have something in mind.

Être en tête.
To be in the lead, in front, ahead.

En avoir par-dessus la tête.
To be sick and tired of something, to have it up to here.

Laver la tête à quelqu'un.
To reprimand somebody (lit. to wash his (her) head).

DEMONSTRATIVE PRONOUNS

57. Forms.

The demonstrative pronoun has the following forms.

singular		**plural**	
masculine	**feminine**	**masculine**	**feminine**
celui-ci *this one*	celle-ci *this one*	ceux-ci *these*	celles-ci *these*
celui-là *that one*	celle-là *that one*	ceux-là *those*	celles-là *those*

There are also neuter forms:

ceci	*this*
cela	*that*
ça	*that (informal)*
ce	*this, that, it, etc.*

See §§286-287.

58. Uses.

A. The forms given in the table above contain the adverbial particles ***-ci, -là*** serving to indicate proximity or distance. These particles can be omitted only in two cases:

1) If the demonstrative pronoun is modified by a *prepositional phrase* (mostly with ***de, en, à***; rarely any other preposition).

Voici mon livre, et voici celui de Paul.
Here is my book, and here is Paul's.

Tu veux la montre en plastique ou celle en or?
Do you want the plastic watch or the gold one?

2) If the demonstrative pronoun is modified by a *relative clause*.

Il me faut un crayon. Celui que tu tiens fera l'affaire.
I need a pencil. The one (that) you are holding will do.

In all other cases, the demonstrative pronouns must contain the adverbial particles.

Donne-moi ce livre-là et garde celui-ci pour toi.
Give me that book and keep this one for you.

Note that the French demonstrative pronoun is used for English *the one* as well as for *this one, that one, these, those.* Note also that a demonstrative pronoun must be used in French to render the English possessive case where the noun is not expressed.

Nous prenons ma voiture et celle de Paul.
We are taking my car and Paul's.

B. *This, that,* used emphatically, are translated ***ceci*** and ***cela***, respectively. When no emphasis is intended, they may be expressed as ***ce*** if the verb is ***être***, *to be.*

Ceci va vous paraître difficile à croire.
This is going to seem difficult for you to believe.

Cela est impossible!
That is impossible!

C'est difficile à croire.
This is difficult to believe. (no emphasis)

In informal language, ***ça*** can be used instead of ***ceci*** or ***cela***, indifferently. However, ***ça*** never precedes directly the verb ***être*** in forms beginning with a vowel.

Ça lui est égal. Ça m'est égal. C'est la même chose.
It's all the same to him. It's all the same to me. It's the same (thing).

Ça n'était pas bien difficile. C'était même très facile.
It (this, that) was not very difficult. It was even very easy.

Ça sera facile. Ça, c'est incroyable!
It will be easy. *That* is incredible!

By itself, ***ça*** is not emphatic. It stresses neither proximity nor distance. It is neutral. Yet it may be emphasised by repetition.

Ça, ça n'a pas d'importance.
That doesn't matter.

Ça, c'est bizarre! C'est bizarre, ça!
That is bizarre!

Ceci, cela and ***ça*** may be used as subject or object of any verb.

Ça, c'est beau! Je n'aime pas cela. Je préfère ceci. Tu aimes ça, toi?
That is nice! I don't like that. I prefer this. Do *you* like that?

C. ***Ce*** is the most frequently used of the demonstrative pronouns. It should be used particularly as the subject of ***être*** in the following cases:

1) To translate *it, this, that,* referring to something vague or general, a scene, an idea, etc., when the predicate following ***être*** is an *adjective.*

C'est beau. Ce n'est pas juste. C'est impossible.
It's beautiful. It's not fair. It's impossible.
Ça, c'est bizarre!
That is weird!

2) To translate *he, she, it,* or *they* referring to a specific noun, provided that the predicate following the verb ***être*** is either a *noun*, a *pronoun*, a *proper noun*, or a *superlative.*

C'est un ami. C'est une étrangère. Ce sont des parents.
He is a friend. She is a foreigner. They are relatives.
C'est lui. C'est elle. Ce sont eux. C'est la mienne. C'est celui-là.
It's he, she, they (that's him, her, them). It's mine. It's that one (that's the one).
C'est Paul. C'est monsieur Jones.
It's Paul (he is Paul). It's (he is) Mr. Jones.
C'est la plus riche des deux. Ce sont les meilleurs.
She is the richest of the two. They are the best.

NOTE: ***Être*** is plural if the predicate is a plural noun (common, proper, or a superlative), or a third person plural pronoun.

Ce sont des vers, ce n'est pas de la prose.
They (these) are verses, they are not (this is not) prose.
C'étaient des étrangers. Ce devaient être des immigrants.
They were foreigners. They must have been immigrants.
C'étaient eux. C'étaient les miens. C'étaient les meilleurs.
They were the ones. They were mine. They were the best.

However, the singular may be used with a plural predicate in familiar or casual language.

C'est eux qui ont cassé la vitre. Ce ne peut être qu'eux.
They broke the windowpane. It can only be they (them).
Ce ne doit pas être eux qui ont fait ça.
It must not be they (them) who did that.
(They must not be the ones who did that.)

Nous and ***vous*** always call for the singular.

C'est nous. C'était vous? Ce sera vous.
It's we (us). Was it you? It will be you.
C'est vous qui serez déçus.
The disappointed ones will be you.

See also §286B1, note.

3) To translate *what* (see §§100-101). When *what* is used as a relative pronoun beginning a noun clause, it must be translated ***ce qui***, ***ce que***, etc., in which ***ce*** serves as the antecedent of the relative pronoun.

Ce qui est arrivé m'a surpris.
What happened took me by surprise.

Dites-moi ce que vous avez fait.
Tell me what you did.

NOTE: As subject of a verb used in a compound tense, the pronoun ***ce*** may precede an auxiliary that begins with the vowel ***a***. ***Ce*** must then be written in its elided form and with a cedilla: ***ç'***.

Ç'aurait été impossible. Ç'avait été long. Ç'aurait pu être un désastre.
It would have been impossible. It had been long. It could have been a disaster.

INDEFINITE PRONOUNS

59. *Forms.*

The indefinite pronouns listed in the following table are detailed individually in sections §§62-77.

singular		plural	
masculine	**feminine**	**masculine**	**feminine**
aucun	aucune	aucuns (rare)	aucunes (rare)
autre	autre	autres	autres
autrui	_	_	_
_	_	certains	certaines
chacun	chacune	_	_
nul	nulle	nuls (rare)	nulles (rare)
on	_	_	_
personne	personne	_	_
_	_	plusieurs	plusieurs
quelque chose	_	_	_
quelqu'un	quelqu'une	quelques-uns	quelques-unes
qui	qui	_	_
quoi	_	_	_
quiconque	quiconque	_	_
rien	_	_	_
tel	telle	_	_
tout	_	tous	toutes

60. *Notes on the use of indefinite pronouns.*

A. The indefinite pronouns must be distinguished from the indefinite adjectives that have identical forms, since the constructions they command are not identical (see §§29-43; §92D2).

Il en avait d'autres d'orange. (autre is a pronoun)
He had others that were orange.

Il avait d'autres oranges. (autre is an adjective)
He had more oranges. He had other oranges.

B. ***Autre*** is the only indefinite pronoun with which a determiner (article, demonstrative, possessive, etc.) must be used. ***Tel*** may be used with an indefinite article.

Un autre. Cette autre. Mon autre. L'autre.
Another (m.). This other one (f.). My other one (m./f.). The other one (m./f.).

C. The indefinite pronouns can have all the functions of regular nouns, except ***on*** and ***nul***, which are always subjects.

D. By meaning, some indefinite pronouns can be only singular, and others only plural. Note also that some have only one invariable form.

E. The final ***s*** in ***tous*** is pronounced as in the English pronoun *us* if ***tous*** is an indefinite pronoun or an indefinite adjective placed *after* the noun (see §43, note 1).

Les hommes sont tous mortels.
All men are mortal.

But the final ***s*** is not pronounced if ***tous*** is an indefinite adjective placed *before* the noun it modifies.

Tous les hommes sont mortels.
All men are mortal. Men are all mortal.

The singular form ***tout*** may be used as a noun meaning *the whole, the totality.*

12 francs de lait, 7 francs de pain et 45 francs de viande, le tout fait 64 francs.
12 francs worth of milk, 7 francs of bread and 45 francs of meat, the total (whole deal, altogether, etc.) is 64 francs.

F. When an indefinite pronoun is modified by one of the prepositional phrases *of us, of you, of them*, the preposition generally used in French is ***d'entre*** (see §§142 and 218).

Plusieurs d'entre vous recevront un billet pour le match.
Several of (among) you will receive a ticket for the game.

61. Features.

Certain features must be observed with the use of indefinite pronouns.

A. ***Ne*** is required before the verb of a clause whenever one of the following indefinite pronouns is used with a negative meaning in the same clause: ***aucun, nul, ni l'un ni l'autre, personne, rien.***

Personne n'est venu. Rien ne bougeait. (subject)
No one came. Nothing moved.

Je ne vois rien. (direct object)
I see nothing.

Je n'ai parlé ni à l'un ni à l'autre. (object of a preposition)
I spoke to neither one.

B. ***De (d')*** must be used directly before an adjective modifying any of the following indefinite pronouns: ***aucun, autre, certains, personne, plusieurs, quelque chose, quelqu'un, qui, quoi, rien. De (d')*** is also added before an adjective describing a noun modified by an expression of quantity (adverb, number, etc.).

Voilà quelque chose d'intéressant. Je n'ai rien de mieux à faire.
That is something interesting. I have nothing better to do.

Qui d'autre est venu? Quelqu'un d'important?
Who else came? Anyone important?

Quoi de neuf? Rien de grave? Personne de blessé?
What's new? Anything serious? Anyone injured?

Combien de personnes y a-t-il eu de blessées?
How many injured (people) were there?

Il n'y a que trois élèves de collés sur quarante.
There are only three students failing (who got F) out of forty.

C. ***En*** must be used directly before the verb that has any of the following indefinite pronouns as an unmodified direct object: ***aucun, autre*, certains, plusieurs, quelques-uns, quelques-unes.***

****Autre*** must be preceded by ***un, une, d',*** or a number. ***En*** is not used if ***autre*** is determined by any other term that diminishes its indefinite quality (definite article, demonstrative, or possessive).

Combien de livres avez-vous achetés? —Je n'en ai acheté aucun.
How many books have you bought? I haven't bought any.

Nous en avons choisi plusieurs.
We chose several.

J'en ai vu d'autres!
I have seen worse! (I have lived through a lot of experiences.)

but: J'ai vu les autres. J'ai vendu quelques-uns de mes timbres.
I saw the others. I've sold a few of my stamps.

D. As object of the verb, the negative indefinite pronouns ***aucun, personne,*** and ***rien*** follow a verb in a simple tense.

Nous n'en vendons aucune.
We aren't selling any.

Ne parlez à personne.
Don't talk to anyone.

Je ne dirai rien. Ne dites rien.
I will say nothing. Don't say anything.

With verbs in compound tenses, ***aucun*** and ***personne*** follow the past participle, but ***rien*** precedes it.

Ils n'en ont vendu aucun.
They didn't sell any.

Nous n'avons vu personne.
We haven't seen anyone.

Nous n'avons rien entendu.
We haven't heard anything.

In infinitive constructions, ***aucun*** and ***personne*** follow the infinitive whereas ***rien*** precedes the main verb (the infinitive if the main verb is a command).

Je ne voulais voir personne. Je n'ai pu parler à personne. Ne laissez entrer personne.
I didn't want to see anyone. I couldn't speak to Don't let anybody in.

Je ne peux en vendre aucun. Je n'aurais osé en manger aucun. N'en laissez jeter aucun.
I can't sell any. I wouldn't have dared to eat any. Don't let any be thrown away.

Elle n'a rien voulu entendre. Elle n'a rien vu passer. Ne faites rien tomber.
She didn't want to listen to any excuses (lit. hear anything). She didn't see anything go by. Don't drop anything (li. make anything fall).

Tout being the opposite of ***rien***, its position is the same as that of ***rien*** in identical circumstances although the regular object position is also possible.

Il sait tout. Il ne sait rien. Qu'il dise tout! Qu'il ne dise rien!
He knows everything. He knows nothing. Let him give it all back! Let him say nothing about it!

Elle a tout cassé. Elle n'a rien fait. Elle a oublié tout. Elle a tout compris.
She broke everything. She didn't do anything. She forgot everything. She understood all of it.

On ne peut tout faire en une seule fois. Faites tout brûler. Faites enlever tout.
One cannot do everything at one time. Have everything burnt. Have everything removed.

(See also §92D and modified negations in §203)

62. *Aucun.*

A. Negative meaning: *None, not any, not a single one.* ***Aucun*** governs a singular verb and may be modified by ***de*** plus an adjective, by a prepositional phrase, or by a relative clause. For additional features associated with the use of ***aucun***, see §61A, B, C.

Aucun de ses amis n'était venu.
None of his friends had come.

Je n'en ai vu aucune de présentable.
I did not see a single one that was presentable.

Nous n'en connaissons aucune qui soit acceptable.
We don't know any that is acceptable.

B. Positive meaning: *any, anyone.* ***Aucun*** has a positive meaning if the verb already has a full two-part negation, or expresses inquiring, doubt, restriction, concession. ***Aucun*** also has a positive meaning if it serves as the second term in a comparison.

Ce garçon est plus malin qu'aucun de vous.
This boy is smarter than any of you.

Je ne pense pas (or: Je doute) qu'aucun de vous réussisse.
I don't think (or: I doubt) that anyone of you will succeed.

Il a plus de bon sens qu'aucun de ces nigauds.
He has more common sense than any of those fools.

(See also ***aucun*** as an indefinite adjective, §30.)

63. Autre.

A. *Other.* ***Autre*** must be preceded by a determiner (article, demonstrative, possessive, etc.) or by ***nous, vous***. Special features are to be observed in clauses containing ***autre*** (see §61B and C).

C'est un beau livre, mais j'en ai d'autres de plus beaux.
That's a beautiful book, but I have others that are more beautiful.

Nous autres, Américains, . . .
We Americans . . . (As for us Americans . . .)

Note the meaning of imminence of the following expressions:

D'un jour à l'autre. D'un moment à l'autre.
Any day. Any moment.

D'une seconde à l'autre. D'une minute à l'autre.
Any second. Any minute.

B. *Both, either one, neither one, one . . . the other,* etc. ***Autre*** is used in combination with ***un*** in the following expressions:

- ***L'un et l'autre*** (*both*). When this expressions is the subject of a verb, the verb must be in the plural.

  L'un et l'autre m'appartiennent.
  Both belong to me.

- ***L'un ou l'autre*** (*either one*). When this expression is the subject of a verb, the verb must be in the singular. But if this expression is used in its plural form ***les uns ou les autres***, then the verb it governs is in the plural.

  L'un ou l'autre me suffira.
  Either one will be enough for me.

Les uns ou les autres lui conviennent.
Either pair suits him (her).

- ***Ni l'un ni l'autre*** (*neither one*). When this expression is the subject of a verb, the verb must be in the singular, unless the expression is in its plural form ***ni les un(e)s ni les autres***.

Ni l'un ni l'autre ne viendra.
Neither one will come.
Ni les uns ni les autres ne viendront.
Neither group will come.

- ***L'un . . . , l'autre . . .*** (*one . . . , the other . . .*), ***les uns . . . , les autres . . .*** (*some . . . , the others . . .*), ***les uns . . . , d'autres . . .*** (*some . . . , others . . .*), ***certains . . . , d'autres . . .*** (*some . . . , others . . .*).

Each half of these four expressions governs one verb.

L'un parle, l'autre écoute. Il flatte l'un, félicite l'autre.
One speaks, the other listens. He flatters one, congratulates the other.
Les uns se cachent, les autres s'enfuient.
Some hide, the others run away.
Les uns se cachent, d'autres s'enfuient.
Some hide, others run away.
On fait confiance aux uns, on méprise d'autres.
One trusts some, one scorns others.

- ***L'un l'autre*** (*each other, one another*). This expression and its plural form ***les uns les autres*** always accompany a plural pronominal verb. Their main use is to make clear the *reciprocal* meaning of the verb instead of its *reflexive* meaning.

Elles ont essayé leurs robes neuves. Elles se sont regardées dans la glace de l'armoire, puis elles se sont regardées l'une l'autre.
They tried on their new dresses. They looked at themselves in the mirror of the armoire, then they looked at each other.
Ils se sont regardés l'un l'autre.
They looked at each other.

L'un l'autre, or ***les uns les autres***, may be added to a verb as a sort of "explanation" of its meaning, particularly when the verb commands a preposition. Observe the word order in the following examples.

Ils se sont assis l'un en face de l'autre.
They sat down facing one another (lit. one in front of the other).
Nous nous lancions la balle (de) l'un à l'autre.
We were throwing the ball to one another (lit. from one to the other).
Les écoliers marchaient l'un derrière l'autre.
The schoolboys walked behind one another (lit. one behind the other).

Les deux vieux s'aidaient à marcher, appuyés l'un au bras de l'autre.
The old couple helped one another walking, leaning against each other's arm (lit. one on the other's arm).

64. Autrui.

Another person, someone else, neighbor, fellow man. ***Autrui*** is used without any article or determiner. It is invariable, and it is seldom used as a subject.

Ne convoitez pas les biens d'autrui.
Do not covet your neighbor's goods.

65. Certains.

Some. ***Certains*** is used without any article or determiner, and only in the plural (masculine or feminine). It may be subject or object. Certain features are to be observed in clauses where ***certains*** is used (see §61B and C.). ***Certains*** is often used in opposition to ***d'autres*** (see §63B.).

Certains sont plus riches que d'autres.
Some are richer than others.

Ses timbres sont beaux, mais certains des miens sont plus beaux.
His stamps are nice, but some of mine are more beautiful.

Voici quelques pommes, mais il y en a certaines de mauvaises.
Here are a few apples, but there are some that are bad.

(See also ***certain***, indefinite adjective, §32.)

66. Chacun.

Everyone, each one, everybody. ***Chacun*** is used without any article or determiner. It stresses each unit of a group individually, whereas plurality is emphasized by ***tous*** (§77). ***Chacun*** is always singular. It is feminine only when it represents each one in an all-feminine group (persons or things).

J'ai lu chacun de ces livres-là.
I have read each one of those books.

Nous avons essayé chacune de ces voitures.
We tried each one of these cars.

Chacun d'eux (chacune d'elles) recevra un certificat.
Each (one) of them will receive a certificate.

Chacun pour soi.
Everyone for himself.

(See also §60F.)

67. Nul.

No one, nobody. ***Nul*** is used without any article or determiner. It is singular (masculine or feminine) and always used as subject. It requires the negative particle ***ne*** before the verb. ***Nul*** should be restricted to formal language. Its informal equivalent is ***personne***.

Nul n'est immortel.
No one is immortal.

La salle était fermée à clé. Personne n'a pu entrer.
The room was locked. No one could get in.

NOTE: ***Nul*** is also a descriptive adjective meaning "zero," "worthless," "void," etc., and found in the phrase ***nulle part*** (*nowhere*) (see §37). ***Annuler*** is the verb corresponding to the indefinite ***nul*** (*to annul, to void, to cancel*).

68. On.

One, people, we, you, they, or in place of passive voice. ***On*** is always subject, and the verb must always be in the third person singular.

On a fini à l'heure. Ici on parle anglais.
We finished on time. English spoken.

Lorsqu'on a tort, on doit l'admettre.
When you are wrong, you must admit it.

On doit toujours faire preuve de respect envers ses parents.
One must always show respect towards one's parents.

En Angleterre on boit du thé. En France on préfère le café.
In England they drink tea. In France people prefer coffee.

On is neutral and invariable, but a predicate adjective may agree with ***on*** in whatever way the context indicates.

On était bien contentes d'avoir chacune un cavalier.
We were very glad to have an escort each.

On is used without any article or determiner, but for reasons of euphony it is sometimes written ***l'on***, especially after ***si, où, ou, et,*** and ***que***. The choice of ***l'on*** instead of ***on*** is always optional.
The personal pronouns corresponding to ***on*** are ***se*** and ***soi***, as is the case with indefinite pronouns in general. But when needed, most other personal pronouns (except ***il, elle, le,***

la, l', lui) may be used to refer to ***on***, as directed by the context, usually the same pronoun as in English.

On doit toujours dire la vérité si l'on veut qu'on nous croie.
One must always speak the truth if one wishes people to believe us.

NOTE: ***On*** is used in French much more frequently than the pronoun *one* in American English. It does not serve only in generalizations or in the expression of universal truths (proverbs, maxims, etc.). Some of the practical uses of ***on*** are to avoid the somewhat delicate choice between ***tu*** and ***vous*** in addressing a person; to avoid using ***je*** when this pronoun might sound too selfish or immodest; to avoid using a clearly identifiable pronoun because of the harshness of a judgment, the bluntness of a remark, an insinuation, an irony or a sarcasm; to avoid using ***nous*** when this pronoun might sound too formal, etc. The most frequent use of ***on*** is in active sentences where all the emphasis is on the action performed, not on the subject who performed it. In English the passive voice serves the same purposes, to avoid mention of the agent by whom the action was performed.

On m'a volé ma voiture.
My car has been stolen.

69. Personne.

A. *No one, nobody, not anybody, not anyone.* ***Personne*** is used without any article or determiner. As a negative word, it must be paired with the particle ***ne*** before the main verb.

Je ne vois personne. Personne ne bouge. Que personne ne sorte!
I see no one. No one is moving. Let no one leave!

Ne parlez à personne!
Don't talk to anybody.

Elle n'avait invité personne. Personne n'était venu.
She had invited no one. No one had come.

There are differences between the position of ***personne*** and that of ***rien*** and other negative indefinite pronouns. ***Personne*** must be placed *after* the past participle in a compound tense and *after* the infinitive in an infinitive construction (details in §61D).

Il n'a rien vu. Il n'a vu personne.
He saw nothing. He saw no one.

Je ne veux rien entendre. Je ne veux voir personne.
I don't want to hear anything. I don't want to see anybody.

Personne is invariable. A modifying adjective or a predicate adjective will normally agree with it in the masculine singular, but if ***personne*** clearly refers to a woman, the modifying adjective or predicate adjective will agree in the feminine singular.

Personne d'autre ici n'est plus coquette.
No one else here is more coquettish.

Certain features are to be observed in clauses where ***personne*** is used (see §61A and B).

B. *Anyone, anybody.* **Personne** has a positive meaning if the verb already has a full two-part negation, or if it expresses inquiring, doubt, restriction, or concession. It also has a positive meaning when it serves as the second term of a comparison. ***Personne*** is then used without ***ne***.

Je doute que personne y parvienne.
I doubt that anyone can manage it.
Je ne doute pas que personne y parvienne.
I do not doubt that someone can manage it. (I know that someone will succeed.)
Elle le connaît mieux que personne.
She knows him better than anyone.

Personne is also a feminine noun meaning *person*. Compare ***personne*** with ***aucun*** (§62), ***nul*** (§67), and ***quiconque*** (§74).

70. Plusieurs.

Several. ***Plusieurs*** is used without any article or determiner. It is always plural (masculine or feminine) and can refer to persons or things.

Je voudrais essayer des chaussures. J'en ai vu plusieurs de jolies dans la vitrine.
I would like to try on some shoes. I saw several that were pretty in the display window.

Certain features are to be observed in clauses where ***plusieurs*** is used (see §61B and C.). ***Plusieurs*** is also an indefinite adjective (§38).

71. Quelque chose.

Something (anything in interrogative and negative sentences). ***Quelque chose*** is used without any article or determiner. It is always singular. Although the noun ***chose*** is feminine, the group ***quelque chose*** is masculine, and any adjective referring to it must agree with it in the masculine singular. An adjective that modifies ***quelque chose*** must be preceded by ***de*** (see §61B).

Il vient de se produire quelque chose d'affreux.
Something awful has just happened.

NOTE: The noun ***chose*** is used in two very common expressions that follow the same rules as ***quelque chose***:

- ***Autre chose***, which is often used to replace ***quelque chose d'autre***: *something else (anything else* in interrogative and in negative sentences), especially with a modifier.
- ***Grand-chose***, which is found only as object of a negative verb: *not much.*

Avez-vous autre chose d'élégant et de pas trop cher à me faire voir?
Have you got anything else elegant and not too expensive to show me?
Non, il ne me reste plus grand-chose (de beau ni de bon marché).
No, I don't have much left any more (that is nice or inexpensive).

72. *Quelqu'un.*

A. *Someone, somebody (anyone, anybody* in interrogative and in negative sentences). ***Quelqu'un*** may be applied in this masculine singular form to any indefinite person.

J'ai vu quelqu'un dans l'escalier.
I saw someone in the stairway.

Quelqu'un may become ***quelqu'une*** if there is a clear reference to a female person.

Quelqu'une de vous a-t-elle perdu un sac à main?
Has any of you lost a purse?

Quelqu'un requires the use of ***de*** before a following unmodified adjective that modifies it (§61B). If the adjective is itself modified, the use of ***de*** is optional.

Y a-t-il quelqu'un d'absent?
Is there anyone absent? (unmodified)
J'ai vu quelqu'un caché derrière le rideau.
I saw someone hiding behind the curtain. (modified)

B. *Some, a few (any* in interrogative and negative sentences). ***Quelqu'un*** in the plural (***quelques-uns, quelques-unes***) applies to both persons and things. Certain features are to be observed in clauses where those plural forms are used (see §61B and C.).

J'en ai vu quelques-uns dans la classe.
I saw a few (of them) in the classroom. (students)
J'ai vu quelqu'un de blessé.
I saw someone wounded.
J'en ai trouvé quelques-unes de magnifiques.
I found a few that were magnificent. (flowers)

NOTE: Negative sentences may contain ***quelqu'un*** or one of its other forms, but ***personne*** (for people) and ***aucun*** (for things) are preferable.

C. *Someone important.* ***Quelqu'un*** used as an unmodified predicate takes on the meaning of *someone important, a person of authority or prestige* (popular language).

Maintenant qu'elle est devenue quelqu'un, elle ne dit plus bonjour à personne.
Now that she has become a big name, she no longer says hi to anyone.

(See also the indefinite adjective ***quelque***, §41.)

73. *Qui, quoi.*

Qui: *Whoever, whomever, no matter who, no matter whom.*
Quoi: *Whatever, no matter what.*

Qui and ***quoi*** must be associated with the relative pronoun ***que*** (rarely any other form) followed by a verb in the subjunctive.

Qui que ce soit. Quoi que ce soit.
Whoever it may be. Whatever it may be.

Quoi que vous fassiez, il sera trop tard.
Whatever you do, it will be too late.

Qui que vous soyez, sortez!
Whoever you are, get out!

À qui que vous parliez, dites bien tout le message.
Whomever you speak to, be sure to give the full message.

However, the expressions ***n'importe qui*** and ***n'importe quoi*** allow these indefinite pronouns to be used without the relative ***que***.

N'importe qui peut se tromper.
Anyone (no matter who it is) can make a mistake.

Il dit n'importe quoi.
He is talking nonsense. (lit. he says just anything, no matter what it is)

Qui and ***quoi*** require ***de*** before a following adjective that modifies them.

Qui de nouveau que vous embauchiez, assurez-vous de son expérience.
No matter whom you hire, verify his or her experience.

NOTE: ***Qui*** and ***quoi*** are also interrogative pronouns (see §§78-81) and relative pronouns (see §§95-103).

74. *Quiconque.*

Any, anyone, anybody (in affirmative sentences). ***Quiconque*** is very similar to ***qui*** (§73 above), and ***n'importe qui*** is a less formal equivalent. ***Quiconque*** is invariable. An adjective modifying ***quiconque*** normally agrees with it in the masculine singular unless the context clearly indicates a feminine. Note that as subject ***quiconque*** (or ***qui*** or ***n'importe qui***) serves as subject of two verbs.

Qui m'aime me suive.
Whoever loves me, let him (her) follow me.

Quiconque veut être hôtesse de l'air doit être prête à voyager.
Whoever (anyone who) wants to be a stewardess must be ready to travel.

Il chante aussi bien que quiconque.
He sings as well as anyone.

Compare ***quiconque*** with ***personne*** (§69B) and with ***aucun*** (§62B).

75. Rien.

A. *Nothing, not anything.* ***Rien*** is invariable. An adjective or participle that modifies it must be in the masculine singular. Certain features are to be observed in clauses where ***rien*** is used (see §61A, B, and D).

Il n'en résultera rien de bon. Rien de bon n'en résultera.
Nothing good will result from it.

B. *Something, anything.* ***Rien*** has a positive meaning if the verb it refers to already has a full two-part negation, or expresses inquiring, doubt, restriction, concession. It also has a positive meaning if it serves as the second term of a comparison. ***Rien*** is then used without ***ne***.

Je ne pense pas qu'il y ait rien de meilleur.
I do not think there can be anything better.

Cela vaut mieux que rien.
It's better than nothing.

NOTE: ***Rien*** is also a masculine noun meaning *a very small amount, a trace, a trifle, etc.*

76. Tel.

Such, such a one. ***Tel*** is used only in the singular when it serves as a pronoun. In the plural, use ***certains*** (§65). ***Tel*** may be used without any article or determiner, or with the indefinite article ***un, une*** to designate a person whose name is unknown: *so-and-so*.

Un tel (une telle) était là.
So-and-so was there.

Tel est présent aujourd'hui qui hier ne l'était pas.
One (someone) (lit. such) is here today who was not yesterday.

Tel is more frequently found as an indefinite adjective (see §42).

77. *Tout.*

A. *All, everything.* In this sense, only the masculine singular form ***tout*** is used.

Tout est arrangé. Vous verrez tout. Tout ce qu'il a dit est vrai.
All is arranged. You will see everything. All that he said is true.

As this meaning is the opposite of ***rien***, the position of ***tout*** is the same as that of ***rien*** in identical circumstances (see §§69A and 75A).

Il n'a rien compris. Il a tout compris.
He understood nothing. He understood everything.
Elle ne voulait rien faire. Elle voulait tout faire.
She wanted to do nothing. She wanted to do everything.

B. *All of us, all of you, all of them.* In this sense, only the plural forms ***tous*** and ***toutes*** are used. *All of them* may refer to persons or things.

A-t-il lu tous ses livres? —Oui, il les a tous lus.
Has he read all his books? —Yes, he has read all of them.
Les fourmis ne bougeaient plus. Toutes étaient mortes. L'enfant les avait toutes tuées.
The ants were no longer moving. All (of them) had died. The child had killed them all.

NOTE: As shown in the above examples, when ***tous*** or ***toutes*** is a direct object, the verb must be preceded by a direct object personal pronoun, not by ***en*** as is the case with most of the other indefinite pronouns (see §61C).
See also ***tout***, indefinite adjective (§43), and the pronunciation note in §60E.

INTERROGATIVE PRONOUNS

78. *Forms.*

The interrogative pronouns are of two kinds: the short forms with ***qui, que, quoi***, and the long forms, which can be described as a substantivation of the interrogative adjectives by the addition of a definite article: ***lequel, laquelle, lesquels, lesquelles***.

Both forms can be used with the interrogative expression ***est-ce que***.

79. *Short forms.*

The short interrogative pronoun has the following forms and functions:

antecedent	**subject**	**direct object**	**after prepositions**
for persons	qui	qui	. . . qui:
for things	(quoi*)	que (quoi*)	. . . quoi*

****Quoi*** is used in the following cases:

A. As subject when the verb is not expressed.

Quoi de neuf? Quoi de plus juste que cette récompense?
What('s) new? What (can be) more fair than this reward?

B As an object (direct or of a preposition) in direct questions, if the question is asked by intonation rather than by structure. ***Quoi*** then follows the verb; if the verb is an infinitive, ***quoi*** precedes the infinitive.

Alors, mon petit (mon gars, mon garçon), tu veux quoi?
Well, my boy, what is it you want?

Quoi dire? Quoi faire? (Que dire? Que faire?)
What to say? What to do?

C. ***Quoi*** is the regular interrogative pronoun to use for things (or neuter) after all prepositions, in all types of constructions.

Dis-moi, un peu, tu penses à quoi?
Tell me now, what is it you are thinking about?

En quoi cela vous concerne-t-il?
In what way does this concern you?

Pour quoi faire?
What for?

À quoi bon?
What's the use?

D. ***Quoi*** is frequently used as a kind of interjection, alone or accompanied by other interjections or adverbs.

Quoi?! Eh quoi?! Hé quoi?!
What?! Well what?! What now?!(etc.)

Quoi donc? Et quoi donc? Et quoi encore?
What now? What next? What more? (etc.)

Qui followed by the verb ***être*** functions as a predicate. Compare with the interrogative adjective ***quel*** (§45B; §46A). Note that in this case the subject and verb are inverted and that both may be in the plural. However, if ***qui*** is the real subject of the verb instead of a predicate of the subject, the verb must be in the third person singular.

Qui sont ces gens-là?
Who are those people?

Qui est là?
Who is there?

80. Long forms.

The long interrogative pronoun differs from the other interrogative pronouns in that it emphasizes the meaning of choice or selection: *which one(s)*. It has the following forms:

	singular	**plural**
masculine	lequel	lesquels
feminine	laquelle	lesquelles

These forms serve in all functions, without any further variation. They can be subject, direct object, or object of a preposition.

Lequel des deux sera le premier?
Which one of the two will be the first?

Voici deux photos. Laquelle choisis-tu?
Here are two pictures. Which one do you choose?

Avec lequel de tes amis es-tu sortie?
With which one of your friends did you go out?

NOTE: Since each of these interrogative pronouns begins with a prefixed definite article, contractions must be made when the preceding preposition is ***à*** or ***de***. The contracted forms are then, with the preposition ***à***:

	singular	**plural**
masculine	auquel	auxquels
feminine	à laquelle	auxquelles

with the preposition ***de***:

	singular	**plural**
masculine	duquel	desquels
feminine	de laquelle	desquelles

See also ***quel***, interrogative adjective (§45).

81. Forms with est-ce que.

The short forms and long forms of the interrogative pronouns can be used with the expression ***est-ce que (est-ce qui*** for subject), which gives them an informal or conversational tone. All the forms thus obtained must be used without any inversion of the verb and subject.

	subject	**direct object**	**after preposition**
for persons	qui est-ce qui lequel est-ce qui	qui est-ce que lequel est-ce que	. . . qui est-ce que . . . lequel est-ce que
for things	qu'est-ce qui lequel est-ce qui	qu'est-ce que lequel est-ce que	. . . quoi est-ce que . . . lequel est-ce que

NOTE: The ***lequel*** form is to be used mainly as object of a preposition, for both persons and things. In other functions, especially as subject, it is preferable to use the single form ***lequel***, without ***est-ce-qui, est-ce que***.

Qui est-ce qui a conduit?
Who did the driving?

Qui est-ce que vous avez vu?
Whom did you see?

À qui est-ce que vous avez parlé?
To whom did you speak?

Qu'est-ce qui s'est passé?
What happened?

Qu'est-ce que vous avez fait?
What did you do?

Avec quoi est-ce que vous l'avez fait?
With what did you do it?

Lequel de ces hommes (est-ce qui) a découvert l'électricité?
Which one of these men discovered electricity?

Lequel est-ce que vous avez vu?
Which one did you see?

Sur lequel est-ce que la pomme est tombée?
On which one did the apple fall?

Parmi ces métaux, lequel (est-ce qui) est le plus précieux?
Among these metals, which one is the most precious?

Lequel est-ce que tu voudrais posséder?
Which one would you like to own?

Avec lequel est-ce qu'on fait les alliances?
With which one are wedding rings made?

See also relative pronouns (§§95-103), interrogative adjectives (§§44-46), interrogative adverbs (§204).

PERSONAL PRONOUNS

82. Forms.

The personal pronouns have the following forms and functions:

person	subject	direct object	indirect object	reflexive reciprocal	disjunctive (stress)
singular					
1st	je	me	me	me	moi
2nd	tu	te	te	te	toi
3rd	il/elle	le/la	lui	se	lui/elle/soi*
plural					
1st	nous	nous	nous	nous	nous
2nd	vous	vous	vous	vous	vous
3rd	ils/elles	les	leur	se	eux/elles/soi*

****Soi*** is the disjunctive personal pronoun used in reference with an indefinite pronoun. For its uses, see §88I.

83. Notes.

A. The table above shows a marked separation between the first four columns, containing the *conjunctive pronouns*, and the last column, which contains the *disjunctive pronouns*.

The *conjunctive* pronouns precede the verb and are always closely linked with it whereas the *disjunctive* pronouns are always separated from the verb, generally by means of a preposition. The only exception occurs with the *affirmative imperative*.

B. When a verb is in the *affirmative imperative*, no personal pronoun can stand before it. The subject pronoun is always left out of the sentence. The direct object, indirect object, and reflexive pronouns must be placed after the verb, and they must be connected to the verb with hyphens. The pronouns ***me, te*** must be replaced by ***moi, toi***, or by ***m', t'*** if ***y*** or ***en*** immediately follows.

Regardez-le. Donnez-la-leur.
Look at it. Give it to them.

Écoute-moi. Donne-m'en quelques-un(e)s.
Listen to me. Give me a few (of them).

Ce livre? Apportez-le-moi.
That book? Bring it to me.

Note that the imperative is an exception only in the *affirmative*. If the imperative verb is negative, the normal position of the pronouns is before the verb.

Ce livre? Ne m'en parle pas!
That book? Don't talk to me about it.

Ne le regardez pas. Ne le leur donnez pas.
Don't look at it. Don't give it to them.

C. The neutral pronoun *it* does not exist in French. When *it* replaces a specific noun, the gender of the noun replaced governs the choice of the pronoun: masculine ***il, le, lui*** (depending on the function) for masculine nouns, and feminine ***elle, la, elle*** (depending on the function) for feminine nouns.

Regardez ce château. Il est très beau.
Look at that castle. It is very beautiful.

Regardez cette maison. Elle est très belle.
Look at that house. It is very beautiful.

If *it* does not replace a specific noun, it may be translated ***ce*** before a form of ***être***, or ***cela*** or ***ça*** before another verb (see §58B, C; §286).

D. The pronouns ***je, me, te, se, le, la*** must be elided when they immediately precede a word (the verb or a second personal pronoun) that begins with a vowel or mute ***h***. Note also the particular case of ***moi*** and ***toi*** in paragraph B, above.

J'attends. Je n'attends pas. Je l'attends.
I'm waiting. I'm not waiting. I'm waiting for him (her).

Elle m'attend. Elle s'habitue à son métier.
She's waiting for me. She is getting used to her job.

E. The English pronouns *they* and *them* serve for masculine and feminine. In the functions where a choice can be made in French between a masculine form and a feminine one, the gender of the noun replaced should be checked and the right pronoun selected.

J'ai vu Jeanne et Élise. J'ai dîné avec elles.
I saw Jeanne and Élise. I had dinner with them.

In the functions where no choice is available, as with ***les, leur, lui***, confusion may result in the French sentence. To avoid this, disjunctive pronouns should be used (see §88G).

J'ai vu Jeanne et Élise. Elles étaient avec Paul et René. Je les ai invitées, elles, mais pas eux.
I saw Jeanne and Élise. They were with Paul and René. I invited them (the girls), but not them (the boys).

84. Inversion.

The subject personal pronouns normally precede the verb. In interrogative sentences, however, there may be inversion of the subject. The subject personal pronoun then follows the verb and is connect to the verb with a hyphen. If the verb is in a compound tense, the subject pronoun is then placed after the auxiliary.

Est-il ici? Où sont-ils? Que fait-elle?
Is he here? Where are they? What is she doing?

Avez-vous fini? Es-tu sorti?
Have you finished? Did you go out?

Il and ***elle*** must be preceded by ***-t-*** if the verb they follow ends in a vowel.

A-t-il travaillé tard? Étudie-t-elle?
Did he work late? Is she studying?

The pronoun ***je*** should not be inverted if the verb ends in a mute ***e***. The interrogation should then be made with the expressions ***est-ce que*** placed before ***je*** and the verb.

Est-ce que je prononce comme il faut?
Do I pronounce correctly? (properly)

but: Puis-je vous accompagner?
May I accompany you?

In formal style, the inversion of ***je*** with a verb ending in a mute ***e*** is allowed. The case is not very frequent in interrogative sentences, however. Inversion is more frequent for some other reason, such as the presence of certain adverbs at the beginning of the sentence or the use of literary tenses in conditional clauses (see §200 and §268A5).

In interrogative clauses where the subject is not a personal pronoun, a direct inversion cannot always be made. The subject must be stated first, then the verb with an inverted second subject—a personal pronoun, which repeats the first one.

Les étudiants ont-ils compris le problème?
Have the students understood the problem?

La vôtre est-elle meilleure?
Is yours better?

This inversion, the "complex inversion" is required in sentences whose subject is something other than a personal pronoun, ***ce***, or ***on*** and that contains no interrogative word.

When the interrogation is made with an interrogative word (interrogative adjective, pronoun, adverb), the inversion may be either direct or complex with all types of subjects, except when ***pourquoi*** is the interrogative word. ***Pourquoi*** requires the inversion to be complex. The choice between direct and complex inversion may depend on style, clarity, and structure. Direct inversion may not be used if the verb has a direct object.

Quand (d'où, comment, etc.) **reviennent vos parents?** (direct inversion)
or: Quand vos parents reviennent-ils? (complex inversion)
When (from where, how, etc.) are your parents coming back?
but: Dans quelle université votre fils fait-il ses études?
In what university does your son study?

When in doubt about the kind of inversion to choose, one may use ***est-ce que***, which governs declarative word order. ***Est-ce que*** begins the clause if no interrogative word is being used. It directly follows the interrogative word or group in clauses where such a word or group is being used.

Est-ce que vous savez nager?
Can you swim?
Quand est-ce que vous partez?
When are you leaving?
Quel livre est-ce que tu as choisi?
What book did you choose?
De quoi est-ce que tu te plains?
What are you complaining about?
Pourquoi est-ce que la bonne n'est pas venue?
Pourquoi la bonne n'est-elle pas venue?
Why didn't the maid come?

See also §83.

85. Direct object.

A. The direct object personal pronoun must be placed immediately before the verb it refers to, except if the verb is in the *affirmative imperative* (see §83B).

Je la vois. Il m'entendra.
I see her. He will hear me.
Regardez-les! Regardez-les courir!
Look at them! Watch them run!

B. When the verb referred to is an infinitive depending on a verb of *perception* or ***faire*** or ***laisser***, the direct object personal pronoun precedes the main verb (see §89A, note 5), not the infinitive. The personal pronoun used in English in this instance is always in the objective case (*me, him, us,* etc.) even though it may really be the subject of the infinitive. The same is true in French.

Je les ai entendus rire.
I heard them laugh. (*They* laughed.)
Je les ai vu couper. Je les ai vu abattre.
I saw them being cut down. (Someone cut *them.*)

For cases where the verb already has a direct object, see §86B. The agreement of the past participle in this type of construction is not obvious. See §273 for details.

C. ***Le*** is used as a neutral pronoun in the following cases:

1) To announce or to recall a whole clause, a phrase, an idea, or an infinitive. This use of ***le*** is optional in comparisons.

Il fait plus chaud que je ne (le) pensais.
It is warmer than I thought (it would be).

Je le pense. Elle me l'a dit.
I think so. She told me so.

Je dois travailler. —Je le dois aussi.
I have to work. —I have to also.

NOTE: When the idea represents assent or dissent (*I think so, I don't think so, etc.*), it is preferable to use the adverbs ***oui, si, non*** instead of ***le***.

Va-t-il chanter? —Je pense que oui. Je crois que non.
Is he going to sing? —I think so (he is). I believe (he is) not.

Il n'est pas parti? —Je crois que si. Je crois que non.
Hasn't he left? —I believe he has. I believe he has not.

2) To recall an adjective or adjectival phrase. ***Le*** is not optional in this case.

Il est riche, je ne le suis pas. (fam.: **Moi, non.** or: **Pas moi.)**
He is rich, I am not.

Nous étions hors d'haleine. Paul ne l'était pas car il n'avait pas couru.
We were out of breath. Paul was not because he had not run.

3) To recall an infinitive that is the direct object of the main verb even though it appears to be object of the preposition ***de***. Be sure to check whether the main verb can have direct objects.

Je lui ai demandé hier de faire un effort. Je le lui demande encore aujourd'hui.
I asked him yesterday to make an effort. I'm asking him again today (asking it of him).

Je crains d'être en retard. —Moi aussi, je le crains. (***craindre*** needs a direct object)
I'm afraid to be late. —I'm afraid of it also.

J'ai peur d'être en retard. —Moi aussi, j'en ai peur. (***avoir peur*** needs a complement introduced by ***de***)
I'm afraid to be late. —I'm afraid of it also.

See also §92C.

86. Indirect object.

The indirect object personal pronoun must be placed immediately before the verb it refers to, except if the verb is in the *affirmative imperative* (see §83).

A. An indirect object personal pronoun normally answers the question "to whom" or "for whom." This is true in French as well as in English. An indirect object personal pronoun may also be used in French in cases where it is not called for in English. One such case is to express possession, or with nonreflexive verbs having for their object (direct or indirect) a part of the body or an article of clothing (§55).

Je lui ai serré la main.
I shook his hand.

Elle m'a tiré les cheveux!
She pulled my hair!

Tu leur en as mis plein la vue! (coll.)
You dazzled them!

Ils lui ont graissé la patte! (idiom.)
They bribed him!

B. Another case is when a verb of *perception* or ***laisser*** or ***faire*** is followed by a dependent infinitive, and each of the two verbs has a direct object of its own. The noun or pronoun that is subject of the infinitive (the action) takes the form of an *indirect object*.

J'ai fait tondre la pelouse à mon fils.
I had my son mow the lawn.

Je la lui ai fait tondre.
I had him mow it. (or: I had it mowed by him.)

There is a tendency in today's informal French to have each object take on its actual direct object form and its normal position in relation to its own verb (see §87B).

J'ai fait mon fils tondre la pelouse. Je l'ai fait la tondre.

C. With some verbs, an indirect object personal pronoun cannot be used. It must be expressed by the preposition ***à*** followed by a *disjunctive pronoun*, placed after the verb.

Je pense à elle. Prenez garde à eux.
I'm thinking of her. Beware of them.

Among the verbs in this category are:

s'abandonner à	yield to
s'accoutumer à	get used to
s'adresser à	speak to, appeal to, inquire with
s'appliquer à	apply to, concern
s'arracher à	tear away from
s'attacher à	grow attached, fond
conduire à	take to, lead to
se consacrer à	devote oneself to
courir à	run to

en venir à	consider the case of
faire attention à	beware of, keep an eye on
se fier à	trust (in)
s'habituer à	get used to
s'intéresser à	get interested in
se joindre à	join
penser à	think of
prendre garde à	beware of
renoncer à	renounce
revenir à soi	regain consciousness
songer à	dream of
tenir à	refuse to part with
venir à	come to

See also §89, §91.

Since the indirect object pronoun ***lui*** translates both *to him* and *to her*, and ***leur*** is both masculine and feminine, a disjunctive pronoun following ***à*** may be added to the verb when clarity is needed (§88G).

87. *Reflexive, reciprocal.*

A. The reflexive pronoun (in English: *myself, yourself, himself, herself, itself, ourselves, yourselves, themselves*) must be placed before the verb, except if the verb is in the *affirmative imperative* (see §83B). The plural pronouns ***nous, vous, se*** may be used with a reciprocal meaning. To avoid the ambiguity, forms of ***l'un l'autre*** are sometimes added after the verb (§63B). To emphasize the reflexive meaning, the pronouns ***moi-même, toi-même, lui-même, elle-même, nous-mêmes, vous-mêmes, eux-mêmes, elles-mêmes*** may be added after a verb, especially if the verb is not an exclusively reflexive one.

Je me suis instruit moi-même. L'enfant est fier de s'être habillé lui-même.
I taught myself. The child is proud to have dressed himself.

Elle s'est photographiée elle-même. Elles se sont photographiées l'une l'autre devant le monument.
She took a picture of herself. They photographed each other in front of the monument.

In dictionaries, a reflexive verb is presented in the infinitive with the reflexive pronoun ***se***. In context such a verb must be preceded by the reflexive pronoun corresponding to its own reference.

Il vient de se lever. Je viens de me lever.
He has just gotten up. I have just gotten up.

Ils m'ont obligé à m'asseoir.
They forced me to sit down.

B. A reflexive infinitive depending on a verb of *perception* or ***laisser*** or ***faire*** will generally be directly preceded by its reflexive pronoun. In some instances, the reflexive pronoun may be left out. But in no case can it be placed before the main verb together with another personal pronoun.

Je l'ai vu se précipiter vers la sortie.
I saw him rush toward the exit.

Ils m'ont fait (m') asseoir.
They made me sit down.

but: Je me le suis fait offrir.
I had it offered to me. (The reflexive here is ***se faire***, not the infinitive ***offrir***.)

See §89A, note 5.

C. The meaning of a French reflexive verb (it should really be called a "pronominal verb") is often neither reflexive nor reciprocal. It may correspond to an English passive construction or to an active construction with a passive meaning, or it may indicate some subjective aspect of the action. English popular language frequently makes use of the reflexive pronouns in this last way: "He got himself fired!" "Have yourself a good time."

See also §304.

To become, to grow, to get followed by an adjective often correspond to French reflexive verbs. This is due to the fact that a French reflexive verb is never static in meaning. It always implies action or progression.

Les jours s'allongent.
The days are getting longer.

Il s'est assis près de nous.
He sat down next to us. (action)

but: Il était assis près de nous.
He was sitting next to us. (position)

Many English verbs with no passive or reflexive or subjective meaning are translated into French by *idiomatic reflexive verbs* (see §304). Many English verbs of action (especially those of movement, or implying movement) are also translated into French reflexive verbs.

Il s'agit de bien se cacher.
It's a question of hiding well. The point is to hide well.

88. Disjunctive.

The *disjunctive* personal pronouns are also called *stressed*, *emphatic*, or *tonic*. They may be modified by ***-même, seul*** (both must agree with the pronoun they modify), or the adverb ***aussi***. These modifiers must directly follow the disjunctive pronoun. ***Même*** must be connected to the pronoun by a hyphen.

Moi-même. Eux-mêmes. Elle seule. Lui aussi.
Myself. Themselves. She alone. He as well.

Nous and ***vous*** may also be modified by the indefinite ***autres***, placed directly after the pronoun.

Nous autres, Américains, . . .
We Americans . . .

Nous, vous, eux, and ***elles*** may also be modified by ***tous*** in the masculine and ***toutes*** in the feminine, or by a cardinal number, placed directly after the pronoun.

Nous tous. Vous trois.
All of us. The three of you.

The disjunctive pronouns have the following uses:

A. The main function of a disjunctive pronoun is that of *object of a preposition*. This is especially true if the verb it refers to cannot accept the indirect object form of a personal pronoun (see §86C).

   Il vient avec moi. Je me suis adressé à lui.
   He is coming with me. I inquired with him.

B. All disjunctive pronouns can be used as subject, provided that a regular subject pronoun or noun precedes the verb. This disjunctive pronoun simply stresses the person and is in apposition to the regular subject. It may begin the clause or end it, being separated in both cases from the rest of the clause by a comma.

   Moi, je suis français. Il est américain, lui.
   I am French. *He* is American.

   Lui and ***eux*** however can be used directly as subject of the verb, without the regular subject pronoun. This is an elliptic construction. A slight pause must be made after ***lui*** or ***eux*** in reading such a clause.

   Moi, je suis français, mais lui est américain et eux sont australiens.
   I am French, but *he* is American and *they* are Australian.

   Lui-même, elle-même, eux-mêmes, may also be used directly as subject of the verb, without the regular subject pronoun.

   Elle-même me l'a dit (or: elle me l'a dit elle-même).
   She told me so herself. She was the one who told me so.

C. Disjunctive personal pronouns must be used in comparisons after ***que*** (*than, as*) and ***comme*** (*as, like*) if no verb is expressed in the second term.

Il est plus grand que toi.
He is taller than you.

Nous ferons exactement comme eux.
We will do exactly as they (do).

D. When an answer is made with a pronoun alone, that pronoun must be disjunctive. This is true also in questions and in exclamations.

Qui est là? —Moi. —Encore toi!
Who is there? —I (me). —You again!

If the answer is emphasized by ***c'est*** (*it is*), the pronoun must also be a disjunctive pronoun.

C'est moi. Est-ce que c'est toi, Paul?
It is I (it's me). Is it (that) you, Paul?

E. Whenever the emphatic construction ***c'est . . . qui, c'est . . . que*** (etc.), is used, the personal pronoun emphasized must be in the disjunctive form. Note that the singular ***c'est*** precedes the pronouns ***moi, toi, lui, elle, nous***, and ***vous***. Only ***eux*** and ***elles*** require the plural ***ce sont***. Note also that the verb following ***qui*** (subject) must agree with the personal pronoun being used.

C'est nous qui sommes (les) coupables.
We are the guilty ones.

C'est moi qui suis l'aîné.
I am the eldest. It is I who am the eldest.

Ce sont eux que nous avons vus.
They are the ones we saw.

F. The disjunctive pronoun is the only kind of pronoun that can be modified by a relative clause. Another kind of personal pronoun may be accompanied by a disjunctive pronoun in apposition (see B above), which is then itself modified by a relative clause.

Il m'a choisi, moi qui suis incapable de réussir.
He chose *me* who am incapable of succeeding.

Il m'a choisi, lui qui m'en veut à mort!
He chose me, and he hates me! (He hates me but he chose me anyway.)

Elle m'a fait signe, à moi qui ne la connais pas!
She waved at me, and I don't know her!

A disjunctive pronoun in apposition may also serve to emphasize a noun, by repeating it as the antecedent of a relative pronoun.

Paul, que j'ai connu enfant, ne m'a même pas dit bonjour.
Paul ne m'a même pas dit bonjour, lui que j'ai connu enfant.
Paul didn't even say hello to me, and I have known him since he was a child.

G. A disjunctive personal pronoun should be used whenever a simple direct or indirect object personal pronoun might be ambiguous. Since ***lui, leur, l'***, and ***les*** may be masculine or feminine, a disjunctive pronoun should be added for clarification. The disjunctive pronoun may stand in apposition, or it may replace the conjunctive pronoun altogether by being placed in emphatic position.

Nous l'attendons, elle (or: lui).
We are waiting for her (or: for him).

Je lui ai parlé, à elle (or: à lui).
I spoke to her (or: to him).

C'est elle que nous attendons.
She is the one we are waiting for.

Ce sont eux qui sont en retard.
They are the ones that are late.

À elles, on ne leur dit jamais rien!
No one ever says anything to *them*!

H. The disjunctive pronouns ***lui, elle, eux, elles*** preceded by the preposition ***à*** must be used to replace the indirect object pronouns ***lui*** and ***leur*** when these might otherwise have to conflict with ***me, te, se, nous, vous, se*** in front of the same verb (see §89, table; see also §86C).

Paul m'a présenté à elle.
Paul introduced me to her.

I. ***Soi*** is either masculine or feminine and either singular or plural. It refers to persons or things and is used mainly with an indefinite or vague antecedent.

Chacun pour soi. Cela va de soi.
Everyone for himself. That goes without saying (lit. goes by itself).

Soi may also be used to refer to a specific antecedent, particularly in cases where a number of possible antecedents might make the use of another pronoun (***lui, elle, eux, elles***) too ambiguous.

Le scout est fier de soi.
A scout is proud of himself.

Paul sentait que le professeur était content de lui.
Paul sensed that the professor was pleased with him.

In this last example, ***lui*** is ambiguous. It may refer to the professor as well as to Paul. Only the general idea of the statement permits us to assume that a professor is more likely to be satisfied with the work of a student than to be self-satisfied (which would be ***content de soi***).

The main function of ***soi*** is to be object of a preposition. Like other disjunctive pronouns, it is often modified by ***-même*** (self). The modified forms ***lui-même, elle-même, eux-mêmes, elles-mêmes*** often replace ***soi***, especially in the plural.

Beaucoup ne pensent qu'à eux-mêmes.
Many think only of themselves.

These forms, like ***soi***, refer to the last antecedent in the sentence and convey the same reflexive idea.

89. Relative position.

A. The normal position of all conjunctive personal pronouns being before the verb, except in the case of a verb in the affirmative imperative (see B), it frequently happens that two pronouns precede the same verb. The pronouns should then be placed in the order indicated in the following table.

me*			
te*			
se*	le	lui*	
	la		y, en
nous*	les	leur*	
vous*			
se*			

The pronouns in the first column always precede those in the other columns. Those in the second column always precede the pronouns in columns three or four. The pronouns in the third column always precede those in the fourth. The pronouns with asterisks may not be used together with a single verb.

Je te les envoie. Je la lui raconte. (cette histoire)
I'm sending them to you. I am telling it to him (her). (this story)
Il s'en moque. Je les y forcerai.
He doesn't care about it. I'll force them to.

Lui and ***leur*** cannot be used together with any of the pronouns shown in the first column of the table. If the case presents itself, ***lui*** must be replaced by ***à lui*** or ***à elle***, and ***leur*** must be replaced by ***à eux*** or ***à elles***. These prepositional objects are placed after the verb (see §86C; §88H).

Je vais vous conduire à lui.
I am going to take you to him.

A verb cannot be preceded by two pronouns from the first column in the table. One of the two must change its form: the direct object pronoun remains before the verb but the indirect object must be replaced by ***à*** and a disjunctive pronoun, placed after the verb. The case presents itself mainly with a certain group of verbs, listed in §86C.

Est-ce que je peux me joindre à vous?
May I join you (your group)?

Vous devez vous adresser à elle.
You must inquire with her. You must get your information from her.

The pronouns ***y*** and ***en*** should not be used together with the same verb, except in ready-made expressions such as the verb phrase ***y en avoir***.

Il y en a. Il y en avait. Il devrait y en avoir.
There is (are) some. There was (were) some. There should be some.

NOTES: 1) The subject pronouns always come first if the sentence contains no inversion (see §84). If the sentence is interrogative, the subject pronoun is inverted with the verb but the object pronouns remain in their respective positions before the verb, the only exception being that of a verb in the affirmative imperative (see B).

Nous les donnera-t-il?
Will he give them to us?

2) In negative sentences, the subject pronoun comes first, then the negative particle ***ne***, then the object pronouns directly before the verb.

Je ne les lui donnerai pas.
I won't give them to him.

The case of a verb in the negative imperative is not different, except that no subject is expressed.

Ne les lui donne pas.
Don't give them to him.

3) The first and second person pronouns obviously refer to persons, but the third persons (singular and plural) do not. In the case of disjunctive pronouns, the notion of human being and that of inanimate object may have to be considered. Animals will fit in either category, depending on the context (see §§90, 91, and 92B).

J'ai une amie et je pense à elle.
I have a girl friend and I think of her.
J'ai des examens et j'y pense.
I have exams and I think of them.
J'ai besoin d'outils. J'en ai besoin tout de suite.
I need tools. I need them right now.
Appelez mes deux filles. J'ai besoin d'elles.
Call my two daughters. I need them.

4) When two personal pronouns are objects of a dependent infinitive, they both precede that infinitive, not the main verb.

Je veux vous les donner.
I want to give them to you.

The main verb at the same time may have its own object pronoun or pronouns (reflexive verb, idiomatic expression, etc.).

Je m'en vais les lui donner.
I'll go and give them to him.

Elle s'est décidée à les lui offrir.
She made up her mind to offer them to him.

If the dependent infinitive is a reflexive verb, its reflexive pronoun must correspond with the subject of the action that the infinitive verb expresses.

Je vous ai vu vous enfuir.
I saw you run away.

5) If the main verb is one of perception (such as ***écouter, entendre, regarder, voir, sentir***) or ***laisser*** or ***faire***, the object pronoun—if there is only one—precedes the main verb. The object pronoun may be the object of either verb, its place is the same.

Je les entends parler. Je les ferai punir.
I hear them talking (*them* is subject of *talking*).
I'll have them punished (*them* is object of *punished*).

Je lui ai fait construire une chaise roulante.
I had a wheelchair built for him (*him* is indirect object of *built*).

If there are two object pronouns, both precede the main verb, provided that the pronoun that is object of the infinitive is ***le, la, l', les, y***, or ***en***.

Il me l'a fait comprendre.
He made it clear to me (lit. made me understand it).

Je ne vous le fais pas dire.
You said it, not I (lit. I don't make you say it).

Vous les lui ferez porter.
You'll have them delivered to him (or: You'll make him carry them).

Passez au palais de justice, vous l'y verrez juger.
Come by the courthouse, you'll see him being judged there.

If the pronoun that is the object of the infinitive is not ***le, la, l', les, y***, or ***en***, then each verb is to be preceded by its own pronoun object.

Je l'entends vous appeler.
I hear him calling you.

Il les a vus s'éteindre.
He saw them die out (lit. extinguish themselves).

Tu le feras te détester.
You will make him hate you.

6) The verb of perception (or ***laisser*** or ***faire***) may itself be a dependent infinitive. In that case, the finite verb should be considered to be only a helping verb, and ***faire, laisser***, or the verb of perception the main verb.

Tu vas le faire te détester.
You are going to make him hate you.
Je veux les lui faire porter.
I want to have them delivered to him (or: to make him carry them).
J'aimerais le lui entendre dire.
I'd like to hear him/her say it.

If the pronoun object of the infinitive is ***le, la, l', les***, and the pronoun object of the main verb (and subject of the infinitive) is also ***le, la, l', les***, the latter become ***lui*** (singular) or ***leur*** (plural) if both precede the main verb.

Je le lui ai fait faire.
I made him do it. (him = ***le*** = ***lui***; it = ***le***)
Je le lui ferai payer cher!
He (She) will pay dearly for it! (lit.: I will make him/her pay dearly for it!)

These statements may become ambiguous, although the immediate context usually helps keep the meaning clear. In the case of verbs of perception, however, each object pronoun should be placed in front of its own verb.

Lui avez-vous écrit une lettre vous-même? —Non, je la lui ai fait écrire.
Did you write him a letter yourself? —No, I had it written to him.
Avez-vous écrit la lettre vous-même? —Non, je la lui ai fait écrire.
Did you write the letter yourself? —No, I had it written to (or: by) him, her.
Il a lu la lettre, vous en êtes sûr? —Oui, j'en suis absolument certain, je l'ai vu la lire.
He read the letter, are you sure? —Yes, I am positive (about it), I saw him read it.

B. If the verb is in the *affirmative imperative*, the object personal pronouns must directly follow the verb and be connected to it and to each other by hyphens. No hyphen is used where there is an apostrophe.

The relative order of the pronouns is then:

DIRECT OBJECT before **INDIRECT OBJECT**
y and ***en*** are always in second position

Me and ***te***, in all functions, must be replaced by ***moi*** and ***toi*** after a verb in the affirmative imperative, or by ***m'*** and ***t'*** respectively before ***y*** or ***en***.

Donnez-les-moi. Apportez-m'en deux.
Give them to me. Bring me two (of them).

Rends-les-nous. Prête-la-leur.
Give them back to us. Lend it to them.
Allons-nous-en. Attendez-nous-y.
Let's leave. Wait for us there.

With the group of verbs that require ***à*** and a disjunctive pronoun instead of an indirect object type pronoun (see §86C), this prepositional object must follow the first pronoun.

If the pronoun ***le*** or ***la*** precedes a word beginning with a vowel that is not a personal pronoun, no elision occurs.

Donne-le à Paul. Mets-le en marche. Mets-toi en route.
Give it to Paul. Get it started. Get on your way.

90. Y and en.

Y and ***en*** are adverbial pronouns. They are pronouns because they can represent nouns, and they are adverbs because they can represent places and quantities.

Like the regular conjunctive personal pronouns, they must precede the verb they refer to, except if the verb is in the affirmative imperative, in which case they directly follow the verb and are connected to it by a hyphen.

Il en vient. Elle y va. Nous y pensons.
He comes from there. She is going there. We are thinking about it.
Allons-y. Prends-en.
Let's go there. Take some.

Y and ***en*** always come *after* any other personal pronoun object referring to the same verb. ***Me, moi, te, toi, le, la,*** and ***se*** become ***m', t', l',*** and ***s'*** when followed by ***y*** or ***en***.

Il les y conduit. Allons-nous-en.
He is taking them there. Let's get away from here.
Conduisez-les-y. Donnez-m'en.
Take them there. Give me some.

Note that after a verb in the affirmative imperative, the two pronouns and the verb are connected by hyphens, unless there is an apostrophe.

Y and ***en*** are rarely used together with the same verb, except in the verbal expression ***y en avoir***, in any tense or construction:

Il y en a. Il y en a eu. S'il y en avait eu. Il aurait pu y en avoir.
There is some. There was some. If there had been some. There could (might) have been some.

With the future and the conditional of the verb ***aller***, the use of the pronoun *y* should be avoided, in order to avoid the clash of ***i*** syllables. ***Y*** can then be replaced by the adverb ***là*** or ***là-bas***, or the verb ***aller*** by a synonym such as ***se rendre***.

J'irai là-bas demain. Je m'y rendrai demain.
I'll go there tomorrow.

91. Y.

The adverbial pronoun *y*, like all pronouns, may represent a noun. But the noun must be object of a verb and meet the following conditions:

- The noun must be preceded by the preposition ***à (au, aux)*** or any preposition of place, even one containing ***de***, such as ***loin de, au milieu de, etc.***
- The noun must represent neither a human being nor an animal.

Allez-vous souvent à Paris? —Oui, j'y vais deux fois par an.
Do you often fly to Paris? —Yes, I fly there twice a year.
Pensez-vous à votre examen? —Oui, j'y pense.
Are you thinking of your exam? —Yes, I am (thinking about it).
Êtes-vous dans le bâtiment? —Oui, j'y suis.
Are you in the building? —Yes, I am (in it).
Allez là-bas, près de la fenêtre, et restez-y.
Walk over there, by the window, and stay there.

If the noun to be replaced represents a human being or an animal, a disjunctive personal pronoun (***lui, elle, eux, elles***) should be used instead of *y*, and the disjunctive pronoun should follow the appropriate preposition.

J'aime ma fiancée, et je pense souvent à elle.
I love my fiancée, and I often think of her.
Une grenouille dans l'herbe? L'enfant aussitôt s'intéresse à elle.
A frog in the grass? The child at once gets interested in it.
Le chien est assis, le chat est couché contre lui.
The dog is sitting, the cat is lying against him.
La mère avait repoussé son petit loin d'elle.
The mother had pushed her young one (cub, calf, chick, etc.) away from herself.

Y may be used to replace a noun representing an animal only if that noun is preceded by the preposition ***à***. ***Y*** then denotes a certain objectivity, detatchment, lack of personal interest, with respect to that animal. The same use of *y* can be observed with nouns representing human beings, especially in the plural, and only after ***à***. Although rare, this use of *y* with reference to human beings shows a speaker that is distant, cold, derogatory, ironical, etc.

On lui a offert un petit lapin, mais il n'y prête aucune attention.
He was given a little rabbit as a present, but he pays no attention to it.

Est-ce qu'il ne s'intéresse pas à lui? —Non, il ne s'y intéresse pas le moins du monde.
Isn't he interested in it? —No, he isn't the least bit interested in it.

Inversely, there are contexts in which nouns representing inanimate objects may be replaced by disjunctive personal pronouns. This may denote that the object is personified, that strong personal feelings are involved, or merely that the object in question is strongly individualized.

NOTES:

1) *Y* translates *here* and *there* when these clearly refer to places previously mentioned. But when no such reference is being made, or when they *point out*, *here* is translated ***ici***, and *there* is translated ***là*** or ***là-bas*** (over there).

2) ***Il y a*** translates *there is, there are* in plain, factual statements. But if these expressions *point out*, both should be rendered by ***voilà***.

Il y a un livre sur votre chaise.
There is a book on your chair.

Voilà vos lunettes.
There are your glasses (here are).

3) With verbs requiring ***à*** before a dependent infinitive, ***y*** may be used to replace the complete prepositional phrase.

N'oubliez pas de me rendre ce livre. —J'y penserai. (i.e., **Je penserai à vous rendre ce livre.**)
Don't forget to return this book to me. —I'll keep it in mind (I'll think of it).

92. *En.*

A. The adverbial pronoun ***en*** stands for any object (or true subject of an impersonal verb) preceded by ***de***. (***De*** must not be part of a multiword preposition such as ***avant de, loin de***, etc.)

La France? J'en reviens.
France? I am coming back from there.

A-t-il envie de parler? —Oui, il en a envie.
Does he want to speak? —Yes, he wants to.

J'ai peu d'argent, toi, tu en as beaucoup.
I have little money, *you* have a lot (of it).

Voulez-vous du pain? —Non, merci, il m'en reste.
Do you want some bread? —No, thank you, I have some left (some is left: subject of impersonal verb).

J'ai beaucoup d'amis, lui, il n'en a pas.
I have lots of friends, *he* doesn't have any.

Il a des ennemis mais moi, je n'en ai pas.
He has enemies but *I* don't have any.

B. The group introduced by the plain preposition ***de*** (not the partitive article) may relate to a verb, an adjective, or a noun. It may be replaced by ***en*** only if the noun it contains does not represent a person.

Il n'est pas coupable de ce crime. Il n'en est pas coupable.
He is not guilty of that crime. He is not guilty of it.

Je suis convaincu de son innocence. J'en suis convaincu.
I am convinced of his innocence. I am convinced of it.

Ce n'est que le début du procès. Ce n'en est que le début.
It is only the beginning of the trial. It is only its beginning.

When the noun in the prepositional group with ***de*** relates to another noun with an idea of possession or close association, a possessive may be used instead of ***en*** provided that the sentence structure makes it possible.

J'imagine la couleur de la mer. J'en imagine la couleur. J'imagine sa couleur.
I imagine the color of the sea. I imagine its color.

La couleur de la mer me rappelle l'émeraude. Sa couleur me rappelle l'émeraude.
The color of the sea reminds me of an emerald. Its color reminds me of an emerald.

If the noun in the prepositional group does represent a person, ***de*** should remain in the sentence, and the noun should be replaced by a disjunctive pronoun following ***de***.

J'ai reçu une lettre de lui, d'elle, d'eux, d'elles.
I have received a letter from him, her, them.

J'ai peur d'eux.
I am afraid of them.

Cette enfant est fragile. Il faut s'occuper d'elle.
This child is frail. One must look after her.

En may be used to represent persons for the purpose of denoting generalization, distance, detachment, indifference, contempt, etc.

Les millionnaires? Je m'en moque!
Millionaires? I don't care a bit about them.

Ce type-là, il vaut mieux s'en débarrasser.
That fellow, we'd better get rid of him.

By the same token, using ***de*** and a disjunctive personal pronoun instead of ***en*** to represent an animal, an inanimate object, or even an idea, will denote that the animal, the object, or the idea is either personified or individualized, or seen in a strongly subjective or affective light.

C. With verbs requiring ***de*** before a dependent infinitive, ***en*** may be used to replace the whole infinitive phrase (including ***de***), but only if the verb or verbal expression that ***en*** is to precede does not normally have a direct object construction.

As-tu envie de boire? —Oui, j'en ai envie.
Do you want to drink? —Yes, I want to. (The verbal expression ***avoir envie*** requires ***de*** at all times. It cannot have a direct object.)

but: Craignez-vous d'être en retard? —Oui, je le crains.
Are you afraid of being late? —Yes, I am (afraid of it). (The verb ***craindre*** requires ***de*** only before dependent infinitives, not before object nouns.)

D. The most common use of ***en*** is to replace a direct object noun (or true subject of an impersonal verb, or complement of ***voici, voilà***) modified by either a partitive article or an expression of quantity.

1) If the modifier is a partitive article (***du, de la, de l', des***, or ***de, d'*** after a negative verb), ***en*** replaces the noun and the partitive article.

De l'argent? —Oui, j'en aurai.
Money? —Yes, I'll have some.

Il mange des escargots. Moi, je n'en mange pas.
He is eating snails. I don't eat any.

Je veux du fromage. En avez-vous?
I want some cheese. Have you got any?

2) If the modifier is an expression of quantity (indefinite article, indefinite adjective, number, adverb of quantity, noun, etc.), ***en*** replaces only the noun. The expression of quantity must be kept. The expression of quantity follows the verb, unless it is an interrogative expression of quantity, in which case it begins the clause.

Combien en avez-vous? —Je n'en ai qu'un.
How many have you got? —I have only one.

Moi, je n'en ai aucun.
I have none (of them, of this or that).

Paul en a encore une douzaine. Il en avait vingt.
Paul still has a dozen. He used to have twenty (of them, this, that).

NOTE: The indefinite adjective ***quelques*** must be changed to its indefinite pronoun form (***quelques-uns, quelques-unes***) when ***en*** replaces the noun, unless an expression of quantity or a substantivized adjective remains present (see 3, below).

The indefinite ***tout*** (and other forms) is never used with ***en***. It is used instead with the personal pronouns ***le, la, l', les***.

3) If the noun to be replaced by ***en*** has other modifiers besides a partitive article or an expression of quantity, the other modifiers may be left out, or they may be kept after the verb. This is true in English as well as in French.

Il a de beaux livres. Il en a de beaux. Il y en a quelques-uns de rares.
He has beautiful books. He has beautiful ones. There are a few rare ones (a few that are rare).

J'ai acheté quelques nouveaux livres. J'en ai acheté quelques nouveaux.
I bought a few new books. I bought a few new ones.

J'ai laissé tomber le paquet d'œufs. Il y en a sept de cassés (or: **il y en a sept qui sont cassés).**
I dropped the package of eggs. There are seven broken (ones).

Regardez ces timbres. En voici d'autres.
Look at these stamps. Here are some more (or: other ones).

NOTE: If the expression of quantity is being modified by a prepositional phrase beginning with ***de*** and containing either the noun in question, or a pronoun standing for it or pointing to it, or an adjective used substantivally in place of the noun, ***en*** cannot be used.

J'ai acheté deux des livres les moins chers.
I bought two of the cheapest books.

J'ai acheté deux des moins chers.
I bought two of the cheapest ones.

Il m'a prêté quelques-uns des siens.
He lent me a few of his.

Donnez-moi encore une livre de ça.
Give me one more pound of that.

4) ***En*** can be found in idiomatic expressions.

s'en aller	to leave, go away
en avoir assez	to be fed up
en avoir marre (fam.)	to be fed up, have reached the limit
en avoir ras-le-bol (pop.)	to have it up to here
il en est ainsi de	that's the way it is with
il en est de même de	it is the same way with
il en est autrement de	it is different with
s'en faire, ne pas s'en faire	to worry, not to worry
Il s'en est fallu de peu!	It was close!
Il s'en faut de beaucoup!	It isn't close at all!
en finir	to get it over with
en revenir	recover from a surpise, a shock
ne pas en revenir	not to believe one's eyes, ears
en vouloir à	to have a grudge against

POSSESSIVE PRONOUNS

93. Forms.

The possessive pronoun has the following forms:

person	**singular**		**plural**	
(English)	**masculine**	**feminine**	**masculine**	**feminine**
mine	le mien	la mienne	les miens	les miennes
yours	le tien	la tienne	les tiens	les tiennes
his, hers, its	le sien	la sienne	les siens	les siennes
ours	le nôtre	la nôtre	les nôtres	les nôtres
yours	le vôtre	la vôtre	les vôtres	les vôtres
theirs	le leur	la leur	les leurs	les leurs

The definite article is an integral part of the possessive pronoun. It cannot be replaced by any other determiner. When a possessive pronoun immediately follows either the preposition ***à*** or the preposition ***de***, the article and the preposition contract (see §1).

NOTE: The choice of the appropriate form of the possessive pronoun depends on the gender and number of the noun replaced (i.e. possessed). The possessor determines only the person indicated in the left column.

94. Uses.

A. As a general rule, the English possessive pronouns correspond to the French ones. There are instances, however, where the constructions do not match.

Je lis mes livres, elle lit les siens.
I read my books, she reads hers.
Ces livres sont à elle, ceux-ci sont à moi.
Those books are hers, these are mine.

As the second example shows, French marks possession by using the verbal phrase ***être à*** followed by a *disjunctive* personal pronoun, whenever the English could be worded "to belong to."

B. The English construction of the type *a friend of mine* is expressed in French in the form *one of my friends*, ***un de mes amis***.

C. The English possessive case of nouns, marked by *'s*, has no equivalent in French. Several constructions are available to express it:

1) If the noun with *'s* is followed by the noun possessed, the two nouns should be inverted and connected with the preposition ***de***. In the French construction, the first noun must be preceded by a definite article.

L'auto de Paul est blanche.
Paul's car is white.

Je n'aime pas la maison de Paul.
I don't like Paul's house.

Elle a rencontré les parents de son amie.
She met her friend's parents.

If the relation between the nouns is one of time rather than one of close relationship or possession, any determiner may be used, as called for by the context.

Un préavis d'un mois. Un mois de préavis.
A month's notice.

Une semaine de paie. La paie d'une semaine.
A week's pay.

Il a perdu tout son salaire du mois (tout son mois de salaire).
He lost his whole month's salary.

There is a definite tendency in today's French to place the emphasis on the term of *time*, so that the order of the words in this case is the same in French as it is in English.

Un mois de congé. Une semaine de vacances.
One month's leave. A week's vacation.

Une journée de route.
A day's ride (drive, travel, walk, etc.).

NOTE: A saint's day is ***la fête de Saint(e) . . .*** or ***la Saint(e) . . .***.

La Saint-Valentin. La Saint-Michel. La fête de Saint-Patrick.
Saint Valentine's day. Saint Michael's day. Saint Patrick's day.

La Sainte-Catherine. La Sainte-Cécile.
Saint Catherine's day. Saint Cecily's day.

but: La sainte patronne de Paris est sainte Geneviève.
The patron saint of Paris is Saint Geneviève.

2) If the noun with *'s* is not followed by the noun possessed and does not indicate a place, the French demonstrative pronoun must be used. The demonstrative pronoun precedes ***de*** and the possessor (the English noun with *'s*).

Voici le livre de Pierre et celui de Paul.
Here are Peter's book and Paul's.

La voiture du président et celle de sa femme.
The president's car and his wife's.

3) If the noun with *'s* is not followed by the noun possessed, but does indicate a place, the French preposition ***chez*** is used. ***Chez*** directly precedes the possessor (the noun with *'s* in English). ***Chez*** replaces both the noun indicating a place and the preposition *to*, *in*, *into*, or *at*. Any other English preposition must be expressed in French before ***chez***.

Only a proper noun or a noun or pronoun representing a *person* may follow ***chez***.

Je vais chez Paul. Tu vas chez lui?
I'm going to Paul's. Are you going to his place?

Je dîne chez Paul.
I'm having dinner at Paul's.

Je reviens de chez Paul.
I am coming back from Paul's.

J'ai acheté ceci chez l'épicier, tu sais, devant chez Paul, en face de chez Pierre, pas loin de chez les Dupont.
I bought this at the grocer's, you know, in front of Paul's, across from Pierre's, not far from the Duponts'.

NOTES: ***Chez*** cannot be used with names of saints designating churches.

I attended mass at Saint Patrick's.
J'ai assisté à la messe à Saint-Patrick.

I worshiped at the First Baptist church.
J'ai assisté au service à (or: de) l'église baptiste.

The preposition *on* used before the date of a saint's day is rendered by either the preposition ***à***, or merely the phrase ***le jour de la Saint(e)-*** . . . .

Les Irlandais portent du vert à la Saint-Patrick.
The Irish wear green on Saint Patrick's day.

À la Saint-Michel, on payait son loyer.
On Saint Michael's day, people used to pay their rent.

RELATIVE PRONOUNS

95. Forms.

The relative pronoun has the following forms and functions:

antecedent	subject	direct object	object of preposition	object of *de*
person	qui	que	qui lequel	dont
not a person	qui	que	lequel	dont
indefinite or *ce*	qui	que	quoi	dont

The relative pronouns normally used are the short forms ***qui, que, quoi, dont***, and ***où***. The latter is an adverbial relative pronoun corresponding to English *where* and *when*, relatives with antecedents of place and time, respectively (see §103).

Only the direct object ***que*** elides to ***qu'*** before a word beginning with a vowel or with a mute ***h***.

The long form ***lequel*** is used mainly as object of a preposition, rarely otherwise (see §97).

Qui, que, quoi, and ***lequel*** are also interrogative pronouns (§§78-81). For ***quoi*** as an interrogative rather than a relative pronoun, see §102.

96. Uses.

A relative pronoun replaces a noun or a pronoun (usually demonstrative), which is called the antecedent. The antecedent is in the main clause, and the relative pronoun begins the relative clause.

The choice of the correct relative pronoun depends on two factors:

- The function it is to have within the relative clause (column headings in the table).
- The nature of the antecedent it is to stand for (row headings on the left in the table).

97. Lequel.

Although ***lequel*** may have any function, it is rarely used as subject or direct object. It is used mainly as object of a preposition for an antecedent that is not a person.

Voici le livre dans lequel j'apprends la chimie.
This is the book in which I learn chemistry.

There is a tendency in everyday French to use ***lequel*** even when the antecedent is a person. It presents an advantage over ***qui*** in that it shows gender and number, thereby allowing a clearer reference to the antecedent.

Voici la fille de M. Dupont, avec laquelle j'ai dansé hier au bal.
Here is Mr. Dupont's daughter, with whom I danced at the ball yesterday.

The use of ***lequel*** in other functions should be restricted to the rare cases where its gender and number might be necessary to avoid ambiguities. Used as subject or as direct object, ***lequel*** is always preceded by a comma.

J'ai dansé avec la belle-fille de M. Dupont, lequel est très sympathique.
I danced with the daughter-in-law of Mr. Dupont, who is very nice. (Mr. Dupont is.)
J'ai dansé avec la belle-fille de M. Dupont, laquelle est très sympathique.
I danced with the daughter-in-law of Mr. Dupont, who is very nice. (She is.)

Lequel is also an interrogative pronoun (§§80-81).

98. Qui, que, quoi, dont.

The form of these relative pronouns depends on their function within the relative clause. In other words, the form of the relative pronoun to be used depends on its function with the verb that it refers to, generally the following verb.

A. Subject: *who, which, that.*

The subject relative pronoun is ***qui***, whatever the nature of the antecedent.

L'homme qui approche est mon frère.
The man who is coming is my brother.
Celui qui arrive est mon frère.
The one who is arriving is my brother.
La voiture qui est dans le fossé est très endommagée.
The car which (that) is in the ditch is heavily damaged.
Ce qui est arrivé était imprévisible.
What (that which) happened was unforeseeable.

B. Direct object: *whom, which, that.*

The direct object relative pronoun is ***que***, whatever the nature of the antecedent (see note in C, below).

La dame que j'ai vue n'est pas sa tante.
The lady whom I saw is not his aunt.

La voiture que j'ai achetée est très rapide.
The car (which, that) I bought is very fast.

Ce que tu portes est élégant.
What (that which) you are wearing is elegant.

C. Object of a preposition (except ***de***): *whom, which.*

The relative pronoun object of a preposition other than ***de*** must be chosen in accordance with the nature of its antecedent.

1) If the antecedent is a *person*, the relative pronoun is ***qui*** or the appropriate form of ***lequel***.

L'homme à qui vous parliez est mon voisin.
L'homme auquel vous parliez est mon voisin.
The man to whom you were speaking is my neighbor.

2) If the antecedent is *neither a person nor ce*, the relative pronoun is the appropriate form of ***lequel***.

Le stylo avec lequel j'écris est tout neuf.
The pen with which I am writing is brand new.

3) If the antecedent is ***ce*** or an indefinite pronoun (***rien, quelque chose***), the relative pronoun is ***quoi***. ***Ce*** often recalls a complete clause or an idea expressed in several words. It is common to find a comma at the end of such a complete clause or idea. It is also common to leave out the recalling pronoun ***ce*** when a preposition governs the relative pronoun ***quoi***.
See also §§100-102.

Il est difficile d'exprimer (ce) à quoi je pense.
It is difficult to express what I am thinking of. (lit.: that of which I am thinking)

Je ne vois rien à quoi (je puisse) m'intéresser.
I see nothing in which I might be interested.

Trouvez-moi quelque chose avec quoi cette étagère puisse être consolidée.
Find me something with which this shelf might be reinforced.

Nous avons visité le Louvre, après quoi nous avons bu un verre dans un café voisin.
We visited the Louvre, after which we had a drink in a nearby café.

Il était certain qu'il tenait la victoire, (ce) en quoi il se trompait.
He was certain that the victory was his, in which he was mistaken.

NOTE: A French relative pronoun cannot be omitted or understood, as it often is in English; nor can the preposition of which it is an object be removed to another place in the clause.

L'homme à qui vous parliez est mon voisin.
The man you were speaking to is my neighbor.

D. Object of ***de***: *whose, of whom, of which (from, about, etc.).*

Whatever the nature of the antecedent, the relative pronoun object of the simple preposition ***de*** should be ***dont***, which contains its own preposition.

L'homme dont je vous parle est étranger.
The man (whom) I'm talking to you about is a foreigner.
La voiture dont je parle est endommagée.
The car of which I speak is damaged.
Ce dont il va parler est fascinant.
What he is going to talk about is fascinating.

The note in C3 above applies to ***dont*** as well as to ***quoi***.

Dont should be the first choice in contemporary French, even though ***de qui*** and ***duquel, de laquelle, desquels, desquelles*** are also possible in many instances with antecedents representing persons. However, ***dont*** cannot be used in the following cases:

1) If the noun or pronoun modified by the relative pronoun (not the antecedent) is itself the object of a preposition.

2) If ***de*** is part of a prepositional expression such as ***en face de, près de, au-dessus de, au milieu de, en dépit de,*** etc.

Dont is then replaced by ***de qui*** or a form of ***duquel*** if the antecedent is a person, or by ***duquel, de laquelle, desquels, desquelles,*** if the antecedent is not a person (see §97, 2nd paragraph).

Le gars au frère de qui j'ai prêté mon livre s'appelle Paul.
The guy to whose brother I lent my book is named Paul.
La malade au chevet de qui j'ai passé la nuit va beaucoup mieux.
The sick woman at whose bedside I spent the night is doing a lot better.
Voilà l'arbre du haut duquel je suis tombé.
That's the tree from the top of which I fell.

99. Whose.

Whenever ***dont*** can be used to translate *whose*, the structure of the French sentence must have the following order:

(1) DONT	(2) subject	(3) verb	(4) objects

La dame *(1) dont (2) la fille (3) se marie* est madame Smith.
The lady whose daughter is getting married is Mrs. Smith.

La dame *(1) dont (2) Paul (3) a épousé (4) la fille* est madame Smith.
The lady whose daughter Paul married is Mrs. Smith.

But if ***dont*** cannot be used (for one of the reasons stated in §98D), the structure of the French relative clause depends on the reason preventing the use of ***dont***.

A. If the noun modified by *whose* (*of which*) is the object of a preposition, the French relative clause then begins with (1) that preposition followed by its object, (2) then ***de qui*** or ***duquel, de laquelle, desquels, desquelles***, (3) then the subject, (4) then the verb and any additional objects.

La dame *(1) avec la fille (2) de qui (3) j' (4) ai dansé hier soir* est madame Smith.
The lady with whose daughter I danced last night is Mrs. Smith.

Le livre de Paul est celui *(1) sur la couverture (2) duquel (3) il (4) a écrit son nom en lettres majuscules.*
Paul's book is the one on the cover of which he wrote his name in capital letters.

B. If the relative pronoun is the object prepositional expression containing ***de***, then the relative clause begins with (1) that prepositional expression, immediately followed by (2) the relative pronoun (from the third column in the table, §95), then (3) the subject, then (4) the verb and any additional objects.

Je n'avais jamais vu l'homme *(1) à côté de (2) qui (3) vous (4) étiez assise.*
I had never seen the man near whom you were sitting.

La forêt *(1) au milieu (2) de laquelle (3) l'avion (4) s'est écrasé* est immense.
The forest in the middle of which the plane crashed is immense.

NOTE: Repeated relative clauses may make the style heavy. Independent clauses are often better. When relative clauses are necessary, their heaviness can be alleviated by inverting the verb and the subject, especially if the latter is of some length. This inversion is possible in all the relative clauses where the relative pronoun is not the subject of the verb.

La colline sur laquelle se dresse cette célèbre chapelle . . .
The hill on which this famous chapel stands . . .

Les auteurs que lisent les étudiants . . .
The authors that the students read . . .

100. What.

As a relative pronoun, *what* is equivalent to *that which*, where the first term is a part of the main clause, and the second belongs in the relative clause. The first term is ***ce***, which may be subject, direct object, or prepositional object in the main clause. The second part is the relative pronoun, which varies according to its function in the relative clause. The two terms combined are as follows:

A. ***Ce qui*** when the relative is subject.

Je comprends ce qui se passe.
I understand what is going on. (that which)

B. ***Ce que*** when the relative is direct object.

J'ai vu ce que tu as fait.
I saw what you did.

C. ***Ce dont, ce . . . quoi*** if the relative is the object of a preposition (often placed at the end of the relative clause in casual English). ***Ce dont*** is used if the French construction requires the preposition ***de*** *within the relative clause.* ***Ce . . . quoi*** is used if the construction of the relative clause requires any preposition other than ***de***. Note that the preposition must be placed *before* ***quoi***.

J'ai entendu ce dont vous parliez.
I heard what you were talking about.
Je devine toujours ce à quoi vous pensez.
I always guess what you are thinking about.

NOTE: This construction with ***quoi*** is frequently expressed as an indirect question (see §102).

101. Which.

For the relative pronoun *which* referring to a specific antecedent, see §§95-98. ***Which***, when its antecedent is an idea or a full clause, is always preceded by a comma. The same is true of its French equivalent.

A. If *which* is the subject of the verb of the relative clause, it is to be translated ***ce qui***.

Il a bien travaillé, ce qui me ravit.
He worked well, which delights me.

B. If *which* is the direct object of the verb of the relative clause, it is to be translated ***ce que***.

Il a bien travaillé, ce que j'apprécie.
He worked well, which I appreciate.

C. If *which* is the object of a preposition governed by a word of the relative clause, it is to be translated ***ce dont*** if the required French preposition is ***de***, and ***. . . quoi*** (without ***ce***) if the required French preposition is any other than ***de***. Note that the preposition in the latter case must precede the relative ***quoi****.

Il a bien travaillé, ce dont je suis content.
He worked well, which I am pleased about. (about which)

Il a bien travaillé, sans quoi il aurait échoué.
He worked well, without which he would have failed.

*Note the difference between the translation of *what* in §100C and *which* in §98C3. This construction is more like that of §98C3, in that ***ce*** may be omitted when a preposition governs ***quoi***, but ***ce*** must be present when the context calls for ***dont***.

102. Indirect questions.

When a question is subordinated to a main clause, it becomes an indirect question. It may not be obvious that the sentence is a question at all since its word order is that of a declarative sentence and since no question mark punctuates it.

Direct question:
Pourquoi est-il parti?
Why did he leave?

Indirect question:
Je me demande pourquoi il est parti.
I wonder why he left.

Certain verbs used in the main clause seem to pose an implicit question:

apprendre	to learn
comprendre	to understand
demander	to ask
deviner	to guess
dire	to say, tell
expliquer	to explain
ignorer	to be unaware, not to know
montrer	to show
raconter	to tell
savoir	to know
se demander	to wonder
sentir	to feel, sense
voir	to see

The interrogative meaning is not apparent in these infinitive forms. It generally comes out when they are accompanied by some other verb or verbal expression of which they are dependent infinitives, in such phrases as *I would like to know, tell me, let me see, I am beginning to understand,* etc.

The subordinate clause containing the substance of the indirect question begins with one of the following words:

comment	how
combien	how much, now many
si (**s'** before ***il, ils***)	if
quel	what (adjective)
ce qui, ce que, ce dont, quoi	what (pronoun)
quand	when
où	where
si (**s'** before ***il, ils***)	whether
quel	which (adjective)
lequel (see note 2, below)	which (pronoun)
qui	who
qui	whom (direct object)
qui	whom (with preposition)
de qui, à qui	whose
pourquoi	why

NOTES:

1) If the pronoun *what* begins the subordinate clause in an indirect question, its function within the subordinate clause determines its form.

- Subject: ***ce qui*** (§100A)
- Direct object: ***ce que*** (§100B)
- Object of a preposition: ***quoi***. The appropriate French preposition must precede the pronoun ***quoi***, which is here an interrogative pronoun, since the antecedent ***ce*** is not being used.

Je me demande ce qui se passe. (subject)
I wonder what's going on.

Je crois comprendre ce que vous faites. (direct object)
I think I understand what you are doing.

Dites-moi de quoi le professeur a parlé. (preposition)
Tell me what the professor talked about.

2) If the pronoun *which (one)* begins the subordinate clause, all its functions are rendered by the appropriate form of ***lequel*** (this is not the *which* of §101 or the *which* of §103).

Paul a essayé deux voitures. Je me demande laquelle est la meilleure et laquelle il préfère.
Paul test-drove two cars. I wonder which one is the best and which one he prefers.

Paul et Marc ont appelé Michelle. Je voudrais bien savoir avec lequel elle sortira.
Paul and Marc called Michelle. I'ld like to know which she'll go out with.

103. Which, when, where.

When the antecedent of a relative pronoun expresses *time* or *place*, the relative pronoun may be *which*, functioning as object of a suitable preposition, or *where*, or *when*.

If the relative is *which*, it should be rendered in French by a form of ***lequel*** preceded by a suitable preposition.

Les arbres dans lesquels il y a trop de branches mortes vont être abattus.
The trees in which there are too many dead branches are going to be felled.

La journée pendant laquelle nous avons visité le Louvre m'a paru très courte.
The day during which we visited the Louvre seemed very short to me.

If the relative is either *where* or *when*, it should be translated ***où***, because ***quand*** cannot be used as a relative in French.

La ville où j'habite n'est pas grande.
The city where I live is not large.

C'est un endroit où il y a peu de touristes.
It is a place where there are few tourists.

C'est arrivé le jour où j'ai eu mon accident.
It happened the day when I had my accident.

Il est venu à une heure où j'aurais préféré ne voir personne.
He came at an hour when I would have preferred to see no one.

PREPOSITIONS

104. Definition.

A preposition is a word serving to introduce an element of a sentence while marking a relation of dependence between that element and another in the sentence.

A preposition is simple if it consists of only one word. It is a locution, or a prepositional expression, if it is made of more than one word.

Of the two terms or elements related by a preposition, the one that precedes the preposition is the main one, and the one that follows it is the dependent one, the *object* of the preposition.

In English, the object of a preposition may be a noun, a pronoun, or a gerund (verbal noun). In French, it may be a noun, a pronoun, or an infinitive. One exception exists in each language: the English preposition *to* may govern an infinitive, and the French preposition ***en*** must precede a present participle.

The group of words formed by the preposition and its object (and modifiers, if any) is called a prepositional phrase. The various functions it may have depend on the main word it is related to.

105. Uses.

The following remarks govern the most frequent occurrences of the various prepositions in English and in French.

A. Most French prepositions can usually have for object either a noun, or a pronoun, or an infinitive, indifferently. But some can govern only an infinitive, and others can never govern an infinitive.

B. Purpose. When *to* precedes an infinitive, it should be translated ***pour*** or ***afin de*** if it expresses strong purpose or intent, unless the word it depends on requires some other preposition.

Pour ouvrir, appuyer ici.
To open, press here.

J'ai attendu deux heures pour (afin de) lui parler.
I waited two hours to speak to her.

J'attends d'avoir reçu ma monnaie.
J'attends qu'on me rende la monnaie.
I'm waiting to get back my change.

C. *After.* When its object is not a noun or a pronoun, ***après*** should be followed by a *past infinitive*. So should all prepositions whenever their object is a verb that expresses a *completed action* presented as *anterior to another action, past or future*.

Après avoir mis de l'essence dans le réservoir, nous nous sommes engagés sur l'autoroute.
After putting some gasoline into the tank, we drove onto the highway.

Vous ne sortirez pas avant d'avoir fini.
You will not leave until you have finished.

D. Personal pronouns. When a personal pronoun is the object of a preposition, it must be a *disjunctive* personal pronoun (see §§82, 88A).

Avec moi. Pour toi. Sans lui. Par elle. Après eux.
With me. For you. Without him. By her. After them (m.).

E. Repetition. Simple prepositions should be repeated before each object in a series. In the case of prepositional expressions, only the last part (generally ***de***) should be repeated. The repetition may be avoided for stylistic reasons.

L'archéologue a découvert des statuettes d'argile, de bronze et de pierre.
The archeologist discovered statues of clay, bronze, and stone.

L'aigle plane au-dessus des montagnes et des plaines, des rivières et des forêts.
The eagle glides over the mountains and the plains, the rivers and the forests.

F. Place of the preposition. The English idiomatic practice of removing the preposition to the end of the sentence has no equivalent in French. A French preposition must always precede its object.

De quoi parlez-vous?
What are you talking about?

À qui penses-tu?
Whom are you thinking about?

G. Single object of several verbs. When several verbs have the same object (direct or prepositional), this object must be placed with the first verb and then repeated in the form of a suitable pronoun with each additional verb.

Il monta dans la voiture et s'y assit.
He got up and sat in the car.

Ils accueillaient les pélerins et leur donnaient à manger.
They welcomed and gave food to the pilgrims.

He caught sight of and walked up to the suspect.
Il aperçut le suspect et le rejoignit.

H. Movement. English prepositions are much more dynamic than French ones. They often have to be "explained" by French periphrases.

An English preposition (or adverb) expressing movement frequently follows a verb expressing manner. French, on the other hand, prefers to express the movement by a simple verb of motion such as ***aller, sortir, entrer, monter, descendre,*** etc., and the manner in which the movement is made by a prepositional phrase—generally ***en*** and a present participle.

Il sortit en hâte de la classe.
He hurried out of the class. (*out*: **sortir**; *hurried*: **en hâte**)

L'enfant traversa la rue en courant.
The child ran across the street. (*across*: **traverser**; *run*: **en courant**)

Nous sommes allés en Italie en avion.
We flew to Italy. (*to*: **aller**; *flew*: **en avion**)

Nous sommes allés à la poste à pied.
We walked to the post office. (*to*: **aller**; *walked*: **à pied**)

NOTE: The manner of the motion is sometimes unnecessary. For example, going to Italy from the United States is obviously by plane nowadays. It is sufficient, therefore, to state "We went to Italy." But from Paris to Rome, the trip could be made by plane, by train, or by car; hence the need for expressing the manner, the means of transportation.

I. Adjectival prepositional phrase. English often modifies nouns with prepositional phrases where French will not. In such cases (usually with any preposition but ***de***), French will have a complete relative clause with ***qui est***, ***qui sont***, etc.

C'est le meilleur élève de ma classe. Connaissez-vous ce roman de Flaubert?
He is the best student in my class. Do you know this novel by Flaubert?

Regardez cette photo. La dame qui est derrière moi est madame Smith.
Look at this picture. The lady behind me is Mrs. Smith.

Le monsieur qui est au téléphone t'a demandé.
The man on the phone asked for you.

See individual prepositions, §§107-170, for additional examples.

J. Clause as object of a preposition. An English preposition may have a full clause for object (noun clause). That English clause should be replaced in French by a suitable French noun (and the necessary modifiers), as suggested by the English word beginning the object clause to be replaced. Such words are *how, what, when, where, whether, which, who, whom, why*. An English gerund with a possessive is also commonly found after a preposition. The following list suggests suitable nouns for their replacement.

1) *How.*

la façon dont . . .
la façon de laquelle. . .
la façon que . . . (avoir) de . . . (infinitive)
la manière dont . . .
la manière que . . . (avoir) de . . . (infinitive)
la manière de laquelle . . .
ma (ta, sa, etc.) façon de . . . (infinitive)
ma (ta, sa, etc.) manière de . . . (infinitive)

Cela dépend de la façon dont il réagira.
Cela dépend de la façon de laquelle il réagira.
Cela dépend de la manière qu'il aura de réagir.
That depends on how he will react.

2) *What.*

ce qui, ce que, ce dont, ce . . . quoi (§100; §102, note 1) or as directed by the context, any suitable noun modified by a prepositional phrase or a relative clause.

Elle est incertaine de ce qu'elle doit faire après.
She's uncertain about *what* to do next.
Il n'a aucune idée des conséquences de sa découverte.
He has no idea of what will come of his discovery.

3) *When.*

le moment où + clause
le moment de + noun
le jour où + clause
le jour de + noun
l'heure à laquelle + clause
l'heure de + noun
l'époque où + clause
l'époque de + noun
l'instant où + clause
l'instant de + noun
la date de + noun

Je ne suis pas sûr de l'heure (du jour, de la date, etc.) de son arrivée.
I am not sure about when he arrived (will arrive).

4) *Where.*

l'endroit où + clause
le lieu où + clause
le lieu de + noun
la place où + clause
la place de + noun
A more precise noun may be suggested by the context.

Nous parlons de l'endroit (la ville, l'hôtel, l'étape, etc.) où nous passerons la nuit.
We are talking about where we'll spend the night.

5) *Whether.* This word is usually found in an indirect question (§102). A main verb requiring no preposition may be chosen so as to permit the use of ***si*** in a direct object clause. Occasionally, the phrase ***le fait que*** may serve as a suitable transition, or the whole structure of the sentence may be changed.

Cela dépendra du fait qu'il aura pris la grand-route ou le raccourci.
It will depend on whether he'll have taken the highway or the shortcut.

Cela dépendra: aura-t-il pris la grand-route ou le raccourci?
That will depend: will he take the highway or a shortcut?

6) *Which.* If *which* is an adjective, the noun it modifies is sufficient as a French antecedent, preceded by a definite article.

Je suis surpris par le trajet qu'il a suivi.
I am surprised at which route he followed.

The French adjective ***quel*** is often the object of a preposition within its own clause.

Je ne sais pas par quelle ville il est passé.
I don't know which city he drove through.

When an English main verb governs a preposition introducing *which* as its object, it is preferable to choose a French verb that will allow the use of a direct object clause as a subordinate, or to change the sentence construction completely in order to improve the style.

Le gouvernement n'avait pas prévu quel secteur serait le plus touché.
The government had not given a thought to which sector would be concerned the most.
Je ne comprends pas le raisonnement qu'il a suivi.
I am amazed at which line of reasoning he followed.
Le raisonnement qu'il a suivi me surprend.
The line of reasoning he followed surprises me.

If *which* is a pronoun, one of the following should be used:

celui (celle, ceux, celles) qui . . .
celui (celle, ceux, celles) que . . .
celui (celle, ceux, celles) dont . . .
celui (celle, ceux, celles) . . . qui . . . (***qui*** is preceded by a preposition and refers to a person)
celui (celle, ceux, celles) . . . lequel . . . (***lequel*** is preceded by a preposition and refers to an antecedent other than a person)

7) *Who.*
la personne qui . . .
l'homme qui . . .
la femme qui . . .
le monsieur qui . . .
la dame qui . . .
(etc., as suggested by the context) or
celui (celle) qui . . .

8) *Whom.*
la personne que . . .
la personne dont . . .
la personne . . . qui . . . (***qui*** is preceded by a preposition)

L'homme, la femme, le monsieur, la dame, le garçon, la fille, le vieillard, la vieille dame, etc. **que . . . , dont . . . , . . . qui . . .**

9) *Why.*
la raison pour laquelle . . .
le motif pour lequel . . .
le motif de . . . (followed by a possessive adjective and a noun translating the English verb)
la raison de . . . (followed by a possessive adjective and a noun translating the English verb)
la cause de . . . (followed by a possessive adjective and a noun translating the English verb)

J'ai des doutes sur la raison (la cause, le motif) de son départ.
I have doubts about why he left.

10) *What . . . for.*
le but de . . . l'objet de . . . l'emploi de . . . etc., or as suggested by the context.

Pouvez-vous vous mettre d'accord sur l'emploi de ces vis?
Can you agree on what these screws will be used for?

In direct object clauses, *what . . . for* may also be rendered by ***dans quel but . . . , pour quelle raison . . . ,*** or ***à quel . . . , dans quel . . . , etc.,*** with a noun appropriate for the context.

Je ne comprends pas pour quelle raison il crie si fort.
I don't understand what he is shouting so loud for.

Dites-moi le but de votre campagne électorale.
Dites-moi dans quel but vous faites une campagne électorale.
Tell me what you are campaigning for.

11) *Possessive and gerund.* This construction may be rendered by a simple infinitive:

Elle a peur d'être en retard.
She is afraid of being late.

It may be rendered by a simple conjunctive clause beginning with ***que***:

Ils sont gênés que vous ayez oublié leur invitation.
They are annoyed at your having forgotten their invitation.

Very frequently it is rendered by a conjunctive clause in the subjunctive beginning with ***à ce que***, when the verb involved wants the preposition ***à***.

Paul s'attend à ce que tu lui téléphones.
Paul counts on your giving him a call.

106. Preposition, adverb, conjunction.

In French as well as in English, a given word may be sometimes a preposition, sometimes an adverb, sometimes a conjunction, depending on its use in the sentence, and this often without any change in spelling.

One should note that a given English preposition (or adverb or conjunction) is never exactly equivalent to a fixed corresponding French preposition (or adverb or conjunction), and vice versa. The use of prepositions is directed much more by custom and tradition than by logic.

In order to translate appropriately from English to French (or from French into English) it is essential to recognize the difference between a preposition, a conjunction, and an adverb.

A. *Preposition* (see definition in §104). Most French prepositions can have for an object either a noun or a pronoun or an infinitive, indifferently. Some can govern only an infinitive, and others can have only a noun or pronoun object.

Il ne reviendra qu'à condition d'être payé d'avance. (infinitive only with ***à condition de***)
He will come back only on condition of being paid in advance.

Nous ne pouvons pas sortir à cause de la neige. (noun only with ***à cause de)***)
We cannot go out because of the snow.

Il est sorti avant la fin du film. (noun only with ***avant***)
He left before the end of the movie.

Mettez votre manteau avant de sortir. (infinitive only with ***avant de***)
Put on your coat before going out.

B. *Adverb*. An adverb modifies the meaning of a verb, adjective, or other adverb. It is usually placed close to the word it modifies (see §199).

J'ai déjà entendu cette histoire.
I have heard that story before.

C'est une histoire très amusante.
It's a very funny story.

Elle conduit extrêmement vite.
She drives extremely fast.

Many of the English adverbs shown in the following pages are also verbal particles. They modify the meaning of a verb to such an extent that the group they form with it becomes an entirely different semantic unit.

to carry	***porter***
to carry out	***exécuter***
to carry on	***continuer***

C. *Conjunction*. A subordinating conjunction can begin only a subordinate clause. It creates a dependence between a main verb (usually preceding) and the verb of the subordinating clause that it begins (which is generally the first verb after the conjunction).

Nous nous mettrons à table dès qu'ils seront arrivés.
We will sit down at the table as soon as they are here.

NOTE: As mentioned in B above, adverbial words like *in, down, off, on, over, up,* etc., used as verbal particles are not translated separately from the verb, but result in a different meaning.

to give	***donner***
to give in	***céder***
to give up	***abandonner***

See §§171-194.

When movement or displacement is involved, a verb with an adverbial addition usually expresses two ideas: movement and manner. A decision must be made, in translating these into French, between expressing both ideas or only one of the two: either the movement or the manner.

Saute!
Jump! Jump in! Jump out! Jump down! (if the manner appears more essential than the movement *in, out,* or *down,* etc.)

Entre!
Come in! Step in! Step inside! Etc.

Descends!
Jump down! Slide down! Step down! Climb down! Etc.

Sors!
Come out! Walk out! Step outside! Move out! Etc.

See also §105H.

107. Prepositions in examples.

In the following paragraphs, only examples of the use of the various prepositions, conjunctions or adverbs will be given, without explanations. The examples provide alternate possibilities. It must be understood that the expressions or portions of sentences placed between double slashes (//) and separated by single slashes (/) may be substituted for one another.

108. About.

There are things about you that I don't understand.
Il y a des choses // sur toi / à ton sujet / chez toi / en toi // que je ne comprends pas.

We talked about you.
Nous avons parlé de vous.

This book is about the philosophy of Sartre.
Ce livre // traite de / parle de / présente / étudie // la philosophie de Sartre.

This novel is about a murder which . . .
Dans ce roman, il // s'agit / est question // d'un meurtre qui . . .

I want to say a word about this book.
Je veux dire un mot // sur / au sujet de / à propos de / en ce qui concerne // ce livre.

About this matter . . .
// Au sujet / À propos / Pour parler // de cette affaire . . .
Un mot en ce qui concerne cette affaire.

We are about to leave.
Nous // allons / sommes sur le point de // partir.

We were about to leave.
Nous // allions / étions sur le point de // partir.

I am certain about this.
Je suis certain // de cela. / à ce sujet. //
J'en suis certain.

It was about ten in the morning.
Il était // environ / à peu près / dans les / vers les // dix heures du matin.

A turnabout, an about-face. To turn around.
Un demi-tour, une volte-face. Faire demi-tour.

To set about doing something.
Se mettre à faire quelque chose.

To bring about.
// Causer. / Soulever. / Faire naître.//

To order someone about.
// Donner des ordres à / Faire marcher / Mener / Commander // quelqu'un.

To wander about.
// Errer. / Aller au hasard. / Aller à l'aventure.//

109. Above.

The sky above our heads.
Le ciel // au-dessus de / par-dessus / sur // nos têtes.

Look above.
Regardez // en haut. / là-haut. / ci-dessus (in a text).**//**

The above passage.
Le passage // ci-dessus. / situé plus-haut.//

110. According to.

According to them, this is not true.
// Selon / D'après // eux, cela n'est pas vrai.

According to what they say, . . .
// D'après / Selon / À // ce qu'ils disent, . . .

111. On account of.

We are late on account of you.
Nous sommes en retard à cause de vous.

He could not come on account of his illness.
Il n'a pas pu venir // à cause de / en raison de // sa maladie.

He is tired on account of his working late every night.
Il est fatigué parce qu'il travaille tard tous les soirs.

112. Across.

They were riding (horses) across the plain.
Ils chevauchaient à travers la plaine. Ils traversaient la plaine à cheval.

We came across a difficult word.
Nous avons // rencontré /trouvé/ découvert // un mot difficile. (fam.: **Nous sommes tombés sur un mot difficile.)**

113. After. Afterward.

Come back after lunch.
Revenez après le déjeuner.

After Denver, we'll stop to have dinner.
Après Denver, nous nous arrêterons pour dîner.

After he has arrived, we'll leave.
Après // son arrivée, / qu'il sera arrivé,// nous partirons.

After hearing the defense, the judge . . .
Après avoir entendu la défense, le juge . . .

Work now, you'll play afterward.
Travaillez maintenant, vous vous amuserez // après. / plus tard. / ensuite.//

He is after me.
Il en a après moi. Il m'en veut. (grudge)
Il me poursuit. (pursuit)
Il est après moi. (waiting line, list)

She looks after him.
Elle // s'occupe de / veille sur / prend soin de // lui.

He takes after his father.
Il // tient de / ressemble à / a tout de // son père.

See also §105C. See *after* as a conjunction in §180.

114. Against.

I hit (bumped) my head against the door.
Je me suis cogné la tête // à / contre // la porte.
Je me suis heurté la tête // à / contre // la porte.

They were fighting against a common enemy.
Ils // se battaient contre / combattaient // un ennemi commun.

They are fighting (against each other).
Ils se battent (l'un contre l'autre).

A race against the clock.
Une course contre la montre.

A ladder leaning against the wall.
Une échelle appuyée // au / contre le // mur.

I am against it.
Je suis // contre. / opposé.//
Je suis // contre / opposé à // cela (ça).

Against a dark (light) background.
// Sur fond sombre (clair). / À contre-jour (if subject is lighted from behind).**//**

To stand out against . . . (a background)
Se détacher sur . . . (un fond)

Against a sunset.
// Devant / Sur // un coucher de soleil.

115. Ahead (of).

Ahead of schedule.
En avance (sur l'horaire).

He walked ahead of us.
Il marchait devant nous.
Il nous // précédait. / a précédés .// (tense from context)

He arrived ahead of us.
Il est arrivé avant nous.
Il nous a précédés.

Stay ahead.
Restez // en tête. / devant. / à l'avant. / en avant.//

Look ahead.
Regardez // devant vous. / devant. / en avant. / vers l'avant.//
Allez de l'avant! (figurative)

Straight ahead.
// Tout droit. / Droit devant vous.//

116. Along.

We were walking along the river.
Nous // marchions le long de / longions // la rivière.

Come along with us.
// Venez avec nous. / Accompagnez-nous.//

To go along with what somebody says.
// Suivre / Admettre / Accepter / Être d'accord avec // ce que dit quelqu'un.

To get along with somebody. We get along well, the two of us.
S'entendre avec quelqu'un. Nous nous entendons bien tous les deux.

117. Among (amongst, amidst).

There is a traitor among us (in our midst).
Il y a un traître parmi nous.

We placed a surprise among the other presents.
Nous avons placé une surprise // au milieu des / parmi les / avec les // autres cadeaux.

Among the Navajo Indians, . . .
Chez les indiens Navajos, . . .

118. Around.

We have shrubs around our house.
Nous avons des buissons autour de notre maison.

Spread the word around.
Faites passer la nouvelle (à la ronde).

I have a house with shrubs all around.
J'ai une maison avec des buissons tout autour.

We have around two thousand records.
Nous avons // environ / à peu près / aux alentours de / approximativement / dans les // deux mille disques.

Turn around.
// Faites demi-tour. / Retournez-vous (face this way). **/ Détournez-vous** (face the other way).**//**

Go around the block.
Faites le tour du pâté de maisons.

Go (all the way) around the building.
Faites le tour du bâtiment.

Go around (to the other side of) the building.
Allez de l'autre côté du bâtiment.

Just around the corner.
Juste au coin de la rue.

What's going on around here? Where is his record?
Qu'est-ce qui se passe (par) ici? Où est son dossier?

119. Aside.

("Aside," in the directions of a play.)
(À part.)

To put aside.
Mettre de côté.

To push aside.
// Refuser. / Repousser. / Rejeter.//

To stand aside.
Rester // de côté. / sur le côté. / hors du chemin.//
// Faire de la place. / Donner de la place.//

To step aside.
Se mettre // de côté. / sur le côté. / hors du chemin.//
Se ranger.
S'écarter.
// Donner / Faire // de la place.

120. At.

See §3H for expressions in which the definite article is omitted.

I am at home.
Je suis // chez moi. / à la maison.//

We are staying at the inn.
Nous sommes (descendus) à l'auberge.

I'll see you at Paul's, at noon.
Je te verrai chez Paul, à midi.

We are looking at the candidate's file (record).
Nous regardons le dossier du candidat.

You are looking at a new world record!
Ce que vous voyez là est un nouveau record du monde!

He is aiming at the target.
Il vise la cible.

Not at all.
Pas du tout.

The dog barks at the mailman.
Le chien aboie après le facteur.

I am angry at you. I am mad at you. I am angry at having listened to you.
Je suis en colère contre toi. Je suis fâché contre (après) toi.
Je suis fâché de t'avoir écouté.

To be exasperated at something.
Être // outré / exaspéré // de quelque chose.

To be furious at . . .
Être furieux // contre (quelqu'un). / de (quelque chose). / de (infinitive).//

To be good at . . .
Être bon // à (infinitive). **/ à** (noun with definite article) **/ en** (subject of study).**//**

To be grieved at
Être peiné de

To be mad at
Être en colère contre

To be sad at
Être triste de (infinitive)

To be surprised at
Être // surpris / étonné // de

To be vexed at
Être vexé de

To be at something.
Être (occupé) // à / à faire // quelque chose.

He is at it again.
Il y est encore.

While I'm at it . . .
Pendant que j'y suis . . .

To swear at somebody.
// Insulter / Lancer des insultes à / Jurer après / Injurier / Lancer des injures à // quelqu'un.

At him, Fido!
// Attaque, / Mords-le, // Médor!

At a time like this!
À un moment pareil!

One thing at a time.
Une chose à la fois.
Chaque chose en son temps.

At best.
Au mieux.

At church.
À l'église.

At close range.
De près.

At hand.
Sous la main.

At first.
// D'abord. / En premier lieu.//

At intervals.
// Par intervalles. / Par moments. / De temps en temps. / Ici et là.//

At last.
// Enfin. / Finalement. / En dernier lieu.//

At last he let us in.
Il a fini par nous laisser entrer.

An attorney at law.
Un // avocat. / avoué.//

At least.
// Au moins./ Du moins.//

At length.
// Longuement. / À fond.//

At most.
Au plus.

At night.
// La nuit. / Le soir. / Pendant la nuit.//

At nightfall.
À la tombée de la nuit.

At no extra charge.
Sans supplément.

At once.
// Tout de suite. / Immédiatement. / Sur le champ.//

At peace.
En paix.

At random.
Au hasard.

At sea.
En mer.

Just a sandwich, and not very large, at that.
Rien qu'un sandwich, et pas très grand, // de plus. / aussi. / encore. / par surcroît.//

At that time.
À ce // moment. / moment-là.//
// À cette époque-là. / En ce temps-là.// (remote: distance in time may be subjective)

At this time.
// En ce moment. / À présent. / Maintenant. / Actuellement.//

At the drop of a hat.
Pour un rien.

At the moment.
En ce moment.

At the table.
À table.

At the same time.
// En même temps. / À la fois. / Au même instant.//

At the time.
// À l'époque. / À ce moment-là.//

At war.
En guerre.

At will.
À volonté.

At worst.
Au pire.

At your request.
Sur votre demande.

121. Because.

Because should be translated ***à cause de*** before a noun or noun phrase and ***parce que*** before a whole dependent clause.

We lost the game because of you.
Nous avons perdu le match à cause de toi.

We lost because you were not there.
Nous avons perdu parce que tu n'étais pas là.

122. Before.

with			
Time	**Place**	**Infinitive**	**Subjunctive**
avant	devant	avant de	avant que

Come back before nightfall.
Revenez avant la nuit.

Brush your teeth before going to bed.
Brosse-toi les dents avant de te coucher.

The defendant was brought before his judges.
L'accusé fut conduit devant ses juges.

It is as I had told you before.
C'est comme je te l'avais dit // avant. / auparavant. / plus tôt.//

Two years before, he had had a similar accident.
Deux ans // plus tôt, / auparavant, / avant, // il avait eu un accident semblable.

Come back here before I lose my temper.
Reviens ici avant que je (ne) me fâche.

Precious minutes had passed before he realized what had happened.
De précieuses minutes s'étaient écoulées avant qu'il (ne) se // rendît / rende / soit rendu / fût rendu // compte de ce qui s'était passé.

Before long he will realize what a fool he has been.
// D'ici peu il se rendra compte de sa bêtise. / Avant longtemps il verra comme il a été bête.//

123. On behalf of.

On behalf of all the members of our staff, I . . .
Au nom de tous les membres de notre équipe, je . . .

124. Behind.

A boy was hiding behind a tree.
Un garçon se cachait derrière un arbre.

Two other cars came behind ours.
Deux autres voitures venaient // derrière / après // la nôtre.

You are still behind in your work.
Vous êtes encore en retard dans votre travail.

Build a fence and hide the trash cans behind.
Construisez une clôture et cachez les poubelles derrière.

We'll leave you behind and you'll catch up with us later.
Nous te laisserons // derrière (nous) / après nous // et tu nous rejoindras plus tard.

Behind schedule.
En retard (sur l'horaire).

125. Below (beneath).

Much of Holland is below sea level.
Une grande partie de la Hollande est au-dessous du niveau de la mer.

Below average, below par.
// Au-dessous de / En dessous de // la moyenne.

Rouen is below (downstream from) Paris. New Orleans is below Saint Louis.
Rouen est // en aval de / au-dessous de / plus bas que / sous // Paris.
La Nouvelle-Orléans est // en aval de / au-dessous de / plus bas que / sous // Saint-Louis.

The Loire river is navigable below Nantes.
La Loire est navigable en aval de Nantes.

Put this down below.
Mettez ceci // en bas. / là-dessous.//

I don't know what floor his office is on. Try below.
Je ne sais pas à quel étage se trouve son bureau. Essayez // dessous. / au-dessous. / en dessous. / plus bas. / en bas (if there is only one floor below).//

Further below.
Plus bas. Encore plus bas.

Far below expectation.
Bien au-dessous de ce qu'on attendait.

The passing grade is 60. Yours is far below.
La note de passage est 60. La vôtre est bien // au-dessous. / en dessous. / plus basse.//

Watch out below!
Attention // dessous! / en bas! / au-dessous! / en dessous! / par terre! / là-dessous! / dans . . .! (in whatever place the people warned are: cellar, hole, street, etc.)//

126. *Beside. Besides.*

She sat beside me.
Elle était assise // à mon côté. / près de moi. / auprès de moi. / à côté de moi.//

He was beside himself with anger.
Il était // fou / aveuglé // de colère.
Sa colère // le mettait hors de lui. / le rendait fou. / l'aveuglait.//

He was beside himself with grief.
Il était effondré de chagrin.

He was beside himself with joy.
Il était // fou / éperdu / transporté // de joie.
Sa joie le rendait fou.

This is beside the point.
// Là / Ce // n'est pas le problème.
Cela n'a rien à voir avec la question .
C'est // à côté du / en dehors du / hors du / hors // sujet.

We cannot wait any longer. Besides, he is not likely to come now.
Nous ne pouvons attendre plus longtemps. D'ailleurs, il ne viendra sans doute plus maintenant.

Besides two escapes from prison, this man has a record of several thefts.
// Outre / En plus de // deux évasions de prison, cet homme a plusieurs vols à son actif (or: **à son casier judiciaire).**

This man has committed several burglaries. Besides, he has made two attempts to escape from prison.
Cet homme a commis plusieurs cambriolages. // De plus / En plus / En outre // il a tenté deux fois de s'évader de prison.

Besides being a liar, he was also a thief.
Non seulement il était voleur, il était aussi menteur.
Il n'était pas seulement voleur, il était aussi menteur.
Ce n'était pas seulement un voleur, c'était // aussi / également // un menteur.

Besides mowing the lawn, I also cleaned the garage.
Non seulement j'ai tondu la pelouse, mais j'ai // aussi / également / encore // nettoyé le garage.
Je n'ai pas fait que tondre la pelouse, j'ai aussi nettoyé le garage.

127. *Between.*

She sat between us.
Elle était assise entre nous (deux).

We can do it between the two of us.
Nous pouvons le faire, à nous deux.

Between the two of us, . . . (confidentially)
Entre nous, . . .

Between the two of us, . . . (be frank!)
De vous à moi, . . .

In between (not good, not bad).
// Moyen. / Pas trop mal.//

In between (time or space between two things).
// Entre les deux. / Dans l'intervalle.//
In between (between two persons).
// Entre les deux. / Entre nous (or: **vous, eux, elles).//**
In between (between two events).
// Entre les deux (événements). / Dans l'intervalle.// Entre-temps. / Dans l'entretemps.//
Choose between swimming and tennis.
Choisissez entre // la nage et le tennis. / vous baigner et jouer au tennis. / la natation et le tennis.//
There is a great difference between loving and liking.
Il y a une grande différence entre aimer et aimer bien.
There is a lot of difference between peeping and spying (between a peeping-tom and a spy).
Il y a loin d'épier à espionner.
D'épier à espionner // il y a loin. / il y a un (grand) pas. / il y a une grande différence.//
No, there is not such a difference between the two.
Non, de l'un à l'autre, il n'y a // qu'un pas. / pas grande différence.//
There is a great distance between Georgia and Oregon.
Il y a loin de la Géorgie à l'Orégon.
De la Géorgie à l'Orégon, la distance est grande.

128. Beyond.

We live beyond that hill.
Nous habitons // au-delà de / de l'autre côté de / là-bas derrière // cette colline.
The sky beyond the roof.
Le ciel // par dessus le toit. / au-dessus du toit.//
Beyond the sea.
// Au delà de la mer. / De l'autre côté de la mer. / Outre-mer (overseas)**.//**
This is beyond me.
Ceci ne dépend pas de moi. (no authority)
Ce n'est pas dans la mesure de mes moyens. (no authority, no capacity, no money)
Ceci me dépasse. (intellectually)
Beyond control.
Incontrôlable.
Qu'on ne peut plus contrôler.
Beyond repair.
Irréparable. (pop.: **Fini)**
Beyond our control.
Indépendant de notre volonté.

129. By.

This picture was painted by Rembrandt.
Ce tableau a été peint par Rembrandt.

Stay by me, by the fire.
Restez près de moi, près du feu.
Restez auprès de moi, à côté du feu.
Restez à côté de moi, // auprès / au coin // du feu.

It is seven-thirty by my watch.
Il est sept heures et demie à ma montre.

A concerto by Mozart.
Un concerto de Mozart.

A novel by Camus.
Un roman de Camus.

He succeeded by working hard.
Il a réussi // en travaillant dur / à force de travail.//

Close by.
// Tout près. / Tout à côté.//

Stand by.
// Attendez. / Restez à l'écoute. (two-way radio) / **Ne quittez pas l'écoute.** (two-way radio) / **Soyez prêt. / Restez là. / Restez à votre poste. / Ne quittez pas.** (telephone: hold on).//

Little by little.
// Peu à peu. / Petit à petit.//

To go by, pass (walk, drive, etc.) by a place.
Passer // à côté d'un / devant un // endroit.
Dépasser un endroit. (go too far, past a place).

To judge by appearances.
Juger sur l'apparence.

Man does not live by bread alone.
L'homme ne vit pas seulement de pain.

To measure three (feet) by five (feet) (3′x5′).
// Mesurer / Faire // trois (pieds) sur cinq.

A 10′ by 12′ room.
Une pièce de 10 pieds sur 12.

This lot is 100 feet long by 50 feet wide.
Ce terrain // mesure / fait // 100 pieds de long sur 50 pieds de large.
Ce terrain // mesure / fait // 100 pieds de longueur sur 50 pieds de largeur.
Ce terrain est long de 100 pieds et large de 50 pieds.

A man by the name of . . .
Un homme du nom de . . .
Un nommé . . .
Un certain . . .

To abide by . . .
// Obéir à / Observer // . . .

One by one, two by two, etc.
Un par un, deux par deux, etc.

By a hair.
// D'un cheveu. / À un poil près. (fam.) / De peu. / De justesse.//

By a narrow margin.
// De peu. / De justesse. / D'un cheveu.//

By a wide margin.
// De loin. / De beaucoup.//

By all means.
// Bien sûr. / Évidemment. / Je vous en prie.//

By and by.
// Bientôt. / Dans un moment. / Tout à l'heure.//

By birth.
// De / Par la // naissance.

By blood.
Par le sang.

By chance.
// Par hasard. / Par chance. (luck) / **par malchance.** (bad luck)//

By day. Day by day.
// De jour. / Le jour./ Au jour le jour.//

By dint of work, of working.
À force de // travail. / travailler.//

By far.
// De loin. / De beaucoup.//

By half.
// De moitié. / D'une moitié. / De la moitié.//

By heart.
Par cœur.

By nature.
// Par la nature. / De nature. (natural tendency)//

By next week.
// Pour / D'ici à // la semaine prochaine.

By night
// De nuit. / La nuit.//

By no means.
// Peu à peu. / Petit à petit.//
// En aucune façon. / En aucun cas. / Pas du tout.//

By now.
Pour maintenant.
À l'heure qu'il est.
À cette heure. (pop.)

By oneself.
// Tout seul. / À soi tout seul.// (See next item.)

By myself (yourself, himself, herself, itself).
// Tout seul. (m.) / Toute seule. (f.) / À moi (toi, lui, elle) seul(e). / À moi (toi, lui, elle) tout(e) seul(e).//

By ourselves (yourselves, themselves).
//Tout seuls (masc.) / toutes seules (fem.) /
à nous (vous, eux, elles) seul(e)s / à nous (vous, eux, elles) tout(es) seul(e)s.//

A by-pass.
// Un détour. / Une rocade. (avoiding a city)//

// Une route / Une avenue / Une voie / Un boulevard / Un / périphérique. (circling a large city)**//**

To by-pass.

// Faire un détour / prendre la rocade (la route, l'avenue, etc. périphérique). / Prendre le périphérique. //

A by-product.

Un sous-produit.

By reason of.

// Pour cause de. / En raison de.//

A bystander.

// Un badaud. / Un curieux. / Un témoin. / Un spectateur.//

By the beginning of.

// Pour le / D'ici au // début de.

By the dozen.

À la douzaine. (selling)
Par douzaines.

By the end of.

// Pour / D'ici (à) // la fin de.

By the pound.

À la livre. (selling)

By the way,

A propos,

By the yard.

Au mètre. (selling)

By tomorrow.

// Pour / D'ici (à) // demain.

130. Considering.

Considering the circumstances, you did quite well.

// Étant donné / Vu // les circonstances, vous vous en êtes très bien tiré.

We accepted the decision considering that it represented the majority's opinion.

Nous avons accepté la décision // étant donné / vu / du moment // qu'elle représentait l'opinion de la majorité.

"Considering that the defendant . . ." "Whereas the defendant . . ."

"Attendu que l'accusé . . ."

131. Despite.

We won despite a strong opposition.

Nous avons gagné // en dépit d'une / malgré une // forte opposition.

We went through despite their trying to stop us.

Nous sommes passés // bien qu'ils aient essayé de / en dépit de leurs efforts pour / malgré leurs efforts pour // nous arrêter.

132. Down.

He fell down the stairs.
Il est tombé // en bas / au bas // de l'escalier.
Il est tombé jusqu'en bas de l'escalier.

Down the road. Down the river.
Le long de la route. Le long de la rivière.

Down river from . . .
En aval de . . .

Down the hill.
// **En descendant** (movement) / **En bas de** (static) // **la côte** (or: **la colline**).

NOTE: *Down* modifying a verb is usually not translated into a separate French word. The verb alone, carefully chosen, is normally sufficient to convey the complete idea (§106, note).

To come down (movement).
Descendre.

To go down (movement).
Descendre.

To come down with the flu.
Attraper la grippe.

To lie down.
// **Se coucher.** (bed) / **S'allonger.** / **S'étendre.**//

To turn down an offer.
Refuser une offre.

To knock down.
// **Mettre / Envoyer // au tapis.** (boxing)
Heurter. (accidental; passive possible)
Faire tomber. (passive not possible)

Keep your head down.
Gardez la tête // en bas. / penchée. / baissée.//

Keep down.
Restez // couché. / baissé. / allongé. / caché. / à l'abri.//

Help me down, please.
Aidez-moi à descendre, s'il vous plaît.

Down with the dictator!
À bas le dictateur!

Down, Fido, lie down!
// Descends, / Par terre, / En bas, // Médor, couché!

The wind dies down.
Le vent // s'apaise. / tombe. / baisse. / diminue.//

The house burnt down (to the ground).
La maison a brûlé (complètement).

My friend let me down.
Mon ami m'a // laissé tomber. / abandonné.//

To put one's name down for something.
// S'inscrire / Se porter volontaire // pour quelque chose.

Down on paper.
Par écrit.

To get down to business.
// En venir aux choses sérieuses. / Se mettre au travail.//

The ups and downs of . . .
// Les hauts et les bas de . . . / Les succès et les déboires de . . .//

Up and down.
De haut en bas et de bas en haut. (vertical)
De long en large. (horizontal)

To go up and down.
Monter et descendre. (actual vertical movement)
Aller et venir. (walking, pacing)

To walk up and down the hallway.
Faire les cent pas dans le couloir.

A down payment.
// Un premier versement / Un acompte / Des arrhes.//

To hunt something down.
Poursuivre quelque chose // jusqu'au bout. / jusqu'à la capture.//

Downstream.
En aval.

Downwind.
// Dans le vent. / Avec le vent. / Au vent. / Dans la direction du vent. / Vent arrière. (sailing)//

To feel down.
Ne pas être en forme.
Avoir le cafard. (fam.: "blue")

To be downtown.
Être // en ville./ au centre de la ville./ au centre-ville.//

The downtown area.
Le centre-ville.

Downward.
Vers le bas.

133. During.

He came during my absence.
Il est venu // pendant / durant // mon absence.

During that time (meanwhile).
Pendant ce temps.

During the ten days that he was here, we had many conversations.
Pendant les dix jours qu'il a passés ici, nous avons eu de nombreuses conversations.

134. *Except (but).*

Write all this except (but) lines three and four.
Écrivez tout ceci // excepté / hormis / sauf // les lignes trois et quatre.

We led the game all along except on one occasion.
Nous avons mené le jeu tout du long // sauf / excepté // en une occasion.

We led the game all along except for one set.
Nous avons mené le jeu tout le temps // sauf / excepté / hormis // dans un set (or: **dans une partie, dans une manche, etc.).**

We played well, all of us, except him.
Nous avons tous bien joué, sauf lui.

Everything went right, except that it rained.
Tout s'est bien passé // sauf / excepté / hormis // qu'il a plu.

All of us played well, not excepting him.
Nous avons tous bien joué // sans l'excepter. / sans exception. / , lui aussi. / , même lui.//

135. *For.*

One for all, all for one.
Un pour tous, tous pour un.

Which is the plane for Paris?
Lequel est l'avion pour Paris?

They left for a week.
Ils sont partis pour une semaine.

What do you take me for? Who do you take me for?
Pour quoi me prenez-vous? Pour qui me prenez-vous?

I am for peace and against war.
Je suis pour la paix et contre la guerre.

Once and for all.
Une fois pour toutes.

What did you do that for?
// Pourquoi / Dans quel but / Pour quelle raison // avez-vous fait cela?

What do you keep this for?
Pour // quoi / que // faire est-ce que vous gardez ceci?

Take my word for it.
Croyez- // moi. / m'en.//
Je vous // (l') assure. / (en) donne ma parole.//

It pays for itself. It is worth the expense.
// Ça / Il / Elle // vaut la dépense.

To fall for something.
Se laisser prendre à quelque chose.

You are in for trouble.
Vous allez avoir des ennuis.
Vous allez vous faire attraper.
Vous n'y coupez pas. (fam.)
Vous êtes bon pour // des ennuis. / un savon. (coll.)//

To hold for certain that . . .
// Être certain que . . ./ Avoir la certitude que . . . //

That's for sure.
Ça, c'est // certain. / sûr.//

Word for word.
Mot pour mot.

An eye for an eye, a tooth for a tooth.
Œil pour œil, dent pour dent.

As for me, . . .
Quant à moi, . . .

As for us, . . .
// Quant à nous, / nous autres, // . . .

Good for him.
Bon pour lui (it will do for him).
It is sufficient for him: **Bon pour lui.**
It fits or suits him: **Ça lui va.**
I'm happy for him: **Tant mieux pour lui.**
It will teach him a lesson: **// Tant pis pour lui. / C'est bien fait pour lui. / Ça lui apprendra. //**

A ticket good for one month.
Un billet // bon pour / valable // un mois.

For a free ride.
// Sans payer. / Pour rien.// (fig.)
Pour un tour (de manège) gratuit. (lit.)

Good for getting rid of mosquitoes.
Bon pour se débarrasser des moustiques.

Good for nothing.
Bon à rien.

Take, choose, elect for a leader.
Prendre, choisir, élire // comme / pour // chef.

Don't take him for a fool.
Ne le prenez pas pour un imbécile.

Send for the doctor.
// Envoyez chercher / Faites venir // le médecin.

To cry for joy.
Pleurer de joie.

It's for you do decide.
C'est à vous de décider.

It is necessary for you to work.
Il faut que vous travailliez.

I'll find something for you to do.
Je vais vous trouver quelque chose à faire.

The best way is for you to ask her yourself.
// Le mieux, / La meilleure solution, // c'est que tu le lui demandes toi-même.

I brought this book for you to read.
Je vous ai apporté ce livre à lire. (matter-of-fact)
Je vous ai apporté ce livre pour que vous le lisiez. (intent)

I was anxious for him to come.
J'étais pressé qu'il vienne.
J'attendais son arrivée avec impatience.

We are waiting for the bus.
Nous attendons le bus.

I asked for a raise.
J'ai demandé une augmentation.

I am looking for my glasses.
Je cherche mes lunettes.

He paid for the meal.
Il a payé le repas.

I don't care for it. I don't care for wine.
Ça ne me dit rien. Le vin ne me dit rien.

The nurse was caring for the wounded.
L'infirmière // s'occupait des / soignait les / prenait soin des // blessés.

Except for.
(See *except*, §134.)

To call for help.
Appeler quelqu'un // au secours. / à l'aide.//

To long for happiness.
Soupirer après le bonheur.
Aspirer au bonheur.

To long for home.
Regretter // la / sa // maison.
Avoir le // mal du pays. / cafard ("blues").//

We have been here for two days.
Nous sommes ici depuis deux jours.
// Il y a / Voilà / Ça fait // deux jours que nous sommes ici.

We had been here for two days when he arrived.
Nous étions ici depuis deux jours quand il est arrivé.
// Il y avait / Ça faisait / Cela faisait // deux jours que nous étions ici quand il est arrivé.

We lived in England for two years before the war.
Nous avons vécu en Angleterre pendant deux ans avant la guerre.
Nous avons vécu deux ans en Angleterre avant la guerre.

Stay here for a while.
Restez ici un moment.

He hesitated, for it was dark.
Il hésita parce qu'il faisait sombre.
Il hésita car il faisait noir.

He was mistaken for a thief.
On l'a pris pour un voleur.
On a cru que c'était un voleur.

He was mistaken for the thief.
On l'a pris pour le voleur.
On a cru // qu'il était / que c'était lui // le voleur.

We take it for granted.
Nous le trouvons tout naturel.
On trouve ça // normal. / naturel.//
Cela ne nous surprend plus.
Cela nous semble // normal. / naturel.//
Nous // croyons / pensons / disons / imaginons // que c'est un dû.

We headed for the mountains.
Nous nous sommes // dirigés vers / mis en route pour // les montagnes.

Not for the world.
Pour rien au monde.

To be fit for . . .
Être bon à . . . (infinitive)
Être bon pour . . . (noun)

To be prepared for . . .
Être // prêt / préparé // à . . . (infinitive)
Être préparé pour . . . (noun)

To be proper for . . .
Être // propre à / convenable pour . . .//

To be ready for . . .
Être // prêt / préparé // à . . . (infinitive)
Être prêt pour . . . (noun)

To be sorry for . . .
Être // navré / désolé / fâché // de . . . (with infinitive)
Être // navré / désolé / fâché // pour . . . (with personal pronoun, proper noun)

Let's go for a walk.
Allons faire une promenade.
Allons nous promener.

They left him for dead.
Ils l'ont laissé pour mort.

For all I care.
Je m'en moque.
Ça ne me dérange pas.

For all I care, . . .
Ça ne me dérange pas que . . . (subjunctive)
Qu'est-ce que ça peut me faire que . . . (subjunctive)

For all I know, he has done his best.
Pour autant que je sache, il a fait de son mieux.

He is the only candidate for the position, for all I know.
Il est le seul à vouloir ce poste, que je sache!

He never returned to see us, for all I know.
Il n'est jamais revenu nous voir, // pour autant que / que // je sache.

For better and for worse.
Pour le meilleur et pour le pire.

Forever.
  Pour toujours.
  À jamais.

Forever and ever.
  Pour toujours et à jamais.

For fear of an accident.
  De // peur / crainte // d'un accident.

For fear that . . .
  De // peur / crainte // que . . . (subjunctive)
  De // peur / crainte // de . . . (infinitive)

For good.
  Pour de bon.

For heaven's sake!
  Mais enfin!
  Tout de même!
  Quand même!

For lack of . . .
  Faute de . . .
  Par manque de . . .
  À cause du manque de . . .

For lease.
  À louer (avec bail).

For life.
  Pour la vie. (promise):
  À vie. (prison, office)

For my part.
  Pour ma part.
  Quant à moi.
  De mon côté.
  En ce qui me concerne.

For my sake.
  Pour // moi. / me faire plaisir.//

For now.
  Pour // le moment. / l'instant. / le présent.//

For myself, himself, etc.
He prepared a sandwich for himself.
  Il s'est préparé un sandwich.

Speak for yourself.
  Parle pour toi-même.

He wanted to see that for himself.
  Il a voulu voir ça // lui-même. / tout seul.//

For one thing . . .
  Et d'abord . . .
  Premièrement . . .
  Du moins . . .
  Pour commencer, . . .

For rent.
  À louer.

For the most part.
Pour la plupart. Dans l'ensemble.

For the present.
Pour // l'instant. / le moment. / le présent.//

For the rest . . .
// Quant au / Pour le / En ce qui concerne le // reste . . .

For sale.
À vendre.

For your information.
Si vous voulez savoir.
Puisqu'il faut vous l'expliquer. (testy)
Pour // vous renseigner. / votre gouverne.//
En guise de renseignement.

For your own good.
Pour votre bien.
Dans votre propre intérêt.

136. From.

See §§167-170 for *from* with geographical names.

They come from Europe.
Ils viennent d'Europe.

Wine is made from grapes.
On fait le vin // avec du raisin / à partir du raisin.//

A scene painted from nature.
Une scène peinte d'après nature.

From beginning to end.
Du // début / commencement // à la fin.

From 1515 on . . .
À partir de 1515, . . .
Dès 1515, . . . (as early as 1515, . . .)

From the XIth century down to the XVIIth century.
Du XIe siècle au XVIIe siècle.
Depuis le XIe siècle jusqu'au XVIIe siècle.

From the XIth century back to the Vth century.
Du XIe siècle au Ve siècle.

From nowhere.
On ne sait d'où.
Comme par miracle.

From day to day.
Gradually: **De jour en jour.**
In the present: **Au jour le jour.**

From time to time.
De temps en temps.

From morning to night.
Du matin au soir. (all day long)

From mouth to mouth.
De bouche à oreille.

From afar. From a distance.
De loin.

From close up.
De près.

From place to place.
// D'un endroit à l'autre. / Ici et là.//

From room to room.
D'une // pièce / salle / chambre // à l'autre.

From here to New York.
D'ici à New York.

To live 20 miles from somewhere.
Habiter à 20 miles de quelque part.

My apartment is only one kilometer from downtown.
Mon appartement n'est qu'à un kilomètre du centre-ville.

From bad to worse.
De mal en pis.
De plus en plus mal.

From hand to mouth.
Au jour le jour.

(From now) until tomorrow, Friday, next week, etc.
D'ici (à) demain, vendredi, la semaine prochaine, etc.

Apart from . . .
// À part / Sans parler de / À l'exception de / Hormis / Excepté / Sauf // . . .

To be different from . . .
Être différent de . . .

To count from one to fifty.
Compter de un à cinquante.

To die from starvation, from the cold, from exhaustion, from despair.
Mourir de faim, de froid, de fatigue, de désespoir.

To die from cancer, tuberculosis, cholera, AIDS.
Mourir du cancer, de la tuberculose, du choléra, du SIDA.

To differ from . . .
Être différent de . . .

To judge from, by appearances.
Juger // sur / selon / d'après // l'apparence.

To keep from . . .-ing.
Éviter de . . . (infinitive)
Se retenir de . . . (infinitive)
S'empêcher de . . . (infinitive)

To keep, prevent someone from doing something.
Empêcher quelqu'un de faire quelque chose.

To keep something from destruction.
// Sauver / Préserver // quelque chose de la destruction.

To know from experience.
Savoir par expérience.

To refrain from . . .-ing.
Éviter de . . . (infinitive)
Se retenir de . . . (infinitive)
S'empêcher de . . . (infinitive)

To save from destruction.
// Préserver / Sauver // de la destruction.

To save someone (or something) from . . .-ing.
Empêcher quelqu'un (ou quelque chose) de . . . (infinitive)

To stay away from . . .
Rester à bonne distance de . . .
Ne pas approcher de . . .
Éviter . . . (noun)
Éviter de . . . (infinitive)

To suffer from starvation, cold, cancer, an ulcer, TB, rheumatism, etc.
Souffrir de la faim, du froid, du cancer, d'un ulcère, de la tuberculose, de rhumatismes, etc.

To take something from someone.
// Prendre / Enlever / Arracher / Voler // quelque chose à quelqu'un.

To tell one thing from another.
Distinguer une chose // d'une autre. / d'avec une autre.//
Faire la distinction entre une chose et une autre.

137. In.

See §§167-170 for *in* with geographical names.

One in ten, twenty, etc.
Un sur dix, vingt, etc.

In stone, brick, wood, cotton, copper, etc.
// En / De // pierre, brique, bois, coton, cuivre, etc.

In color, mourning, white, etc.
// En / De // couleur, deuil, blanc, etc.
(*de* is preferred if the prepositional phrase modifies a noun.)

In Sunday best.
En costume de dimanche.
En dimanche.

In Milton, Corneille, Shakespeare, etc.
// Chez / Dans l'œuvre de // Milton, Corneille, Shakespeare, etc.

In all.
En tout.

In any case.
En tout cas.

Not in a million years.
Pour rien au monde.

In a good humor (mood).
De bonne humeur.

In brief . . .
Bref . . .
En somme . . .

In cash.
Comptant.
Au comptant.
En (argent) liquide.

Indeed.
En effet.
Le fait est que . . .

In excess of . . .
Plus de . . .
Au-dessus de . . .

Is in excess of . . .
Dépasse . . .

In exchange for . . .
En échange de . . .

In fashion.
À la mode.

In front of.
// En face de. / Devant.//

In fact.
En fait.

In folds.
// Plissé. / Tout en plis.//

In good spirits.
De bonne humeur.
En forme. (coll.)

In honor of . . .
En l'honneur de . . .

In hope of . . .
Dans l'espoir de . . .

. . . in number.
Au nombre de . . .

In order to . . .
// Afin de / Pour . . .// (infinitive)

In order that . . .
// Afin / Pour // que . . . (subjunctive)

In packages of twenty.
// En / Par // paquets de vingt.

In particular.
En particulier.

In quest of . . .
En quête de . . .
À la recherche de . . .

In short.
Bref.
En résumé.
En somme.

Insofar as, inasmuch as . . .
Dans la mesure où . . .

In spite of . . .
// En dépit de / Malgré . . .// (noun)

In tears.
En larmes.

. . . in that you failed to deliver the goods in time.
. . . // puisque / du moment que / du fait que / en ce que // vous n'avez pas livré la marchandise à temps. (with indicative)

In truth.
À la vérité.
En vérité.

In the back, rear, bottom of . . .
//Au fond de / À l'arrière de // . . .

In the distance.
// Au loin. / À l'horizon.//

In use.
En usage. (custom)
En service. (being used)

In view of the fact that . . .
// Vu / Considérant / Étant donné // le fait que . . .

In the opposite direction.
// En / Dans le // sens inverse.

In the sun.
Au soleil.

In the rain.
Sous la pluie.

In autumn.
En automne.

In summer.
En été.

In the summer.
Pendant l'été.

In spring.
Au printemps.

In winter.
En hiver.

In 1989.
En 1989.

In January, etc.
// En / Au mois de // janvier, etc.

In the daytime.
// Le jour. / Pendant la journée.//

In the morning.
// Le matin. / Pendant la matinée.// (modifies a verb)
Du matin. (10:00 a.m.: 10h du matin)

In the afternoon.
// L'après-midi. / Pendant l'après-midi.// (with verb)
De l'après-midi. (4:00 p.m.: 4h de l'après-midi)

In the evening.
// Le soir. / Pendant la soirée.// (with verb)
Du soir. (10:00 p.m.: 10h du soir)

In the night.
// La nuit. / Pendant la nuit.// (with verb)
De la nuit. (with noun)

In time.
Not late: **À temps.**
Eventually: **// Avec le / en son // temps.**

In the shade.
À l'ombre.
Dans l'ombre. (may be figurative)

In the dark.
Dans l'obscurité.
Dans l'ombre. (shade, darkness)
Dans la pénombre. (half darkness)
Dans le noir. (at night; not in the know)

To be in earnest.
// Être sérieux. / Parler sérieusement. / Ne pas rire. / Parler sans rire. / Ne pas plaisanter.//

To be in business.
To be a businessperson: **Être dans les affaires.**
Open for business: **Être ouvert (au public).**

We're in business, now!
// Ça / L'affaire // commence à marcher.

To be in demand.
Être (très) demandé.

To be in. Mrs. Smith is in.
Madame Smith est // là. (here) **/ chez elle.** (at home) **/ à son travail.** (at her job) **/ dans son bureau.** (in her office) **/ rentrée.** (is back home) **//**

Peaches are in.
Les pêches sont de saison.
C'est la saison des pêches.
Les pêches sont arrivées.

Pink is in.
Le rose est à la mode.

You are in for . . .
Vous êtes bon pour . . .
Vous pouvez vous attendre à . . .

We believe in God.
Nous croyons en Dieu.

He believes in love.
Il croit à l'amour.

She believes in sharing.
Elle croit au partage.
Selon elle, il faut partager.
Son avis est qu'il faut partager.

His work consists in sorting the mail.
Son travail consiste à trier le courrier.

He indulged himself in a pound of chocolate.
Il s'est laissé aller à manger une livre de chocolat.

We deal in lost causes.
Nous nous occupons des causes perdues.
Les causes perdues, c'est notre affaire.

We deal in cars, new and used.
// Nous faisons le commerce des / Nous vendons des // voitures, neuves et d'occasion.

Have confidence in me, trust (in) me.
Ayez confiance en moi.
Faites-moi confiance.
Fiez-vous à moi.

She confides in me.
Elle se confie à moi.
Elle me fait ses confidences.
Je suis son confident.

We are lacking in (short of) space, room.
Nous manquons // de place. / d'espace.//

We succeed in . . .-ing
Nous réussissons à . . . (infinitive)

To be in a bathing suit, a dress, shorts, etc.
Être en maillot de bain, robe, short, etc.

138. Inside.

Inside your pocket.
Dans votre poche.

From inside your pocket.
De votre poche.

Get (step, walk, come, go, etc.) inside.
Entrez.
// Allez / Venez // à l'intérieur.

Inside out.
À l'envers.
Sens dessus-dessous. (upside down, topsy-turvy)

It is nicer inside the house.
C'est mieux // dans / à l'intérieur de // la maison.
The house is nicer inside.
La maison est // plus belle / mieux // à l'intérieur.
Number 13 is on the inside (horse race).
Le 13 est à la corde.
The inside of . . .
// L'intérieur / Le dedans // de . . .

139. Instead.

I bought four instead of three.
J'en ai acheté quatre au lieu de trois.
Why me instead of him?
Pourquoi moi // au lieu de lui? / à sa place?//
He went to play tennis instead of working.
Il est allé jouer au tennis au lieu de travailler.
You were in instead of out.
Vous étiez à l'intérieur au lieu d'être dehors.
Vous étiez dedans au lieu d'être à l'extérieur.
I brought you this instead.
Je vous ai apporté ceci // à la place. / en échange.//
I'd rather die instead!
J'aimerais mieux mourir!
Plutôt mourir!

140. Near. Nearly.

Nearby.
// Tout près. / À proximité. / Dans le voisinage. Dans le coin. (coll.)//
He nearly killed himself.
Il s'est presque tué.
Il a failli se tuer.
Come near me.
Viens près de moi.
He is near-sighted.
Il est myope.
Near here.
Près d'ici.
Christmas is near.
Noël est proche.
The Near East.
Le Proche-Orient.
They stayed nearly a month.
Ils sont restés // près d'un / presqu'un // mois.

It is not nearly as good.
Il est loin d'être aussi bon.

141. Notwithstanding.

See *despite*, **§131.**

142. Of.

The wheel of the car.
La roue de la voiture.

The wheel of a car.
Une roue de voiture.

A person of quality.
Une personne de qualité.

The coast of Florida. (and other feminine place names)
La côte // de / de la // Floride.

The coast of Texas. (and other masculine place names)
La côte du Texas.

A wall of brick.
Un mur // de / en // brique.

A piece of cloth.
Un morceau de tissu. Un morceau d'étoffe.

To make a fool of someone.
Tourner quelqu'un en ridicule.

To make . . . of . . .
See *to do, to make,* §294.

He was robbed of his money. (See §304D for similar passive constructions.)
On lui a volé son argent.

Who(m) are you thinking of?
À qui pensez-vous?

What are you thinking of?
À quoi pensez-vous?

I am thinking of her.
Je pense à elle.

What do you think of him, of her?
Que pensez-vous de lui, d'elle?

A kind of . . . , a type of . . . , . . . of sorts.
// Un type de / une sorte de / une espèce de / un genre de // . . .

Of age.
En âge de // comprendre. / savoir vivre. / raisonner. // etc.
Majeur. (legal age)
Adulte.

. . ., of all things!
. . . , // vraiment! / tout de même! / quand même! / pensez donc!//

Of importance.
Important.
D'importance.

Of little importance.
// De peu / Sans trop // d'importance.

Of no importance.
// Sans / D'aucune // importance.

Of necessity.
Par nécessité.
Par obligation.

Of old.
// Jadis. / Autrefois.// (with verb)
// De jadis. / D'autrefois.// (with noun)

All of us, all of you, all of them.
Nous tous, nous toutes, vous tous, vous toutes, eux tous, elles toutes.

All three of us, of you, of them.
Nous trois, vous trois, eux trois, elles trois.

Both of us, of you, of them.
Nous deux, vous deux, eux deux, elles deux.

Both of them were singing.
Tous (Toutes) deux chantaient.
Ils (Elles) chantaient tous (toutes) les deux.
Tous (Toutes) les deux, ils (elles) chantaient.

Both of you failed.
Vous avez échoué tous (toutes) les deux.
Tous (Toutes) les deux, vous avez échoué.

All of the men.
Tous les hommes.

All of the girls.
Toutes les filles.

All of it.
En entier.
. . . tout entier. (masc.)
. . . tout entière. (fem.)

One of us.
Un (une) // de / d'entre // nous.
L'un (l'une) // de / d'entre // nous.

One of them.
Un (une) d'entre eux (elles).

With the following expressions, the preposition *of* should be expressed as ***d'entre*** before the personal pronouns ***nous, vous, eux*** and ***elles***. The use of ***de*** is also possible in many cases, but may be unacceptable in others.

a few	**quelques-uns**
a great number	**un grand nombre**
another one	**un autre**
any (one)	**n'importe qui, n'importe lequel**

each (one)	**chacun**
either one	**l'un ou l'autre**
enough	**assez**
every one	**chacun**
half	**la moitié**
lots	**beaucoup, un grand nombre**
many	**beaucoup**
most	**la plupart**
neither (one)	**ni l'un ni l'autre**
none	**aucun, nul**
not one	**pas un (seul), personne**
only one	**un seul**
one, two, three, ten, etc.	**un, deux, trois, dix, etc.**
one-fourth	**le quart**
(twenty-five) percent	**(vingt-cinq) pour cent**
several	**plusieurs**
some	**certains, quelque-uns**
the best	**les meilleurs**
the best one	**le meilleur**
the first	**les premiers**
the first one	**le premier**
the last	**les derniers**
the last one	**le dernier**
the majority	**la majorité**
too many	**trop**

Note:

Who among you?	**Qui d'entre vous? Qui de vous?**
Whoever among them . . .	**Quel que soit celui d'entre eux qui . . .**
Which one among them?	**Lequel d'entre eux?**
Which one among you?	**Lequel d'entre vous?**

Both of us are here.
Nous sommes // tous deux / tous les deux // ici. (fem.: toutes)

Both of them are here.
Ils sont ici tous les deux.
Elles sont ici toutes les deux.

He saw both of us.
Il nous a vus tous les deux.
Il nous a vues toutes les deux.

143. Off.

Keep off.
Défense d'entrer.

Keep off the grass.
Défense de marcher sur le gazon.

The tire came off the wheel.
Le pneu est sorti de la jante.
La roue a perdu son pneu.

The house is just off the road.
La maison est // peu à l'écart / à peu de distance // de la route.
La maison n'est pas loin de la route.

It is a mile off.
C'est à un mile // de distance. / d'ici. / de là.//

Get off this property.
Sortez // d'ici. / de cette propriété.//

Get off my back.
Cesse de m'embêter.
Tu m'agaces.
Tu me casses les pieds. (coll.)

Get off the stove.
Éloignez-vous de la cuisinière.

Get off my horse.
Descends de mon cheval.

To turn off the light, the radio, the TV, etc.
Éteindre la lumière, la radio, la télé, etc.

To turn off the power.
Couper le courant.

To turn off the water.
Fermer le robinet.
Coupez l'eau.

Off the coast.
Au large.
À distance de la côte.

10% off.
Réduction de 10%.
Solde: 10%.

Off duty.
Libre. (taxi)

I am off duty.
Je ne suis // pas / plus // de service.

Off and on.
Place: **// Ici et là /çà et là.//**
Time: **De temps // à autre / en temps.//**
An occurrence: **Par // intermittence / intervalles.//**

To be well off.
Être à l'aise.
Avoir // de la fortune. / de l'argent.//

He fell off the ladder.
Il est tombé de l'échelle.

To be far off.
Guessing: **Être loin.**
Traveling: **Être au loin.**

To show off.
Faire le malin.
Faire son // malin. / intéressant.// (children)
Se vanter.
Crâner.

To show off something.
// Faire étalage de / Exhiber / Vanter // quelque chose.

The light went off.
La lumière s'est éteinte.

The bomb went off.
La bombe a explosé.

He went off.
Il est parti.
Il s'en est allé.

Off you go!
// Vas-y! / Va-t'en!//
// Allez-y! / Allez-vous-en!/
En route!
Allez, ouste! (rough)

The game is off.
Le match est annulé. (will not take place)

I must be off.
Il faut que // je parte. / je m'en aille. / je me sauve.//

Our supplies were cut off.
On nous a coupé les vivres. (especially allowance)
On ne nous fournit plus. (merchandise)

Offshore.
Au large.
Loin // de la côte. / du rivage.//

Offshore drilling.
Forage en mer.

Offhand.
Sans y réfléchir.
De but en blanc.
Comme ça. (familiarly, and vague)

To be off schedule.
Ne plus être à l'heure.
Être en retard sur l'horaire.

144. On.

To be on the lookout.
Faire attention.
Être sur ses gardes.
Ouvrir l'œil.

To be on the move.
Être // en action. / en marche.//
// Se déplacer. / avancer. / bouger. / remuer.//

I'm on my way.
// J'arrive. / J'y vais. / Je suis en route.//

On the way, we saw . . .
En chemin, nous avons vu . . .

I have my checkbook on me.
J'ai mon carnet de chèques sur moi.

What is going on?
Qu'est-ce qui se passe?

Don't stop, go on.
Ne vous arrêtez pas, continuez.

Go on in!
Entrez donc!

We went on talking.
Nous avons continué à parler.

Keep on . . .-ing.
Continuer à . . . (+ infinitive.)

Burn on, roll on, walk on, etc.
Continuer à brûler, rouler, marcher, etc.

On arriving (On arrival), we saw them.
// En arrivant / À notre arrivée // nous les avons vus.

He has his hat on.
Il porte son chapeau.
Il a son chapeau sur la tête.

Hold on.
Ne quittez pas. (telephone)
Tenez bon.
Ne lachez pas. (don't let go)

What's on?(TV, movies, etc.)
Quel film // y a-t-il? / joue-t-on?//
Quel est le programme?
Qu'est-ce qu'on présente?

The contact is on.
Le contact est mis.

The power (electricity) is on.
Il y a // de l'électricité. / du courant.//
Ça marche! (after cut off, blackout, or blown fuse)

The film is on.
Le film passe // en ce moment. / actuellement.// (showing this week)

The show is on.
Le programme est commencé. (in progress)

The gas is on.
Le gaz est // ouvert. / en marche. // (someone forgot to turn it off)
Il y a du gaz. (it's not cut off)
Ça marche! (after cut off)

The light is on.
Il y a de la lumière.
La lumière est allumée.

The motor (engine) is on.
Le moteur // est en marche. / tourne.//

The show is on.
Le spectacle est commencé. (has begun)
On va présenter le spectacle. (not canceled)

The water is on.
Il y a de l'eau.
L'eau coule. (someone left it running)
Ça marche! (after cut off)

Go right on.
Continuez.
Faites comme si je n'étais pas là.

Right on!
// Exactement! / C'est ça!//
En plein // dedans! / dessus!//
En plein dans le mille! (bull's-eye)

From 1918 on.
// À partir de / Après // 1918.

To be on one's toes.
Être // sur les dents. / en éveil.//
Faire très attention.

It gets on my nerves.
Ça me tape sur les nerfs.
Ça m'énerve.

On account of . . .
À cause de . . .

. . . is on course.
La trajectoire de . . . est parfaite.
. . . suit la trajectoire prévue.

To be on duty.
Être de // service. / garde.//

While on duty.
Pendant // le service. / les heures de service.//

On fire.
En feu.

To set something on fire.
Mettre le feu à quelque chose.

On foot.
À pied.

On one's back.
Sur le dos.
Sur son dos.

On one's knees.
À genoux. (static: be on one's knees)
S'agenouiller. (movement: get down on one's knees)

On purpose.
Exprès.

On sale.
À vendre. (regular selling: for sale)
En // réclame. / solde.// (special, discount)

To be on strike.
Être en grève.

To go on strike.
// Se mettre en / Faire // grève.

The people on strike.
Les grévistes.

On time.
À l'heure.

On the average.
En moyenne.
Dans l'ensemble.

On the board.
Au tableau. (blackboard)
Au panneau d'affichage. (bulletin board)
// Au conseil de . . . / Membre du conseil de . . .// (member of the council, of the board of directors)

On board.
À bord. (ship, plane)
Dans // le train. / le bus. / le car. / l'avion. / etc.//

Get on board (aboard) the train, plane, etc. (to board)
Monter dans le train, l'avion, etc. (embarquer)

On the floor.
// Par terre. / Sur le sol. / Sur le plancher.//

On the left.
À gauche. (with verb)
De gauche. (with noun)

On the morning of May 16.
Le matin du 16 mai.
Le 16 mai au matin.

On the right.
À droite. (with verb)
De droite. (with noun)

On the wall.
// Au mur. / Sur le mur.//

On the whole.
Dans l'ensemble.

On wheels.
En voiture. (to travel on __)
Sur roues. (mounted on __)

145. Opposite.

Opposite our house.
// En face de / Devant // notre maison.
// En face de / Devant // chez nous.

The opposite side.
Le côté // opposé. / d'en face.//
L'équipe adverse. (opposite team)

The opposite direction.
La direction opposée.
Le sens // opposé. / contraire. / inverse.//

In the opposite direction.
En sens inverse.

146. Out.

One out of a hundred.
Un sur cent.

Outdoors.
// À l'extérieur. / En plein air.//

To look out the window.
Regarder par la fenêtre.

To come out of a place.
Sortir d'un endroit.

To be out of breath.
Être // à bout de souffle. / essoufflé. / hors d'haleine.//
Avoir le souffle coupé.

I am out of cigarettes.
Je n'ai plus de cigarettes.

To be out of danger.
Être hors de danger.

To be out of date.
Être // démodé. / dépassé. / périmé. / obsolète.//

To be out of fashion.
Être démodé.
Ne plus être à la mode.

You are out of line.
Vous n'y êtes plus.

You are out of luck.
Vous n'avez // pas / plus // de chance.
Votre chance est terminée.

She ran out of sugar. (result: she is out of sugar)
Elle est à court de sucre.
Elle n'a plus de sucre.
Il lui manque du sucre.

We ran out of time.
Nous avons été pris de court.

To be out of office.
Être sortant.
Avoir fini son mandat.

To be out of order (machine).
Ne plus // marcher. / être en état de marche.//
Être // cassé. / détraqué. / en panne.//

To be out of order (person).
Ne plus y être.
Être en dehors du sujet.

He is out of order.
Il n'y est plus.
// Sa conduite / Son attitude // est déplacée.
Ses paroles sont déplacées.

To be out of service.
Être hors d'usage.

To be out of sight.
Être // hors de vue. / caché.//

Out of sight! (coll.)
// Formidable! / Terrible! / Fantastique! // etc.

To be out of trouble.
Être hors // d'affaire. / de danger.//
Être // sauf. / sauvé. / tranquille.//
Ne plus avoir d'ennuis.
S'être tiré d'affaire.

To get out of trouble.
Se tirer d'affaire.

To get out of it (alive).
// S'en tirer. / En réchapper.//

To be out of work.
Être // en chômage. / sans travail. / sans emploi.//

He is out of his mind.
Il a perdu // la tête. / la raison.//
Il ne sait plus ce qu'il dit.
Il est hors de lui. (See §126, *beside himself.***)**

147. Outside.

Outside the house.
// Hors de / En dehors de / À l'extérieur de / Devant // chez soi (or: **la maison).**

Go outside.
// Sortez. / Allez dehors.//

It is nicer outside the house.
C'est mieux // à l'extérieur / hors // de la maison.

The house is prettier outside.
La maison est plus jolie à l'extérieur.

Come outside.
Sortez.
Venez // dehors. / à l'extérieur.//

The outside of . . .
// L'extérieur / Le dehors // de . . .

148. Over.

To jump over the fence.
Sauter par-dessus la clôture.

To fall overboard.
Tomber par-dessus bord.

A cloud over my head.
Un nuage au-dessus de ma tête.

Over fifty dollars.
Plus de cinquante dollars.

Over the river.
// Par-dessus / De l'autre côté de // la rivière.

People over 65.
Les personnes // de plus / qui ont plus // de 65 ans.

Over the weekend.
Pendant le week-end.
Tout le week-end.
Jusqu'à la fin du week-end.
Jusqu'à lundi. (this weekend)
Jusqu'au lundi. (that weekend)

Sophomore is over freshman.
Sophomore est au-dessus de freshman.

To stay overnight.
Rester passer la nuit.

To change overnight.
Changer // en une / pendant la // nuit.
Changer du jour au lendemain. (rapidly)

An overall impression.
Une impression d'ensemble.

To do something over.
// Refaire / Recommencer // quelque chose.
Recommencer.

To paint something over.
Repeindre quelque chose.

To turn something over.
Retourner quelque chose.

To turn something over to someone.
// Donner / Rendre / Livrer // quelque chose à quelqu'un.

Over and over (again).
Plusieurs fois // de suite. / de rang.//
À plusieurs reprises.

Over again.
Encore une fois.
De nouveau.
Une fois de plus.

To take over.
Prendre le commandement.

To take something over.
Prendre quelque chose en charge.

To take someone, something over to a place.
Conduire quelqu'un quelque part.
Porter quelque chose quelque part.

To ask someone over.
Inviter quelqu'un à venir.
Demander à quelqu'un de venir.

I asked them over.
Je leur ai demandé de venir chez nous.
Je les ai invités à venir chez nous.

It's (all) over.
C'est // fini. / terminé.//
Tout est // fini. / terminé.//

School, the day, the week is over.
L'école, la journée, la semaine est finie.

1991 is over.
1991 est // fini. / passé.//

He had sunglasses over his eyes.
Il portait des lunettes de soleil.
Il avait des lunettes de soleil sur les yeux.
Il avait les yeux cachés par des lunettes de soleil.
Des lunettes de soleil // cachaient / couvraient // ses yeux.

He had a viser over his eyes.
Il avait une visière au-dessus des yeux.

She had a shawl over her shoulders.
Elle portait un châle sur les épaules.

Move over. (depends on direction of movement)
// Avance-toi. / Recule-toi. / Éloigne-toi. / Approche-toi.//
Fais-moi de la place.

Over. (two-way radio)
À vous.

Over and out. (two-way radio)
Terminé.

Let's get it over with.
Finissons-en.

Over dinner.
// En mangeant. / Pendant le repas.//

Let's discuss this over dinner.
Parlons de cela pendant le dîner.
Discutons cela en mangeant.
Allons dîner, nous en discuterons pendant le repas.

She is over at Paul's.
Elle est chez Paul.

Come over to dinner.
Venez dîner // chez nous. / ici.//

He came over from Paris.
Il est venu de Paris pour nous voir.

To fight over something.
Se battre // pour / au sujet de // quelque chose.

A stopover.
The action: **Un arrêt // à mi-chemin. / temporaire.//**
Une escale.
The place:// **Un point d'arrêt. / Une escale.//**

Left over.
// En / De // trop.
De reste.

Leftovers.
// Un reste / Des restes // de . . .

We have some chicken left over from lunch.
Il nous reste du poulet du déjeuner.
Nous avons // un reste / des restes // de poulet du déjeuner.

We have some chicken left over.
// Il nous reste / Nous avons encore // du poulet.

Drop over to see us.
Venez nous voir // quand vous voudrez. / n'importe quand. / à l'improviste.//

All over the country.
// Dans / À travers // tout le pays.
// D'un bout à l'autre / Sur toute l'étendue // du pays.
Partout dans le pays.

Over here.
// Ici. / De ce côté-ci. / De ce côté-là.//

I am over here, under the tree.
Je suis // ici, / là, // sous l'arbre.

Over there.
// Là. / Là-bas. / De ce côté-là. / Plus loin là-bas.//

NOTE: The prefix *over-* corresponds to several French prefixes:

to overdo	**exagérer**
to overestimate	**surestimer**
to overflow	**déborder**
to overuse	**abuser**

149. Past.

We walked (drove, ran, etc.) past their house.
Nous sommes passés devant leur maison.
Nous avons dépassé leur maison. (went farther than)

He lived past 100.
Il a dépassé la centaine.
Il a vécu plus de cent ans.

A plane flew past our house.
Un avion est passé au-dessus de chez nous.

It's half past ten.
Il est dix heures et demie.

It is five past three.
Il est trois heures cinq.

I shall not wait past the hour.
Je n'attendrai pas // après l'heure / une fois l'heure passée / quand l'heure sera passée.//

It is ten past, a quarter past, half past. (past the present hour: the statement is left incomplete)
Il est dix, le quart, la demie.

Drive past those hills.
Allez // au-delà de / de l'autre côté de / plus loin que // ces collines.

Past a certain age.
//Au delà d'un / Passé un / Après un / Quand on a dépassé un // certain âge.

150. Per.

Percent.
Pour cent.

Rounds per minute.
Tours à la minute.

They cost $2 per pound.
Ils coûtent deux dollars la livre.

He makes $6.25 per hour.
Il gagne six dollars vingt-cinq de l'heure.

He is driving at 60 miles per hour.
Il roule à 60 miles à l'heure.

You will get one free copy per fifty ordered.
Vous recevrez un exemplaire gratuit pour chaque commande de cinquante.

Per se.
En soi.

Per annum (per year). Per day. Per week. Per month.
Par an. Par jour. Par semaine. Par mois.

. . . per child.
. . . par enfant.

151. Round.

See *around*, **§118.**

152. Save.

See *except*, **§133.**

153. Since.

I have been here since yesterday. (see also *how long, for, since*, §291 and *for*, §135)
Je suis ici depuis hier.

I had been in New York since the day before.
J'étais à New York depuis la veille.

He has not said a word since you left.
Il n'a pas dit un mot depuis // votre départ. / que vous êtes parti.//

You don't have to come, since you have work to do.
Tu n'es pas obligé de venir, puisque tu as du travail à faire.

You are not responsible, since *he* was on duty, not you.
Vous n'êtes pas responsable, // puisque / du moment que / étant donné que // c'est lui qui était de service, et non vous.

154. In spite of.

See *despite*, **§131.**

155. Through.

To look through the window. To look out the window.
Regarder par la fenêtre.

To hear the neighbors through the wall.
Entendre les voisins à travers le mur.

To travel through the country.
Voyager à travers le pays.

The bullet went through his heart.
La balle // lui a traversé le cœur. / est passée à travers son cœur.//

To look at something through a microscope.
Regarder quelque chose au microscope.

We walked through the night.
Nous avons marché dans la nuit.

We walked through the rain.
Nous avons marché // dans / sous // la pluie.

We walked through the door.
Nous avons franchi (le seuil de) la porte.

The burglar came in through the window.
Le cambrioleur est entré par la fenêtre.

He slept through the lecture.
Il a dormi // pendant toute / d'un bout à l'autre de // la conférence.

Can you see through this fabric?
Peut-on voir à travers cette étoffe?

Monday through Friday.
Du lundi au vendredi (inclusivement).
Les jours ouvrables. (: on working days)

Choose a number from 1 through 20.
Choisissez un nombre de 1 à 20 (inclusivement).

To go through college.
Faire ses études // universitaires. / supérieures.//
Faire ses études.

Let's go through this chapter again.
Relisons ce chapitre.

Let's go through this scene again.
Répétons cette scène (encore une fois).

Let's go through this problem again.
// Refaisons / Revoyons // ce problème. (math class)

I don't think we can get through.
Je ne crois pas que nous puissions // passer. / traverser.//

Through no fault of mine.
Sans aucune faute de ma part.
Sans que ce soit ma faute.

An idea flashed through his mind.
Une idée lui // est venue / a traversé // l'esprit.

Let me through.
Laissez-moi passer.

He ran his fingers through her hair.
Il passait ses doigts dans ses cheveux.

To read through.
Lire en entier.
Lire d'un bout à l'autre.

To read through and through.
Lire et relire.

Evil through and through.
Foncièrement mauvais.
Mauvais // des pieds à la tête. / d'un bout à l'autre. / de fond en comble.//

Are you through?
Avez-vous fini?

A through train.
Un (train) // direct. / rapide. / express.//

To go through with something.
Continuer quelque chose.
Aller jusqu'au bout de quelque chose.

156. Throughout.

Throughout the year.
Toute l'année.
L'année entière.
// Tout au long / D'un bout à l'autre // de l'année.

Throughout the land.
// D'un bout à l'autre / Sur toute l'étendue // du pays.
// À travers tout / Partout dans / Dans tout // le pays.
Dans le pays tout entier.

Throughout his carreer.
// Tout au long de / Pendant toute // sa carrière.

Throughout her life.
Tout au long de sa vie.
Sa vie durant.
Durant // toute sa vie. / sa vie entière.//

157. Till. Until.

Not until then had they . . .
Ce n'est qu'à ce moment qu'ils . . .
Avant // cela, / ce moment, // ils ne . . . pas . . .

Until then, . . .
// Jusqu'à ce moment, / Jusqu'alors, / Jusque-là, / Auparavant, / Avant cela, / Avant, // . . .

Wait until next week.
Attendez (jusqu'à) la semaine prochaine.

Don't wait until next week.
N'attendez pas (jusqu'à) la semaine prochaine.

It's 25 (20, 15, 10, 5) till the hour.
Il est moins 25 (20, le quart, 10, 5).

It's 25 till eleven.
Il est onze heures moins 25.
Il est dix heures 35.

He went on walking until he found help.
Il a continué à marcher jusqu'à ce qu'il ait trouvé de l'aide.

He did not turn around until he saw the signal.
Il ne s'est pas retourné avant d'avoir vu le signal.

Work until you hear the bell.
Travaillez jusqu'à ce que vous entendiez la sonnerie.

Don't move until I tell you to.
Ne bougez pas avant que je vous le dise.

He won't last (live) until tomorrow.
Il ne durera (vivra) pas jusqu'à demain.

158. To.

See §§167-170. for *to* with geographical names.

To give something to someone.
Donner quelque chose à quelqu'un.

To bring something to an end.
// Finir / Terminer / Achever // quelque chose.
Mener quelque chose à bonne fin.

To fall to the ground.
Tomber // à / par // terre.

To love to distraction (to death).
Aimer à la folie.

To starve to death.
Mourir de faim.

To cut to pieces.
Couper en morceaux.

To perfection.
À la perfection.

To the last breath.
Jusqu' // à son / au // dernier souffle.

On to the end.
Jusqu' // au bout. / à la fin.//

The score is 13 to 7.
Le score est de 13 à 7.

Made to order.
Fait sur // mesure. / commande.//

True to life.
// Véritable. / Réel. / Véridique.//

To one's liking.
À son goût.

What is it to you?
Qu'est-ce que cela vous fait?
En quoi cela vous regarde-t-il?

Here's to you.
À votre santé.

There is an end to the story.
L'histoire a une // fin. / morale. / conclusion.//

I wish to God that . . .
Fasse le ciel que . . . (with subjunctive)
Si seulement . . . (with imperfect indicative)

To take to . . .
Begin, take up: **Se mettre à . . .**
Start to like: **S'habituer à . . .**

To come to. (from fainting)
Reprendre ses esprits.
Revenir à soi.

Go home if you want to.
Rentrez chez vous si vous (le) voulez.

I tried to, but I couldn't.
J'ai essayé, mais je n'ai pas pu (le faire).
J'ai essayé (de le faire), mais je n'ai pas pu.

Who(m) are you talking to?
À qui parlez-vous?

Would you like to?
// Voudriez-vous / Aimeriez-vous // le faire?
Ça vous plairait (de le faire)?

Yes, I'd love to.
Oui, ça me plairait beaucoup.
Oui, j'aimerais bien // ça. / le faire.//

159. Toward. Towards.

Flowers turn toward the sun.
Les fleurs se tournent vers les soleil.

We must be good toward one another.
Nous devons être bons les uns envers les autres.

We must be good toward everyone, toward our neighbor.
Nous devons être bons envers tout le monde, envers autrui.

Toward midnight.
Vers minuit.

To save money toward college.
Économiser de l'argent // en vue de / pour / dans le but de // faire ses études.

160. Under. Underneath.

Put your feet under the table.
Mets tes pieds sous la table.

I can swim under water.
Je sais nager sous l'eau.

This car costs under $10,000.
Cette voiture // coûte moins de / ne coûte pas // 10.000 dollars.

This amount is under what we expected.
Cette somme est au-dessous de ce que nous avions prévu.

To go under (water).
// Sombrer. / Couler. / S'enfoncer sous l'eau.//

To go under (financially).
Faire faillite.

To speak under one's breath.
// Murmurer. / Parler à voix basse.//

To be under consideration. (file, record, application, etc.)
Être à l'étude. (project)
On examine // le dossier / le cas / la candidature // de . . . (person)

Under penalty of death.
Sous peine de mort.

Under repair.
En réparation.

Under certain circumstances.
Dans certaines circonstances.

Under the circumstances.
Dans les circonstances actuelles. (now, today)
Dans les circonstances // du moment. / en question.// (then, at that time)

Under certain conditions.
Dans certaines conditions.

Under other circumstances.
En d'autres circonstances.

To be under the impression that . . .
// Avoir l'impression / Croire // que . . .

Under oath.
Sous serment.

The underdog.
Le non favori. (individual)
L'équipe non favorite. (team)
Celui qui part perdant.

161. Until.

See *till*, §157.

162. Up.

Up in the air.
En l'air.

High up in the air.
Très haut dans le ciel.

One floor up.
Un étage plus haut.
À l'étage au-dessus.
À l'étage du dessus.

Look up.
Levez les yeux.
Regardez là-haut.

Look up the word.
Cherchez le mot (dans le dictionnaire).

To look up to someone.
Admirer quelqu'un.
Considérer quelqu'un avec respect.

Up there.
Là-haut.

To be up.
Être // levé. / debout.// (not in bed)

To stay up (late).
Rester // debout. / tard.//
Ne pas se coucher.

To be up to something.
Avoir une idée en tête.
Manigancer quelque chose.

To be up to . . .
Se préparer // à (infinitive) **/ à faire** (noun).**//**

I don't feel up to . . .
Je ne me sens pas // de taille / d'humeur // à . . .

It is up to you to . . .
C'est à vous de . . . (infinitive)
C'est de vous que dépend . . . (noun)

It's (all) up to you.
Cela dépend de vous.
Cela ne dépend que de vous.
C'est à vous de décider.

What's up?
Quoi de neuf?
Qu'est-ce qui se passe // de neuf? / de nouveau?//

Up and down.
De haut en bas (et de bas en haut).

To walk up and down.
Aller et venir.
Faire les cent pas.
Marcher de long en large.

To be up against . . .
Être en face de . . .
Confronter . . .
Faire face à . . .
Se trouver face à face avec . . .

Time is up.
L'heure est passée.
Il est l'heure.

163. *Upon.*

See *on*, §144.

164. *With.*

Come with me.
Venez avec moi.

To be filled with . . .
Être // rempli / plein // de . . .

To be lined with . . . (lining of dress, box, wall, etc.)
Être // doublé / recouvert / tapissé // de . . .

To be lined with . . . (border, hem; with line of trees, etc.)
Être bordé de . . .

To be covered with . . .
Être // couvert / recouvert // de . . .

We live with our in-laws.
Nous habitons chez nos beaux-parents.

To compare with . . .
Comparer // à / avec . . .//

Compare my work with yours.
Comparez mon travail // au / avec le // vôtre.

The two cannot compare with one another.
On ne peut pas comparer ces deux choses.
Il n'y a pas de comparaison (possible entre ces deux choses).

To differ with . . .
Ne pas être // de l'avis de / du même avis que // . . .

A girl with blue eyes.
Une fille aux yeux bleus.

The girl with the red hair.
La fille aux cheveux roux.
La rousse.

The man with the green hat.
L'homme au chapeau vert.

A boy with freckles.
Un garçon qui a des taches de rousseur.

The boy with the freckles.
Le garçon aux taches de rousseur.

The man with his hands in his pockets.
L'homme qui a les mains dans les poches.

He came in with his hands in his pockets.
Il est entré les mains dans les poches.

I have no money with me.
Je n'ai pas d'argent sur moi.

Drive with caution.
Conduisez // avec prudence. / prudemment.//

To fight with . . .
Se battre // avec / contre // . . .
Combattre . . .

To part with . . .
// Se séparer de / Quitter // . . .

I am with you on this point.
Je suis // avec vous / de votre avis // sur ce point.
Je vous approuve sur ce point.

To be delighted with . . .
Être ravi de . . .

To be busy with . . .
Être occupé à . . .

What does this have to do with me?
En quoi cela me regarde-t-il?
Qu'est-ce que cela a // à faire / à voir // avec moi?
En quoi cela me concerne-t-il?

With that, he proceeded to . . .
// Là-dessus, / Sur ces mots, // il se mit à . . .
// Là-dessus, / Sur ces mots, // il se mit en devoir de . . .

Down with the dictator!
// À bas / À mort // le dictateur!
Mort au dictateur!

Nature was a favorite source of inspiration with the romantic poets.
La nature était une source d'inspiration favorite chez les poètes romantiques.

165. Within.

Inquire within.
S'adresser à l'intérieur.
// Renseignez-vous / Adressez-vous // à l'intérieur.

Stay within the house.
Restez // dans / à l'intérieur de // la maison.

It will be done within the hour.
Ce sera fait en moins d'une heure.

He will be back within an hour.
Il sera de retour dans moins d'une heure.

Within range.
À portée.

Within sight.
À portée du regard.

Within reach.
À portée de la main.

Within reason.
Raisonnable.
Dans les limites de la raison.

To live within one's income, one's means.
Vivre selon ses moyens.
Ne pas vivre au-dessus de ses moyens.

Within a month of his birthday.
Moins d'un mois après son anniversaire.

166. Without.

Without difficulty.
Sans difficulté.

Without doubt.
Sans doute. (: probably)
Certainement. (: no doubt)

That goes without saying.
Cela va sans dire.

It goes without saying that . . .
Il va sans dire que . . .

The man without a hat.
L'homme qui n'a pas de chapeau.

He left without an umbrella.
Il est parti sans parapluie.

I'll have my coffee with cream but without sugar.
Je prendrai mon café avec du lait mais sans sucre.

He left without saying a word.
Il est parti sans dire un mot.

He left without my being able to say a word.
Il est parti sans que j'aie pu dire un mot.

He left without our having had the time to explain the situation.
Il est parti sans que nous ayons pu expliquer la situation.

167. Prepositions with geographical names.

A. The use of prepositions with proper names of places depends on whether those names are masculine or feminine. In addition, other elements must be considered, such as whether the name begins with a consonant or a vowel, whether it is well known or not, whether the place is a country, a city, an island, etc.

Since it is sometimes difficult to decide which type of preposition should be used, the following list offers the French spelling of a good number of countries, states, provinces, islands, etc., and the preposition to be used with each name in view of the various elements mentioned above.

Three prepositional constructions may be used with a geographical name to translate *in* or *to*, according to the degree of familiarity with, knowledge of, or frequency of use of the name in question:

1) ***Dans le (la, l', les) . . . de* . . . .***

Dans le territoire du Yukon.
In the Yukon Territory.

Dans la République du Mali.
In the Mali Republic.

Dans l'île de Java.
In the island of Java.

This construction is used when the speaker feels the need to "explain" the name he uses to his audience.

*See §169C.

2) ***Dans le (la, l', les) . . .***

Dans l'Alabama. Dans le Wyoming. Dans la Ruhr.
In Alabama. In Wyoming. In the Ruhr.

This construction may be used with most names that are considered to be somewhere between unfamiliar and clearly universally known. It is particularly used with the names of the divisions of larger countries: states, provinces, departments, etc.

3) ***En . . .*** (with feminine names)
au . . . (with masculine names)
aux . . . (with plural names, masculine or feminine)

En France. En Angleterre. En Floride.
In France. In England. In Florida.

Au Japon. Au Canada. Au Texas.
In Japan. In Canada. In Texas.

Aux États-Unis. Aux Philippines.
In the United States. In the Philippines.

This construction is the *standard* preposition to express *in* or *to*. It should be used with nearly all the major nations of the world, the five continents, and a number of other places standardized by French usage (see details in §168).

B. With most Canadian provinces, most states of the Union, and most islands, it is safer to use the first construction: ***dans la province de, dans l'état de, dans l'île de,*** since relatively few of them have been standardized by French usage. This is especially the case of the few states and provinces whose names is that of their major city (Québec, New York).

C. With the names of seas and oceans and the names of mountains, use only constructions A1 and A2.

Dans l'océan Atlantique. Dans le Pacifique.
In the Atlantic Ocean. In the Pacific.
Dans les Alpes. Dans les montagnes de l'Oural.
In the Alps. In the Ural mountains.

Note that most geographical terms relating to the sea are "explained" in the prepositional expression.

Dans le golfe du Mexique. Dans la rade de Brest.
In the Gulf of Mexico. In the bay of Brest.

168. In, to, from, with geographical names.

NAME	IN, TO	FROM	EXAMPLES
masculine singular **masculine plural**	au aux	du des	Canada, Japon, Pérou États-Unis
feminine singular **feminine plural**	en aux	de (d') des	France, Italie, Floride Philippines, Açores, Baléares
cities, some islands*	à	de (d')	Rome, Cuba

*Cities and islands whose names contain an article must keep that article at all times. The prepositions ***à*** and ***de*** must contract to ***au*** and ***du*** with the article ***le***, and to ***aux*** and ***des*** with the article ***les***. No contraction is made with the articles ***l'*** and ***la***.

Nous arrivons du Havre.
We are arriving from Le Havre.
Nous revenons de La Nouvelle-Orléans.
We are coming back from New Orleans.

169. Notes.

Nearly all the names of continents, countries, states, provinces, etc., ending in a mute ***e*** are feminine. A few notable exceptions are ***le Cambodge, le Maine, le Mexique, le Nouveau Mexique, le Mozambique, le Zaïre, le Zimbabwe*** (see §170). The mute ***e*** is followed by ***s*** in feminine plural names: ***les Philippines, les Antilles, les Açores.*** Most names with other endings are masculine. Names of islands are feminine, however, because of implicit references to the words **île** and **colonie**, which are both feminine. Notice that many singular names of islands are used in the same way as names of cities (see individual names in §170).

A. Names of cities have no definite gender. No article is used with a city unless it is an integral part of the name. Since it may be difficult to make the agreement of a modifying adjective with the name of a city, it is safer to use a prepositional expression containing the word ***ville***, feminine (or ***île*** for *island*, or any other appropriate word), and make the adjective agree with the word chosen.

Paris est une grande ville. La ville de Paris est grande.
Paris is a large city.

Le territoire de Monaco est indépendant. La principauté de Monaco est indépendante. Monaco est un territoire indépendant.
Monaco is independent. The territory of Monaco is independent. The principality of Monaco is independent.

B. The standard prepositions should be replaced by ***dans*** and a definite article before a name uncommonly modified.

Nous trouverons un hôtel dans le Paris des étudiants.
We will find a hotel in the Paris of the students.

This can also be done with unmodified names to emphasize strongly the meaning of "inside," when no movement is involved. In other words, it translates *in* but not *to*.

Il y a peu de villes dans le Groenland.
There are few cities inside Greenland.

C. When an expression of the type ***dans l'état de . . ., dans la province de . . .*** (in or to the state of . . ., the province of . . .) or ***de l'état de . . ., de la province de . . .*** (from the state, the province of . . .) is being used, the name that follows must be preceded by one of the following:

du	if the name is masculine
de	if the name is feminine
des	if the name is plural (masculine or feminine)

Dans l'état du Colorado. Dans la province d'Alberta. Dans le territoire du Yukon. Dans l'état de Floride. Dans l'archipel des Bahamas.

170. Places.

The following list contains, in alphabetical order, and in their French spelling, the names of most major countries, states of the Union, Canadian provinces, and French departments and provinces, as well as the names of some cities and islands. Each name is followed by the preposition (or prepositions) normally used with it to translate *in* or *to*. To translate *from*, refer to the following table:

IN, TO	FROM
en*	de (d′)
au	du
aux	des
dans le	du
dans l′	de l′
dans la (à la)	de la
dans les	des

*With names of cities, use **à**.

The names accompanied by a number are the French departments, ranked in alphabetical order from 1 to 90. Recent changes in the Paris area have brought on the creation of new departments, numbered 91 and up. These numbers are used as the first two digits in the official French postal codes. The same two digits serve in the registration of cars (the last two digits on car plates). French overseas departments have 3-digit numbers (971 to 975).

Açores (aux)
Afghanistan (en)
Afrique (en)
Afrique (en)
Afrique du Nord (en)
Afrique du Sud (en)
Ain, 01 (dans l′)
Aisne, 02 (dans l′)
Alabama (en, dans l′)
Alabama (en, dans l′)
Alaska (en, dans l′)
Albanie (en)
Alberta (dans l′)
Algérie (en)
Allemagne (en)
Allemagne de l′Est (en)
Allemagne de l′Ouest (en)
Allier, 03 (dans l′)
Alpes (dans les)
Alpes-de-Haute-Provence, 04 (dans les; former Basses-Alpes)
Hautes-Alpes, 05 (dans les)
Alpes-Maritimes, 06 (dans les)
Alsace (en)
Amazone (dans l′)
Amazonie (en)
Amérique (en)
Amérique Centrale (en)
Amérique Latine (en)
Amérique du Nord (en)
Amérique du Sud (en)
Andorre (country: en; city: à)
Angleterre (en)
Angola (en, dans l′)
Anjou (en)
Antilles (aux, dans les)
Arabie Saoudite (en)
Ardèche, 07 (en, dans l′)
Ardenne (en, dans l′)
Ardennes, 08 (dans les)
Argentine (en)
Ariège, 09 (en, dans l′)
Arkansas (en, dans l′)
Arménie (en)
Artois (en, dans l′)
Aube, 10 (dans l′)
Aude, 11 (dans l′)
Aunis (dans l′)
Australie (en)
Auvergne (en)
Aveyron, 12 (dans l′)
Avignon (à, en)
Azerbaïdjan (en)

Bahamas (aux)
Bahreïn (country: au; city: à)
Baléares (aux)
Barbade (à la)
Bas-, Basse-, Basses- (see main name)
Bavière (en)
Béarn (dans le)
Belfort, 90 (dans le territoire de)
Belgique (en)
Bélize (à, dans le)
Bengale (au)
Bengladesh (au, dans le)
Bénin (au, dans le; former Dahomey)
Bermudes (aux)
Berry (dans le)
Bhoutan (dans le)
Biélorus (en; former Biélorussie)
Birmanie (en)
Bolivie (en)
Bornéo (à)
Bosnie-Herzégovine (en)
Botswana (dans le)
Bouches-du-Rhône, 13 dans les)
Bourbonnais (dans le)
Bourgogne (en)
Brésil (au)
Bretagne (en)
Bulgarie (en)
Burkina-Faso (dans le; former Haute-Volta)
Burundi (dans le)

Californie (en)

Calvados, 14 (dans le)
Cambodge (au; see Kamputchea)
Cameroun (au)
Canada (au)
Canaries (aux)
Cantal, 15 (dans le)
Caroline du Nord (en)
Caroline du Sud (en)
Ceylan (à; see Sri-Lanka)
Champagne (en)
Charente, 16 (en)
Charente-Maritime, 17 (en)
Cher, 18 (dans le)
Chili (au)
Chine (en)
Chypre (à)
Colombie (en)
Colombie-Britannique (en, dans la)
Colorado (dans le, en)
Communauté des États Indépendants (dans la; abbreviated CEI; former USSR)
Congo (au)
Connecticut (dans le)
Corée (en)
Corfou (à)
Cornouaille (en)
Corrèze, 19 (en, dans la)
Corse (former 20; en)
Corse-du-Sud, 2A (en, dans la; created in 1976)
Haute-Corse, 2B (en, dans la; created in 1976)
Costa Brava (sur la)
Costa Rica (au, dans le)
Côtes-d'Armor, 22 (dans les; former Côtes-du-Nord)
Côte d'Azur (sur la)
Côte d'Ivoire (en)
Côte-d'Or, 21 (en, dans la)
Côtes-du-Nord (dans les; see Côtes-d'Armor)
Crète (en, à)
Creuse, 23 (dans la)
Croatie (en)
Cuba (à)

Dahomey (au; see Bénin)
Dakota du Nord (dans le)
Dakota du Sud (dans le)
Danemark (au)
Dauphiné (dans le)
Delaware (dans le)
District de Columbia (dans le)
Dordogne, 24 (en, dans la)
Doubs, 25 (dans le)
Drôme, 26 (dans la)

Écosse (en)
Égypte (en)
Elbe (à l'île d'; dans or sur l'île d')
Équateur (en, dans l')
Espagne (en)
Essonne, 91 (dans l', en)
Estonie (en)
États-Unis (aux)
Éthiopie (en)
Eure, 27 (dans l')
Eure-et-Loir, 28 (en, dans l')

Finistère, 29 (dans le)
Finlande (en)
Floride (en)
France (en)

Gabon (au)
Galles (see Pays de Galles)
Gard, 30 (dans le)
Haute-Garonne, 31 (en, dans la)
Gascogne (en)
Géorgie (en)
Gers, 32 (dans le)
Ghana (au)
Gibraltar (à)
Gironde, 33 (en, dans la)
Grande Bretagne (en)
Grèce (en)
Groenland (au, dans le)
Guadeloupe, 971 (à la)
Guatémala (au)
Guernesey (à)
Guinée (en)
Guyane Britannique (en, dans la)
Guyane Française, 973 (en, dans la)
Guyane Hollandaise (en, dans la; see Surinam)
Guyenne (en)

Haïti (à, dans la république d', en)
Haut . . . (see main name)
Haute-Volta (dans l'ancienne, en; see Burkina-Faso)
Hauts-de-Seine, 92 (dans les)
Hawaii (à)
Hérault, 34 (dans l')
Hollande (en)
Honduras (dans le)
Honduras Britannique (dans l'ancien, dans le; see Bélize)
Hong-Kong (à)
Hongrie (en)

Idaho (dans l')
Ile-de-France (en, dans l')
Ille-et-Vilaine, 35 (en, dans l')
Illinois (dans l', en)
Inde (en)
Indes (aux)
Indiana (dans l')
Indonésie (en)
Indre, 36 (dans l')
Indre-et-Loire, 37 (en, dans l')
Iowa (dans le, dans l')
Irak (en)
Iran (en)
Irlande (en)
Isère, 38 (dans l')
Islande (en)
Israël (en)
Italie (en)

Jamaïque (à la)
Japon (au)
Java (à)
Jordanie (en)
Jura, 39 (dans le)

Kamputchea (dans le;

former Cambodge)
Kansas (au, dans le)
Kazakhstan (au, dans le)
Kentucky (au, dans le)
Kénya (au)
Kirghizie (en)
Koweït or Kuwait (country: au, dans le; city: à)
Kurdistan (dans le)

Labrador (au, dans le)
Landes, 40 (dans les)
Languedoc (dans le)
Laos (au)
Lesotho (dans le)
Lettonie (en)
Liban (au)
Libéria (au, dans le)
Libye (en)
Liechtenstein (dans le)
Limousin (dans le)
Lituanie (en)
Loir-et-Cher, 41 (dans le)
Loire, 42 (dans la)
Haute-Loire, 43 (en, dans la)
Loire-Atlantique, 44 (en, dans la)
Loiret, 45 (dans le)
Lorraine (en)
Lot, 46 (dans le)
Lot-et-Garonne, 47 (dans le)
Louisiane (en)
Lozère, 48 (en, dans la)
Luxembourg (city: à; country: dans le)

Macao (à)
Madagascar (à)
Madère (à)
Maine (dans le)
Maine-et-Loire, 49 (dans le)
Majorque (à, dans l'île de)
Malaisie (en)
Malawi (dans le)
Maldives (aux, dans les)
Mali (au)
Malte (à, dans l'île de)
Manche, 50 (dans la)
Mandchourie (en)
Manitoba (dans le)
Marne, 51 (dans la)
Haute-Marne, 52 (en, dans la)
Maroc (au)
Martinique, 972 (à la)
Maryland (dans le)
Massachusetts (dans le)
Massif Central (dans le)
Mauritanie (en)
Mayenne, 53 (en, dans la)
Mayotte (à)
Meurthe-et-Moselle, 54 (en dans la)
Meuse, 55 (dans la)
Mexique (au)
Michigan (dans le)
Midi (dans le)
Minnesota (dans le)
Moldavie (en)
Mongolie (en)
Monte-Carlo (à)
Morbihan, 56 (dans le)
Moselle, 57 (en, dans la)
Mozambique (au, dans le)

Namibie (en)
Nebraska (dans le)
Népal (au)
Nevada (dans le)
New . . . (see also Nouveau, Nouvelle . . .)
Newfoundland (see Terre-Neuve)
New Hampshire (dans le)
New Jersey (dans le)
New York (city: à; state: dans l'état de)
Nicaragua (au)
Nièvre, 58 (dans la)
Niger (au)
Nigéria (au, dans le; used to be: en, dans la)
Nivernais (dans le)
Nord, 59 (dans le)
Normandie (en)
North . . . (see main name)
Norvège (en)
Nouveau-Brunswick (dans le)
Nouveau-Mexique (au, dans le)
Nouveau Monde (dans le)
Nouvelle-Angleterre (en, dans la)
Nouvelle-Calédonie (en)
Nouvelle-Écosse (en)
Nouvelle-Guinée (en)
Nouvelles-Hébrides (aux)
La Nouvelle-Orléans (à)
Nouvelle-Zélande (en)
Nova Scotia (see Nouvelle-Écosse)

Oise, 60 (dans l')
Oman (à, dans le territoire d', dans le sultanat d')
Orne, 61 (dans l')
Ouganda (en, dans l')
Ouzbékistan (en)

Pakistan (au)
Palestine (en)
Panama (city: à; country: au, dans le)
Paraguay (au)
Pas-de-Calais, 62 (dans le)
Pays-Bas (aux)
Pays de Galles (au, dans le)
Pennsylvanie (en)
Périgord (dans le)
Pérou (au)
Perse (en)
Picardie (en)
Poitou (en, dans le)
Pologne (en)
Polynésie (en)
Porto Rico (à)
Portugal (au)
Prince-Édouard (dans l'île du)
Provence (en)
Puy-de-Dôme, 63 (dans le)
Pyrénées (dans les)
Pyrénées-Atlantiques, 64 (dans les; former Basses-Pyrénées)
Hautes-Pyrénées, 65 (dans les)
Pyrénées-Orientales, 66 (dans les)

Qatar (dans le, au)

République Centrafricaine (en dans la)
La Réunion, 974 (à)
Bas-Rhin, 67 (dans le)
Haut-Rhin, 68 (dans le)
Rhodésie (en; see Zimbabwe)
Rhode Island (dans le)
Rhône, 69 (dans le)
Rouergue (dans le)
Roumanie (en)
Roussillon (dans le)
Ruanda or Rwanda (au, dans le)
Russie (en; see also Communauté des États Indépendants)

Sahara (au, dans le)
Saint-Marin (à)
Saint-Domingue (à)
Saint-Pierre-et-Miquelon, 975 (à)
Sainte-Hélène (à)
Salvador (au; au El Salvador)
San Marino (see Saint-Marin)
Santo Domingo (see Saint-Domingue)
Haute-Saône, 70 (en, dans la)
Saône-et-Loire, 71 (en, dans la)
Sardaigne (en)
Sarthe, 72 (dans la)
Saskatchewan (dans le)
Savoie, 73 (en)
Haute-Savoie, 74 (en, dans la)
Seine, 75 (dans la)
Seine-Maritime, 76 (en, dans la)
Seine-et-Marne, 77 (en, dans la)
Seine-et-Oise, 78 (en, dans la; see "Yvelines")
Seine-Saint-Denis, 93 (en, dans la)
Sénégal (au)
Serbie (en)
Deux-Sèvres, 79 (dans les)
Sibérie (en)
Sicile (en)
Sierra Leone (en, dans la, dans le)
Singapour (à)
Somalie (en, dans la)
Somme, 80 (dans la)
Soudan (au)
South . . . (see main name)
Sri Lanka (au, dans le; former Ceylan)
Suède (en)
Suisse (en)
Sumatra (à)
Surinam (dans le, au; former Guyane Hollandaise)
Swaziland (dans le)

Tadjikistan (au, dans le)
Tahiti (à)
Tanzanie (en, dans la)
Tasmanie (en)
Tarn, 81 (dans le)
Tarn-et-Garonne, 82 (dans le)
Taïwan (à)
Tchad (au)
Tennessee (au, dans le)
Terre-Neuve (à)
Texas (au)
Thaïlande (en)
Tibet (au)
Togo (au)
Transkei (dans le)
Tunisie (en)
Turquie (en)
Turkménistan (au, dans le)

Ukraine (en)
Union Soviétique, URSS (see Communauté des États Indépendants)
Uruguay (en, dans l')
Utah (en, dans l')

Val-de-Marne, 94 (dans le)
Val-d'Oise, 95 (dans le)
Vallée de la Loire (dans la)
Var, 83 (dans le)
Vatican (au)
Vaucluse, 84 (dans le)
Vendée, 85 (en)
Venezuela (au)
Vermont (dans le)
Vienne, 86 (dans la)
Haute-Vienne, 87 (en, dans la)
Viêt-Nam (au)
Virginie (en)
Virginie de l'Ouest (also: Virginie-Occidentale) (en, dans la)
Vosges, 88 (dans les)

Washington (D.C.: à; state: dans l'état de)
Wisconsin (dans le)
Wyoming (dans le)

Yémen (au)
Yonne, 89 (dans l')
Yougoslavie (en)
Yukon (dans le)
Yvelines, 78 (new name for part of Seine-et-Oise; dans les)

Zaïre (au, dans le)
Zambie (en)
Zimbabwe (au, dans le)

CONJUNCTIONS

171. Definition.

There are two kinds of conjunctions: the coordinating conjunctions and the subordinating conjunctions.

The *coordinating conjunctions* serve to connect two words, groups of words, or clauses, creating a link but no actual dependence. The terms connected are of identical and equal value.

The *subordinating conjunctions* serve to connect clauses only. They create between the verbs of those clauses a dependence, the nature of which is particular to each conjunction (cause, consequence, condition, time, comparison, etc.). The two terms connected by a subordinating conjunction are not of equal value: the term following the conjunction is dependent on the term preceding it.

172. Coordinating conjunctions.

The main coordinating conjunctions are

et	and
mais	but
car	for
ou	or
donc	so, therefore
ne . . . ni . . . ni . . .	neither . . . nor . . .

There are a number of other coordinating conjunctions. Some are strictly conjunctions, others are also adverbs, and others are also prepositions.

The French coordinating conjunctions are used in the same way as English ones, and they have no bearing on the grammatical structure of the sentence in which they are being used.

173. Subordinating conjunctions.

Subordinating conjunctions may be simple (if they are made of only one word), or compound (if they consist of two or more words). Compound conjunctions are also called conjunctive expressions or conjunctive locutions. The general term *conjunction* may designate both simple and compound conjunctions, when no distinction is necessary.

The main English conjunction is *that.* The main French conjunction is ***que*** (***qu'*** before a word beginning with a vowel or a mute ***h***).

When using a French conjunction, it is necessary to determine whether the verb it governs (the *subordinate* or dependent verb) must be in the *indicative* or in the *subjunctive.* Each conjunction has its own requirement. As for the simple conjunctions ***que***, its case is studied in the chapter on verbs, §280.

A number of conjunctions require a subordinate verb in the indicative, others a subordinate verb in the subjunctive, and a few may accept a subordinate verb in the indicative or the subjunctive or even in the conditional.

174. Conjunctions with the subjunctive.

The following conjunctions require a subordinate verb in the subjunctive:

although	**bien que (§177), quoique (§177)**
before	**avant que* (§178)**
on condition that	**à condition que (§178)**
even though	**encore que (§177)** See *although.*
for fear that	**de crainte que* (§178), de peur que* (§178)**
for (you, me, etc.) to	**pour que (vous, je, etc.), que (vous, je, etc.)**
however (with adjective, adverb)	**quelque . . . que (§176), si . . . que (§176), pour . . . que (§176)**
in order that	**afin que (§178), pour que (§178)**
in such a way that	**de façon que (§175), de manière que (§175), de sorte (§175)**
lest	See *for fear that.*
no matter . . .	See *however, whatever, whenever,* etc.
no matter why	**pour quelque raison que**
not that	**non pas que, non que, ce n'est pas que**
provided that	**pourvu que, à condition que (§178)**
so that	See *in order that, in such a way that.*
supposing that	**à supposer que**
that (showing purpose)	See *in order that.*
though	See *although.*
unless	à moins que* (§178)
until	**avant que* (§178), jusqu'à ce que* (§178)**
whatever	**quoi que** (object), **quoi qui** (subject), **quel que (être) . . .** (with *to be*) **(§39),** **quelque . . . que** (with a noun) **(§41C)**
whenever	**à quelque moment que**
wherever	**où que, à quelque endroit que, en quelque lieu que**
whether . . . or . . .	**que . . . ou que . . .**
whether . . . or not.	**que . . . ou non**
whether . . ., or whether . . .	**que . . ., ou que . . .**
while (waiting for . . . to . . .)	**en attendant que (§178)** See also §179.
whichever	See *whatever.*

whoever, whosoever	**qui que ce soit qui,** **quel que . . . être . . .** (with *to be*) **(§39),** **qui que . . . être . . .** (with *to be*) **(§73)**
whomever, whomsoever	**qui que ce soit que, qui que (§73)**
without	**sans que (§178)**

*The conjunctions ***avant que, à moins que, de crainte que,*** and ***de peur que*** may have their subordinate verb in the subjunctive preceded by ***ne,*** which is not negative in this case. It is called expletive or redundant ***ne,*** and its use is optional.

Cachez-vous vite avant qu'il ne vous voie.
Hide quickly before he sees you.

175. De façon que, de manière que, de sorte que.

These three conjunctions are followed by a subordinate verb in the subjunctive only if they express purpose or intent. If they express result, the verb should be in the indicative. If they express eventuality, the verb should be in the conditional.

Retrouvons-nous devant le Café de la Paix, de façon que nous puissions prendre le même taxi pour aller à l'aéroport.
Let's meet in front of the Café de la Paix, so that we may take the same taxi to go to the airport.

Faites vite, de manière que nous soyons à l'heure.
Hurry, so that we may be on time.

Il avait invité aussi son amie, de sorte que nous étions maintenant treize à table.
He had also invited his girl friend, so that there were now thirteen of us at table.

Je pourrais prendre ton fou, de sorte que ton roi serait alors en échec.
I could take your bishop, so that your king would then be in check.

NOTE: These conjunctions often take the form of ***de telle façon que, de telle manière que, de telle sorte que,*** for emphasis.

176. Quelque . . . que, pour . . . que, si . . . que.

The conjunctive expressions ***quelque . . . que, pour . . . que,*** and ***si . . . que*** translate *however, no matter how* modifying an adjective or an adverb. In French, the adjective or the adverb immediately follows ***quelque, si,*** or ***pour,*** which are invariable.

Si loin qu'il soit, je le rattraperai.
No matter how far he is, I'll catch up with him.

Quelque riches qu'ils soient, ils ne sont pas heureux.
However rich they are, they are not happy.

The expression ***quelque . . . que*** may also be used with a noun, following the word ***quelque,*** which in this case is variable and must agree with the noun. The conjunctive expression translates *no matter what, no matter which, whatever, whichever* (see §41C and D).

Quelques preuves que vous lui donniez, ce têtu ne vous croira jamais.
Whatever proofs you may give him, that stubborn fellow will never believe you.

Si . . . que and ***pour . . . que*** may be found with a verb in the indicative or in the conditional, to insist on the reality or the eventuality of a fact, respectively. But this use should be considered exceptional in the extreme, and attempted only by the very proficient student.

177. Bien que, quoique, encore que.

The subordinate verb following the conjuntions ***bien que, quoique,*** and ***encore que*** is normally in the subjunctive mood.

Elle veut aller en Italie bien qu'elle n'ait pas de quoi faire le voyage.
She wants to visit Italy although she does not have the money for the trip.
Encore qu'il soit pénible en général, il a parfois des idées géniales.
Although he is generally a bore, he has sometimes fantastic ideas.

The subordinate verb following these conjunctions may be in the indicative or in the conditional, to show the reality of a fact or the eventuality of a fact, respectively.

Tu peux passer le week-end chez nous si tu veux, quoique je serai absente le samedi à cause d'un congrès.
You may spend the weekend at our house if you wish, although I will be absent on Saturday because of a convention.
Je vais me promener, bien que je guérirais plus vite si je restais couché.
I am going for a walk, although I would get well faster if I stayed in bed.

178. Conjunction versus preposition.

A. A conjunction (see definition in §171) can introduce only a conjugated verb (i.e. in a *finite* form), whereas a preposition (see definition in §104) can introduce a noun, a pronoun, or a verb in a *non-finite* form (infinitive or present participle).

B. When the verb of the main clause and the verb of the subordinate clause have the same subject, tighter style is achieved when the conjunction is replaced by a corresponding preposition and the verb in the subjunctive is turned into an infinitive. This change of structure is possible only with the conjunctions that have corresponding prepositions, as shown in the following list:

CONJUNCTION	PREPOSITION
à condition que	à condition de
à moins que	à moins de
afin que	afin de
après que	après (§180)
avant que	avant de
de crainte que	de crainte de
de façon que	de façon à
de manière que	de manière à
de peur que	de peur de
en attendant que	en attendant de
pour que	pour
sans que	sans
jusqu'à ce que*	jusqu'à
à ce que**	à

*The change to an infinitive structure with ***jusqu'à*** is not as frequent as with the other expressions due to a slight semantic difference between the conjunction and the preposition. The use of the conjunction with a verb in the subjunctive is quite appropriate even if both verbs have the same subject. Note however the expression ***aller jusqu'à*** (*to go so far as . . .-ing, to go so far as to . . .*).

Elle est allée jusqu'à poser nue pour obtenir ce rôle.
She went so far as to pose nude to get that part.
She went as far as posing nude in order to get that part.

The conjunction ***à ce que* is a variation of the simple conjunction ***que***. It is used to introduce a subordinate clause after a main verb that requires the preposition ***à*** before a dependent infinitive or a noun object.

Je tiens à passer le week-end avec vous.
I really want to spend the weekend with you.
Je tiens à ce que vous passiez le week-end avec moi.
I really want you to spend the weekend with me.

À ce que is used when the subject of the subordinate verb is not a repeat of the subject or the direct object of the main verb.

Je me suis décidé à payer mes dettes.
I made up my mind to pay my debts.
Je les encouragerai à rendre visite à leurs grands-parents.
I will encourage them to visit their grandparents.
but: Je veillerai à ce qu'ils ne fassent pas de bruit en rentrant.
I'll make sure that they won't make any noise when then come home.

179. Conjunctions with the indicative.

The following list contains subordinating conjunctions, each governing a subordinate verb in the indicative or in the conditional, depending on the meaning sought. Note that most are expressions ending with ***que***, and that many are also adverbs or prepositions.

according as, according to whether	**selon que, suivant que**
after (§180; §184)	**après que**
although	See §177.
as (§181)	**que, comme, puisque, en tant que, alors que, tandis que, pendant que, à mesure que, ainsi que, de même que, tout . . . que** (see *however*).
as . . . as (§185)	**aussi . . . que**
not as . . . as, not so . . . as (§185)	**pas aussi . . . que, pas si . . . que**
the more . . . as (§187)	**d'autant plus . . . que**
the . . .-er as (§187)	**d'autant plus . . . que**
the less . . . as (§187)	**d'autant moins . . . que**
as far as (§182)	**autant que**
as far as I am concerned	**en ce qui me concerne**
as far as I know	**pour autant que je sache**
as if (§183)	**comme si**
as long as (§184)	**tant que** (time) **du moment que** (cause)
as much as (§185)	**autant que**
as soon as (§184)	**aussitôt que, dès que**
as though (§183)	**comme si**
as well as (§185)	**ainsi que, aussi bien que, autant que**
because	**parce que**
the more . . . because (§187)	**d'autant plus . . . que**
the . . .-er because (§187)	**d'autant plus . . . que**
the less . . . because (§187)	**d'autant moins . . . que**
besides (§188)	**outre que.** See also §126.
but (§186)	**si . . . ne.** See also §134, *except (but).*
certainly, surely	**certainement que***
considering that	**étant donné que, vu que, attendu que** (law)
despite the fact that	**en dépit du fait que, malgré le fait que**
even if (§183)	**même si, quand** (with conditional: see §268A2)
even though (§177)	**bien que, quoique, encore que**
except if (§183)	**sauf si**
except that	**sauf que, excepté que, hormis que, si ce n'est que**
fortunately, luckily	**heureusement que***
how (§189)	**comment**
however (with adj. or adv.)	**tout . . . que (§43, note 3)** See also §176.
how much (§189)	**combien**
if (§183)	**si**
inasmuch as, insofar as	**étant donné que, attendu que** (law)
notwithstanding that	**en dépit du fait que, malgré le fait que** See *although*, §177.

no matter . . .	See §176.
perhaps, maybe	**peut-être que***
probably	**probablement que***
probably, undoubtedly	**sans doute que***
seeing that	**vu que, étant donné que**
since (§190)	**depuis que** (time), **puisque** (cause). **du moment que** (cause; see §184)
so . . . as (§185)	**aussi . . . que**
not so . . . as (§185)	**pas si . . . que**
so that (result; see §175)	**de façon que, de manière que, de sorte que**
so . . . that (§185)	**si . . . que, tellement . . . que**
so much that (§185)	**tellement que, tant que**
surely, certainly	**sûrement que***
than (§191)	**que**
that (§192)	**que, de ce que**
though	See *although*, §174, §178.
when (§184)	**quand, lorsque**
whereas (§193)	**tandis que, alors que, attendu que** (law)
whether (§189)	**si** See also §174.
while (§193)	**pendant que, cependant que, tandis que**
why (§189)	**pourquoi**

* These expressions are not really conjunctions. They contain the conjunction ***que***, but since they begin a sentence, no main verb is expressed. Their use should be limited to spoken or informal language. Notice that the English equivalent is only an adverb, which can often be inserted inside the full clause.

Heureusement qu'il n'a pas plu.
Fortunately, it did not rain.
It is fortunate that it did not rain.

Sans doute qu'il viendra par le train de nuit.
He will probably come on the night train.

180. After.

The conjunction ***après que*** should be followed by a verb in the indicative mood.

It is not uncommon nowadays to find, instead, a subordinate verb in the subjunctive. This is due on the one hand to the fact that the conjunctions ***avant que***, its opposite, requires a subordinate verb in the subjunctive; and on the other hand to the fact that the only appropriate tense is the *passé antérieur*, which is a very formal and literary tense. This combination of facts has led to the relatively recent creation of a new tense, the *passé surcomposé*, the only tense suitable to express both the completion of an action and an informal tone.

When the subject of the subordinate verb is the same as that of the verb it is dependent on, the conjunction ***après que*** may be replaced by the preposition ***après*** (§113), and the subordinate verb by an infinitive, generally a *past infinitive* (see §178B).

Après qu'ils eurent fendu le bois, ils se reposèrent.
Après avoir fendu le bois, ils se reposèrent.
Après qu'ils ont eu fendu le bois, ils se sont reposés.
After having split the wood, they rested.

Notice that the passé simple, as a narrative tense, must be paired with its matching compound tense, the passé antérieur (in the first example above). If the narrative tense is the passé composé, the matching compound tense should be the passé surcomposé if an infinitive construction is not possible (see §267, note 1).

181. As.

The choice of the French conjunction equivalent to *as* depends on the meaning of *as* in the sentence.

J'ai acheté le même livre que toi.
I bought the same book as you.

Ce château n'est pas aussi beau que je (le) croyais.
This castle is not so beautiful as I thought.

Je ferai comme vous dites.
I shall do as you say.

Comme il entrait, il s'est cogné la tête à la porte.
As he was entering, he hit his head against the door.

Comme il n'est pas là, je vais le remplacer.
As he is not here, I am going to replace him. (since)

Puisqu'il pleut, restons chez nous.
As it is raining, let us stay home. (since, because)

Alors qu'il travaillait, moi, je ne faisais rien.
As he was working, I was doing nothing. (while, whereas)

Pendant qu'il travaillait, moi, je m'amusais.
As he was working, I was playing. (while, whereas)

À mesure que le ballon monte, son volume augmente.
As the balloon rises, its volume increases. (in proportion, at a proportional rate of progression)

Tout riche qu'elle est, elle n'est pas heureuse.
Rich as she is, she is not happy. (though)

Ainsi que je vous l'ai dit, j'ai visité Paris.
As I told you, I visited Paris.

J'ai visité la Suisse ainsi que l'Italie.
I visited Switzerland as well as Italy.

J'avais une bonne situation en tant que président de cette société.
I had a good situation as president of that company.

Il travaillait comme employé de bureau.
He worked as a clerk. (job description)

Il travaillait comme un esclave.
He worked as a slave. (comparison)

182. *As far as.*

Autant que may govern a subordinate verb in the indicative as well as in the subjunctive. In today's French, the conjunction ***autant que*** is often preceded by ***pour*** and a preference is shown for a subordinate verb in the subjunctive.

Il ne s'est rien passé, pour autant que je sache.
Nothing happened, as far as I know.

La pluie va bientôt cesser, autant que je puis en juger d'ici.
The rain is going to stop, as far as I can tell from here.

The phrase *as far as he is concerned* is rendered in French as ***en ce qui le concerne***. Note the use of a direct object personal pronoun before the French verb.

See ***autant***, comparative adverb, §213.

183. *If.*

A. ***Si*** translates both *if* and *whether*. *If* expresses a condition, whereas *whether* expresses an alternative.

When ***si*** expresses a condition, alone or in ***même si*** or ***comme si***, the subordinate verb cannot be in any future or conditional tense. Those tenses must be replaced in the following manner:

future	by	present indicative
future perfect	by	passé composé (indicative)
present conditional	by	imperfect indicative
past conditional	by	pluperfect indicative

Notice that these tenses match those used in English.

S'il pleut, nous resterons ici.
If it rains, we shall stay here.

S'il pleuvait, nous resterions ici.
If it rained, we would stay here.

S'il avait plu, nous serions restés ici.
If it had rained, we would have stayed here.

S'il a fini à temps, il pourra venir avec nous.
If he has finished in time, he can come with us.

Même si tu montes dans l'arbre, tu ne les verras pas.
Even if you climb up the tree, you won't see them.

Même si tu montais dans l'arbre, tu ne les verrais pas.
Even if you climbed up the tree, you wouldn't see them.

Même si tu étais monté dans l'arbre, tu ne les aurais pas vus.
Even if you had climbed up the tree, you wouldn't have seen them.

Même si tu n'as pas fini à temps, tu pourras venir avec nous.
Even if you haven't finished in time, you can come with us.

Tu ne pourras pas venir avec nous sauf si tu as fini à temps.
You can't come along with us except if you have finished on time.

B. Conditions may be expressed by other structures than those with ***si***.

1) The use of ***quand*** with a verb in the *conditional* is a literary way of expressing a condition. The stressed forms ***quand même*** and ***quand bien même*** may also be used.

Quand bien même vous seriez beau, je ne vous aimerais pas!
Even if you were handsome, I would not love you!

2) Literary inversion of the subject and verb, with a verb in the conditional, or in the imperfect or pluperfect subjunctive, can be substituted for ***si*** and the tenses it requires. The inversion is simple if the subject is a personal pronoun or ***ce*** or ***on***. It is complex otherwise (see §84).

"Eussiez-vous capitulé, je vous aurais banni," dit la reine.
"Had you capitulated, I would have banished you," said the queen.

Le général eût-il capitulé, la reine l'aurait banni.
Le général eût-il capitulé que la reine l'aurait banni.
If the general had capitulated, the queen would have banished him.
Had the general capitulated, the queen would have banished him.

In this literary construction, if the verb ends in a mute ***e*** in the first person singular of the tense being used, an acute accent is added over the ***e***, so as to permit an easier pronunciation of the inverted group.

Dussé-je en souffrir, je continuerai l'expérience.
Were I to suffer from it, I shall continue with the experiment.

3) The preposition ***à*** followed by an infinitive provides an idiomatic way of expressing a condition.

À vous entendre, on croirait que la maison brûle!
If anyone heard you, he would think the house was on fire!
Anyone hearing you would think the house was on fire!

4) The gerund and present participle constructions may also be used to express conditions.

En vendant ce terrain, vous risquez de perdre l'avantage.
By selling (if you sell) that parcel of land, you stand to lose your advantage.

C. French constructions containing ***si*** may be expressed in English forms without *if*:

Faites comme si je n'étais pas là.
Just ignore me. (Do, act, behave, etc., as if I were not here)

Faisons comme s'il n'existait pas. Faisons semblant de ne pas le voir.
Let's ignore him. Let's pretend we don't see him.

184. As long as, as soon as, when, after.

Contrary to English usage, future tenses must be used in French after the conjunctions ***aussitôt que, dès que, lorsque, quand, tant que,*** and ***après que*** whenever futurity is meant. To the English present tense corresponds the French future, and to the English present perfect corresponds the French future perfect.

Quand j'arriverai à Paris, je visiterai le Louvre.
When I arrive in Paris, I shall visit the Louvre.

Dès qu'il aura fini son travail, il pourra sortir.
As soon as he has finished his work, he can go out.

With ***tant que***, the future perfect appears only in negative clauses.

Il ne sortira pas tant qu'il n'aura pas fini son travail.
He will not go out as long as he has not finished his work.

Tant qu'il refusera de signer, nous ne pourrons rien faire.
As long as he refuses to sign, we won't be able to do anything.

Note that *as long as* expressing cause is rendered in French as ***du moment que***, which must also be followed by future tense if futurity is meant. ***Du moment que*** also translates *since* (see §190).

Du moment que c'est vous qui le dites, ça doit être vrai.
As long as *you* say so, it must be true.

Du moment que vous êtes d'accord sur le prix, nous pouvons commencer les travaux.
As long as you agree on the price, we can begin construction.

Je ne vois pas d'inconvénient à ce qu'ils sortent, du moment qu'ils seront rentrés avant minuit.
I see no reason for them not to go out, as long as they are back by midnight.

With ***après que***, the future tense is always the *future perfect*. However, if the subordinate verb and the verb it depends on both have the same subject, ***après que*** may be replaced by the preposition ***après*** and the subordinate verb by a *past infinitive*.

Après qu'il aura fini son travail, il pourra sortir.
Après avoir fini son travail, il pourra sortir.
After he has finished his work, he can go out.

185. As much as, as well as, as . . . as, so . . . as, so . . . that, etc.

These comparative expressions function in the same manner in French as in English.

Je travaille autant (aussi bien) que vous.
I work as much (as well) as you.

Il est aussi grand que moi, mais pas aussi lourd que toi.
He is as tall as I, but not so heavy as you.

Nous étions si fatigués, nous avions tant travaillé, que nous nous sommes endormis tout de suite.
We were so tired, we had worked so much, that we fell asleep immediately.

Les extrémistes de droite aussi bien que ceux de gauche sont souvent dangereux.
The extremists of the right as well as those on the left are often dangerous.

For more on the comparative, see §§22, 209.

186. But.

But is generally a coordinating conjunction corresponding to ***mais*** in French. It is also used as a conjunction related to some negative word in the sentence, and it may be rendered in French by a relative pronoun, a conjunction, a preposition, or an adverb. For *but* as a preposition, see §134, *except (but)*.

Relative pronoun:

Pas un oiseau qui ne s'arrêtât de chanter à l'approche de l'orage.
Not a bird but stopped singing as the storm grew near.

Conjunction:

J'aurais pu être à l'heure si je n'avais été retenu par le directeur.
I could have been on time but that I had been detained by the director.

Je ne peux rien faire d'autre que d'attendre.
I can do nothing but wait. I cannot but wait.

Tu ne peux que sourire.
You can but smile.

Personne d'autre que moi n'y arrive.
No one but me can do it.

Rien que de la publicité dans le courrier.
Nothing but advertising in the mail.

Preposition:

Tout le monde avait fui, sauf moi.
Everyone had fled, but me.

Sans cela, je serais déjà loin.
But for that, I would already be far away.

Adverb:

Nous avons reçu seulement une lettre aujourd'hui.
We received but one letter today.

187. The more...as, the more...because, etc.

J'en suis d'autant plus navré que cela me touche personnellement.
I am all the more sorry about it as (or: because) it concerns me personally.

Il avait d'autant moins d'espoir qu'on était déjà dans la deuxième semaine des recherches.
He was all the less hopeful as (or: because) the search was already into its second week.

188. Besides.

As a conjunction, *besides* may be rendered by the French conjunction ***outre que***, but mainly in formal style. For the informal constructions, see §126. *Besides* is also a preposition and an adverb (§126).

Outre qu'il avait une belle voix, il s'accompagnait lui-même au piano.
Besides having a beautiful voice, he accompanied himself on the piano.

189. How, how much, why, whether.

The interrogative words *how, how much*, and *why* are conjunctions in indirect questions.

Je me demande comment il va s'en tirer.
I wonder how he is going to get out of it.

Il m'a demandé pourquoi j'avais pris son livre.
He asked me why I had taken his book.

Je veux savoir combien coûte le voyage.
I want to know how much the trip costs.

Whether (***si***) in indirect questions does not indicate a condition, but an alternative; in this case ***si*** may be followed by the future or the conditional when needed.

Je me demande s'il voudra participer au concours.
I wonder whether he will want to participate in the competition.

Compare with ***si***, §183. See also indirect questions, §102 and §105J.

190. Since.

Since expressing time is translated ***depuis que*** as a conjunction, ***depuis*** as a preposition (§153). Its use in time sentences is studied in sections §§291-293.

Je me sens seul depuis que vous êtes partis.
I feel lonely since you left.

When it expresses cause, *since* is translated ***puisque, du moment que*** (§184).

Puisque vous êtes là, donnez-nous un coup de main.
Since you are here, give us a hand.

Du moment qu'il a téléphoné à ses parents, c'est que tout va bien.
Since he called his parents, it means that everything is fine.

191. Than.

Than is translated ***que*** whenever the term it governs in a comparison is not a number.

Il travaille plus que moi.
He works more than I.

If the second term of the comparison is a number, *than* is expressed as ***de***.

Ce souvenir coûte plus de vingt francs.
This souvenir costs more than twenty francs.
Allons, ce n'est pas assez, j'en veux plus d'une bouteille.
Come on, now, it's not enough, I want more than one bottle of it.

When the two terms compared and connected by *than* are to be rendered in French by *infinitives*, the construction depends on the functions of the infinitives. If the first infinitive is a subject or a direct object, the second one is generally preceded by ***que de*** instead of ***que*** alone.

Je préfère lire que de regarder la télé.
I prefer to read than to watch television.
Lire un bon livre vaut mieux que de regarder la télé.
Reading a good book is more worthwhile than watching TV.

If the first infinitive is the object of a preposition, the same preposition should be repeated after ***que*** before the second one.

C'est plus facile à dire qu'à faire.
It is more easily said than done.

See comparative adverbs in §209.

192. That.

A. ***Que***. The simple conjunction ***que*** translating *that* unrelated to any word but the main verb is studied in sections §§279-285. §279; §280A2b, note 1; §280B1a, note; §281.

That is often combined with another word to form a conjunctive locution. See the word it is combined with in the lits in sections §174 and §179.

As a conjunction expressing strong purpose, *that* is the same as *in order that, so that* (see §178).

B. ***De ce que***, a variation of the simple conjunction ***que***, may be used after a main verb that requires the preposition ***de*** when it has a dependent infinitive or a noun object.

Je m'étonne de ce qu'il est déjà arrivé chez lui.
I am surprised that he has already reached home.

It is by no means compulsory. ***Que*** is sufficient to indicate the dependence of the subordinate verb on the main one. But with the type of main verb in question, a subordinate verb in the subjunctive is generally required if ***que*** is used, whereas ***de ce que*** is followed by a subordinate verb in the indicative (or conditional, if called for).

De ce que means *of the fact that*. It should not be mistaken for *of what*.

Je suis content de ce que l'école est finie.
I am pleased that school is over. (with the fact that)
Je suis content de ce que vous avez fait pour moi.
I am pleased with what you did for me.

That is also a relative pronoun (§98), a demonstrative adjective (§§25-27), a demonstrative pronoun (§§57-58), an adverb (§27 and §212).

193. While, whereas.

Whereas stresses opposition, contrast, difference. *While* emphasizes the time element, simultaneity. ***Tandis que*** and ***alors que*** stress opposition, contrast, difference.

Il continuait son discours tandis qu'une pluie de projectiles s'abattaient autour de lui.
He was proceeding with his speech while (or: even though) a hail of projectiles fell around him.
Elle a continué à se battre, alors que toi, tu as fui!
She kept on fighting, whereas *you* ran away!

Pendant que stresses the simultaneity of two different actions, but keeps the actions separate from one another.

Cependant que also emphasizes simultaneity, but it adds to it a note of closeness between the two actions, or a note of difference or subjectivity.

Il lisait pendant que je regardais la télé.
He was reading while I was watching TV.
Nous lisions tranquillement cependant qu'au dehors le vent soufflait.
We were reading quietly while outside the wind was blowing.

Whereas has a particular use in legal documents; the French counterpart is generally ***attendu que***. For additional meanings, see also §130.

194. Repetition.

Each conjunctive subordinate clause added to a sentence or coordinated or juxtaposed with another should be preceded by its own conjunction. To avoid the awkward repetition of a long conjunctive expression, it is usual to repeat only ***que***.

Aidez-le afin qu'il finisse vite et qu'il soit libre d'aller s'amuser.
Help him so that he will finish quickly and be free to go play.

Que also serves to avoid repeating simple conjunctions like ***quand, lorsque***, and ***puisque***.

Quand il neige et qu'il fait très froid, je reste chez moi.
When it snows and it is very cold, I stay home.

Puisque vous êtes têtu et que vous refusez de parler, . . .
Since you are stubborn and you refuse to talk, . . .

To express two coordinated conditions, one may use ***si*** (or ***même si, comme si***) before each of them in normal style.

Si la nuit tombait et si nous étions loin de la maison, nous pourrions nous perdre.
If night came and we were far from home, we might get lost.

In formal style, ***si (même si, comme si)*** may be replaced in the second of the two conditions by ***que*** with a verb in the subjunctive mood. This construction should be limited to two conditions coordinated by ***et, ou***, or ***mais***.

Si la nuit tombait et que vous fussiez loin de la maison, trouvez un abri pour y passer la nuit.
If night came and you were far from home, find a shelter in which to spend the night.

S'il part tôt et qu'il soit là-bas avant nous, . . .
If he should start early and be there before us, . . .

NOTE: Repetition is a principle that should be applied also in the case of determiners (articles, demonstratives, possessives, etc.) and prepositions. Two major reasons motivate this practice: clarity of the text and grammatical necessity.
The presence of a repeated word (conjunction, preposition, article, subject pronoun, etc.) signals the beginning of a new item as well as the end of the preceding one. This makes it easier for the reader to see clearly the pattern and the syntax of a sentence. The grammatical reason is that each item in a series has its own gender and number (in the case of substantives), and that these must be identified by different forms of the various determiners or pronouns.

ADVERBS

195. Definition.

An adverb is a word or phrase that is added to a verb, an adjective, or another adverb to modify its meaning.

The adverbs may be divided in three groups:

- The adverbs of circumstance, by far the largest group. It comprises adverbs of manner, place, time, quantity, degree, etc.
- The adverbs of opinion: negation and affirmation.
- The adverbs of interrogation.

As in English, the French adverbs may be single words, phrases, adjectives used as adverb, or adjectives transformed into adverbs by the addition of a suffix.

196. Formation of adverbs with the suffix -ment.

The French adverbs formed with the suffix ***-ment*** generally correspond to the English adverbs ending in *-ly*, the adverbs of manner.

A. The suffix ***-ment*** is added to the *feminine singular* of the adjective.

masculine singular	**feminine singular**	**adverb in *-ment***
actif	active	activement
affreux	affreuse	affreusement
beau	belle	bellement
doux	douce	doucement
facile	facile	facilement
fin	fine	finement
fou	folle	follement
gai	gaie	gaiement
général	générale	généralement
mou	molle	mollement
nouveau	nouvelle	nouvellement
premier	première	premièrement
sot	sotte	sottement
vif	vive	vivement

B. Several adverbs in ***-ment*** are formed in an irregular manner, most of them because their masculine singular form ends in a vowel sound. These should be memorized individually.

aisé	(aisée)	aisément
assuré	(assurée)	assurément
éperdu	(éperdue)	éperdûment
gentil	(gentille)	gentiment
joli	(jolie)	joliment
poli	(polie)	poliment
résolu	(résolue)	résolument
vrai	(vraie)	vraiment

Several common adverbs, most of which are formed on the feminine singular form of the adjective, present the irregularity of an acute accent on the ***e*** preceding the suffix ***-ment***.

aveugle	(aveugle)	aveuglément
commun	commune	communément
confus	confuse	confusément
énorme	énorme	énormément
exprès	expresse	expressément
immense	immense	immensément
obscur	obscure	obscurément
précis	précise	précisément
profond	profonde	profondément
profus	profuse	profusément
uniforme	uniforme	uniformément

The adverbs ***brièvement*** (*briefly*) and ***grièvement*** (*seriously*) are based on adjectives that have disappeared from modern French. They correspond to the adjectives ***bref*** and ***grave*** (cf. English *brief, grief*).

C. If the adjective ends in ***-ant*** or ***-ent*** in its masculine singular form, ***nt*** changes to ***m*** before the suffix ***-ment*** is added.

constant	constam-	constamment
évident	évidem-	évidemment
prudent	prudem-	prudemment
puissant	puissam-	puissamment
exceptions:		
lent	lente	lentement
présent	présente	présentement
content. *See below.*		

D. Many adjectives have failed to develop adverbial forms in ***-ment***. For these, it is necessary to use a prepositional phrase: ***d'un ton . . ., d'un air . . ., d'une façon . . ., d'une manière . . ., etc.***

Elle ajouta d'un air content: "Revenez vite, hein!"
She added gleefully: "Hurry back, now!"

197. Adjectives used as adverbs.

In the language of everyday, and particularly in the popular language, a number of adjectives are used with an adverbial value. The following expressions are examples of such use.

BAS les pattes (coll.)!
Hands off!

Ça sent BON. Ça sent MAUVAIS.
It smells good. It smells bad.

Tenez BON! Tenez FERME!
Hold on tight! Resist! Keep your position!

Cette voiture coûte CHER.
This car costs a lot.

Ça va lui coûter CHER!
He will pay for it dearly! (figuratively)

Je ne vois pas CLAIR, allume! Allume les phares!
I can't see clearly, turn the light on! Turn the headlights on!

Dites lui CLAIR et NET ce que vous voulez dire.
Just tell him clearly and precisely what you mean.

Couper COURT à quelque chose.
To cut something short. (To interrupt.)

S'habiller COURT, LONG.
To wear short, long clothes (dresses, skirts).

Filer DOUX.
To go straight, behave (be submissive).

Marcher DROIT.
To go straight, behave (under orders, the law).

Aller, marcher, rouler TOUT DROIT.
To go, walk, drive straight ahead.

Travaillez DUR!
Work hard!

Il chante FAUX. Il chante JUSTE.
He sings out of tune. He sings in tune.

Allez-y FERME!
Go at it without hesitation!

Tenez FERME! Tenez BON!
Hold on tight! Resist! Keep your position! Etc.

Travaillez FERME!
Work hard!

Parlez plus FORT, plus HAUT.
Speak up, speak louder, raise your voice.

Cela est FORT beau.
That is very nice.

Vous y allez trop FORT!
You are overdoing it!

Ça va lui coûter GROS!
It will cost him a bundle! (financially)

Il joue GROS.
He makes large bets.

Il risque GROS.
He takes big risks.

Il gagne GROS.
He makes a lot of money. He is winning big (gambling).

HAUT les mains!
Hands up!

Parlez plus HAUT, plus FORT.
Speak up, speak louder, raise your voice.

Il chante JUSTE. Il chante FAUX.
He sings in tune. He sings out of tune.

Ça ne vaut pas LOURD.
It isn't worth much.

Casser, briser NET.
To break suddenly, clean. (To snap.)

S'arrêter NET.
To stop short, suddenly, on the spot.

Ça sent MAUVAIS. Ça sent BON.
It smells bad. It smells good.

Il a les cheveux coupés RAS.
His hair is cut very short (almost shaved).

Ce gars-là boit SEC!
That guy drinks a lot (and straight)!

Il m'a répondu SEC.
He answered me roughly. (He snapped back at me.)

Aller, marcher, rouler TOUT DROIT.
To go, walk, drive straight ahead.

La petite fille était TOUT en larmes.
The little girl was all in tears.

Un livre TOUT neuf.
A brand new book.

Casser, briser TOUT NET.
To break suddenly, clean. (To snap.)

NOTE: In compound adjectives, the first term is often an adjective used as an adverb, in which case it remains invariable. But if it is an adjective with full adjectival value, it should agree with the noun it refers to.

In the case of ***grand, nouveau, frais, tout, premier, dernier*** used adverbially in compound adjectives, the agreement is observed as if they were strictly adjectives.

Les enfants premiers-nés.
The firstborn children.

Des fenêtres grandes-ouvertes.
Wide-open windows.

Les nouvelles-venues.
The newcomers (girls).

Des fleurs fraîches cueillies.
Freshly picked flowers.

For ***tout***, see §43, notes 2 and 3.

198. Adverbial phrases.

It frequently happens that one needs to use several adverbs in sequence to modify the same word, particularly the same verb. In order to avoid repetitions of sounds (the ending ***-ment*** for instance), or an awkward rhythm in the constrution, it is useful to know that adverbs can be replaced advantageously by adverbial phrases.

Adverbial phrases may be formed with words of various natures. The most common type of adverbial phrase is also called *prepositional phrase.* A list of common adverbs, adverbial phrases, prepositions, prepositional expressions, conjunctions, and conjunctive expressions is given in §306.

199. Position of adverbs.

In general, an adverb should be placed near the word it modifies.

In French as in English, emphasis may be achieved by placing an adverb at the very beginning or at the very end of a clause. It may also be achieved by choosing a synonymous expression of less usual character, such as a prepositional phrase, instead of the ordinary adverb.

The following rules govern the position of French adverbs:

A. An adverb precedes the adjective or the adverb it modifies.

Il fait très froid. Vous marchez trop vite.
It is very cold. You walk too fast.

B. An adverb modifying a verb in a simple tense must follow the verb.

Vous marchez vite. Elle travaille trop.
You walk fast. She works too much.

C. When they modify a verb in a compound tense, most simple adverbs not ending in ***-ment*** are placed between the auxiliary and the past participle.

Il a encore reçu le premier prix.
He was awarded the first prize again.

Nous avons souvent visité le Louvre.
We have often visited the Louvre.

Alors vous avez déjà vu la Joconde?
So you have already seen the Mona Lisa?

The following adverbs are placed *after* the past participle:

aujourd'hui	today	**devant**	in front
autrefois	formerly	**hier**	yesterday
davantage	more	**ici**	here
dedans	inside	**là**	there
dehors	outside	**loin**	far away
demain	tomorrow	**partout**	everywhere
derrière	behind	**près**	near
dessous	under, below	**tard**	late
dessus	on, on top	**tôt**	early

The adverb ***puis*** (*then*) must precede the subject of the verb it modifies.

Il est resté derrière. Je l'ai rencontré hier.
He stayed behind. I met him yesterday.

D'abord, il s'est assis là, puis il regardé partout.
First, he sat down there, then he looked everywhere.

D. Most adverbial phrases and adverbs ending in ***-ment*** either begin the clause or come after the verb (and its objects, if any), except the following, which may be placed between the auxiliary and the past participle in the case of compound tenses, or immediately after the verb in a simple tense. The choice of the position for these is a matter of emphasis and style. This list is by no means exhaustive. It is always possible, for stylistic reasons, to change the place of most adverbs and adverbial phrases.

à moitié	half(way)	**peut-être**	perhaps, maybe
à peine	hardly, scarcely	**probablement**	probably
à peu près	approximately, about	**quand même**	all the same, anyway
brusquement	abruptly, suddenly	**rarement**	rarely, seldom
certainement	certainly	**récemment**	recently
chaque fois	every time	**sans doute**	no doubt, probably
d'abord	first, at first	**seulement**	only
d'ailleurs	besides, moreover	**soudain**	suddenly
de même	also, in the same way	**soudainement**	in a sudden manner
de nouveau	again, once more	**tour à tour**	by turns
d'habitude	usually	**tout à coup**	suddenly
en vain	in vain	**tout à fait**	completely, quite
immédiatement	immediately	**tout de suite**	at once, immediately
par conséquent	consequently, therefore	**tout d'un coup**	all of a sudden
petit à petit	little by little	**vraiment**	really, truly
peu à peu	little by little		

200. *Peut-être, à peine, aussi.*

The conjunction ***aussi***, meaning *so, therefore*, must begin the clause it governs and requires an inversion of the subject and verb in that clause. In other positions, ***aussi*** means *also, too, as, so*, etc.

L'orage approchait, aussi décidèrent-ils de rentrer.
The storm was approaching, therefore they decided to go back home.

Peut-être and ***à peine*** (see §199D) may be placed at the beginning of the clause whose verb they modify, in which case they require the inversion of the verb and subject.

À peine avais-je le dos tourné qu'il a disparu.
J'avais à peine le dos tourné qu'il a disparu.
Hardly had I turned my back than he was gone.
S'il doit pleuvoir, peut-être vaudrait-il mieux ne pas sortir.
S'il doit pleuvoir, il vaudrait peut-être mieux ne pas sortir.
S'il doit pleuvoir, peut-être qu'il vaudrait mieux ne pas sortir. (See the footnote on the table at §179.)
If it is going to rain, perhaps we'd better not go out.

The inversion required by the initial position of ***peut-être*** may be avoided by using ***que***:

S'il doit pleuvoir, peut-être qu'il vaudrait mieux ne pas sortir.

201. *Aussi, non plus, encore. Toujours, même.*

The words ***aussi*** (*also, too, as well*), ***non plus*** (*neither, not either*), ***encore*** (*again, still*), ***toujours*** (*still, always*), and ***même*** (*even*) may be directed toward a noun or pronoun instead of a verb. This is obvious when no verb is expressed in the clause.

A. ***Aussi*** and ***non plus*** always follow the word they are directed toward when no verb is expressed, and ***encore, toujours***, and ***même*** always precede it.

Lui aussi. Lui non plus.
He too (so does he). He neither (neither does he).
Encore toi? —Oui, toujours moi.
You again? —Yes, always me.
Même eux? —Oui, eux aussi.
Even they? —Yes, they also.
Les enfants aussi? —Oui, même les enfants.
The children too? —Yes, even the children.

Note that the personal pronouns must be of the *disjunctive* kind, and may be immediately followed by ***aussi*** or ***non plus***, or immediately preceded by ***encore, toujours***, or ***même***.

B. When a verb is expressed, if it is clearly the verb itself that is being modified, the position of ***aussi, non plus, encore, toujours,*** and ***même*** should be as described in §199.
But if it is the subject or the object of the verb that is being given the emphasis, the position is as follows:

- To give emphasis to a *noun* or *pronoun* (other than personal), ***aussi*** and ***non plus*** are placed after the noun or pronoun; ***encore*** and ***toujours*** are placed before the noun or pronoun, but are themselves reinforced by ***c'est . . . qui*** (subject), ***c'est . . . que*** (object); ***même*** may either precede or follow the noun or pronoun. Note that ***même*** is attached to a personal pronoun with a hyphen, and means *self.*

Paul aussi est venu.
Paul came also.

J'ai visité le Louvre aussi.
I visited the Louvre also.

Nos amis non plus n'ont pas été invités.
Our friends were not invited either.

Ils n'ont pas invité nos amis non plus.
They did not invite our friends either.

C'est encore Paul qui a fini le dernier.
Paul finished last again.

C'est toujours à Paul qu'on fait des reproches.
It's always Paul who gets the blame.

Même les enfants (or: les enfants même) travaillaient dans la mine.
Even the children used to work in the mine.

Voyez vous-mêmes!
See for yourselves!

- To give emphasis to a personal pronoun, the personal pronoun must be repeated in its *disjunctive* form, and the modifiers ***aussi, non plus, encore, toujours,*** and ***même*** are added to the disjunctive pronoun in the manner described in paragraph A above.

Je l'ai vu, moi aussi. Moi aussi, je l'ai vu.
I, too, saw him.

Je l'ai vu, lui aussi. Lui aussi, je l'ai vu.
I saw *him* too.

The third person subject pronouns ***il, elle, ils, elles,*** may be replaced altogether—not merely reinforced—by the disjunctive pronouns ***lui, elle, eux, elles,*** modified by ***aussi*** or ***non plus.***

Lui aussi est venu. Elles non plus n'y ont pas pensé.
He came too. They did not think of it either.

202. Adverbs of opinion.

Negation, affirmation, dissent, and approval may be expressed with the following adverbs:

A. *Yes, no:* There are two French adverbs to translate *yes*. The first one, ***oui***, is used to answer a regular question. The second one, ***si***, is used to answer a negative question, or to oppose a negative statement. ***Non*** translates *no* in all cases.*

Avez-vous fini? —Oui, j'ai fini. Non, je n'ai pas fini.
Have you finished? —Yes, I have. No, I haven't.

N'avez-vous pas fini? —Si. Si, j'ai fini. Non. Non, je n'ai pas fini.
Haven't you finished? —Yes. Yes, I have. No. No, I haven't.

Ce n'est pas vrai. —Si, c'est vrai.
That isn't true. —Yes, it is. (It is too!)

C'est vrai, n'est-ce pas? —Oui, c'est vrai. Oui.
It is true, isn't it? —Yes, it is. Yes.

Ce n'est pas vrai, si? —Si, c'est vrai. Si.
It isn't true, is it? —Yes, it is. Yes.

**No*, used without a verb, should not be confused with *no* modifying another word, as in "no money," "no good," etc. (See indefinite adjectives, §30, §37; see also §7A.)

Pas d'argent. Pas bon (du tout). Je n'ai pas d'argent.
No money. No good. I have no money.

B. *Neither, nor, not . . . either* are rendered by ***non plus*** (see §201). When correlated with one another, *neither* and *nor* are rendered by ***ne . . . ni . . . ni . . .*** (with objects), or by ***ni . . . ni . . . ne . . .*** (with subjects), or by ***ne . . . ni ne . . .*** (with verbs).

Ni Paul ni Pierre ne fume.
Neither Paul nor Peter smokes.

Il ne fume ni ne boit.
He neither smokes nor drinks.

(Ni) moi non plus. L'évêque non plus.
Neither do I. Neither does the bishop.

Ils ne s'intéressent ni à l'art ni à la politique.
They are interested neither in art nor in politics.

C. *Not.* The French negative adverb that modifies a verb is made of two parts: ***ne*** and ***pas***. ***Ne*** (***n'*** before a vowel or mute ***h***) always precedes the verb, and ***pas*** generally follows the verb (the auxiliary in a compound tense).

Il ne parle pas bien.
He does not speak well.

Je n'ai pas fini.
I have not finished.

If the verb is an infinitive, both negative words precede the infinitive.

On est prié de ne pas fumer.
You are asked not to smoke.

If the negation is directed toward the subject rather than the verb, ***pas*** precedes the subject while ***ne*** remains before the verb.

Pas un seul article ne manquait.
Not a single item was missing.

If a verb has two complements, one in the affirmative and the other in the negative, the negative is preceded by ***pas, non pas***, or ***non*** preceded by ***et, mais***, or a comma. The choice is subjective and based on style, rhythm, and euphony. Other negative or restrictive words may also be used in this elliptical construction.

On vous demande de parler, pas de crier!
You are asked to speak, not to shout!

Elle a mis les fourchettes, mais pas les couteaux.
She did set the forks, but not the knives.

Nous avons mangé une fois chez Troisgros, jamais chez Pic.
We ate at Troisgros' once, never at Pic's.

C'est à Pierre que j'ai parlé, et non (pas) à Paul.
It was Pierre I spoke to, not Paul.

Il a pris trois brêmes, mais aucune truite.
He caught three bream, but no trout.

NOTE: ***Ne*** may be used without ***pas*** with ***cesser, oser,*** and ***pouvoir*** when these are followed by an infinitive.

Elle ne cesse de pleurnicher. Je ne puis le supporter davantage.
She won't stop whining. I can't take it anymore.

Ne is also used without ***pas*** in a number of phrases and expressions among which are ***si ce n'est*** (*except*), ***qu'à cela ne tienne*** (*never mind that*), ***je ne saurais*** + ***infinitive*** (*I wouldn't know how to*), ***si je ne me trompe*** (*if I am not mistaken*).

Ne without ***pas*** appears also in subordinate clauses in the subjunctive after certain conjunctions and after main verbs expressing fear. See §174 and §280A1.

D. *Never, no one, none, nothing, nobody, no . . ., hardly, scarcely, not . . . any, not . . . anyone*, etc., are all made of two parts in French, like the basic negation ***ne . . . pas***.

Except for ***personne*** (*no one, nobody, not anyone, not anybody*), and ***aucun*** (*none, not any, no . . .*), their position is the same as that of ***ne . . . pas***.

Personne and ***aucun*** are never to be placed between the auxiliary and the past participle in compound tenses.

Je n'ai rien vu. Je n'ai vu personne. Je n'ai vu aucun ennemi.
I saw nothing. I saw nobody. I saw no enemy.

203. Modified negations.

A. French negations are often modified in an idiomatic way. The following list offers examples of the most frequently used modified negations.

Il ne pleut guère dans cette région.
It hardly (ever) rains in this area.

Il n'y a guère que deux clients dans la salle d'attente.
There are only (just) two customers in the waiting room.

Il ne gèle jamais ici.
It never freezes here.

Tu ne me fais jamais aucun compliment.
You never pay me any compliment.

Il ne se passe jamais grand-chose.
Nothing much ever happens.

Je n'ai jamais insulté personne.
I have never insulted anyone.

Nous ne le verrons jamais plus.
We shall never see him again.

Je ne lui prêterai jamais plus aucun livre.
I shall never lend him any book again.

Je ne parlerai jamais plus à personne.
I shall never speak to anyone again.

Après ça, il ne m'a jamais plus rien dit.
After that, he never said anything to me again.

Tu ne me dis jamais que des bêtises.
You never tell me anything but nonsense.

On ne me dit jamais rien.
I am never told anything.
They never tell me anything.

Je n'ai entendu ni le tonnerre ni la grêle.
I heard neither the thunder nor the hail.

Je n'aime pas le thé.
I don't like tea.

Je n'aime pas beaucoup ce genre de remarque.
I don't like this kind of remark very much.

Il ne m'a pas aidé du tout. Il ne m'a pas du tout aidé.
He did not help me at all.

Je n'ai pas encore passé l'examen.
I have not taken the exam yet.

Ça ne vous a pas servi à grand-chose.
It was not much use to you.

Vous n'avez pas dit grand-chose.
You haven't said much.

Nous ne parlons plus de cet incident.
We no longer mention that incident.

Je ne l'ai plus revu après cet incident.
I didn't see him again after that incident.

Je ne veux plus de vin rouge.
I don't want anymore red wine.

Il ne reviendra plus.
He will not come back anymore.

Il ne me reste plus aucun espoir.
I have no hope left anymore.

Il ne me reste plus du tout d'argent.
I have no money left at all anymore.

Après ça, il ne m'a plus dit grand-chose.
After that, he didn't tell me much anymore.

Après ça, il ne m'a jamais plus parlé.
After that, he never spoke to me again.

D'ailleurs, il ne parle plus à personne.
Besides, he no longer talks to anyone.

Il ne reste plus qu'un mois avant Noël.
There is only one month left before Christmas.

Je n'ai plus qu'un examen à passer.
I have only one exam left to take.

Moi, je n'ai plus rien à faire. J'ai réussi à tous les miens.
I have nothing more to do. I passed all of mine.
I have nothing left to do anymore. I passed all of mine.

Cela ne m'étonne point. (literary or regional)
That does not surprise me at all.

Je n'ai revu presque aucun de mes anciens amis.
I met almost none of my former friends.

Ils ne viennent presque jamais dans cette ville.
They hardly ever come to this town.

Il ne parle presque jamais d'aucun de ses projets.
He hardly ever talks about any of his projects.

D'ailleurs, il ne parle presque jamais à personne.
Besides, he hardly ever talks to anyone.

Elle ne sort presque jamais plus.
She hardly ever goes out anymore.

Il ne dit presque jamais rien.
He hardly ever says anything.

Il ne dit presque jamais plus rien.
He hardly ever says anything anymore.

Il ne mange presque rien.
He hardly eats (anything).

Il n'y a presque personne.
There is hardly anybody.

Il n'y a presque plus personne.
There is hardly anyone left.

Nous ne sortons presque plus jamais.
We hardly ever go out anymore.

Nous ne voyons presque plus personne.
We hardly ever see anyone anymore.

Elle ne fait presque plus rien.
She hardly does anything anymore.

B. Some negative words may be used as subjects of the verb. In that case, the negative word begins the sentence and is followed by *ne* and the verb.

Nul n'est infaillible.
No one is infallible.

Nul homme n'est immortel.
No man is immortal.

Aucun candidat ne sera admis dans la salle après le début de l'épreuve.
No applicant will be admitted to the room after the test has begun.

Personne ne sait où je suis.
No one knows where I am.

Rien n'est plus difficile.
Nothing is more difficult.

Pas un d'entre vous n'est capable de le faire.
Not one among you is capable of doing it.

Plus rien ne m'étonne.
Nothing astonishes me anymore.

Presque personne n'est venu nous voir, nous rendre visite.
Hardly anybody came to see us, to visit us.

C. A negative subject may be accompanied by a negative object, but ***pas*** cannot be associated with any other negative term.

Personne ne te fera plus aucun mal.
No one will hurt you anymore.

Personne ne s'est rendu compte de rien.
Nobody noticed anything.

D. The combination ***ne . . . que*** is only restrictive, not absolutely negative. Therefore no change of article is made before the direct object of a verb modified by ***ne . . . que*** (see §5B, §7A).

Il ne mange que des légumes.
He eats only vegetables.

Nous ne voulons que la justice et l'égalité.
All we want is justice and equality.
We want only justice and equality.

Dépêchez-vous, nous n'avons qu'une minute!
Hurry up, we have only one minute.

The expression ***ne . . . que*** is also used in idiomatic expressions.

Il ne font que s'amuser.
All they do is play. They merely play.

Vous le saviez? Moi, je ne fais que l'apprendre.
You knew it? *I* have just now found out.

Tu ne fais rien d'autre que de perdre ton temps.
You do nothing but waste your time.
All you do is waste your time.
You are merely wasting your time.

Cet endroit est détestable. Il ne fait que pleuvoir.
This place is awful. All it does is rain.

Ce garçon ne fait que se plaindre.
That boy does nothing but complain.

Tu n'as rien d'autre à faire que d'appuyer sur ce bouton.
All you have to do is press on this button.

Tu n'avais qu'à l'avertir. Maintenant il est trop tard.
All you had to do was warn him. Now it is too late.

Tu n'as qu'à être prêt à l'heure, c'est tout.
Just be ready on time, that's all.

204. Interrogative adverbs.

Interrogative adverbs are used to formulate questions as well as to introduce subordinate clauses in indirect questions.

The interrogative adverbs are actually ordinary adverbs of place, quantity, time, etc., or conjunctions, used in asking questions. Only the idiomatic expression ***est-ce que*** can really be considered a true interrogative adverb.

The main interrogative adverbs are ***combien*** (*how much, how many*), ***comment*** (*how*), ***où*** (*where*), ***pourquoi*** (*why*), and ***quand*** (*when*). They are frequently used in ready-made interrogative phrases:

<u>Combien</u>

combien de temps	how long (action completed)
depuis combien de temps	how long (action still going on at moment considered)
dans combien de temps	how long until how long before

après combien de temps — how long (will it be) until, before
how long (was it) until, before
how long (would it be) until, before
(other tenses as needed)

en combien de temps — how long . . . take (any tense)

pour combien de temps — for how long
how long . . . intend to . . .

combien de — how much, how many (with noun)

<u>Comment</u>

Comment se fait-il que (+ subjunctive) — how come, how does it happen that

<u>Où</u> (See §247.)

d'où — from where, whence

jusqu'où — how far

par où — which way
in what direction

<u>Pourquoi</u>

(mais) pourquoi donc — but why; why on earth

<u>Quand</u>

de quand (date) — what is the date of origin

jusqu'à quand — how long (with future)
until when

après quand — after what date, day, hour

à partir de quand — starting when, at what time

depuis quand — how long (with past tense)
since when

There are also interrogative adjectives (see §44-46) and pronouns (see §78-81).

All interrogative words and phrases require the inversion of the verb and subject (see §84), unless they are or contain the subject, or unless they are found in an indirect question (see §102).

Depuis quand ne l'avez-vous pas vu?
How long (has it been) since you've seen him?
Dans combien de temps est-ce que vous serez prêt?
How long (will it be) until you are ready?
Demande-lui combien d'argent il lui faut.
Ask her how much money she needs.

205. Adverbs of quantity.

Like any expression of quantity, the adverbs of quantity may be used with ***de*** before a noun. Only two expressions require a full article: ***la plupart*** (*most, most of*) and ***bien*** (*lots of, a lot of*).

Beaucoup de livres. Une douzaine de roses.
Many books. A dozen roses.
Il y avait bien du monde à la réunion.
There were lots of people at the meeting.
La plupart des vedettes de cinéma vivent à Beverly Hills.
Most movie stars live in Beverly Hills.

Some adverbs of quantity stress degree or intensity and therefore are never used with nouns, unless these nouns are a part of verbal expressions such as ***avoir besoin, avoir faim, avoir froid, avoir soif*** (§3H; see also §206, §213, and §215 for use of ***très, si*** and ***trop*** with these expressions).

Elle est très sensible, et si frêle!
She is very sensitive, and so frail!
J'ai assez faim, très soif, trop chaud, et extrêmement hâte d'arriver.
I'm rather hungry, very thirsty, too hot, and in an extreme hurry to arrive.

206. Much, many, a lot, lots. Very, most, quite.

Beaucoup and ***bien*** can both modify adjectives or adverbs involved in comparative statements, but only ***bien*** can modify adjectives or adverbs that are not being used in a comparison.

Ce roman est beaucoup (or: bien) plus intéressant que je ne croyais.
This novel is a lot more interesting than I thought.
Il est bien intéressant en effet.
It is very (most, quite) interesting indeed. (no comparison)

Bien, très, and ***fort*** are synonymous as adverbs of degree. ***Très*** is appropriate with all levels of speech. ***Bien*** is lest frequent in familiar language (it often suggests a subjective observation), and ***fort*** is strictly formal and literary.

Cunégonde était très grande, bien grasse et fort laide.
Cunégonde was very tall, quite fat, and most ugly.
Candide était bien malheureux de la savoir morte.
Candide was quite sad to learn that she was dead.

Beaucoup should never be modified by another adverb of quantity, degree, or intensity, especially not by ***très***.

Merci bien. Je vous remercie beaucoup.
Thanks a lot. Thank you very much.

Beaucoup can modify verbs. It gives them a note of degree or intensity. ***Bien*** can do so only with verbal expressions containing a noun, where ***très*** or ***grand*** sometimes replaces it.

J'ai beaucoup travaillé. J'ai bien envie de me reposer. J'ai grand besoin de repos.
I have worked a lot. I feel very much like resting. I very much need rest.

Elle avait très soif en sortant de la mine.
She was very thirsty when she came out of the mine.

With verbs that do not contain nouns, ***bien*** indicates the manner in which the action is performed.

J'ai bien travaillé.
I have worked well.

Beaucoup can be used with ***de*** and a noun. ***Bien*** can be used with ***des*** and a noun, in the plural most of the time. Used with ***du, de l', de la*** and a singular noun, in the place of ***beaucoup de***, ***bien*** generally implies some subjective idea. See also §§216,217.

J'ai beaucoup de livres, et beaucoup de patience.
I have many books, and a lot of patience.

Il faut bien de la patience pour lire tant de livres!
It takes a great deal of patience to read so many books!

Bien des gens vivent au jour le jour. Beaucoup de gens vivent au jour le jour.
Many people live from hand to mouth.

Elle se fait bien du souci. Elle se fait beaucoup de souci.
She worries a lot.

207. How, how much, how many. So much, so many.

Combien, que, comme may modify a verb, an adjective, or an adverb. But they are generally separated from the word they modify, since they must begin the clause to which they belong. All three serve as exclamatory adverbs. ***Combien*** can also be an interrogative adverb and can thus be found in indirect questions.

Combien il souffre! Comme il souffre! (verb)
He suffers so much!

Qu'il est triste! Comme il a l'air triste! (adjective)
How sad he is! How sad he looks!

Comme elle est partie vite! Qu'elle écrit peu! (adverb)
How fast she left! How little she writes!

J'aimerais savoir combien il est riche. (adjective)
I would like to know how rich he is.

Mon Dieu! Qu'il saigne! Comme il saigne! Combien il saigne! (Ce qu'il saigne! pop.) (verb)
My God! He is bleeding so much!

Combien used with ***de*** and a noun, generally begins a question or an exclamation. Only direct questions require the inversion of the verb and subject.

Combien de fois m'avez-vous appelé?
How many times did you call me?

Combien de jours y a-t-il dans le mois de février?
How many days are there in the month of February?

but: Dites-moi combien de cerises il vous faut.
Tell me how many cherries you want.

The noun with ***de*** normally comes immediately after ***combien***, but may be placed after the verb. Note the difference in agreement of the past participle when the direct object precedes or follows the verb.

Combien de fautes il fait!
He makes so many mistakes!

Combien il fait de fautes!
He makes so many mistakes!

Combien a-t-il fait de fautes?
Combien de fautes a-t-il faites?
How many mistakes has he made?

Que, used with ***de*** and a noun (singular or plural), begins an exclamation. If the noun is part of a verbal expression such as ***avoir besoin, avoir faim, avoir froid, avoir soif, que*** is used without ***de***.

Que d'eau! Que de monde (quelle foule)! Que de moustiques!
So much water! So many people (such a crowd)! So many mosquitoes!

Que j'ai faim! Que j'ai envie de manger!
How hungry I am! (I am so hungry!) I feel so much like eating!

208. More.

Davantage and ***plus*** both mean *more*. Both can modify a verb or precede ***de*** and a noun, but only ***plus*** can modify an adjective or an adverb. ***Davantage*** should be substituted for ***plus*** when style and euphony demand it, as well as in contexts where ***plus*** might be perceived as a negative word.

Il a plu davantage hier.
It rained more yesterday.

Je voudrais pouvoir faire davantage pour vous.
I wish I could do more for you.

Il y aura davantage de monde dimanche prochain.
There will be more of a crowd next Sunday.

Il est plus riche que moi, il travaille davantage.
He is richer than I, he works more.

Il court plus vite.
He runs faster.

Davantage also means *more time, longer, more often*, etc.

Restez davantage. Venez nous voir davantage.
Stay a while longer. Drop in more often.

Écrivez-nous davantage. Donnez-nous davantage de nouvelles de votre famille.
Write to us more. Give us more news about your family.

See also the expressions with ***plus*** in §211.

209. Comparative adverbs.

A. *More, as, less*:

Plus, aussi, and ***moins*** are the adverbs of quantity used in the comparison of adjectives and adverbs.

Plus (*more*) is used to form the comparative of superiority.

Paul est plus grand que Pierre.
Paul is taller than Pierre.

Il court plus vite que moi.
He runs faster than I.

Aussi (*as*) is used to form the comparative of equality. After a negative verb, ***aussi*** is sometimes reduced to ***si***.

Elle est aussi grande que toi.
She is as tall as you.

Tu n'es pas si fort que tu crois.
You are not so strong as you think.

Il n'y a rien de si bon qu'un café fort le matin.
Nothing is so good as a cup of strong coffee in the morning.

Moins (*less*) is used to form the comparative of inferiority.

Pierre court moins vite que Paul.
Pierre runs less fast than Paul.

Il est moins rapide que lui.
He is less fast than he.

Plus, aussi, and ***moins*** must precede the adjective or adverb they modify. The second term of the comparison is introduced by ***que*** (*as, than*).

B. *Than*:

When ***plus*** and ***moins*** are used with expressions of quantity, especially numbers, *than* should be expressed as ***de*** instead of ***que***.

Paul a plus de dix mille dollars en banque.
Paul has more than ten thousand dollars in the bank.

J'ai fait ce travail en moins de dix minutes.
I did this job in less than ten minutes.

Que may introduce a subordinate clause instead of a second term of comparison of the same nature as the first. In this case the verb is often preceded, in the subordinate clause, by an expletive ***ne***, except if the comparative adverb is ***aussi*** or ***si***.

Il est bien plus malade que je ne croyais.
He is far more seriously ill than I thought.

When the two terms of the comparison are infinitives, if the first one is preceded by ***à***, ***de***, or no preposition, as required by the verb or adjective on which it depends, the second one must also be preceded by ***à***, ***de***, or no preposition, respectively. However, if the main verb governing the two infinitives compared is ***préférer***, ***aimer mieux***, ***valoir mieux***, ***aimer autant***, ***valoir autant***, ***avoir mieux à faire***, or one of the many forms of these, then the second infinitive is usually preceded by ***que de***.

Il est plus important d'écouter que de parler.
It is more important to listen than to talk.

Je m'attends plus à échouer qu'à réussir.
I expect more to fail than to pass.

Il est plus facile de rire que de pleurer.
It is easier to laugh than to cry.

Cette porte est moins difficile à fermer qu'à ouvrir.
This door is less difficult to shut than to open.

Les enfants sont plus enclins à jouer qu'à travailler.
Children are more inclined to play than to work.

but: Je préfère finir maintenant que de recommencer demain.
I prefer to finish now than to start all over tomorrow.

J'aimerais mieux mourir que de manger du foie de veau!
I'd rather die than eat calves' liver!

J'ai bien d'autres choses à faire que d'écouter vos sornettes.
I have better things to do than listen to your silly stories.

When the two terms compared are subordinate clauses, the second one may be turned into an infinitive phrase introduced by ***que de***, so as to avoid the contact of ***que*** (*than*) with a second ***que*** (*that*) introducing the subordinate clause.

Il vaudrait mieux qu'il s'arrête que de s'épuiser en vain.
He'd do better to stop than exhaust himself in vain.

Que de in this case is often reinforced by ***plutôt*** (*rather*).

Il vaut mieux qu'il s'arrête plutôt que de s'épuiser en vain.
He'd do better to stop rather than exhaust himself in vain.

If an ambiguity of subjects is feared, the infinive ***voir***, preceded by a personal pronoun, can be used to prevent it.

Je préfère que vous travailliez encore un peu avec moi plutôt que de vous voir échouer à l'examen.
I prefer that you work some more with me rather than see you flunk the exam.

210. Superlatives.

The superlative of adjectives and adverbs is formed with ***le plus*** (*the most, the . . .-est*) and ***le moins*** (*the least*).

Le plus beau. Le plus facilement.
The most beautiful. The most easily.
The prettiest. The easiest.

The article in ***le plus, le moins*** must show agreement with the noun referred to when the superlative applies to an adjective. When it applies to an adverb, the article is always ***le***.

Jeanne est la plus jolie fille de la classe.
Jeanne is the prettiest girl in the class.
C'est aussi l'étudiante la plus intelligente.
She is also the most intelligent student.
C'est elle qui court le plus vite.
She is the one that runs the fastest.

A few adverbs have irregular comparative and superlative forms:

normal	comparative	superlative
beaucoup much, many	***plus*** more	***le plus*** the most
peu little, few	***moins*** less, fewer	***le moins*** the least
bien well	***mieux*** better	***le mieux*** the best
mal bad, badly	***pis**** worse	***le pis**** the worst
loin far	***plus loin*** farther further**	***le plus loin*** the farthest the furthest

****Pis*** and ***le pis*** are used only in ready-made expressions and idioms. In general, one should use the regular comparative and superlative forms ***plus mal*** and ***le plus mal***.

Tant pis. De mal en pis.
Too bad (so much the worse). From bad to worse.

C'est lui qui conduit le plus mal.
He is the one who drives the worst.

Farther* is translated ***plus loin when the meaning is actually that of distance in space. *Further* is used in figurative expressions as well as in expressions of time, and may be expressed idiomatically rather than with ***plus loin***. *Furthermore* is synonymous with *besides, moreover*: ***de plus, en outre***.

Ils n'iront pas plus loin. N'allez pas plus loin (n'avancez plus).
They won't go any farther. Don't go any further.

See comparative and superlative of adjectives in §22-23.

211. Expressions.

the more . . . the more . . .	***plus . . . plus . . .***
the less . . . the less . . .	***moins . . . moins . . .***
more and more . . .	***de plus en plus . . .***
less and less . . .	***de moins en moins . . .***

Plus on est de fous, plus on rit.
The more, the merrier. (The more jesters, the more laughter.)
Plus il boit, plus il a soif.
The more he drinks, the thirstier he gets.
La pollution est de plus en plus grave.
Pollution is more and more serious.
Il y a de moins en moins d'arbres dans la forêt vierge.
There are fewer and fewer trees in the rain forest.
La population mondiale augmente de plus en plus vite.
The world population increases more and more rapidly.

212. As, so, also. That (adverb).

Aussi and ***si*** are used to form the comparative of equality of adjectives and adverbs. The second term of the comparison is introduced by ***que*** in French (by *as* in English).

Le plomb n'est pas aussi léger que l'aluminium.
Lead is not as light as aluminum.
Personne n'est aussi naïf que Candide.
No one is as naive as Candide.

Aussi modifying a verb means *also*, and may be replaced by ***également***.

Il ne suffit pas de parler, il faut aussi agir.
It is not enough to talk, it is also necessary to act.

When ***that*** is used as an adverb to modify an adjective or another adverb, it is translated ***si . . . que cela, si . . . que ça*** (informal), or ***. . . à ce point***.

Il n'est pas si malin que ça.
He is not that smart.

Also and *too* modifying personal pronouns are studied in §201.

213. As much, as many. So much, so many. That much, that many.

Autant and ***tant*** both translate *as much, as many,* as well as the negative *not as (so) much, not as (so) many.* Both can modify a verb or precede ***de*** and a noun. Both can be correlated with ***que***, but ***autant*** is preferred if the comparison is between terms of similar natures.

Paul ne boit pas autant de lait que son petit frère.
Paul does not drink as much milk as his little brother.

Il ne boit pas tant qu'on le dit.
He does not drink as much as people say he does.

Pierre travaillait tant qu'il est tombé malade.
Pierre was working so much that he became ill.

Il a tant de soucis qu'il n'en dort plus.
He as so many worries that he no longer can sleep.

That much, that many are translated ***tant que cela (ça), tant de . . . que cela (ça), à ce point*** (see §212).

Il ne boit pas tant que ça.
He does not drink that much.

A few idiomatic expressions contain ***tant*** and ***autant***:

pas tant que	not so much as
d'autant que, d'autant plus que	all the more as (because)
d'autant moins que	all the less as (because)
d'autant mieux que	all the better as (because)
. . . pour autant.	. . . for it, . . . for that reason.
(pour) autant que (subjunctive)	as far as (§182)
(pour) autant que je sache	as far as I know
tant mieux	so much the better
tant pis	too bad, so much the worse
si tant est que	inasmuch as, if at least
tant . . ., tant . . .	as . . ., so . . .
tant soit peu	little as it may be

Si, tant, and ***tellement*** are adverbs of intensity or degree. They can be used as exclamatory adverbs: ***si*** with an adjective or an adverb; ***tant*** with a verb; and ***tellement*** with all three.

Tant and ***tellement*** can also precede ***de*** and a noun.

Il fait si chaud aujourd'hui!
It is so hot today!

Il a tant parlé! Il a tellement travaillé!
He talked so much! He worked so much!

Il y a tellement de monde et tant de bruit!
There is such a crowd and so much noise!

By exception, ***si*** may be used instead of ***tellement*** to modify verbal expressions containing a noun (see §3H), like ***avoir faim, avoir froid, avoir peur,*** and ***avoir soif.*** (See §205 and §215 for use of ***très*** and ***trop*** with these expressions.)

Tant, si, and ***tellement*** are frequently correlated with ***que*** and a subordinate clause.

Il est tellement (or: si) riche qu'il ne sait que faire de son argent.
He is so rich that he does not know what to do with his money.

J'ai tant (or: tellement) couru que je suis tout essoufflé.
I ran so much that I am completely out of breath.

In this type of sentence where the subordinate clause expresses a consequence of the main clause, a personal pronoun is frequently used to recall the idea of the main clause. The personal pronoun immediately precedes the subordinate verb.

Il a tellement (or: tant) de soucis qu'il en est tombé malade.
He has so many worries that he became ill (because of it).

Il est si riche qu'il en perd la tête.
He is so rich that he is losing his mind (on account of it).

214. Enough, rather, quite.

Assez means *enough, rather, quite.* It can be used before an adjective, an adverb, or ***de*** and a noun (if the noun is part of a verbal expression such as ***avoir besoin, avoir faim, avoir froid,*** then ***assez*** may modify it directly, without ***de***). ***Assez*** may also be used after a verb in a simple tense (between the auxiliary and the past participle in a compound tense).

J'avais assez faim mais j'ai assez mangé. Ce poulet était assez bon.
I was reather hungry but I have eaten enough. This chicken was quite good.

Je travaille assez, je réussirai assez facilement.
I work enough, I shall succeed easily enough.

See §215B for comments on infinitive complements with ***assez*** and ***trop***. *Rather* and *quite* can also be translated ***plutôt*** and ***tout à fait***, respectively.

Pas mal, originally negative, is now quite frequently used without ***ne*** to mean *enough, rather, quite, much, a lot, a good deal, a lot of, a good deal of,* etc., but should be restricted to conversation or very informal language. It can be used by itself with the value of an adjective or an adverb; or it can precede an adjective, an adverb, or ***de*** and a noun; or it can follow a verb in a simple or a compound tense, or follow the auxiliary in a compound tense.

Il pleut pas mal dans cette région.
It rains quite a bit in this region.

Ce costume est pas mal.
This suit is quite nice-looking.

J'ai pas mal de choses à faire.
I have a good deal of things to do.

Nous sommes pas mal nombreux.
There are rather a good many of us.

Nous avons pas mal voyagé. Nous avons voyagé pas mal.
We traveled quite a bit.

215. Too, too much, too many, too long, too far, too often.

A. ***Trop*** can be used before an adjective, an adverb, or ***de*** and a noun (if the noun is part of a verbal expression such as ***avoir besoin, avoir faim, avoir froid,*** then ***trop*** may modify it directly, without ***de***). ***trop*** can also be used after a verb in a simple tense (after the auxiliary in a compound tense).

Vous attendez trop. Vous avez trop attendu.
You are waiting too long. You waited too long.

Vous êtes trop bavard, vous parlez trop vite et trop souvent.
You are too talkative, you talk too fast and too often.

Il y a trop de choses à voir.
There are too many things to see.

J'ai trop faim. J'ai trop besoin de manger.
I am too hungry. I am too much in need of food.

B. ***Trop*** (and ***assez*** as well) often call for a conclusion by an infinitive. The preposition *to* of the English infinitive must be translated ***pour***, provided that the infinitive in question is not a mere modifier of the word modified by ***trop*** or ***assez***.

C'est trop beau pour être vrai.
It is too good to be true.

J'ai assez d'argent pour payer mon billet.
I have enough money to pay for my ticket.

but: J'ai trop peur d'être en retard.
I am too afraid of being late.

216. One too many, once too often, in excess, one more, one less

En trop, de trop, en plus, de plus, en moins, and ***de moins*** can be used as modifiers of a noun or pronoun, if the noun or pronoun is indefinite or follows a number. They can also be used as modifiers of numbers.

Il n'y a rien de trop.
There is nothing extra (in excess, unnecessary).

J'ai une carte de trop dans mon jeu.
I have one card too many in my hand.

Il fallait écrire un paragraphe de plus.
You should have written one more paragraph.

Hier j'avais huit disques; j'en ai deux de moins aujourd'hui.
Yesterday I had eight records; I have two less today.

Le joueur du far-west est mort. Il avait triché une fois de trop.
The frontier gambler is dead. He had cheated once too often.

217. *Many other . . .; many others.*

Many other . . . (adjective), *many others* (pronoun), can be rendered by ***beaucoup d'autres*** . . . (adj.), ***beaucoup d'autres*** (pron.), or ***bien d'autres . . ., bien d'autres***. This is the only instance in which ***bien*** is used with ***de*** and no article (see §206), possessive, or demonstrative (see §218).

218. *Most, most of, lots of, many.*

La plupart and ***bien*** can be used with ***des*** and a noun, a possessive pronoun, or an adjective used as a noun.

La plupart des gens.
Most people.

Tu as encore tous tes livres? Moi, j'ai vendu la plupart des miens.
You still have all your books? *I* have sold most of mine.

La plupart des jeunes ont des voitures de nos jours.
Most young people own cars nowadays.

La plupart and ***bien*** can also be used with ***de*** and either a possessive adjective or a demonstrative adjective before a noun; also with a demonstrative pronoun.

La plupart de ces livres. La plupart de vos livres. La plupart de ceux-ci.
Most of these books. Most of your books. Most of these.

Bien des livres. Bien de vos livres. Bien de ceux-là.
Many of these books. Many of your books. Many of those.

Most of and *many of* before a personal pronoun are translated ***la plupart d'entre, beaucoup d'entre*** with a disjunctive personal pronoun. As subjects, they command verbs in the third person plural, even when the personal pronoun is ***nous*** or ***vous***. ***D'entre*** is generally used before a disjunctive personal pronoun after indefinite expressions of quantity and also after numbers (see §60F and §142).

La plupart d'entre eux pensent déjà aux vacances.
Most of them are already thinking of the holidays.

Beaucoup d'entre nous sont des nouveaux.
Many of us are freshmen (newcomers).

La moitié d'entre eux partiront le matin.
Half of them will leave in the morning.

Trois d'entre vous resteront après les autres.
Three of you will remain after the others.

219. All, completely, entirely. However, no matter how.

Tout (§43, notes 2 and 3), ***quelque*** (§41D), and ***si, pour*** (§176) are often used in correlation with ***que***. They modify an adjective or an adverb, and they mean *however, no matter how*.

Tout riche qu'elle est, elle manque de goût.
However rich she is, she lacks good taste.

Quelque juste que soit votre décision, elle ne me satisfait pas.
No matter how fair your decision may be, it does not satisfy me.

Completely and *entirely* are ordinary adverbs: ***complètement, entièrement***. They may also be expressed as ***tout***.

Tes coudes sont tout troués.
Your elbows are completely worn out (worn through).

220. Little, few. A little, a few.

Peu (*little*), ***un peu*** (*a little*) may be used to modify a verb, even if it is a verbal expression containing a noun.

Il travaille peu. Il réfléchit un peu.
He works little. He thinks a little.

J'ai eu un peu peur, et j'ai un peu soif.
I got scared a little, and I am a little thirsty.

Intensified forms may be used: ***un petit peu*** (*a little bit*), ***un tout petit peu*** (*just a little bit*).

J'ai très peu dormi. Je suis un petit peu fatigué.
I slept very little. I am a little bit tired.

All these may also be used to modify adjectives or adverbs.

Il parle un tout petit peu trop vite pour moi.
He speaks just a tiny bit too fast for me.

J'en voudrais un tout petit peu plus.
I'd like to have just a little bit more.

Note that ***peu*** (*little*) is hardly ever used to modify an adjective or an adverb: the meaning is better expressed with ***pas très*** (*not very*). Two expressions, however, make use of ***peu***:

peu probable	unlikely, showing little probability or likelihood
peu vraisemblable	unlikely, showing little verisimilitude or reality

Peu, however, is frequently used with verbs in cases where English usage prefers a negative turn with *not much.*

Il ne parle pas très bien cette langue.
He does not speak that language very well.

Il étudie peu. Il est peu probable qu'il réussisse.
He doesn't study much. It is unlikely that he will pass.

The meaning "few" occurs only when the French expression is used with ***de*** preceding a noun. Here, the distinction between "few" and "little" appears in the English, not in the French:

Il nous reste peu de temps pour prendre une décision.
We have little time left to make a decision.

Ils avaient peu de voisins.
They had few neighbors.

Voulez-vous un peu de café, un peu de gâteau, un peu de glace, un fruit?
Would you like some coffee, some cake, some ice cream, a fruit?

Note that *few* is expressed as ***peu de***, but that *a few* is ***quelques***.

Il reste peu de gorilles en Afrique.
There are few gorillas left in Africa.

J'ai encore quelques minutes pour acheter mon billet.
I still have a few minutes to purchase my ticket.

221. Scarcely, not much.

Guère is used to form a negation (§203A). It is slightly different from ***pas***, the regular negative adverb, in that it conveys more clearly the notion of quantity. It can be compared to English *not much, scarcely.*

Je n'ai guère le temps de vous expliquer la situation.
I scarcely have the time to explain the situation to you. (apologetic for: I do not have the time)

Je n'ai guère de temps à perdre.
I don't have much time to lose.

Je n'ai guère envie de rire.
I don't feel much like laughing.

222. *Almost, nearly, hardly.*

Presque is an adverb that can follow a simple verb or auxiliary or precede an adjective or another adverb.

Elle dort presque.
She is almost asleep.

La bouteille est presque vide.
The bottle is nearly empty.

Cela se fait presque automatiquement.
That is done almost automatically.

Vous aviez presque manqué le train.
You had nearly missed the train.

In combination with negative words, ***presque*** expresses *hardly*.

Je ne bois presque jamais de vin blanc.
I hardly ever drink white wine.

Tu n'as presque pas mangé!
You hardly ate anything!

Hardly in affirmative contexts is rendered by the expression ***à peine*** (see §200).

J'ai à peine commencé mon roman.
I have hardly begun my novel.

Il nous reste à peine dix minutes.
We have hardly ten minutes left.

Nous étions à peine assis que le film a commencé.
We were hardly seated when the film began.

À peine étions-nous assis que le film a commencé.
Hardly were we seated when the film began.

NOTE: The concept of "near miss" or "close call" is expressed very well by the French idiomatic verb ***faillir***. The use of this verb implies that something unfavorable or unpleasant was narrowly avoided, and that the conclusion is therefore a favorable, fortunate, or pleasant one.

Cat Ballou a failli être pendue!
Cat Ballou was nearly hanged!

Nous avons failli avoir un accident!
We nearly had an accident.

223. *About, some, . . . or so (with numbers).*

Environ is used almost exclusively to modify numbers and expressions of quantity preceded by ***un, une***.

Il nous reste une caisse de bière environ.
We have about one case of beer left.

Et environ un demi paquet de cacahuètes.
And about half a pack of peanuts.

J'ai environ trois cents dollars en poche.
I have some three hundred dollars in my pocket.

Il est parti il y a trois heures environ. Il est parti il y a environ trois heures.
He left about three hours ago.

Il y avait pas mal de monde, deux cents personnes environ.
There were a good many people, two hundred people or so.

À peu près is a common substitute for ***environ***. It also means *about, some, . . . or so, approximately, almost,* or *nearly.* Unlike ***environ***, it can modify verbs, adjectives, and adverbs, although ***presque*** is preferable.

J'ai à peu près fini. Il est à peu près minuit.
I have nearly finished. It is about midnight.

Le réservoir est à peu près vide.
The tank is just about empty.

Presque implies that the mark is almost reached, whereas ***à peu près*** implies that it is either almost reached or slightly passed.

Vers is a preposition that expresses approximation.

Vers midi. Vers dix heures. Vers les six heures.
Around noon. At about ten. At six o'clock or so.

Ça s'est passé vers Pâques.
It happened around Easter.

224. Adverbs of time.

The following is a listing of the most common adverbs of time.

a long time	**longtemps**
a moment ago	**tout à l'heure**
afterward(s)	**après, plus tard**
again	**encore, de nouveau**
all of a sudden	**tout à coup, soudain, brusquement**
already	**déjà**
always	**toujours**
at first	**d'abord**
at last	**enfin, finalement**
at once	**aussitôt, tout de suite, à l'instant**
at the moment	**à présent, maintenant, actuellement**
at times	**quelquefois, parfois**
before	**avant, auparavant**
earlier	**avant, auparavant, plus tôt**
early	**tôt, de bonne heure**

ever	**jamais**
finally	**enfin, finalement**
first	**d'abord, premièrement**
forever	**à jamais, pour toujours**
formerly	**jadis, autrefois**
from now on	**désormais, dorénavant**
from then on	**dès lors**
from time to time	**de temps en temps**
henceforth	**désormais**
in a moment	**tout à l'heure**
in our times	**actuellement, de nos jours**
in the meantime	**entre-temps**
in the old days	**jadis, autrefois**
last, lastly	**enfin, finalement**
later	**plus tard, après**
late	**tard**
long	**longtemps**
more	**encore, davantage**
never	**jamais**
next	**ensuite, puis**
not long ago	**naguère**
now and then	**de temps en temps**
now . . ., now . . .	**tantôt . . ., tantôt . . .**
nowadays	**actuellement, de nos jours, maintenant, aujourd'hui**
now	**à présent, maintenant, actuellement**
often	**souvent**
once	**une fois**
presently	**à présent, maintenant, actuellement**
previously	**auparavant, avant, précédemment**
right away	**tout de suite, à l'instant**
right now, right then	**à l'instant, tout de suite**
seldom	**rarement**
since	**depuis**
sometimes	**parfois, quelquefois**
soon	**bientôt, sitôt**
still	**encore, toujours**
suddenly	**soudain, brusquement**
the day after tomorrow	**après-demain**
the day before yesterday	**avant-hier**
then (next)	**ensuite, puis, lors** (literary)
then (so)	**alors**
today	**aujourd'hui**
tomorrow	**demain**
twice	**deux fois**
when	**quand**
yesterday	**hier**
yet	**encore**

See also §306.

225. *Encore.*

Encore has various meanings conveying ideas of time and quantity (see §201). It is also used with the conjunction ***que*** to introduce a concessive clause (see §177).

Donnez-moi encore une livre de pêches, et encore quatre bananes.
Give me one more pound of peaches, and four more bananas.
Give me another pound of peaches, and another four bananas.

Jouez-moi encore cette mélodie. Jouez-moi cette mélodie (cet air) encore une fois.
Play that melody for me one more time.

Je me suis encore trompé. Je me suis trompé encore une fois.
I made a mistake again. I made another mistake.

Il pleut encore!
It is raining again! It is still raining!

Il pleut encore?
Is it still raining?

J'en ai encore trois.
I have three left. I still have three.

Il fait encore plus chaud aujourd'hui.
It is even warmer today.

Il a travaillé encore moins (plus, mieux, plus mal, etc.) aujourd'hui.
He worked even less (more, better, worse, etc.) today.

Ce n'est pas encore la saison des fraises.
Strawberries are not yet in season.

Elles ne sont pas encore arrivées.
They haven't arrived yet.

Je te donne une minute, et encore!
I give you one minute, and even that! (i.e. and I wonder if that is not too much)

Encore vous! Si encore vous vouliez bien m'aider . . .!
You again! If only you were willing to help me . . .!

Vous le trouverez sans doute chez lui, encore qu'il soit un peu tard.
You will probably find him at home, even though it is a bit late.

Si encore il savait de quoi il s'agit!
If only he knew what it's all about!
If at least he knew what it was all about!

NOTE: "*Encore*" as a call at the end of a performance is expressed in French by the Latin adverb ***"bis."***

226. *First, then.*

D'abord means *first*. ***Tout d'abord*** means *first of all*. These expressions begin balanced sentences in which the second part is introduced by either ***puis, ensuite,*** or ***alors*** and the third part by ***enfin***.

Puis and ***ensuite*** mean *then* in the sense of *next* and should be used when the sequence of actions is smooth, unbroken, unstressed.

Alors means *then* in the sense of *therefore* and should be used to mark opposition, contrast, rupture of sequence, relation of cause to effect, etc., between the actions.

D'abord il a frappé, ensuite il a ouvert la porte. Il a hésité quelques secondes, puis il est entré.
First he knocked, then (next) he opened the door. He hesitated for a few seconds, then he stepped in.

Il a frappé et il a attendu. Il a frappé de nouveau. Rien ne bougeait. Alors il a compris qu'il n'y avait personne.
He knocked and he waited. He knocked again. Nothing stirred. Then he understood than no one was home.

Si personne ne m'écoute, alors je m'en vais.
If no one listens to me, then I am leaving.

Note that ***puis, ensuite, alors,*** and ***enfin*** may be used without the initial ***d'abord.***

What next?, what then?, can be rendered by ***et maintenant?, et après?, et ensuite?, quoi d'autre?, et puis quoi encore!***

Then what?, so what?, can be rendered by ***et alors?, et après?*** All these expressions may constitute insolent remarks.

D'abord tu veux mon livre, ensuite c'est ma chaise, et puis quoi encore!
First you want my book, then it is my chair, and then what!

L'émission n'était pas intéressante, alors je suis allé me coucher.
The (TV) show was not interesting, so I went to bed.

NOTE: ***Donc***, meaning *so*, should be used only went the statement is intended as very argumentative, as in syllogisms. In general, ***alors*** is quite sufficient.

227. *Soon, late, early. Now, then.*

Tôt ou tard translates the phrase *sooner or later*, leaving out the comparative form.

Early can be rendered by ***tôt*** or by ***de bonne heure***. However, the latter cannot show the comparative form *earlier*, whereas ***tôt*** can, as ***plus tôt*** (do not confuse with ***plutôt***, meaning "rather"). The phrase ***au plus tôt*** means "at the earliest." The modified forms of the expression ***de bonne heure*** should be limited to:

de très bonne heure	*very early*
de trop bonne heure	*too early*
d'assez bonne heure	*rather early, quite early*

Nous nous sommes levés tôt (or: de bonne heure).
We got up early.

Il est arrivé plus tôt que prévu.
He arrived earlier than expected.

Certain English expressions with *early* must be rendered by corresponding French adjectives or adjectival phrases or idioms.

Une personne matinale. Une personne qui se lève tôt.
An early riser.

Une visite matinale.
An early (morning) visit.

Le début de la période Gothique.
The early Gothic period.

Au début des années vingt. Dans les premières années vingt.
In the early twenties.

Les primeurs. Les légumes précoces.
Early vegetables.

Late in a given period of time can be translated ***tard*** (especially within the day or the night), or ***vers la fin de . . .*** (with longer periods of time: week, month, year, etc.).

Il est rentré tard hier soir.
He came home late last night.

Vers la fin du 18e siècle. Dans les dernières années du 18e siècle.
Late in the 18th century. In the late 18th century.

Vers la fin du mois de mai. Dans les derniers jours du mois de mai.
Late in May. Late in the month of May.

Les clients de fin de matinée étaient surtout des ménagères.
The late-morning shoppers were mostly housewives.

Revenez nous voir en fin d'après-midi.
Come back to see us in the late afternoon.

Late in relation to a set time is translated ***en retard***, and *early* is then translated ***en avance***.

Hier il était en retard pour le dîner, mais aujourd'hui il est en avance.
Yesterday he was late for supper, but today he is early.

Late, as an adjective, often must be rendered in French by some other corresponding adjective, adjectival expression, or idiomatic phrase.

La dernière représentation. La toute dernière représentation.
The late show. The late performance.

Le tout dernier film. La dernière séance.
The late show. The late movie.

Feu Monsieur X. Feu son père. Feu sa mère. (archaic)
The late Mr. X. His late father. His late mother.

Sitôt (*soon*) and ***sitôt que*** (*as soon as*) are equivalent to ***aussitôt*** and ***aussitôt que***. The latter forms are more common than the former. The phrase ***de sitôt*** (*very soon, in the near future*) appears exclusively with a negative context.

Sitôt qu'il fut à quelques pas, il cria: "Tu ne me reverras pas de sitôt!"
As soon as he was a few steps away, he shouted: "You won't see me again very soon!"

Compare with ***si*** and ***aussi*** (§209A).

Tantôt is generally repeated to create a balanced statement with the meanings *now . . ., then . . .; now . . ., now . . .; here . . ., there . . .; sometimes . . ., sometimes . . .*; etc.

On voyait tantôt des prairies, tantôt des forêts.
We could see now pastures, now forests.

Tantôt de verts pâturages apaisaient ses regards, tantôt il côtoyait des gouffres sans fond.
Now green pastures offered him a peaceful sight, now he walked on the edge of bottomless chasms.

228. *From . . . on, henceforth.*

Désormais and ***dorénavant*** both mean *from now on.* ***À l'avenir*** can mean *from now on, from then on, in the future*, with a point of reference established by the tense of the main verb in the sentence.

Dès lors means only *from then on*, the point of reference being either in the past or in the future.

Dès and ***à partir de*** are prepositions generally used with dates to mean *beginning in . . ., as early as . . ., from . . . on.*

Dès le XVe siècle, la Renaissance . . .
As early as the XVth century, the Renaissance . . .

Lors is rarely used by itself. Besides its use in ***dès lors***, it also serves to form the preposition ***lors de*** (*on the occasion of, at the time of*), and the conjunction ***lorsque*** (*when*—not an interrogative).

229. *Sometimes, formerly, once, twice.*

Quelquefois and ***parfois*** are synonymous. Both mean "sometimes, at times," but ***parfois*** is slightly more vague than ***quelquefois***.

Jadis and ***autrefois*** are also synonymous and mean "formerly, in olden times, long ago."

Once, twice, three times, etc. are translated ***une fois, deux fois, trois fois***, etc.

Il était une fois corresponds to the standard *once upon a time.* Note that the French expressions contains a verb. Thus it actually corresponds to *once upon a time, there was.*

At once has several possible French equivalents:

aussitôt, tout de suite, immédiatement	immediately, right away
d'un seul coup, en une seule fois, en même temps, à la fois	in one single time, all at once, in one sweep

Viens ici tout de suite!
Come here at once!

Aussitôt il s'est mis en colère.
At once he became angry.

J'en ai tué sept d'un seul coup!
I killed seven of them all at once!

230. *Today, nowadays, now, presently.*

Aujourd'hui means *today*. It also means *in this age, nowadays*, even though the expressions ***de nos jours, à l'heure actuelle, actuellement*** render that meaning more accurately.

Actuellement should not be confused with the adverb *actually*, which translates ***vraiment, en réalité, en fait***. ***Actuellement*** translates *presently, now, at this time, at this moment*. The corresponding adjective ***actuel*** means *present, happening now, of today*, and the plural noun ***les actualités*** means *the current events, today's news* and applies also to the "newsreel" of the former movie theater programs.

Maintenant is used to translate *now* when the period considered is rather short.
Now, repeated to create a balanced description, is rendered as ***tantôt*** (see §227).

231. *Déjà, enfin.*

The normal equivalent of ***déjà*** is *already*. ***Déjà*** may be used in conversation as an idiomatic way to ask someone to repeat a statement that he or she has—or pretends to have—forgotten.

Comment vous appelez-vous, déjà?
What did you say your name was again?

Enfin (*finally, at last*) is sometimes used as a kind of interjection to conclude a conversation, with the meaning of *oh, well!, for heaven's sake!* It is also frequently used after ***car*** and after ***mais***, with the general meaning of *after all, in the end* used as a filler.

Mais enfin, que voulez-vous donc?
What is it you want (then)?

Il nous faut de l'essence, car enfin, à quoi sert une voiture sans essence?
We need gasoline, because in the end, what good is a car without gasoline?

232. *Toujours.*

The several possible meanings of ***toujours*** are shown in the following examples.

Il pleut toujours dans ce maudit pays!
It is always (constantly) raining in this darn country!

Ce matin il pleuvait, et regarde, il pleut toujours.
This morning it was raining, and look, it is still raining.

Parle toujours, on verra bien qui a raison.
Keep on talking (all you want), we'll see who is right in the end.

Il raconte toujours la même histoire.
He always (continually, repeatedly) tells the same story.

Ce n'est toujours pas moi qui vais la faire encore, cette corvée, je l'ai déjà faite hier.
It is certainly not I who will do that chore again, I did it yesterday already.

Depuis toujours, les hommes se sont fait la guerre.
Since the beginning of times, men have fought wars against one another.

Mon copain m'a donné ça pour toujours.
My pal gave me that for good (for keeps, forever).

. . .; toujours est-il que vous n'y avez pas pensé.
. . .; one thing is sure, however: you did not think of it.

. . .; toujours est-il que vous devriez faire attention.
. . .; one thing is sure, however: you ought to pay attention.

233. *Jamais.*

Jamais is generally used in a negative sentence containing ***ne***. It may also be used in an affirmative sentence with the meaning of *ever*, or in questions.

Avez-vous jamais entendu parler de Jean 1er?
Have you ever heard about John the First?

Il nous a quittés à jamais.
He has left us for ever.

Si jamais vous le voyez, parlez-lui de moi.
If ever you see him, speak to him about me.

234. *Again, back.*

Again in affirmative contexts corresponds to the French expressions ***encore, encore une fois, une fois de plus, de nouveau*** (see §225). *Again and again* is usually expressed in idiomatic phrases such as ***avoir beau*** and infinitive or an adverbial expression.

Essayez encore une fois.
Try again.

Il a regardé de nouveau dans ses jumelles.
He looked again through his binoculars.

Vous en entendrez parler de nouveau.
You'll hear about it again.

Nous en avons parlé une fois de plus.
We talked about it again.

J'ai eu beau essayer, je n'ai pas eu de chance.
I tried again and again, without luck.
I tried and tried again, without luck.

Il vous répétera l'histoire cent fois (mille fois, sans arrêt).
He will tell you the story again and again (a hundred, a thousand times, etc.).

The most common equivalent of *again* consists of the prefix ***re-*** added to a great variety of verbs. That prefix indicates a repeat of the action of the verb, and may be understood as meaning "again" for a simple iteration, and "back" for a reversal of the action. The prefix is reduced to the single letter ***r*** when attached to a verb beginning with a vowel sound. It is expanded to ***res-*** with verbs beginning with the letter ***s***.

The following are only a few examples of the verbs to which the prefix ***re-*** may be added:

appeler	**rappeler**	to call again, to call back, recall
envoyer	**renvoyer**	to send back, return
faire	**refaire**	to do again, make again, remake
habiller	**rhabiller**	to put clothes back on
naître	**renaître**	to be born again
mettre	**remettre**	to put back
ouvrir	**rouvrir**	to open again, reopen
passer	**repasser**	to pass (by) again, etc. (with ***être***) to iron, to press clothes (with ***avoir***)
prendre	**reprendre**	to take back
sortir	**ressortir**	to go out again; to stand out
voir	**revoir**	to see again

235. Emphasis.

Emphasis can be achieved with most adverbs by placing them at the very beginning or at the very end of the clause in which they belong, or by opening the clause with the emphatic expressions ***c'est . . . que***.

C'est alors que l'accident s'est produit.
It was then that the accident happened.

C'est là que vous avez eu tort.
That's where you made a mistake.

Hier, j'ai rencontré monsieur Smith.
Yesterday, I met Mr. Smith.

Ils se sont trompés, quelquefois.
They made mistakes, sometimes.

Note that the stress expressions ***c'est . . . qui, c'est . . que*** are generally in the present tense. ***C'est*** is not the main verb. It should not be changed to match the tense of the

English sentence. On occasions, however, it may be matched with the simple tense of the French subordinate verb.

C'est en 1769 que Napoléon est né.
It was in 1769 that Napoleon was born.
Qui sera de garde? —C'est vous (qui serez de garde).
Who will be on duty? —It will be you.
Ce sera en l'an 2000 qu'elle prendra sa retraite. (matched tenses)
It's in the year 2000 that she will retire.
but: Ce furent là ses dernières paroles. (main verb)
Those were his last words.

See also §88E.

236. Inversion.

When an English sentence begins with an adverb of negative or restrictive value (*never, neither, nor, hardly, scarcely,* etc.), it is customary to invert the subject and the verb. In French, this type of an inversion is in order only if the sentence or the clause begins with the adverbs ***à peine*** or ***peut-être*** or with the conjunction ***aussi*** (*so, therefore*). See §200.

Je n'ai jamais rien vu d'aussi répugnant.
Jamais je n'ai rien vu d'aussi répugnant.
Never have I seen anything so disgusting.
Il était exténué, aussi voulut-il s'allonger.
He was exhausted, therefore he decided to lie down.

237. Adverbs of place.

The following is a list of the most common adverbs of place.

against	**contre**
anywhere	**n'importe où**
	quelque part
	nulle part
anywhere else	**ailleurs**
	autre part
around	**alentour, autour**
ahead	**avant**
away	**loin**
back, backward	**arrière**
behind	**derrière**
below	**dessous**
by, close by	**près, tout près**
down there	**là-bas, en bas**
elsewhere	**ailleurs**
	autre part
everywhere	**partout**
everywhere else	**partout ailleurs**
far	**loin**
forward	**avant**
here	**ci, ici**
inside	**dedans**
in there, in (it)	**dedans**
near, nearby	**près, tout près**
nowhere	**nulle part**
out, outside	**dehors**
over, on	**dessus**
over there	**là-bas**

somewhere	**quelque part**	under	**dessous**
somewhere else	**ailleurs**	up there	**là-haut, en haut**
there	**là**	where?	**où**
this way, that way	**par ici, par là**		

These adverbs of place may be used alone, but most are found in adverbial phrases (see §306). French adverbial phrases sometimes correspond to English single-word adverbs, and vice-versa. ***Ailleurs*** has a synonym in the expression ***autre part*** (elsewhere, somewhere else). *Somewhere* is matched by ***quelque part***, and *nowhere* by ***nulle part***.

238. Alentour.

Alentour is rarely used by itself. However, it is quite frequently used as a noun in the expressions ***aux alentours de*** (a preposition meaning *around, in the area surrounding*) and ***aux alentours*** (an adverb meaning *in the surrounding area*).

Ne vous éloignez pas, restez aux alentours.
Don't go far, stay in the neighborhood.

239. Ci, là.

The two adverbial particles ***ci*** and ***là*** are used in the formation of demonstrative adjectives (§25) and demonstrative pronouns (§57). ***Ci*** indicates proximity, ***là*** indicates distance. Both are used in the formation of adverbial expressions as well:

ci-après	hereafter
ci-contre	opposite (on the opposite page)
ci-dessous	hereafter, below
ci-dessus	aforesaid, above
ci-devant (rare today)	formerly
là-bas	over there
là-haut	up there
là-dedans	in there, therein
là-dessous	under there, thereunder
là-dessus	on there, thereon, thereupon

- *Here and there* may be translated ***par-ci par-là, de-ci de-là, ici et là, çà et là.***
- *So-so* in reply to *how do you do?* is translated ***comme ci, comme ça.***
- *Here is (are), there is (are)* are described in §288.
- *There* may also be rendered by the pronouns ***y*** and ***en***. See §91, notes 1, 2; §92A.
- ***Par là*** may mean "that way, in that direction." It may also mean "by that, by those words."
- ***De là*** means "from there, thence" and may be replaced by ***d'où*** (see §247).
- ***Là*** is also a regular adverb and may be used alone with the meaning of *there.*

240. *Ailleurs.*

Ailleurs (*elsewhere, somewhere else*)—see also §§31, 41—should not be confused with ***d'ailleurs***, which means "besides, moreover, in addition."

Anywhere else is translated ***ailleurs*** or, with emphasis, ***n'importe où ailleurs***, anytime the meaning sought is "it does not matter where else" (i.e. when the key word is else). This is the case mainly in affirmative contexts.

Mettez cette caisse ailleurs, n'importe où ailleurs.
Put this crate elsewhere, anywhere else.
N'importe où ailleurs, sa conduite aurait été condamnée.
Anywhere else his conduct would have been condemned.

If the context is negative or interrogative, *anywhere else* should be rendered merely by ***ailleurs***

Mettez cette chaise ici, ne la mettez pas ailleurs.
Put this chair here, don't put it anywhere else.
Nous ne vendons pas cet article. Je ne pense pas que vous le trouviez ailleurs non plus.
We do not carry this item. I don't think you'll find it anywhere else either.
Avez-vous fait des voyages ailleurs?
Have you traveled anywhere else?
Peut-on voir des éléphants en liberté ailleurs qu'en Afrique?
Can one see elephants in the wild anywhere else but in Africa?

For *anywhere* without else, see §§31, 37, and 41.

241. *Arrière.*

By itself, ***arrière*** is mainly used as a technical term in navigation. Its main use is as a noun in adverbial expressions:

En arrière	backwards, in a backwards direction, toward the back, in the rear
À l'arrière	at the back, in the back, in the rear, behind, behind the others, behind the rest
En arrière de, à l'arrière de (prepositions)	at the back of, behind, in the rear of

The adjective *rear* (or: *hind*) is translated ***arrière*** (invariable), or ***de derrière*** (invariable expression).

Les feux arrière d'une voiture.
The rear lights of a car.
Les pattes de derrière d'un animal.
The hind legs of an animal.

242. *Avant.*

Avant, which is more commonly used as an adverb of time, may also mean *above, further back* and is generally modified by another adverb or serves to form adverbs, prepositions, and conjunctions (see §121, §177). Modified, its meaning may vary.

Les garçons s'avancèrent trop avant (plus avant) dans la forêt.
The boys ventured too far (farther) into the forest.

Ce travail nous a gardés bien avant dans la nuit.
That work kept us until late into the night.

Other expressions:

en avant	ahead, forward
en avant de	ahead of, in front of, before
à l'avant	in front, at the front
à l'avant de	in the front (part) of
aller de l'avant	to go ahead, go forth
(pas) plus avant	(not) farther, (no) further

Avant is also used as a modifier meaning "front, forward," the opposite of "rear, hind" (see §241, above).

Les feux avant, les roues avant d'une voiture.
The front lights (headlights and other), the front wheels of a car.

but: Les pattes de devant d'un animal.
The front legs of an animal.

243. *Autour.*

The adverb ***autour*** is generally modified by ***tout***. It translates *around* in a more general way than the adverb ***alentour***. It is also a preposition.

Il y avait des gens tout autour.
There were people all around. (adverb)

Tout autour de nous, il y avait du monde.
All around us, there were people. (preposition)

244. *Contre.*

The general meaning of ***contre*** is "against." As in English, it may express opposition between two things or indicate the contact of two things. It is generally a preposition.

Ils se sont battus contre leurs ennemis.
They fought against their enemies.

Ils étaient appuyés contre le mur.
They were leaning against the wall.

As an adverb, ***contre*** is rarely used alone. It serves to form adverbial expressions, and in several idiomatic expressions it is used as a noun or as a preposition. It is common also as a prefix denoting opposition.

Envers et contre tout.
In spite of all.

Faire contre mauvaise fortune bon cœur.
To remain optimistic in spite of adversity.

Par contre, . . .
On the other hand, . . .

Le pour et le contre.
The pro and the con. The arguments in favor and those against.

245. *Ici.*

Ici is the opposite of ***là*** (§239). It is used in expressions of time as well as place and also serves in several adverbial and prepositional expressions.

Nous aurons fini d'ici (à) demain. Jusqu'ici, tout va très bien.
We'll be through by tomorrow. Until now (up to now), everything is all right.

Ici, Paul Smith.
Paul Smith speaking (on the telephone).

D'ici peu, il sera promu général.
Before long, he will be promoted to general.

Par ici, s'il vous plaît.
This way, please.

Notre vie est dure, ici-bas.
Our lives are difficult, on this earth (opposed to heaven).

246. *Loin, près.*

Loin (*far*) and ***près*** (*near*) are more often used in adverbial and prepositional expressions than alone with a verb:

de loin	from a distance, by a wide margin, by far
au loin	in the distance, far away
de loin en loin	at great intervals, wide apart (time or place)
de près	from close up, from a short distance
tout près	very close by
loin de	far from, away from
près de	near, close to; nearly, about, almost
plus loin	farther, further

Ne cherchez pas plus loin.
Look no further.

247. *Où.*

Où is an interrogative adverb (§204), as well as a relative pronoun (§103). It can be used alone or in combination with certain prepositions: ***d'où*** (*from where, from which, from there*), ***jusqu'où*** (*how far, to what extent*), ***par où*** (*which way*). It is also found in the expression ***n'importe où*** (*anywhere, no matter where*).

Où en êtes-vous?
How far did you get? (: at what point of it are you?)

Vous êtes arrivé en retard trois fois de suite, d'où je conclus que vous ne faites pas d'effort.
You came in late three times in a row, from which I conclude that you are not making an effort.

D'où venez-vous? Par où êtes-vous passés? —Nous venons de Venise. Nous sommes passés par la Suisse.
Where are you coming from? Which way did you travel? —We are coming from Venice. We traveled through Switzerland.

Jusqu'où comptez-vous aller? —Jusqu'en Espagne.
How far do you intend to go? —As far as Spain.

248. *Partout.*

Partout is used only as an adverb. It means "all over, everywhere, throughout." ***Partout où*** means "wherever, everywhere that."

Partout où vous irez, je vous suivrai.
Everywhere (or: wherever) you go, I'll follow you.

When the English expressions ***all over, everywhere, throughout*** are followed by names of places, it is preferable not to use ***partout***. The expressions ***dans tout, à travers tout, sur tout, de tout,***, followed by the name of the place, may be used instead of ***partout***.

Il semble qu'il y ait un sentiment de déception dans tout le pays.
There seems to be a feeling of disappointment throughout the country.

Une vague de froid s'est étendue sur tout le nord des États-Unis.
A cold wave has spread all over the north of the United States.

On sent maintenant les effets de la sécheresse dans toute la Californie.
The drought is now felt everywhere in California.

INTERJECTIONS

249. Definition.

An interjection is a word or group of words used as a kind of exclamation to express a feeling or emotion. An interjection has no grammatical function in the sentence. The words and the arrangements of letters representing the various noises, and the sounds and cries made by animals, are also interjections.

250. Main interjections.

Many interjections that were of current usage at a certain period of time may no longer be in use today. For that reason, only the main interjections that have more permanence are presented in the following list.

Pain or grief

Aïe!	Ouch!
Hélas!	Alas!
Ah!	Ah!

Disgust

Pouah!	Yuk! Yeccch!

Relief

Ouf!	Whew!

Surprise

Hein! (Hein?)	Well! (What?)
Ah! Oh!	Ah! Oh!
Eh! Eh bien!	Well! Well now!
Ça alors!	Well, well!
Ça par exemple!	Well, I'll be . . .!
Ho!	Yi!

Scorn, disapproval

Allons, allons!	There, there! Now, now!
Stupide! Ridicule!	Nonsense! Ridiculous!
Hou!	Boo!

Approval, admiration, encouragement

Allez! Allez, les . . . (name)!	Come on, come on! Go . . . (team name)
Allez! Allez . . . (name)!	&Kmn. Go . . . (player's name)
Bien! Très bien! Ah!	Ok! All right! Great! Very good! Ah!
Bravo! (applause)	Bravo! Hurray!
Hip hip hip hourra!	Hip hip hurrah!
Bis!	Encore!
Vive . . .!	Long live . . .! Hurray for . . .!

Doubt, embarrassment, impatience

Ah, oui?	Oh, yeah?
Allons!	Come on! Come now!
Allez!	Come on! Come now!
Heu . . . (hesitation)	Er . . .
Hum!	Ahem!
Ah!	Ah!
Enfin!	Come on, now!
Ouste! Allez, ouste!	Out! Get out! Get out at once!
Suffit! Ça suffit!	Cut it out! Enough! Quit it!
Zut! Zut alors!	Oops! Darn! Shoot! etc.

Insult

Espèce de . . .!	You . . .!

Strong surprise

Sapristi! Tonnerre!	Darn it! I'll be . . .!
Tonnerre de Brest!	Doggonit! etc.
Mince! Mince alors!	Shoot! Darn! I'll be . . .!

Calls, greetings

Hé! Hé là-bas!	Ho! Hey! You there!
Salut!	Hi! Hello!
Allo . . . (telephone)	Hello . . .
Bonjour.	Good morning. Good day.
Bonsoir	Good evening. Good night.
Au revoir.	Good bye.
Adieu!	Farewell!
À . . .	See you . . . (date, time)
Au secours!	Help!
Au feu!	Fire!
Au voleur!	Thief!
À l'assassin!	Murder!
Écoute! Écoutez!	Listen! There!
Attention!	Watch out! Careful! Look out!
Arrête! Arrêtez!	Stop! Hold it! Wait!
Arrêtez-le!	Stop him!

Chut!	Silence! Hush! Quiet!
Silence! La paix!	Silence! Quiet! Keep quiet!
Doucement!	Easy! Steady! Slowly!

Animal noises and cries:

English	French	verb	sound
birds	oiseaux	chanter	cui-cui
cat	chat	miauler	miaou
cow	vache	meugler, beugler	meuh
dog	chien	aboyer	ouaf
dog, wolf	chien, loup	hurler	houhouhou . . .
donkey	âne	braire	hi-han
duck	canard	*none*	couin couin
frog	grenouille	croasser	croâ
goat	chèvre	bêler	bée or bêêê
hen	poule	caqueter	cot cot cot . . .
horse	cheval	hennir	*none*
owl	hibou, chouette	ululer	hou-hou . . .
pig	cochon	grogner	groin, groin . . .
rooster	coq	chanter	cocorico
sheep	mouton	bêler	bée or bêêê
sparrows	moineaux	gazouiller	cui-cui
turkey	dindon	glousser	glouglou

Miscellaneous sounds and noises:

clock	montre, horloge, pendule	tic-tac
knock on the door	frapper à la porte	toc toc toc
a gunshot	un coup de feu	pan
a paddling	une fessée	pan-pan
a kiss	un baiser, une bise	cuic
strangle, hang	étrangler, pendre	couic
break	casser, briser	crac
thunder, explosion	tonnerre, explosion	boum, badaboum
picture taking	photographier	clic, clic-clac
fall in water	tomber dans l'eau	plouf

VERBS

251. Verb groups.

The French verbs are divided into three major groups, recognizable from their infinitive endings and the type of conjugation they follow:

Group 1: infinitife ending in ***-er***.

Group 2: infinitive ending in ***-ir***, with present participle in ***-issant***.

Group 3: infinitive ending in ***-ir***, with present participle in ***-ant***; and infinitive ending in ***-re***.

chanter	first group
finir (finissant)	second group
sentir (sentant)	third group
répondre	third group

The part of the verb that precedes the ending is called the stem.

Regular verbs (in any of the three groups) have only one basic stem, found in the infinitive form. Irregular verbs have several differents stems.

252. Moods and tenses.

There are six moods in the French conjugation: ***indicative, subjunctive, conditional, imperative, participle***, and ***infinitive***. Each mood represents an aspect of the verb, but does not in any way tell about the timing of what is expressed in the verb. The "aspect" of a mood is described in its name:

Indicative is the mood of verbs used to "indicate" facts, actions, events, etc.

Subjunctive is the mood of verbs having an "underlying" (sub) "connection" (junctive) with something previously stated, particularly a feeling or an emotion.

Conditional is the mood of verbs tied to a condition.

Imperative is the mood of verbs expressing commands, wishes, and the like.

Participle is the mood of verbs that take part in two natures: at times verbs, at times adjectives.

Infinitive is the mood of verbs whose form has a fixed, invariable ending.

The timing is given by the tenses, which cover the three general areas of past, present, and future. In addition, the tenses are divided by form into two categories: the simple tenses and the compound tenses. A simple tense consists of one single word. A compound tense is composed of an *auxiliary* and a *past participle.* To each simple tense corresponds a compound tense. The most common of the moods, the indicative, contains a total of eight tenses: four simple and four compound, in the following manner:

INDICATIVE	
4 simple tenses (one word)	**4 compound tenses (auxiliary + past participle)**
présent *present*	passé composé *compound past*
imparfait *imperfect*	plus-que-parfait *pluperfect/past perfect*
futur *future*	futur antérieur *future anterior/future perfect*
passé simple *simple past*	passé antérieur *past anterior/past perfect*

As mentioned earlier, each compound tense corresponds to a simple tense: the *auxiliary* of the compound tense is in the corresponding simple tense (on the same line in the preceding table). Thus the following correspondences are noticeable in the indicative mood:

Présent is the tense of the auxiliary in the ***passé composé.***
Imparfait is the tense of the auxiliary in the ***plus-que-parfait.***
Futur is the tense of the auxiliary in the ***futur antérieur.***
Passé simple is the tense of the auxiliary in the ***passé antérieur.***

There are only four tenses in the ***subjunctive*** mood (the top four in the preceding table). Thus the table of the tenses in the subjunctive is as follows:

SUBJUNCTIVE	
2 simple tenses (one word)	**2 compound tenses (auxiliary + past participle)**
présent	passé composé
imparfait	plus-que-parfait

Each of the other moods has only two tenses: a simple one, the present tense, and its corresponding compound tense, the ***passé composé***.

CONDITIONAL	
1 simple tense (one word)	**1 compound tense (auxiliary + past participle)**
présent	passé composé

IMPERATIVE	
1 simple tense (one word)	**1 compound tense (auxiliary + past participle)**
présent	passé composé

INFINITIVE	
1 simple tense (one word)	**1 compound tense (auxiliary + past participle)**
présent	passé composé

PARTICIPLE*	
1 simple tense (one word)	**1 compound tense (auxiliary + past participle)**
présent	passé composé

*The participle has a second simple tense, the common past participle or "participe passé". It is in fact the participle portion of the passé composé, used without the auxiliary. It is not shown in the table as a separate simple tense because its function is to accompany the auxiliaries ***être*** and ***avoir*** in the formation of all compound tenses. Used alone, it is mainly an adjective, although its function as a verb must not to be overlooked (see §271B).

253. Endings.

The following table shows the endings of the various persons, tenses, and moods of the French verb system.

For each of the simple tenses of each mood, the *stem* of the verb and its *ending* indicate the person, the tense, and the mood in which the verb is being used.

There are six endings for each simple tense of the indicative, subjunctive, and conditional moods. They indicate if the verb is in the first, second, or third person singular or in the first, second, or third person plural.

There are three endings for the present imperative: second person singular, and first and second persons plural.

Infinitive and participle tenses have no personal endings. They are nonfinite forms. Their endings vary only according to the group to which they belong.

In some tenses, the endings of group 1 verbs may be different from those of the verbs in groups 2 and 3.

	person					
	singular			plural		
	1st	2nd	3rd	1st	2nd	3rd
tense	**INDICATIVE mood**					
présent, gr. 1	-e	-es	-e	-ons	-ez	-ent
group 2	-is	-is	-it	-issons	-issez	-issent
group 3	-s(x)	-s(x)	-t(d)	-ons	-ez	-ent
imparfait	-ais	-ais	-ait	-ions	-iez	-aient
futur	-ai	-as	-a	-ons	-ez	-ont
passé simple, gr. 1	-ai	-as	-a	-âmes	-âtes	-èrent
group 2	-is	-is	-it	-îmes	-îtes	-irent
group 3	-is	-is	-it	-îmes	-îtes	-irent
	-us	-us	-ut	-ûmes	-ûtes	-urent

tense	**SUBJUNCTIVE mood**					
présent	-e	-es	-e	-ions	-iez	-ent
imparfait, gr. 1	-sse	-sses	-ât	-ssions	-ssiez	-ssent
group 2	-sse	-sses	-ît	-ssions	-ssiez	-ssent
group 3	-sse	-sses	-ît	-ssions	-ssiez	-ssent
	-sse	-sses	-ût	-ssions	-ssiez	-ssent

tense	**CONDITIONAL mood**					
présent	-ais	-ais	-ait	-ions	-iez	-aient

tense	**IMPERATIVE mood**		
présent, gr. 1	-e (es)	-ons	-ez
groups 2 and 3	-s	-ons	-ez

tense	PARTICIPLE	
présent	group 1 group 2 group 3	-ant -issant -ant
passé	group 1 group 2 group 3	-é -i -i or -u or irregular

tense	INFINITIVE	
présent	group 1 group 2 group 3	-er -ir -ir -re

For each of the compound tenses of each mood, it is necessary to know the simple tense of ***avoir*** (§255) or ***être*** (§256). Each of these two verbs is an *auxiliary*, used in the formation of half of the complete conjugation system.

254. Stem, principal parts.

The endings presented in the preceding table are to be added to a suitable *stem.*

In order to obtain the suitable stem for a given tense, certain basic forms must be known. They may be called *principal parts* because they contain the stems needed for the conjugation of all the tenses of a given verb, in all the moods and persons. The principal parts are:

A. The infinitive
B. The present participle
C. The past participle
D. The present indicative
E. The passé simple indicative

(In the list of irregular verbs of §258, only these parts are given, since they are sufficient to form the rest of the conjugation of each.)

A. The *infinitive* provides the stem needed for the formation of the *future* indicative and the *present conditional.* The stem is the infinitive up to and including the last ***r*** it contains.

chanter	the stem is	chanter-
prendre	the stem is	prendr-

To form the future or the present conditional, the endings of those two tenses are added to the stems thus obtained.

chanter-	future:	je chanter-ai tu chanter-as il chanter-a etc.
prendr-	present conditional:	je prendr-ais tu prendr-ais il prendr-ait etc.

Several verbs have irregular stems for the formation of the future and the present conditional. Such irregular stems are given in parentheses immediately after the infinitive in the list of irregular verbs (§258).

aller (ir-)	future	j'ir-ai tu ir-as il ir-a nous ir-ons etc.

B. The *present participle* does not provide any stem, but gives an indication of the group of the verb in question (-issant / -ant). It also is identical in stem with the first person plural of the present indicative for all verbs except ***être*** and ***savoir***.

finir	present participle: present indicative:	finissant nous finissons vous finissez
prendre	present participle: present indicative:	prenant nous prenons vous prenez
vouloir	present participle: present indicative:	voulant nous voulons vous voulez

C. The *past participle* is used in the formation of all the *compound tenses*, as well as in the formation of the *passive voice*.

finir	past participle:	fini
	passé composé:	ils ont fini
	past subjunctive:	que j'aie fini
	past conditional:	tu aurais fini
	past infinitive:	avoir fini
	passive voice (future tense):	il sera fini

D. The *present indicative* provides the stems for three other tenses:

1) The imperative, formed by taking from the present indicative the three persons that it is made of: the second person singular and the first and second persons plural. No subject pronouns are used in the imperative.

prendre (to take)

present indicative:	je prends	nous prenons
	tu prends	vous prenez
	il prend	ils prennent
imperative:	prends, prenons, prenez	

aller (to go)

present indicative:	je vais	nous allons
	tu vas (note 1)	vous allez
	il va	ils vont
imperative:	va, allons, allez	

écouter (to listen)

present indicative:	j'écoute	nous écoutons
	tu écoutes (note 1)	vous écoutez
	il écoute	ils écoutent
imperative:	écoute, écoutons, écoutez	

NOTES: 1) If the second person singular ends in ***-es***, then the final ***s*** is dropped, unless ***y*** or ***en*** follows. The irregular second person singular of ***aller (tu vas)*** follows the same rule (: ***va***).

2) A few verbs borrow the three imperative forms from the subjunctive. Among those are ***être, avoir, pouvoir, savoir,*** and ***vouloir***.

2) The imperfect indicative, formed from the stem provided by the first person plural after dropping the ending ***-ons*** (exception: ***être***).

prendre (to take)

present indicative:	nous prenons	
imperfect indicative:	je prenais	nous prenions
	tu prenais	vous preniez
	il prenait	ils prenaient

boire (to drink)

present indicative:	nous buvons	
imperfect indicative:	je buvais	nous buvions
	tu buvais	vous buviez
	il buvait	ils buvaient

3) The present subjunctive, formed with the stem obtained by dropping ***-ent*** from the third person plural.

There are several exceptions. In each case, the irregular stem to be used is indicated in the parentheses immediately after the third person plural in the list of irregular verbs (§258).

• When the first and second persons plural of the present indicative (nous, vous) have a common stem different from the stems of the other persons in the same tense, that same common stem will also be used in the first and second persons plural of the present subjunctive. The verbs in which this occurs are marked with a bullet (•) in the listing of §258.

attendre (to wait)

present indicative:	j'attends	nous attendons
	tu attends	vous attendez
	il attend	ils attendent
present subjunctive:	que j'attende	que nous attendions
	que tu attendes	que vous attendiez
	qu'il attende	qu'ils attendent

devoir (to have to)

present indicative:	je dois	nous *dev*ons
	tu dois	vous *dev*ez
	il doit	ils doivent•
present subjunctive:	que je doive	que nous *dev*ions
	que tu doives	que vous *dev*iez
	qu'il doive	qu'ils doivent

E. The *passé simple* provides the stem needed for the formation of the *imperfect subjunctive*. The stem is obtained by dropping the final ***t*** (if any) from the third person singular.

aller	passé simple (3rd person singular):	il alla
	stem for the imperfect subjunctive:	***alla-***
venir	passé simple (3rd person singular):	il vint
	stem for the imperfect sunjunctive:	***vin-***
prendre	passé simple (3rd person singular):	il prit
	stem for the imperfect subjunctive:	***pri-***
vouloir	passé simple (3rd person singular):	il voulut
	stem for the imperfect subjunctive:	***voulu-***

The endings of the imperfect subjunctive (see table of endings in §253) are then added to the stems thus obtained:

stem ***alla-***	que j'allasse	que nous allassions
	que tu allasses	que vous allassiez
	qu'il allât	qu'ils allassent
stem ***vin-***	que je vinsse	que nous vinssions
	que tu vinsses	que vous vinssiez
	qu'il vînt	qu'ils vinssent
stem ***pri-***	que je prisse	que nous prissions
	que tu prisses	que vous prissiez
	qu'il prît	qu'ils prissent
stem ***voulu-***	que je voulusse	que nous voulussions
	que tu voulusses	que vous voulussiez
	qu'il voulût	qu'ils voulussent

F. *Summary.* On the next two pages, the letters and numbers in parentheses refer to the above paragraphs (§254A-E), and the boxes contain the essential endings necessary to form the other simple tenses (see §253).

<u>Diagram of principal parts:</u>

futur

-ai	-ons
-as	-ez
-a	-ont

conditionnel, imparfait

-ais	-ions
-ais	-iez
-ait	-aient

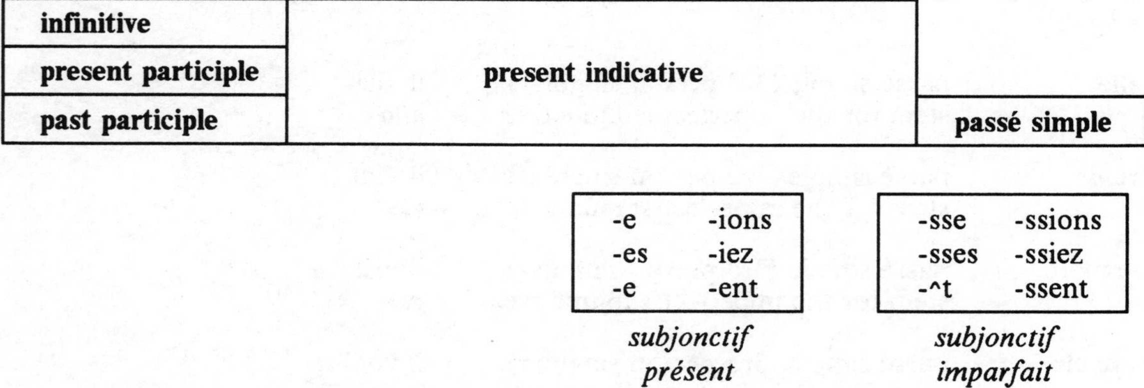

subjonctif présent

subjonctif imparfait

Principal parts of a regular verb of the first group:

futur		*conditionnel, imparfait*	
-ai	-ons	-ais	-ions
-as	-ez	-ais	-iez
-a	-ont	-ait	-aient

chanter (A)	**je chante**	**nous chantons (D1, D2)**	
chantant (B)	**tu chantes (D1)**	**vous chantez (D1)**	
chanté (C)	**il chante**	**ils chantent (D3)**	**il chanta (E)**

subjonctif présent		*subjonctif imparfait*	
-e	-ions	-sse	-ssions
-es	-iez	-sses	-ssiez
-e	-ent	-ât	-ssent

Principal parts of a regular verb of the second group:

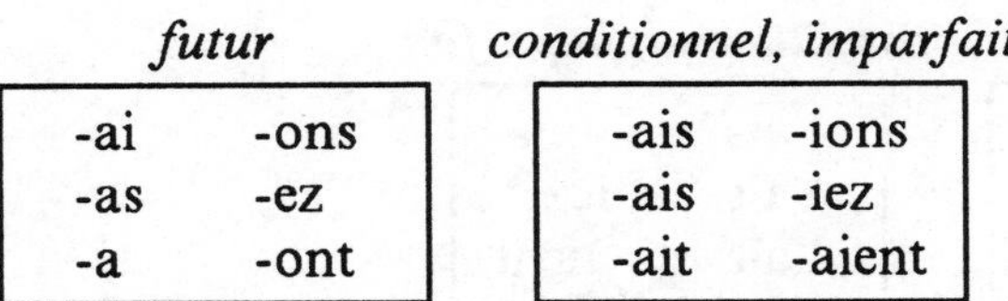

futur		*conditionnel, imparfait*	
-ai	-ons	-ais	-ions
-as	-ez	-ais	-iez
-a	-ont	-ait	-aient

finir (A)	**je finis**	**nous finissons (D1, D2)**	
finissant (B)	**tu finis (D1)**	**vous finissez (D1)**	
fini (C)	**il finit**	**ils finissent (D3)**	**il finit (E)**

subjonctif présent		*subjonctif imparfait*	
-e	-ions	-sse	-ssions
-es	-iez	-sses	-ssiez
-e	-ent	-ît	-ssent

Principal parts of a regular verb of the third group:

futur	
-ai	-ons
-as	-ez
-a	-ont

conditionnel, imparfait	
-ais	-ions
-ais	-iez
-ait	-aient

vendre (A)	**je vends**	**nous vendons (D1, D2)**	
vendant (B)	**tu vends (D1)**	**vous vendez (D1)**	
vendu (C)	**il vend**	**ils vendent (D3)**	**il vendit (E)**

subjonctif présent	
-e	-ions
-es	-iez
-e	-ent

subjonctif imparfait	
-sse	-ssions
-sses	-ssiez
-ît	-ssent

Principal parts of an irregular verb of the third group:

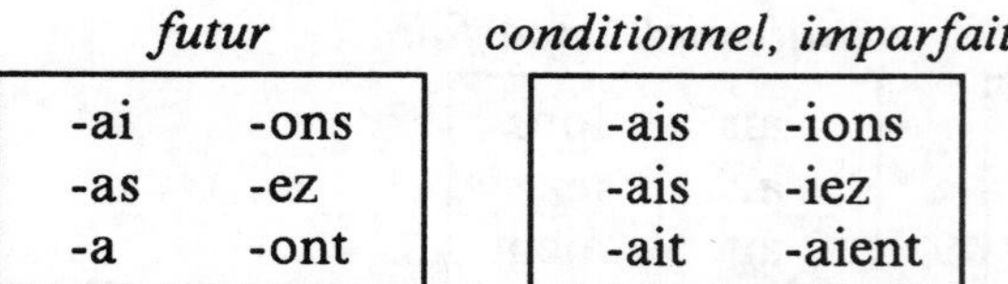

futur	
-ai	-ons
-as	-ez
-a	-ont

conditionnel, imparfait	
-ais	-ions
-ais	-iez
-ait	-aient

mourir (mourr-)(A)	**je meurs**	**nous mourons (D1, D2)**	
mourant (B)	**tu meurs (D1)**	**vous mourez (D1)**	
mort (C)	**il meurt**	**ils meurent• (D3)**	**il mourut (E)**

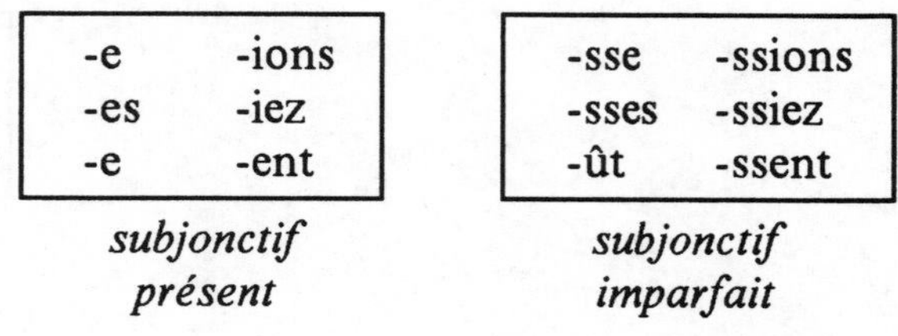

subjonctif présent	
-e	-ions
-es	-iez
-e	-ent

subjonctif imparfait	
-sse	-ssions
-sses	-ssiez
-ût	-ssent

255. *To be: être.*

INDICATIVE	
présent	***passé composé***
je suis tu es il est nous sommes vous êtes ils sont	j'ai été tu as été il a été nous avons été vous avez été ils ont été
imparfait	***plus-que-parfait***
j'étais tu étais il était nous étions vous étiez ils étaient	j'avais été tu avais été il avait été nous avions été vous aviez été ils avaient été
futur	***futur antérieur***
je serai tu seras il sera nous serons vous serez ils seront	j'aurai été tu auras été il aura été nous aurons été vous aurez été ils auront été
passé simple	***passé antérieur***
je fus tu fus il fut nous fûmes vous fûtes ils furent	j'eus été tu eus été il eut été nous eûmes été vous eûtes été ils eurent été

SUBJUNCTIVE	
présent	***passé composé***
que je sois que tu sois qu'il soit que nous soyons que vous soyez qu'ils soient	que j'aie été que tu aies été qu'il ait été que nous ayons été que vous ayez été qu'ils aient été
imparfait	***plus-que-parfait***
que je fusse que tu fusses qu'il fût que nous fussions que vous fussiez qu'ils fussent	que j'eusse été que tu eusses été qu'il eût été que nous eussions été que vous eussiez été qu'ils eussent été

CONDITIONAL	
présent	***passé composé***
je serais tu serais il serait nous serions vous seriez ils seraient	j'aurais été tu aurais été il aurait été nous aurions été vous auriez été ils auraient été

IMPERATIVE	
présent	***passé composé***
sois soyons soyez	aie été ayons été ayez été

PARTICIPLE	
présent	***passé composé***
étant	ayant été

INFINITIVE	
présent	***passé composé***
être	avoir été

256. To have: avoir.

INDICATIVE	
présent	***passé composé***
j'ai tu as il a nous avons vous avez ils ont	j'ai eu tu as eu il a eu nous avons eu vous avez eu ils ont eu
imparfait	***plus-que-parfait***
j'avais tu avais il avait nous avions vous aviez ils avaient	j'avais eu tu avais eu il avait eu nous avions eu vous aviez eu ils avaient eu
futur	***futur antérieur***
j'aurai tu auras il aura nous aurons vous aurez ils auront	j'aurai eu tu auras eu il aura eu nous aurons eu vous aurez eu ils auront eu
passé simple	***passé antérieur***
j'eus tu eus il eut nous eûmes vous eûtes ils eurent	j'eus eu tu eus eu il eut eu nous eûmes eu vous eûtes eu ils eurent eu

SUBJUNCTIVE	
présent	***passé composé***
que j'aie que tu aies qu'il ait que nous ayons que vous ayez qu'ils aient	que j'aie eu que tu aies eu qu'il ait eu que nous ayons eu que vous ayez eu qu'ils aient eu
imparfait	***plus-que-parfait***
que j'eusse que tu eusses qu'il eût que nous eussions que vous eussiez qu'ils eussent	que j'eusse eu que tu eusses eu qu'il eût eu que nous eussions eu que vous eussiez eu qu'ils eussent eu

CONDITIONAL	
présent	***passé composé***
j'aurais tu aurais il aurait nous aurions vous auriez ils auraient	j'aurais eu tu aurais eu il aurait eu nous aurions eu vous auriez eu ils auraient eu

IMPERATIVE	
présent	***passé composé***
aie ayons ayez	aie eu ayons eu ayez eu

PARTICIPLE	
présent	***passé composé***
ayant	ayant eu

INFINITIVE	
présent	***passé composé***
avoir	avoir eu

257. *Principal parts of avoir and être.*

avoir (aur-)	j'ai	nous avons	
ayant	tu as	vous avez	
eu	il a	ils ont	il eut

present subjunctive:		
	que j'aie	que nous ayons
	que tu aies	que vous ayez
	qu'il ait	qu'ils aient

imperative (borrowed from the subjunctive): aie, ayons, ayez

être (ser-)	je suis	nous sommes (ét-)	
étant	tu es	vous êtes	
été	il est	ils sont	il fut

present subjunctive:		
	que je sois	que nous soyons
	que tu sois	que vous soyez
	qu'il soit	qu'ils soient

imperative (borrowed from the subjunctive): sois, soyons, soyez

258. *Principal parts of major irregular verbs.*

See §254 for an explanation.

infinitive / present participle / past participle	present indicative		passé simple (il)
acquérir (acquerr-)	j'acquiers	nous acquérons	
acquérant	tu acquiers	vous acquérez	
acquis	il acquiert	ils acquièrent•	il acquit
aller (ir-)	je vais	nous allons	
allant	tu vas	vous allez	
allé	il va	ils vont (aill-)•	il alla
asseoir (assoir-)	j'assois	nous assoyons	*(See note 1.)*
assoyant	tu assois	vous assoyez	
assis	il assoit	ils assoient•	il assit
asseoir (assiér-)	j'assieds	nous asseyons	*(See note 1.)*
asseyant	tu assieds	vous asseyez	
assis	il assied	ils asseyent	il assit

attendre	j'attends	nous attendons	
attendant	tu attends	vous attendez	
attendu	il attend	ils attendent	il attendit
battre	je bats	nous battons	
battant	tu bats	vous battez	
battu	il bat	ils battent	il battit
boire	je bois	nous buvons	
buvant	tu bois	vous buvez	
bu	il boit	ils boivent•	il but
bouillir	je bous	nous bouillons	
bouillant	tu bous	vous bouillez	
bouilli	il bout	ils bouillent	il bouillit
conclure	je conclus	nous concluons	
concluant	tu conclus	vous concluez	
conclu	il conclut	ils concluent	il conclut
conduire	je conduis	nous conduisons	
conduisant	tu conduis	vous conduisez	
conduit	il conduit	ils conduisent	il conduisit
connaître	je connais	nous connaissons	
connaissant	tu connais	vous connaissez	
connu	il connaît	ils connaissent	il connut
coudre	je couds	nous cousons	
cousant	tu couds	vous cousez	
cousu	il coud	ils cousent	il cousit
courir (courr-)	je cours	nous courons	
courant	tu cours	vous courez	
couru	il court	ils courent	il courut
craindre	je crains	nous craignons	
craignant	tu crains	vous craignez	
craint	il craint	ils craignent	il craignit
croire	je crois	nous croyons	
croyant	tu crois	vous croyez	
cru	il croit	ils croient•	il crut
croître	je croîs	nous croissons	
croissant	tu croîs	vous croissez	
crû	il croît	ils croissent	il crût
cueillir (cueiller-)	je cueille	nous cueillons	
cueillant	tu cueilles	vous cueillez	
cueilli	il cueille	ils cueillent	il cueillit

devoir (devr-)	je dois	nous devons	
devant	tu dois	vous devez	
dû	il doit	ils doivent•	il dut
dire	je dis	nous disons	
disant	tu dis	vous dites (*See note 2.*)	
dit	il dit	ils disent	il dit
dormir	je dors	nous dormons	
dormant	tu dors	vous dormez	
dormi	il dort	ils dorment	il dormit
écrire	j'écris	nous écrivons	
écrivant	tu écris	vous écrivez	
écrit	il écrit	ils écrivent	il écrivit
envoyer (enverr-)	j'envoie	nous envoyons	
envoyant	tu envoies	vous envoyez	
envoyé	il envoie	ils envoient•	il envoya
faire (fer-)	je fais	nous faisons	
faisant	tu fais	vous faites	
fait	il fait	ils font (fass-)	il fit
falloir (faudr-)	. . .	. . . (il fallait)	
. . .	. . .	. . .	
fallu	il faut	. . . (qu'il faille)	il fallut

(**Falloir** is impersonal: only the 3rd person singular exists.)

fuir	je fuis	nous fuyons	
fuyant	tu fuis	vous fuyez	
fui	il fuit	ils fuient•	il fuit
haïr	je hais	nous haïssons	
haïssant	tu hais	vous haïssez	
haï	il hait	ils haïssent	il haït
lire	je lis	nous lisons	
lisant	tu lis	vous lisez	
lu	il lit	ils lisent	il lut
mentir	je mens	nous mentons	
mentant	tu mens	vous mentez	
menti	il ment	ils mentent	il mentit
mettre	je mets	nous mettons	
mettant	tu mets	vous mettez	
mis	il met	ils mettent	il mit

mourir (mourr-)	je meurs	nous mourons	
mourant	tu meurs	vous mourez	
mort	il meurt	ils meurent•	il mourut
mouvoir (mouvr-)	je meus	nous mouvons	
mouvant	tu meus	vous mouvez	
mû	il meut	ils meuvent•	il mut
naître	je nais	nous naissons	
naissant	tu nais	vous naissez	
né	il naît	ils naissent	il naquit
ouvrir	j'ouvre	nous ouvrons	
ouvrant	tu ouvres	vous ouvrez	
ouvert	il ouvre	ils ouvrent	il ouvrit
plaire	je plais	nous plaisons	
plaisant	tu plais	vous plaisez	
plu	il plaît	ils plaisent	il plut
pleuvoir (pleuvr-)	. . .	. . . (il pleuvait)	
pleuvant	. . .	. . .	
plu	il pleut	. . . (qu'il pleuve)	il plut

(**Pleuvoir** is impersonal: only the 3rd person singular exists.)

pouvoir (pourr-)	je peux / je puis	nous pouvons	*(See note 3.)*
pouvant	tu peux	vous pouvez	
pu	il peut	ils peuvent (puiss-)	il put
prendre	je prends	nous prenons	
prenant	tu prends	vous prenez	
pris	il prend	ils prennent•	il prit
recevoir (recevr-)	je reçois	nous recevons	
recevant	tu reçois	vous recevez	
reçu	il reçoit	ils reçoivent•	il reçut
résoudre	je résous	nous résolvons	
résolvant	tu résous	vous résolvez	
résolu	il résout	ils résolvent	il résolut
rire	je ris	nous rions	
riant	tu ris	vous riez	
ri	il rit	ils rient	il rit
savoir (saur-)	je sais	nous savons	
sachant	tu sais	vous savez	
su	il sait	ils savent (sach-)	il sut

(imperative borrowed from the subjunctive: sache, sachons, sachez)

soustraire	je soustrais	nous soustrayons	
soustrayant	tu soustrais	vous soustrayez	
soustrait	il soustrait	ils soustraient	(none)
suffire	je suffis	nous suffisons	
suffisant	tu suffis	vous suffisez	
suffi	il suffit	ils suffisent	il suffit
suivre	je suis	nous suivons	
suivant	tu suis	vous suivez	
suivi	il suit	ils suivent	il suivit
tenir (tiendr-)	je tiens	nous tenons	
tenant	tu tiens	vous tenez	
tenu	il tient	ils tiennent•	il tint
vaincre	je vaincs	nous vainquons	
vainquant	tu vaincs	vous vainquez	
vaincu	il vainc	ils vainquent	il vainquit
valoir (vaudr-)	je vaux	nous valons	
valant	tu vaux	vous valez	
valu	il vaut	ils valent (vaill-)•	il valut
venir (viendr-)	je viens	nous venons	
venant	tu viens	vous venez	
venu	il vient	ils viennent•	il vint
vivre	je vis	nous vivons	
vivant	tu vis	vous vivez	
vécu	il vit	ils vivent	il vécut
voir (verr-)	je vois	nous voyons	
voyant	tu vois	vous voyez	
vu	il voit	ils voient•	il vit
vouloir (voudr-)	je veux	nous voulons	
voulant	tu veux	vous voulez	
voulu	il veut	ils veulent (veuill-)•	il voulut

NOTES: 1) ***Asseoir*** has two conjugations. The first one listed (***j'assois***) is considered to be of popular usage. (Note that the letter ***e*** of the infinitive is dropped in all the other forms of the verb.)

The second conjugation listed (***j'assieds***) is preferred.

2) Only ***dire*** and ***redire*** have their second person plural on the pattern ***vous dites, vous redites*** in the present indicative and in the imperative. The other compounds of ***dire*** listed in §259 have a regular second person plural: ***vous contredisez, vous dédisez, vous interdisez, vous médisez, vous prédisez***.

The verb ***maudire***, however, has become irregular:

maudire	je maudis	nous maudissons	
maudissant	tu maudis	vous maudissez	
maudit	il maudit	ils maudissent	il maudit

3) ***Puis*** is an alternate form of the first person singular of the present indicative ***je peux***. It is used in formal and literary style. It is required in the inverted construction ***puis-je*** (*may I, can I*).

259. Other irregular verbs.

The following irregular verbs are conjugated on the models listed in the preceding section (§258). Most verbs not in this list are conjugated on the models given in §254, immediately preceding ***être*** and ***avoir***: ***chanter, finir,*** and ***vendre*** according to ending: ***-er*** on ***chanter***, ***-ir*** on ***finir***, and ***-re*** on ***vendre***. The learner should be careful to recognize prefixes in order to choose the appropriate model verb.

Verb	Pattern	Verb	Pattern
abattre	battre	construire	conduire
abstenir (s′)	tenir	contenir	tenir
accourir	courir	contraindre	craindre
accueillir	cueillir	contredire	dire *(note)*
acquérir	*model*	contrefaire	faire
admettre	mettre	convaincre	vaincre
aller	*model*	convenir	venir
apercevoir	recevoir	coudre	*model*
apparaître	connaître	courir	*model*
appartenir	tenir	couvrir	ouvrir
apprendre	prendre	craindre	*model*
assaillir	cueillir	croire	*model*
asseoir	*model*	croître	*model*
astreindre	craindre	cueillir	*model*
attendre	*model*	débattre	battre
atteindre	craindre	décevoir	recevoir
avoir	§§256-257	découvrir	ouvrir
battre	*model*	décrire	écrire
boire	*model*	dédire	dire *(note)*
bouillir	*model*	déduire	conduire
combattre	battre	défaire	faire
commettre	mettre	défaillir	cueillir
comprendre	prendre	démentir	mentir
compromettre	mettre	dépeindre	craindre
concevoir	recevoir	déplaire	plaire
conclure	*model*	descendre	attendre
conduire	*model*	déteindre	craindre
connaître	*model*	détenir	tenir
conquérir	acquérir	détruire	conduire
consentir	mentir	devenir	venir

devoir	*model*	partir	mentir
dire	*model*	parvenir	venir
discourir	courir	peindre	craindre
disparaître	connaître	pendre	attendre
distraire	soustraire	perdre	attendre
dormir	*model*	permettre	mettre
écrire	*model*	plaindre	craindre
élire	lire	plaire	*model*
émettre	mettre	pleuvoir	*model*
émouvoir	mouvoir	poursuivre	suivre
endormir	dormir	pourvoir *(note 1)*	voir
enfreindre	craindre	pouvoir	*model*
enfuir (s')	fuir	prédire	dire *(note)*
entendre	attendre	prendre	*model*
entreprendre	prendre	prescrire	écrire
entretenir	tenir	pressentir	mentir
entrevoir	voir	prévenir	venir
entr'ouvrir	ouvrir	prévoir *(note 1)*	voir
envoyer	*model*	produire	conduire
éteindre	craindre	promettre	mettre
être	§255, §257	proscrire	écrire
étreindre	craindre	provenir	venir
exclure	conclure	recevoir	*model*
extraire	soustraire	reconduire	conduire
faire	*model*	reconnaître	connaître
falloir	*model*	recueillir	cueillir
feindre	craindre	réduire	conduire
fuir	*model*	rejoindre	craindre
geindre	craindre	remettre	mettre
haïr	*model*	renvoyer	envoyer
inclure	conclure	répandre	attendre
inscrire	écrire	repartir	mentir
interdire	dire *(note)*	repentir (se)	mentir
intervenir	venir	répondre	attendre
introduire	conduire	reprendre	prendre
joindre	craindre	résoudre	*model*
lire	*model*	ressentir	mentir
maintenir	tenir	restreindre	craindre
maudire	dire *(note)*	retenir	tenir
médire	dire *(note)*	revenir	venir
mentir	*model*	revoir	voir
mettre	*model*	rire	*model*
mourir	*model*	satisfaire	faire
mouvoir	*model*	savoir	*model*
naître	*model*	secourir	courir
obtenir	tenir	séduire	conduire
offrir	ouvrir	sentir	mentir
omettre	mettre	servir	dormir
ouvrir	*model*	sortir	mentir
paraître	connaître	souffrir	ouvrir
parcourir	courir	soumettre	mettre

sourire	rire	tenir	*model*
souscrire	écrire	traduire	conduire
soustraire	*model*	transmettre	mettre
soutenir	tenir	tressaillir	cueillir
souvenir (se)	venir	vaincre	*model*
suffire	*model*	valoir	*model*
suivre	*model*	vendre	attendre
surprendre	prendre	venir	*model*
taire *(note 2)*	plaire	vivre	*model*
teindre	craindre	voir	*model*
		vouloir	*model*

NOTES: 1) ***Pourvoir*** and ***prévoir*** differ from ***voir*** only in the stems for the future and the conditional, which are ***pourvoir-*** and ***prévoir-***, respectively. Future: ***je pourvoirai, je prévoirai,*** etc. Conditional: ***je pourvoirais, je prévoirais,*** etc.

2) ***Se taire*** is modeled after ***plaire*** except for the third person singular of the present indicative, which has no circumflex accent: ***il se tait.***

3) It should be noted that a few verbs of the third group (theoretically) are conjugated on the pattern of second-group verbs, model ***finir***. It is the case with the following:

asservir	to enslave, subdue
assortir	to match, suit, coordinate
impartir	to impart
maudire	to curse (see §258, note)
répartir*	to distribute, divide in shares
ressortir*	to be under the jurisdiction of

*The verbs ***repartir*** (no accent!) meaning "*to retort, reply quickly*, or *to leave again*" and ***ressortir*** meaning "*to go out again*, or *to come out, stand out against a background*" are to be conjugated like ***partir*** and ***sortir***, respectively.

260. The present indicative.

The present indicative indicates what is or happens now. The present indicative shows a fact, event, or action that is incomplete. It translates the regular English present, the English present progressive or continuous, and also the emphatic form of the present.

Je parle français.
I speak French.
I am speaking French.
I do speak French.

The French present indicative should be used in the following cases:

A. As in English in place of the future, when a word or expression in the sentence points to a precise time, or if the action is in the not-too-distant future.

Je sors ce soir. Je reviens tout de suite.
I am going out tonight. I am returning right away.

B. In sentences with ***depuis*** (*for, since*) if the action, fact, or event begun in the past is still going on at this time (English uses the present perfect tense in this case).

Nous sommes en vacances depuis hier.
We have been on vacation since yesterday.

Elle est au soleil depuis une demi-heure.
She has been in the sun for half an hour.

C. In clauses beginning with ***si*** if the verb of the main clause is in the present, the future, or the imperative.

S'il pleut, la chaussée sera glissante.
If it rains, the road will be slippery.

Si la chaussée est glissante, ralentissez.
If the road is slippery, slow down.

D. In clauses with ***pendant que*** (*while*) if the verb of the main clause is in the present indicative (or imperative implying *right now*).

Il s'amuse pendant que moi, je travaille.
He is playing while *I* work.

Faites attention pendant que j'explique le problème.
Pay attention while I explain the problem.

NOTE: The actual progression of an action (present progressive or present continuous in English) can be emphasized by using the expression ***être en train de*** with an infinitive. The verb ***être*** in that expression must be in the present indicative if present is meant.

Je suis en train de travailler.
I am working. I am busy working.

If the action is situated in the past, ***être*** must be in the imperfect indicative. And if the action is situated in the future, ***être*** must be in the future indicative.

J'étais en train de travailler.
I was working. I was busy working.

Je serai en train de travailler.
I shall be working. I'll be busy working.

Occasionally, ***être*** may be in the conditional or in the subjunctive, if either a condition or conjecture is stated, or the clause it forms is a subordinate that must be in the subjunctive.

Si j'étais en vacances, je ne serais pas en train de travailler!
If I were on vacation, I would not be busy working!

Dommage qu'il soit en train de perdre son temps!
What a pity that he is wasting his time!

261. The imperfect indicative.

The imperfect indicative indicates what was, or was happening, or happened regularly, in the past. The imperfect indicative shows a fact, event, or action that is incomplete (im-perfect).

The imperfect indicative emphasizes time, habit, repetition, aspect, condition, or state, not the fact itself. It does not present an action only as an action: it stresses an aspect of it, a circumstance surrounding it, such as its being in progress, its repetition, or its duration.

The imperfect indicative should be used in the following cases:

A. If the verb *describes a state of being, a physical or mental state or condition, an attitude* (as opposed to a movement), *a circumstance* surrounding an event, etc., especially with verbs like the following:

aimer	to like, to love	**connaître**	to know
avoir besoin	to need	**désirer**	to wish, to want
avoir chaud	to be warm, hot	**être**	to be
avoir envie	to feel like	**préférer**	to prefer
avoir faim	to be hungry	**savoir**	to know
avoir froid	to be cold	**vouloir**	to want
avoir soif	to be thirsty	**se trouver**	to be located

These verbs usually describe states of being, physical conditions, or states of the mind. But when the emphasis is placed on the *sudden appearance* of such states, or on the *sudden awareness* of them, or on a *change* to them, then the verb should be in the passé composé instead of the imperfect.

J'avais faim.
I was hungry.
This is merely the statement of a fact, the expression of my state of being, of my physical condition.

J'ai eu faim.
I was hungry. I became hungry. I suddenly became aware of my hunger.
The emphasis is no longer on the condition itself, but on its sudden appearance, on the idea of time, on consequence, etc.

B. If the verb stresses a habit, or the repetition of an action, especially when the English sentence contains frequentative constructions with *would* or *used to.*

Il pleuvait tous les jours où nous habitions.
It would rain every day where we used to live.

Would and *used to* may not be expressed. The repetition or the recurrence of the action may be marked by a word or phrase such as *often, every night, every week,* etc. but it should be possible to introduce *would* or *used to* into the sentence. If not, the emphasis is not on the habitual or repetitive characteristic of the action: it is on the accumulation of individual actions (or facts, or events) seen as accomplished within a completed period of time, which requires the use of a *perfect* tense: the passé composé.

Tous les soirs, il faisait une promenade.
Every evening, he would go for a walk. (he went)
This example clearly emphasises a habit.

L'été dernier, il lisait le journal tous les jours.
Last summer, he read the paper every day.
This example stresses a habit, or the repeatedness of an action. Thus, the verb is in the imperfect, even though "last summer" represents a limited period of time (it is not emphasized).

L'été dernier, il a lu le journal tous les jours.
Last summer, he read the newspaper every day.
With the verb in the passé composé, the emphasis is on the mere fact as a daily accomplishment, accumulating into a large number of completed actions. There is no stress on any habit.

C. If the time factor is vague and emphasis is placed on duration. Especially if the verb expresses an action seen in the course of its duration (progressive), and no mention is made of whether the action ended or when it ended.

Il vivait au Mexique.
He lived in Mexico. He was living in Mexico.
At the time, he was living in Mexico. No mention is made of whether he stopped living there afterwards, or still does.

Il a vécu au Mexique.
He lived in Mexico.
He lived there for a certain time, and then he went to another country. He no longer lives in Mexico.

D. In sentences with ***depuis*** (*for, since*) if the action considered, begun in the past, was still going on at a certain moment of the past taken as a point of reference (implied or expressed by a verb or by a time expression).

Je travaillais depuis dix minutes.
I had been working for ten minutes.

Je travaillais depuis dix minutes quand il est entré.
I had been working for ten minutes when he came in.

J'étais ici depuis deux ans au moment de ce scandale.
I had been here for two years at the time of that scandal.

In this case, the French imperfect indicative translates the English pluperfect (or past perfect). Compare with the use of the present indicative in sentences with ***depuis*** (§260B).

E. In clauses beginning with ***si*** (*if*) when the verb of the main clause is in the present conditional.

S'il travaillait, il réussirait.
If he worked, he would succeed.

Est-ce que je pourrais vous accompagner si j'avais ma journée?
Could I go with you if I had the day off?

F. In clauses beginning with ***pendant que*** (*while*) if the main verb is in a past tense: the shorter action is begun and completed (passé composé) while the longer one is in progress (imparfait).

Pendant que j'écrivais, il lisait le journal.
While I wrote, he was reading the newspaper.
Il a lu le journal pendant que j'écrivais cette lettre.
He read the (whole) paper while I wrote (was writing) this letter.

262. The future indicative.

The future indicative indicates what will be, or will happen, or will be happening. It corresponds to the English tense formed with the auxiliaries *shall* and *will.* But not all the meanings of *shall* and *will* can be rendered by the French future indicative (see §299).

A. The future indicative should be used in the following cases:

1) Generally as in English to express simple futurity.

Il viendra demain. Elle s'arrêtera. Nous vaincrons.
He will come tomorrow. She will stop. We shall overcome.
Il dit qu'il arrivera vers huit heures.
He says that he will arrive around eight o'clock.

NOTE: In reported speech (the last example above), the future tense may be used in the subordinate clause only if the main verb is not in a past tense. For cases where the main verb is in a past tense, see §268A7.

2) Contrary to English practice, after the conjunctions ***tant que*** (*as long as*), ***aussitôt que, dès que*** (*as soon as*), ***quand, lorsque*** (*when*), ***pendant que*** (*while*), and ***après que*** (*after*) whenever futurity is meant.

Quand tu seras vieux, tu ne travailleras plus.
When you are old, you will no longer work.
Dès que je la verrai, je lui en parlerai.
As soon as I see her, I'll talk to her about it.

NOTE: This rule applies also to the verbs following ***que*** when this word represents one of the conjunctions listed above. See §194.

B. The future indicative should *not* be used in the following cases:

1) After ***si*** (meaning *if*, not *whether*) expressing a condition, not an alternative (i.e. *if*, not *whether*).

S'il vient lundi, il me trouvera chez moi.
If he comes by on Monday, he'll find me at home.

2) In subordinate clauses in which the verb must be in the subjunctive. The present subjunctive has the meaning of the future indicative.

J'ai peur qu'il ne vienne pas.
I am afraid he will not come.

NOTE: The "near future" or "immediate future" expressed in *to be going to, to be about to,* is formed in French with the verb ***aller*** followed by an infinitive.

Je vais partir. J'allais partir.
I am going to leave. I was about to leave.

The expression ***être sur le point de***, followed by an infinitive, insists even more on the immediacy of the future action.

Le mur est sur le point de s'écrouler.
The wall is about to crumble (on the verge of crumbling).

263. The passé simple indicative.

The passé simple indicative is used only in literary or formal style. It is never used in conversation, and very rarely in informal writing. It should be used instead of the passé composé as the action tense in story writing (story-telling, short story, novel, etc.) but not in correspondence.

The passé simple is also called passé défini, and corresponds to the English preterit or definite past.

Conversation uses the passé composé to replace the passé simple. However, the passé simple situates an action or an event in the past in a very "detached" way, whereas the passé composé, with its present tense auxiliary, connects the passé composé action with the present. See §264 for examples.

264. The passé composé indicative.

The passé composé indicative indicates what happened, or has happened. It corresponds to the English past, or the the present perfect, but there are important differences in their respective uses.

The passé composé stresses *fact* and excludes all descriptive aspects of the action. It should be considered the opposite of the imperfect indicative, in that it always implies that the actions is *completed* ("perfect" versus "imperfect").

The passé composé and the passé simple differ in their form (one is a simple tense, the other is compound), and in their names (in English, the passé simple is called past definite; the passé composé is called past indefinite). They also differ from one another in that one (the passé simple) is used only in writing and in formal style, whereas the other (the passé composé) is the normal tense of conversation and informal writing. Otherwise, the same reasons or circumstances govern their use.

The passé composé indicative (or the passé simple in literary contexts) should be used in the following cases:

A. If the elements of *rapidity and suddenness* are emphasized or obvious.

Le livre est tombé. La lumière s'est éteinte.
Le livre tomba. La lumière s'éteignit.
The book fell. The light went out.

B. If the time when the action took place is known, and if the action is seen merely as a *completed fact*, without any emphasis on its aspects (duration, progression, repetition, etc.).

Il a plu hier.
It rained yesterday.
The statement considers the rain as a past, completed event. Yet the passé simple could not be used here because the adverb "hier" connects the past event with today: it is not detached enough.

Il pleuvait hier.
It rained (was raining) yesterday.
The statement considers the rain a circumstance, not an event. It "describes" yesterday's weather.

The passé composé is obviously the tense to use if the end of the action is expressed, or clearly implied, and if again the mere *completed fact* is being considered.

Hier, il a plu jusqu'à trois heures.
Yesterday, it rained until three o'clock.

The passé composé may be used instead of the imperfect to change what would normally be the description of a state or condition (see §261A, B, C), into the statement of a *completed fact* with all the implications it entails.

Elle était belle.
She was pretty.
At the time considered, and she may still be so.

Elle a été belle.
She was pretty.
Once, long ago. This is a completed fact. She is no longer pretty. The passé simple would be inappropriate, even in a literary context, because the statement implies that now she is no longer pretty, a suggestion that would not be present in the passé simple with its "detachment".

C. If what seems to be a simple description of a state or condition (see imperfect, §261) is in reality the sudden awareness of it, with emphasis on *suddenness*, or the expression of a *change of state or condition*, or the expression of a *result or consequence.*

Il a voulu sortir de l'autobus.
Il voulut sortir de l'autobus.
He wanted to get out of the bus.
He suddenly felt the urge, or made up his mind to go out. Some external event caused him to decide to leave.

but: Il voulait sortir de l'autobus.
He wanted to leave the bus.
His mind was set on getting out. This is the description of a state of mind (§261A). Yet how long this state of mind prevailed is immaterial. "Imperfect" implies "un-concerned" with length of time or with beginning or end.

D. If several verbs indicate actions that are performed in a consecutive, chronological, or logical manner, each action forwarding the plot, each action being completed before the next one begins, thus serving as a *limit* for the others.

Il s'est assis, il a pris un livre, et il s'est mis à lire.
Il s'assit, il prit un livre, et il se mit à lire.
He sat down, he took a book, and he began to read.

Note that if this example showed a habit, the three verbs would be in the imperfect.

E. In sentences with ***depuis*** (or an indication of time elapsed), if the verb stresses the *occurrence*, or the *recurrence*, or the *absence* of a fact or action in a period of time ending *now.* (The absence of a fact or action is generally indicated by a negative sentence.)

Je ne l'ai pas vu depuis dimanche dernier.
I haven't seen him since last Sunday.

Je l'ai vu très souvent ces derniers jours.
I have seen him very often these last few days.
(The passé simple would be inappropriate here because of the word ***depuis****, which connects the past event or fact with the present.)*

F. After ***depuis que*** (*since*, before a verb), to mark the time when another action began. The verb of the main clause is in the present indicative if the action begun is still going on now, and in the passé composé if the action begun has already ended, or is considered so.

Je travaille depuis qu'il est sorti.
I have been working since he went out.

J'ai travaillé depuis qu'il est sorti.
I did some work since he went out.
(The passé simple would be inappropriate here because of the word ***depuis****, which connects the past event or fact with the present.)*

G. In a main clause preceding ***pendant que*** (*while*) and a verb in the *imperfect.* The subordinate clause with ***pendant que*** serves as a descriptive background for the action in the main clause, which begins, progresses, and ends while the other merely goes on. The verb in the imperfect may be replaced by an expression of time, after the preposition ***pendant*** (*during*).

J'ai travaillé pendant qu'il se reposait.
I worked while he was resting.

J'ai travaillé pendant les vacances de Pâques.
I worked during Easter vacation.

Il s'échappa pendant que le garde dormait.
He escaped while the guard was sleeping.

Il s'échappa pendant la relève.
He escaped during the changing of the guard.

H. After ***si*** (meaning *if*, not *whether*) if the condition to fulfill will have to be completed before the other action is performed. The verb of the main clause is normally in the future in this case, but a clause with ***si*** must not be in the future perfect: this tense must be replaced by the passé composé.

Si j'en ai parlé à mes parents avant huit heures, nous pourrons certainement aller voir cette pièce.
If I speak (have spoken) to my parents about it by eight o'clock, we shall certainly be able to go see that play.
(The passé simple would not be appropriate in this conditional context.)

I. After ***combien de temps*** (*how long, how much time*) if the question is about the length of time it took to complete an action that has just ended, or ended recently, or was performed last among several, but is not considered as having ended prior to something else (which would require a verb in the pluperfect).

Combien de temps avez-vous passé en France?
How much time did you spend in France?

Combien de temps vous a-t-il fallu pour résoudre ce problème?
How long did it take you to solve this problem?

Combien de temps les Romains restèrent-ils en Gaule?
How long did the Romans remain in Gaul?

Combien de temps fallut-il à Jules César pour vaincre Vercingétorix?
How long did it take Julius Cesar to defeat Vercingetorix?

265. The pluperfect indicative.

The pluperfect indicative indicates what had been, had happened, or had been happening *prior* to something else that is implied or expressed by an adverb of time, a phrase, or another event or action (verb).

Le 4 mai, il a paru très inquiet. La veille, il avait reçu un télégramme.
On May 4, he appeared very worried. The day before, he had received a telegram.

The pluperfect indicative should be used in the following cases:

A. In sentences with ***depuis*** (*since, for, in*) if the verb stresses the occurrence or the recurrence (not a habit) of a fact or action in a period of time that ended in the past, *prior* to a date of the past (time expression) or an event of the past (verb), implied or expressed.

Je ne l'avais pas vu depuis deux ans (quand je l'ai rencontré cet été-là).
I had not seen him in two years (when I met him that summer).

B. After ***depuis que*** (*since*, conjunction marking time), to indicate the beginning time of an action. The verb preceding ***depuis que*** (i.e., the verb of the main clause) is generally in the imperfect indicative: the action begun was still going on at the moment chosen as a reference in the past (it may also be in the pluperfect indicative: see A, above).

Je ne travaillais plus depuis qu'ils avaient fait faillite.
I had not been working since they had gone bankrupt.

Elle n'était jamais sortie depuis que son mari était mort.
She had never gone out since her husband had died.

C. After ***si*** indicating a condition, not an alternative (i.e., *if*, not *whether*), when the main verb is in the past conditional.

S'il avait essayé, il aurait réussi.
If he had tried, he would have succeeded.

D. After ***combien de temps*** (*how long, how much time*), if the question is about the length of time it took to complete an action that ended *prior* to something else, expressed or implied. (The following examples assume a conversational context in which a narrative is interrupted to ask a question about an event that occurred earlier in time than the point of interruption.)

Combien de temps aviez-vous passé à Paris?
How much time had you spent in Paris?

Combien de temps vous avait-il fallu pour réparer la voiture?
How much time had it taken you to repair the car?

266. The future anterior indicative.

The future anterior or future perfect indicative indicates that an action will be completed before another one (expressed or implied) is performed.

Si nous maintenons notre moyenne, nous serons arrivés avant la tombée de la nuit.
If we keep up our average speed, we shall have arrived before nightfall.

The future anterior indicative should be used in the following cases:

A. Contrary to English practice, after the conjunctions *as long as* (***tant que***), *as soon as* (***dès que, aussitôt que***), *when* (***quand, lorsque***), and *after* (***après que***) to indicate that the action considered will be completed before another one is performed.

Tant qu'il n'aura pas mangé sa soupe, il ne pourra pas sortir.
As long as he has not eaten his soup, he won't be allowed to go out.

Quand j'aurai fini ce livre, je te le prêterai.
When I have finished this book, I'll lend it to you.

B. In a conjecture, where it translates *probably* followed by a past tense.

Il n'est pas encore là? Il aura manqué le dernier métro.
Isn't he home yet? He probably missed the last subway train.

267. The past anterior indicative.

The past anterior indicative has roughly the same meaning as the pluperfect indicative, but it is used only in literary or formal style like its corresponding simple tense, the passé simple indicative.

The past anterior cannot be used in all the cases where the pluperfect is called for. Each has some of the nuances of its respective corresponding simple tense (see imperfect, §261, and passé simple, §263).

The past anterior indicative should be used after the conjunctions *after* (***après que***), *as soon as* (***dès que, aussitôt que***), *when* (***quand, lorsque***), *as long as* (***tant que***—see note 2), to indicate that an action was completed before another was performed. The other action is expressed by a verb in the passé simple.

Dès qu'il eut fini son livre, il le remit dans la bibliothèque.
As soon as he had finished his book, he put it back in the bookcase.

NOTES: 1) In informal writing and in conversation, the past anterior is inappropriate due to the fact that the auxiliary verb used to form it is in the passé simple, a literary tense. Besides, the third person singular of the past anterior is almost identical to the same person in the pluperfect subjunctive. Thus the past anterior tends to be replaced in today's French by the *passé surcomposé*. This tense is formed with an auxiliary in the passé composé and the past participle of the verb. The conversational value of the passé composé auxiliary is transferred to the passé surcomposé, which must be paired with the passé composé.

Dès qu'il a eu fini son livre, il l'a remis dans la bibliothèque.
As soon as he had finished the book, he put it back in the bookcase.

2) The case of ***tant que*** occurs only with a negative subordinate verb.
For the construction of sentences with ***après que***, see §180, §184.

268. The conditional.

The present and the past conditional are generally used as in English to present an action as the possible consequence of a condition or supposition.

The French conditional tenses translate the English forms composed of *should* and *would*, although not all the meanings of these two words can be rendered by the mere conditional tenses (see B, below, and §302).

A. The present and past conditional should be used in the following cases:

1) After ***si*** expressing an alternative (*whether*).

Je ne savais pas s'il viendrait (ou non).
I did not know whether he would come (or not).

Il se demandait s'il aurait pu visiter le Louvre.
He was wondering whether he would have been able to visit the Louvre.

2) After ***quand, quand même, quand bien même*** meaning "even if, even though."

Quand il serait le diable en personne, je n'aurais pas peur.
Even if he were the devil in person, I would not be scared.

This construction is more emphatic and more literary than the construction with ***même si*** (§§183A and 268B, below).

3) To translate ***could*** plus a verb in interrogative clauses of conjecture. Also to translate *could, could have, might, might have* (§301).

Aurait-il déjà fini?
Could he already have finished?

Aurait-il oublié son rendez-vous?
Could he have forgotten his appointment?

4) In requests and orders, to attenuate the force of an order or the bluntness of a request.

Pourriez-vous me prêter ce livre?
Could you lend me this book?

Voudriez-vous me passer le beurre (s'il vous plaît)?
Would you (please) pass me the butter?

Auriez-vous la bonté de fermer la porte?
Would you be so kind as to shut the door?

Would may occasionally be rendered by an indicative tense of the verb ***vouloir***, if the idea is only that of willing, without any condition.

Voulez-vous fermer la porte?
Would you please shut the door?

Il m'a demandé si je voulais bien monter ses chevaux pour lui, pour leur donner de l'exercice.
He asked me if I would ride his horses for him, to exercise them.

However, ***vouloir*** in the indicative may sound like a strong order, if it is not accompanied by a polite formula, even when it is attenuated by the adverb ***bien***.

Voulez-vous bien fermer la porte, s'il vous plaît?
Would you please shut the door?

5) When an English inverted construction begins a conditional clause, it should be translated into French by an identical inverted construction, with a verb in the *imperfect* or in the *pluperfect* of the *subjunctive mood*, but only in literary or formal style.

Dussé-je mourir, je n'hésiterais pas.
Were I to die, I would not hesitate.

Fût-il venu plus tôt, la bataille eût été gagnée.
Had he come sooner, the battle would have been won.

Note that the conditional (ordinary or formal) is used also in the clause expressing the result or consequence of the condition or the supposition.

6) When *should* means *ought to*, the conditional of the verb ***devoir*** should be used, followed by an infinitive (see §302).

Vous devriez partir tout de suite.
You should leave at once.

Vous auriez dû partir tout de suite.
You should have left at once.

7) In reported speech, expressing an event later in time than the main verb, if the main verb is in a past tense.

Il a dit qu'il arriverait lundi.
He said that he would arrive on Monday.

Elle a répondu qu'elle aurait fini avant midi.
She replied that she would be through before noon.

NOTE: After a main verb in a past tense, the subordinate verb may be in a future tense instead of the prescribed conditional to indicate that the fact or event, which could have taken place between the moment of the main verb and now, has not yet taken place, and therefore necessarily belongs in the future. This is very frequent in English, but should be restricted in French to the most obvious contexts.

On m'a dit qu'il viendra me voir dès son arrivée.
I have been told that he will come to see me as soon as he arrives.
(With the main verb in the passé composé, the subordinate verb in the future tense is easily understood. But if the main verb is in the passé simple, or in the pluperfect, a subordinate verb in the future is no longer acceptable.)

Le chevalier jura qu'il sauverait la jeune princesse.
The knight swore that he would rescue the young princess.

Elle m'avait assuré qu'elle serait à l'heure.
She had assured me that she would be on time.

B. The following are cases in which the present and past conditional should *not* be used:

1) After ***si, même si, comme si*** (*if, even if, as if*). Instead of the present conditional, use the *imperfect indicative*, and instead of the past conditional, use the *pluperfect indicative*.

Si vous veniez la voir, elle serait contente.
If you came to see her, she would be pleased.

Si vous étiez venu la voir, elle aurait été contente. Vous lui manquez beaucoup.
If you had come to see her, she would have been pleased. She misses you a lot.

Comme si and ***même si*** may be followed by a verb in the pluperfect subjunctive, which is considered a second form of the past conditional, a formal construction.

Il refusa de parler, comme s'il eût craint que sa voix le trahît.
He refused to speak, as if he had feared that his voice would (or: might) betray him.

2) To translate *would* meaning *used to*. Instead of the present conditional, use the imperfect indicative.

Il arrivait toujours à cinq heures précises.
He would always arrive at five o'clock sharp.

269. The imperative.

The imperative has three persons: the second person singular, the first person plural, and the second person plural.

Écoute. Sors. Écoutez. Sortez.
Listen. Go out.

Partons. Ne restons pas là.
Let's leave. Let us not remain here.

When a command or a simple wish needs to be made in another person, a form of the subjunctive is used preceded by the conjunction ***que***, suggesting the understating of a formula such as "je veux," "il faut," "j'ordonne," etc.

Qu'il parte!
Let him leave! Make him go!

Que je sois pendu!
May I be hanged! I'll be . . .!

Qu'ils entrent!
Have them come in! Let them in!

NOTES: 1) First-group verbs and verbs with an ***-es*** ending in the second person of the present indicative, lose the ***s*** of that ending in the second person singular of the imperative, except directly before the adverbial pronouns ***y*** and ***en***.

2) When personal pronouns accompany a verb in the imperative, they must precede the verb in all its forms except in the affirmative imperative, in which case they must immediately follow the verb and be connected to it by hyphens (see §89B).

3) No subject pronoun should be used in French with the imperative forms.

Fais-le tout de suite, autrement . . .!
Fais-le tout de suite, sinon . . .!
You do it right away, or else . . .!

4) The infinitive is often preferred to the imperative on written signs, for references, in cooking recipes, etc.

Ne pas toucher à la marchandise.
Do not handle the merchandise.
S'adresser en face.
Inquire across the street.
Voir le numéro 89.
See number 89.
Mélanger le sucre et les jaunes.
Blend the sugar and the yokes.

270. Present participle.

The present participle has three functions:

A. It is an *adjective* if it accompanies a noun, with or without the aid of a verb. It gives the noun a permanent quality, generally with an active meaning. As an adjective, the present participle must agree in gender and number with the noun it refers to (see position of adjectives, §20A).

Des livres intéressants. Cette histoire est amusante.
Interesting books. This story is amusing.
Le dessert était une île flottante.
Dessert was a floating island.
Il n'y a qu'une place gratuite. L'autre est payante.
There is only one free seat. The other one is paying (i.e., to be paid for).

B. It is a *verb* if it expresses a real action performed by a subject. The present participle is particularly recognizable as a verb if it has a direct object. As a verb, it is invariable and is never preceded by any preposition, including ***en***.

Mon ami étant malade, j'ai dû voyager seul.
My friend being ill, I had to travel alone.

The use of the present participle as a verb is the same in French as in English. In both languages, however, other constructions, such as conjunctive subordinate clauses may be preferred.

Comme mon ami était malade, j'ai dû voyager seul.
As my friend was ill, I had to travel alone.

The present participle construction has the advantage of emphasizing the simultaneity of the two facts or actions involved, an emphasis that cannot be obtained with a subordinate clause. Yet there are cases where a subordinate clause may not be avoided.

Je ne peux pas dire une parole sans que tout le monde se moque de moi.
I cannot utter a word without everyone making fun of me.

C. It is a *gerund* when it follows the preposition ***en***, or its stressed form ***tout en***. The present participle is then invariable. ***En*** translates *while, by, on, upon, when*, etc., preceding a gerund, or even a gerund alone. ***Tout en*** stresses simultaneity. It may be used only where timing is considered and it is inappropriate to render the construction *by + gerund*, which emphasizes manner or cause.

Ces dames tricotaient tout en regardant les exécutions.
These ladies used to knit while watching the executions.

Il s'est blessé en jouant.
He injured himself (while) playing.

En arrivant, j'ai dû me changer parce que j'étais trempé.
On (upon) arriving, I had to change clothes because I was soaking wet.

C'est en prenant le train de nuit qu'il a pu arriver à temps.
It is by taking the night train that he was able to arrive in time.

The present participle with ***en*** should be used only if *simultaneity* is implied, besides meanings of *manner, consequence, means, time*, etc. It should *not* be used in the following cases:

1) After prepositions other than ***en***. It must then be replaced by the <u>infinitive</u>.

Je m'amuse (m'occupe) à faire des mots croisés.
I keep busy by doing crossword puzzles.

Après avoir frappé, on peut entrer.
After knocking, one may enter.

Il se tue à travailler.
He kills himself with working.

On frappe avant d'entrer.
One knocks before entering.

2) To translate an English gerund when no simultaneity is involved, especially in the case of gerunds used as the subject or object of a verb or modified by possessives. A *noun*, a *clause*, or an *infinitive* should be used in French.

Son retard ne m'inquiète pas. Ça ne m'inquiète pas qu'il soit en retard. (note: subjunctive)
His being late does not worry me.

Ça ne l'avancera à rien qu'il se mette en colère.
His getting angry won't get him anywhere.

Pourquoi tenez-vous tant à dépenser une fortune pour eux?
Why do you insist so much on spending a fortune on them.

Ça ne servira pas à grand-chose de courir maintenant.
Running now won't help much.

Ça ne me dérange pas que vous fumiez.
I don't mind your smoking. Your smoking doesn't bother me.

Défense de fumer. Il est inderdit de fumer. Prière de (Merci de) ne pas fumer.
No smoking. Smoking prohibited. Thank you for not smoking.

J'aime travailler ici. Ça me plaît de travailler ici.
I like working here. I enjoy working here.

Il a commencé à pleuvoir.
It began raining. It started raining.

Ça me fait peur de penser à l'avenir.
Thinking about the future scares me. It scares me to think about the future.

271. Past participle.

The past participle, like the present participle, may have three functions.

A. It is an *adjective* if it describes the state or condition of a noun, with or without the aid of a verb. It generally has a passive meaning, and it must agree in gender and number with the noun it describes.

Une homme fatigué. Une jeune fille passionnée.
A tired man. A passionate young lady.

La leçon est finie.
The lesson is finished.

See position of adjectives, §20A.

B. It is a *verb* if, being used without an auxiliary, it expresses a real action and has a subject or an object. The action may be active or passive in meaning. (The past participle in this case stands for a circumstantial clause with a conjunction.)

The past participle used in this function must agree in gender and number with its subject, whatever the position of the latter.

Fatiguée de mes remarques, elle est partie.
(Parce qu'elle était fatiguée de mes remarques, . . .)
Fed up with my remarks, she left.

L'examen fini, nous sommes allés boire un verre.
(Une fois que l'examen a été fini, . . .)
Once the exam was over, we went out for a drink.

NOTE: This type of construction is not common in modern English. Modern English uses the past participle as a verb without an auxiliary mainly after certain conjunctions and adverbs (*if, when, once,* etc.). French translates these constructions into full conjunctive clauses. However, the expressions ***une fois*** (*once*), and ***à peine*** (*hardly, scarcely*) may be found with past participle constructions in which no auxiliary is expressed. Note that in such cases, the subject of the past participle must also be the subject of the verb of the other clause.

À peine arrivée, elle parlait déjà de rentrer.
Scarcely had she arrived when she talked of going back home.

but: Si on le déplace, ce récipient pourrait se briser.
If moved, this container might break.

Une fois terminé, ce mur sera très solide.
Once (or: when) finished, this wall will be very strong.

but: Quand il sera terminé, ce mur sera très solide.
When finished, this wall will be very strong.

It is more common in English to find a past participle preceded by an auxiliary in its present participle form (a compound past participle or "passé composé" participle). This construction is rendered in French by a simple past participle, provided that the meaning sought is that of a circumstantial clause (of time, especially), and that both the participle and the verb of the other clause have the same subject.

Devenu roi, il fit de grandes choses.
Having become king, he did great things.

Restées seules loin des autres, elles se crurent perdues.
Having remained alone away from the others, they thought they were lost.

If the circumstantial clause in the participle has an active meaning and a direct or indirect object, the same construction can generally be used in English and in French. The participle in French may be either a simple present participle or a compound past participle.

Prenant son manteau, il ouvrit la porte et partit.
Taking his coat, he opened the door and left.

Ayant remarqué mon absence, il interrogea mes collègues.
Having noticed my absence, he questioned my colleagues.

M'ayant demandé des excuses, elle me regardait fixement.
Having asked me for an apology, she was staring at me.

C. It is a *verb* in all the compound tenses and in the passive voice, where it is always used with an auxiliary. In English, the compound tenses of the active voice are all formed with the auxiliary *to have*, and all the tenses (simple and compound) of the passive voice are formed with the auxiliary *to be*. In French, the auxiliary for the passive voice is also *to be*, ***être***, in all tenses. But in the active voice, the auxiliary may be either *to have*, ***avoir***, or *to be*, ***être***.

1) The auxiliary is ***avoir*** for most verbs.

J'ai compris. Il a entendu. Vous avez fini? Ils n'ont rien fait.
I have understood. He has heard. Have you finished? They haven't done anything.

2) The auxiliary is ***être*** with all *pronominal verbs* (reflexive or reciprocal) and with the following intransitive verbs:

accourir	to run to, to hasten to
aller	to go
arriver	to arrive, to happen
descendre*	to go (come) down, etc.
redescendre*	to go (come) down, etc., again
entrer	to go (come) in, enter
rentrer*	to go (come) back in, go (come) home
monter*	to go (come) up
remonter*	to go back up, come up again
mourir	to die
naître	to be born
partir	to leave, to depart, to go away
repartir	to leave again
rester	to stay, to remain
rester (impersonal)	to have (something) left
retourner*	to return, to go back
sortir*	to go (come) out
ressortir*	to go (come) out again
tomber	to fall
retomber	to fall again
venir	to come
devenir	to become
redevenir	to become again
intervenir	to intervene; to occur
parvenir	to attain, to reach, to succeed
revenir	to come back
survenir	to occur, happen suddenly or unexpectedly

*These verbs are frequently used transitively (i.e., with an object). When they are used with an object, they mean *to carry, to take, to send* the object ***up, down, out***, etc.; the French verb must then form its compound tenses with the auxiliary ***avoir***.

À huit heures, nous sommes descendus déjeuner. (intransitive)
At eight o'clock, we came down for breakfast.

Le domestique a descendu nos valises. (transitive)
The servant carried our suitcases downstairs.

Je suis remonté dans ma chambre.
I went back up to my room.

J'ai remonté la pendule.
I wound up the (table) clock.

La bonne a remonté une de mes valises.
The maid brought one of my suitcases back up.

J'ai ressorti mon costume de la valise.
I took my suit out of the suitcase again.

272. Agreement of participles.

Present and past participles used as *adjectives* must agree with the noun they modify.

Une femme âgée. Des voyageurs fatigués.
An old (elderly) lady. Tired travelers.

Une histoire amusante. Des discours fatigants.
An amusing story. Tiring (boring) speeches.

A number of present participles show a difference of spelling for their functions as adjective and verb. The following examples are only a few, but among the most commonly used.

ADJECTIVE	VERB
convaincant	convainquant
équivalent	équivalant
fatigant	fatiguant
négligent	négligeant
précédent	précédant
provocant	provoquant

Used as a verb and without any auxiliary, a present participle is invariable, but a past participle must agree in gender and number with its subject whatever its position.

Oubliant ma promesse, j'ai refusé de l'accompagner.
Forgetting my promise, I refused to accompany him.

Ballottée par les vagues, la barque allait couler.
Tossed about by the waves, the rowboat was going to sink.

Used with an auxiliary, the past participle must follow certain rules of agreement, which are as follows:

A. If the auxiliary is ***avoir***, the past participle must agree only with a *preceding direct object.* The case is frequent with interrogative adjectives and pronouns, with personal pronouns, and with relative pronouns.

Quels livres avez-vous lus?
What books have you read?

Voici les livres que j'ai lus.
Here are the books that I have read.
Moi aussi, je les ai lus.
I have read them also.

B. If the auxiliary is ***être*** and the verb is *not a reflexive or reciprocal verb*, the past participle must agree with the *subject*, whatever its position.

Elle a été blessée dans un accident d'auto.
She was injured in a car accident. (passive voice)
Sont-elles parties?
Have they left? (verbs listed in §271C2)

C. If the auxiliary is ***être***, and the verb is reflexive or reciprocal, the past participle normally agrees with a *preceding direct object.* In most cases, the reflexive or reciprocal pronoun is the direct object. But it is often difficult to detect the direct object of a French reflexive verb. The reflexive pronoun does not appear to represent the object of an action. It seems instead to have become attached to the verb in an essential way, to express a concept different from that of the non-pronimal verb: ***douter*** means *to doubt*; ***se douter*** means *to suspect.* The corresponding English verb does not necessarily express a reflexive or reciprocal idea. *To get up*, for instance, has no reflexive pronoun, whereas its French counterpart ***se lever*** has one. The same is true of ***se demander*** (*to wonder*), ***se presser*** (*to hurry*), ***se dépêcher*** (*to hurry*), ***s'en aller*** (*to leave, to go away*), ***s'enfuir*** (*to flee, to run away*), ***se passer*** (*to happen*), and a good number of other verbs. For practical purposes, especially in the case of infrequent reflexive and reciprocal verbs, apply one of the following three rules of agreement of the past participle:

The past participle of a reflexive or reciprocal verb agrees directly with its subject:

1) If the English translation must include *myself, yourself, itself,* etc., or *each other, one another* as a direct object.

Elle s'est blessée en tombant.
She hurt herself falling.
Anne et Léa se sont comprises tout de suite.
Anne and Lea understood each other right away.

2) If it is one of the verbs in the following list.

s'absenter	s'attaquer à	s'ébattre	s'entendre
s'abstenir	s'attendre à	s'échapper	s'entendre à qqch
s'acharner	s'avancer	s'écouler	s'éprendre de
s'adonner à	s'aviser de	s'écrier	s'étonner
s'affaiblir	se battre	s'écrouler	s'évader
s'agenouiller	se blottir	s'efforcer	s'évanouir
s'en aller	se cacher	s'emparer de	s'évaporer
s'apercevoir	se coucher	s'empresser	s'éveiller
s'approcher	se dépêcher	s'endormir	s'évertuer à
s'arrêter	se disputer	s'enfuir	s'empresser
s'attacher à	se douter	s'ennuyer	s'extasier

se féliciter	se lever	se raviser	se saisir
se hâter	se méfier de	se réfugier	se sauver
s'habiller	se méprendre	se réjouir	se sentir
s'habituer	se moquer	se rencontrer	se servir de
s'ingénier à	s'oublier	se rendre	se soucier de
s'insurger	se perdre	se rendre à	se souvenir de
se joindre	se plaindre	se repentir	se suicider
se jouer de	s'en prendre à	se résoudre à	se taire
se lamenter	s'y prendre	s'en retourner	se tromper
se laver	se presser	se réveiller	se vendre

Elle s'est dépêchée. Ils se sont enfuis.
She hurried. They fled.

Elles s'étaient rendues en ville.
They (the girls) had gone downtown.

Jeanne s'en est allée.
Jeanne went away.

Nous nous sommes aperçus de notre erreur.
We (boys) noticed our mistake.

Elle s'était souvenue de l'histoire.
She had remembered the story.

Nous nous sommes trompées.
We (girls) made a mistake.

3) If there is a preceding direct object other than the reflexive or reciprocal pronoun (relative pronoun, interrogative group), the past participle must agree with that preceding direct object.

Ils avaient encore les lettres qu'ils s'étaient écrites à quinze ans.
They still had the letters that they had written to one another at fifteen.
*(The past participle agrees with the preceding direct object **qu'**, a relative pronoun the antecedent of which is **les lettres**, feminine plural.)*

but: Elles se sont lavé les mains.
They (girls) washed their hands.
*(The direct object **les mains** does not precede the verb, therefore no agreement is necessary.)*

Cette phrase? Il se l'est répétée toute la nuit.
That sentence? He repeated it to himself all night long.
*(The past participle agrees with the preceding direct object **l'**, a personal pronoun representing **cette phrase**, feminine singular.)*

but: Il s'est répété cette phrase toute la nuit.
He repeated that sentence to himself all night long.
*(The direct object **cette phrase** does not precede the verb, therefore no agreement is necessary.)*

NOTES: 1) ***Se parler, se plaire,*** and ***se ressembler*** never show past participle agreement because their reflexive or reciprocal pronoun is an indirect object and they cannot have a direct object.

2) In ***se rendre compte***, the word ***compte*** is a direct object that follows the verb. Therefore, no agreement is shown in the past participle.

273. *Notes on the agreement of past participles.*

A. In the causative construction ***faire*** + ***infinitive***, if ***faire*** is in a compound tense, the past participle ***fait*** is invariable.

Ils nous ont fait arrêter. Je les ai fait parler.
They had us arrested. I made them talk.

Quelles corvées vous a-t-il fait faire?
What chores did he have you do?

Tu as vu la fosse qu'elle lui a fait creuser?
Did you see the hole that she had him dig?

B. When a verb in a compound tense is followed by an infinitive, the past participle agrees with *its own preceding direct object*, not the direct object of the infinitive.

Où sont les enfants? Je ne les ai pas entendus jouer.
Where are the children? I haven't heard them playing.
*(The pronoun **les** is the direct object of the verb **ai entendus**, and at the same time the subject of the infinitive **jouer**, not its object.)*

Je connais cette mélodie, je l'ai déjà entendu chanter.
I know that melody, I have already heard it sung.
*(Literally: I have already heard someone sing it. The pronoun **l'**, representing the feminine noun **mélodie**, is here the direct object of the infinitive **chanter**. Therefore, there is no agreement.)*

C. When the pronoun ***en*** precedes a verb in a compound tense, the past participle never agrees with it. But ***en*** may be a preposition meaning "from there," in which case the verb may be preceded by a direct object of another sort, with which the past participle should agree.

Regarde ces belles robes! Et j'en ai vu de plus jolies dans la vitrine.
Look at these beautiful dresses! And I have seen prettier ones in the window.

but: Je reviens de France; voici les souvenirs que j'en ai rapportés.
I am just back from France. Here are the souvenirs that I brought back from there.
*(The past participle **rapportés** agrees with its preceding direct object **que**, a relative pronoun, the antecedent of which is **les souvenirs**, masculine plural.)*

D. It should be remembered that many verbs having direct objects in English require prepositional objects in French, and vice versa.

Dans quelle salle du musée sommes-nous entrés?
Which room of the museum did we enter?

Il a encore changé de chemise!
He changed shirts again!

Tu ressembles à ton frère.
You resemble your brother.

Je cherche la gare.
I am looking for the railway station.

Regardez-moi!
Look at me!

Ils ont demandé une table pour quatre.
They asked for a table for four.

Nous les avons attendues au Café du Port.
We waited for them (girls) at the Café du Port.

Je m'attendais à un échec.
I expected a failure.

274. Infinitives.

The three groups of verbs are recognizable from their *infinitive endings.*

- The first-group verbs end in ***-er***.

- The second-group verbs end in ***-ir***, and have a present participle ending in ***-issant*** (infix ***-iss-***).

- The third-group verbs end in ***-ir*** or in ***-re***.

The infinitive, up to and including the last ***r*** it contains, serves as the stem of the ***future indicative*** and of the ***present conditional*** (see §254A).

The infinitive of reciprocal and reflexive verbs is always listed with the pronoun ***se***; but in context, the pronoun ***se*** must be changed to correspond to the person actually performing the action expressed by the infinitive (see §87).

275. Notes on the spelling of verbs of the first group.

Many verbs of the first group have irregularities in their spelling, due to the presence of a mute ***e*** either in an ending or in a stem.

A. Verbs ending ***-cer*** in the infinitive will add a cedilla to the ***c***: ***ç***), whenever the next letter is ***a*** or ***o***.

Lancer (*to cast, to throw*): je lance - nous lançons - il lançait - nous lancions - tu lanceras - en lançant.

B. Verbs ending in ***-ger*** in the infinitive will add ***e*** after ***g*** to avoid the contact of ***g*** with ***a*** or ***o***.

Nager (*to swim*): je nage - nous nageons - il nageait - vous nagiez - en nageant.

C. Verbs ending in ***-guer*** in the infinitive will keep ***u*** after ***g*** throughout the complete conjugation.

Distinguer (*to distinguish, perceive, notice*)**: il distingue - nous distinguons - ils distinguaient - vous distinguiez.**

D. Verbs ending in ***-yer*** in the infinitive will change ***y*** to ***i*** whenever a mute ***e*** follows, whether final or not. Verbs in ***-ayer*** (like ***payer***) may keep ***y*** through the complete conjugation, or change it to ***i***.

broyer (to grind):	je broie	nous broyons
	tu broies	vous broyez
	il broie	ils broient

future: je broierai, tu broieras, il broiera, etc.
conditional: je broierais, tu broierais, etc.

payer (to pay):	je paie/paye	nous payons
	tu paies/payes	vous payez
	il paie/paye	ils paient/payent

future: je paierai/payerai, tu paieras/payeras, etc.
conditional: je paierais/payerais, tu paierais/payerais, etc .

E. *e-stem verbs*: If, after dropping the ***-er*** ending of the infinitive, the last vowel in the stem is a mute ***e***, that mute (or "voiceless") ***e*** must be turned into a "voiced" one anytime the next syllable also contains a mute ***e***. Such is the case in the present and future indicative, in the present subjunctive, and in the present conditional. This is done in two ways depending on the verb in question.

1) For most verbs, a grave accent is marked over the ***e*** of the stem: ***è***.

infinitive **se promener** (stem **promen-**)

present indicative:	je me promène	nous nous promenons
	tu te promènes	vous vous promenez
	il se promène	ils se promènent
present subjunctive:	que je me promène	que nous nous promenions
	que tu te promènes	que vous vous promeniez
	qu'il se promène	qu'ils se promènent
future indicative:	je me promènerai	nous nous promènerons
	tu te promèneras	vous vous promènerez
	il se promènera	ils se promèneront
present conditional:	je me promènerais	nous nous promènerions
	tu te promènerais	vous vous promèneriez
	il se promènerait	ils se promèneraient

infinitive **acheter** (stem **achet-**)

present indicative:	j'achète	nous achetons
	tu achètes	vous achetez
	il achète	ils achètent
present subjunctive:	que j'achète	que nous achetions
	que tu achètes	que vous achetiez
	qu'il achète	qu'ils achètent
future indicative:	j'achèterai	nous achèterons
	tu achèteras	vous achèterez
	il achètera	ils achèteront
present conditional:	j'achèterais	nous achèterions
	tu achèterais	vous achèteriez
	il achèterait	ils achèteraient

The following is a list of the most common mute ***e*** -stem verbs following the pattern of ***acheter*** (it is safe to assume that any ***-eler*** or ***-eter*** verb not in the list follows the pattern of ***appeler***, below):

amener	to bring, take
assener	to give, deliver (a violent blow, a shock)
celer	to conceal
ciseler	to chisel
congeler	to freeze (food)
déceler	to notice, discover
dégeler	to thaw
geler	to freeze (weather)
élever	to rise up, lift up, raise
s'élever	to rise
enlever	to remove, take away
emmener	to take away, carry
haleter	to pant, huff and puff
harceler	to harass, torment
lever	to raise, lift
se lever	to get up, rise
marteler	to hammer
mener	to lead
modeler	to model
peler	to peel
prélever	to withhold
ramener	to bring back, take back
receler	to hide stolen goods
relever	to put up again, raise again
se démener	to move violently, be very active
se promener	to take a walk
soulever	to lift up
surgeler:	to freeze:
produits surgelés	frozen foods

2) For a group of verbs in ***-eler*** and ***-eter***, the consonant ***l*** or ***t*** ending the stem is doubled.

infinitive **appeler** (stem **appel-**)

present indicative:	j'appelle tu appelles il appelle	nous appelons vous appelez ils appellent
present subjunctive:	que j'appelle que tu appelles qu'il appelle	que nous appelions que vous appeliez qu'ils appellent
future indicative:	j'appellerai tu appelleras il appellera	nous appellerons vous appellerez ils appelleront
present conditional:	j'appellerais tu appellerais il appellerait	nous appellerions vous appelleriez ils appelleraient

infinitive **jeter** (stem **jet-**)

present indicative:	je jette tu jettes il jette	nous jetons vous jetez ils jettent
present subjunctive:	que je jette que tu jettes qu'il jette	que nous jetions que vous jetiez qu'ils jettent
future indicative:	je jetterai tu jetteras il jettera	nous jetterons vous jetterez ils jetteront
present conditional:	je jetterais tu jetterais il jetterait	nous jetterions vous jetteriez ils jetteraient

F. Verbs with ***é*** as the last vowel in the stem (***e*** with acute accent) change that ***é*** to ***è*** whenever the next syllable is a *final mute **e*** syllable. This will apply only in the present indicative and in the present subjunctive.

infinitive **espérer** (stem **espér-**)

present indicative:	j'espère tu espères il espère	nous espérons vous espérez ils espèrent

present subjunctive:	que j'espère	que nous espérions
	que tu espères	que vous espériez
	qu'il espère	qu'ils espèrent

Among the verbs following this pattern are ***céder, préférer, refléter, repérer***.

276. Notes on the spelling of verbs of the second group.

Except for the use of the infix ***-iss-*** in the present participle, in the present indicative and in the tenses derived from it, the verbs of the second group are regular. The model verb for all the second group verbs is ***finir***.

The verb ***haïr***, however, keeps its diaeresis (tréma in French) over the letter ***i*** in all persons and tenses except in the singular of the present indicative, and therefore also in the second person singular of the present imperative (see §258).

277. Notes on the spelling of verbs of the third group.

The verbs of the third group are all irregular in one form or other. The following generalizations may be helpful in remembering the irregularities by subgroups instead of individually.

A. Verbs in ***-indre*** keep the letter ***d*** only in the future and in the conditional, where the infinitive serves as a stem. They also change ***-nd-*** to ***-gn-*** before vowel endings in all the other tenses (see ***craindre***).

B. Verbs in ***-soudre*** keep the ***d*** only in the future and in the conditional, where the infinitive serves as a stem. They also change ***-soud-*** to ***-solv-*** before vowel endings in most other tenses, with the exception of the passé simple (and its derived tense, the pluperfect subjunctive) and the past participle, where the ***v*** of ***-solv-*** disappears (see ***résoudre***).

C. The other verbs ending in ***-dre*** keep the letter ***d*** in the singular of the present indicative. In fact, most ***-dre*** verbs keep ***d*** in all persons and tenses—compare ***attendre*** with ***prendre***.

D. Several verbs in ***-ir*** modeled on ***dormir*** drop the last consonant of their stem in the singular of the present indicative. They include

dormir	to sleep
mentir	to lie
partir	to leave
se repentir	to repent
sentir	to smell, feel, sense
servir	to serve
sortir	to go out

Bouillir also belongs to this group, with the special feature that in the singular of the present tense, it loses the consonant sound ending its stem (spelled ***-ill-***). See §258 for its principal parts.

E. The verbs ending in ***-aître*** or in ***-oître*** keep the circumflex accent over the ***i*** only in the tenses and persons in which ***i*** is followed by ***t***. The verb ***croître***, however, keeps ***î*** with the circumflex accent in all persons and tenses in which it might be mistaken for the verb ***croire*** (*to believe*). See §258.

F. The verbs ***croire, fuir, voir*** and their compounds change the letter ***i*** to ***y*** whenever the ending begins with a vowel other than a mute ***e***.

278. Uses of the infinitive.

The French infinitive is used in the following ways:

A. As object of all prepositions except ***en*** (see §270C). English uses a gerund here. The preposition ***après*** requires a *past infinitive*.

Je suis habitué à dîner tard.
I am accustomed to having supper late.

Avant de partir, donnez-moi votre adresse.
Before leaving, give me your address.

Après avoir visité le Louvre, nous sommes allés à Versailles.
After visiting the Louvre, we went to Versailles.

B. English uses the gerund to indicate cause, reason, purpose, manner of spending one's time, etc. If simultaneity is not emphasized or apparent, the French structure in this case is always ***à*** + infinitive. If simultaneity is apparent, emphasized, or necessary, see §270C.

Il s'amuse à compter les voitures qui passent.
He keeps busy by counting the passing cars.

Je dois vous ennuyer à parler tant.
I must be boring you (by) talking so much.

Il se tue à travailler.
He is killing himself by working (so much).

C. After a great number of verbs, to translate the English structure *that* and a subordinate clause, or a dependent infinitive, or a dependent gerund (see also F, above). Also after a good number of adjectives used with *to be* in personal and impersonal constructions (see the adjective table after the verb table, below).

Three dependent infinitive constructions should be observed. The first and most common is one in which the main verb requires the preposition ***de*** to introduce the dependent infinitive.

J'ai décidé de partir le 15 mai.
I have decided to leave on May 15.

Je viens d'acheter mon billet.
I have just purchased my ticket.

The second construction is one in which the main verb requires the preposition ***à*** to introduce the dependent infinitive.

J'ai commencé à faire ma valise.
I have begun packing.
J'apprendrai à parler français.
I will learn to speak French.

The third construction is one in which the main verb requires no preposition before the dependent infinitive.

Je veux visiter la Bourgogne et l'Alsace.
I want to visit Burgundy and Alsace.
Je vais revenir le 22 juin.
I am going to come back on June 22.

These French infinitive patterns are used to render three basic English structures:

Main Verb	+	*to* Infinitive
Main Verb	+	*that* Subordinate Clause
Main Verb	+	Gerund

J'essaierai d'être à l'heure.
I'll try to be on time.
Il commence à comprendre.
He is beginning to understand.
Nous voudrions voir les Jeux Olympiques.
We would like to see the Olympic Games.
Vous devrez passer la nuit là-bas. Vous serez obligé de passer la nuit là-bas.
Il vous faudra passer la nuit là-bas. Il faudra que vous passiez la nuit là-bas.
It will be necessary for you to stay overnight.

Je regrette de ne pas être parti plus tôt.
I regret that I did not leave sooner.
Il ne s'attend pas à trouver ce nouveau guide touristique facilement.
He doesn't expect that he will find this new guidebook easily.
J'admets avoir triché un peu.
I confess that I have cheated a bit.

Ils l'accusent d'avoir triché.
They accuse him (her) of cheating. (having cheated)
Il fait en sorte de ne pas être le dernier.
He avoids being last.
Elle n'est pas de taille à finir ce travail à temps.
She is not up to completing this job on time.

Ne me reproche pas de les avoir avertis!
Don't blame me for warning them! (having warned)

When using verbs from the list in the following pages, it would be wise to refer to the examples given below as possible structural patterns, observing the presence or absence of a direct or indirect object—beside the reflexive or reciprocal pronoun— in addition to the dependent infinitive.

Object Construction		
A. None	**B. Direct Object**	**C. Indirect Object**
Main Verb (+ prep.) + Infinitive	*Main Verb (+ prep.) + D.O. + Inf.*	*Main Verb (+ prep.) + I.O. + Inf.*
J'ai essayé de comprendre.	J'ai prié Paul de venir.	Je lui demande de répondre.
Il s'habitue à conduire.	Je l'ai obligé à payer.	Il apprend aux élèves à compter.
Nous voulons entrer.	Nous regardons passer les gens.	Nous leur ferons faire l'exercice.

VERBS WITH DEPENDENT INFINITIVES			
English Main Verb	**French Main Verb**	**Prep.**	**Object**
abstain from + *ger.*	**s'abstenir**	**de**	*none*
accept to + *inf.* accept + *ger.*	**accepter** **consentir** **s'accorder**	**de** **à** **à**	*none* *none* *none*
accuse someone of + *ger.*	**accuser**	**de**	direct
accuse oneself of + *ger.*	**s'accuser**	**de**	*none*
accustom someone to + *ger.*	**habituer**	**à**	direct
accustom oneself to + *ger.*	**s'habituer**	**à**	*none*
accustomed (get) to + *ger.*	**s'habituer**	**à**	*none*
admit + *ger.* admit that	**admettre**	**de**	*none*
advise someone to + *inf.*	**conseiller**	**de**	indirect
advise someone not to + *inf.*	**déconseiller**	**de**	indirect
afford to + *inf.*	**se permettre**	**de**	*none*
agree to + *inf.*	**accepter** **consentir** **s'accorder** **convenir**	**de** **à** **à** **de**	*none* *none* *none* *none*
aid someone to + *inf.* aid (help) someone in + *ger.*	**aider**	**à**	direct
aim at + *ger.*	**viser**	**à**	*none*
allow someone to + *inf.*	**permettre** **autoriser**	**de** **à**	indirect direct
. . . almost . . .	**faillir (past tense)** **manquer**	 **de**	*none* *none*
apologize for + *ger.*	**s'excuser**	**de**	*none*

arrange (it) so that	**faire en sorte** **s'arranger**	**de** **pour**	*none* *none*
ask someone to + *inf.*	**demander** **prier**	**de** **de**	indirect direct
ask to + *inf.*	**demander**	**à**	indirect
aspire to + *inf.*	**aspirer**	**à**	*none*
assert (claim) that	**affirmer**		*none*
attempt to + *inf.*	**tenter** **essayer** **tâcher**	**de** **de** **de**	*none* *none* *none*
attempt in vain to + *inf.*	**avoir beau** **s'évertuer**	 **à**	*none* *none*
authorize someone to + *inf.*	**autoriser**	**à**	direct
avoid + *ger.*	**éviter** **faire en sorte**	**de** **de ne pas**	*none* *none*
be + *adjective* + *infinitive*	See also **Adjective Table** (§278D).		
be about to + *inf.*	**aller** **être sur le point**	 **de**	*none* *none*
be accustomed to + *ger.*	**avoir l'habitude**	**de**	*none*
be amazed to + *inf.*	**s'étonner**	**de**	*none*
be anxious to + *inf.*	**avoir hâte**	**de**	*none*
be appointed to + *noun* be appointed to + *inf.*	**être nommé** **être nommé**	**à (noun)** **pour**	*none* *none*
be ashamed to + *inf.* be ashamed of + *ger.*	**avoir honte** **rougir**	**de** **de**	*none* *none*
be bound to + *inf.*	**avoir l'obligation**	**de**	*none*
be careful to + *inf.*	**ne pas manquer**	**de**	*none*
be careful not to + *inf.*	**faire attention** **prendre garde** **se garder**	**à ne pas** **de** **de**	*none* *none* *none*
be caught + *ger.*	**être pris** **être attrapé** **être pris en train** **être attrapé en train** **se faire prendre**	**à** **à** **de** **de** **à**	*none* *none* *none* *none* *none*
be dying to + *inf.*	**mourir d'envie**	**de**	*none*
be early to + *inf.*	**être de bonne heure**	**à**	*none*
be enough to + *inf.*	**suffire**	**à**	
be equivalent to + *ger.*	**correspondre** **équivaloir**	**à** **à**	*none* *none*
be fortunate to + *inf.*	**avoir le bonheur** **avoir la chance**	**de** **de**	*none* *none*
be glad to + *inf.*	**avoir le plaisir**	**de**	*none*
be grateful to someone for + *ger.*	**savoir gré**	**de**	indirect
be going to + *inf.*	**aller**		*none*

be hopeful to + *inf.*	**avoir l'espoir** **espérer**	**de**	*none* *none*
be hurried/in a hurry to + *inf.*	**avoir hâte**	**de**	*none*
be a long time + *ger.* take a long time to + *inf.*	**mettre longtemps**	**à**	*none*
be lucky to + *inf.*	**avoir la chance** **avoir de la chance**	**de** **de**	*none* *none*
be prone to + *ger.*	**avoir tendance**	**à**	*none*
be quick to + *inf.*	**ne pas perdre de temps** **ne pas traîner**	**à** **à**	*none* *none*
be reluctant to + *inf.*	**hésiter** **avoir peu envie** **montrer de la réticence**	**à** **de** **à**	*none* *none* *none*
be scheduled to + *inf.*	**devoir** (in active voice)		*none*
be slated to + *inf.*	**devoir** (in active voice)		*none*
be sorry to + *inf.* be sorry for + *ger.*	**regretter**	**de**	*none*
be suitable to + *inf.*	**convenir**	**à**	*none*
be supposed to + *inf.*	**devoir**		*none*
be the best (most) at + *ger.*	**exceller**	**à**	*none*
be to + *inf.*	**devoir**		*none*
be up to + *ger.* (ability)	**être de taille** **être à même**	**à** **de**	*none* *none*
be up to + *ger.* (mood)	**être d'humeur** **être à même**	**à** **de**	*none* *none*
be worth + *ger.* (passive meaning)	**valoir la peine** (with passive voice)	**de**	*none*
bear to + *inf.* bear + *ger.*	**supporter**	**de**	*none*
beg someone to + *inf.*	**prier** **supplier** **conjurer**	**de** **de** **de**	direct direct direct
begin to + *inf.* begin + *ger.*	**commencer** **se mettre**	**à** **à**	*none* *none*
believe that (see §285)	**croire** **penser** **estimer**		*none* *none* *none*
beseech someone to + *inf.*	**supplier** **implorer**	**de** **de**	direct direct
blame someone for + *ger.*	**blâmer** **reprocher**	**de** **de**	direct indirect
blame oneself for + *ger.*	**se reprocher**	**de**	*none*
boast of + *ger.*	**se vanter**	**de**	*none*
brag of + *ger.*	**se vanter**	**de**	*none*
bring to + *inf.*	**apporter**	**à**	direct

bring someone down to + *ger.*	**réduire**	**à**	direct
can + *inf.*	**pouvoir** **savoir** (know how)		*none* *none*
can see + *inf.* can see + *ger.*	**voir** **pouvoir voir**		direct direct
can feel + *inf.* can feel + *ger.*	**sentir** **pouvoir sentir**		direct direct
can hear + *inf.* can hear + *ger.*	**entendre** **pouvoir entendre**		direct direct
can't wait + *inf.*	**avoir hâte** **être impatient**	**de** **de**	*none* *none*
care about + *ger.*	**se soucier** **veiller**	**de** **à**	*none* *none*
not care about + *ger.*	**se moquer (bien)** **ne pas se soucier**	**de** **de**	*none* *none*
cause to + *inf.*	See *make, have* someone do something		
cease + *ger.* cease to + *inf.*	**cesser** **arrêter** **s'arrêter** **s'interrompre**	**de** **de** **de** **de**	*none* *none* *none* *none*
choose to + *inf.*	**choisir**	**de**	
claim to + *inf.* claim that	**prétendre** **affirmer** **assurer** **dire** **déclarer**		*none* *none* *none* *none* *none*
come and (§278G)	**venir**		*none*
come back and (§278G)	**revenir**		*none*
command someone to + *inf.*	**commander** **ordonner** **sommer**	**de** **de** **de**	indirect indirect direct
complete + *ger.*	**finir** **achever**	**de** **de**	*none* *none*
condemn someone to + *ger.*	**condamner**	**à**	direct
condescend to + *inf.*	**condescendre** **s'abaisser** **daigner**	**à** **à**	*none* *none* *none*
confess (to) + *ger.*	**avouer** **s'accuser** **confesser** **reconnaître**	 **de**	*none* *none* *none* *none*
congratulate someone for + *ger.*	**féliciter**	**de**	direct
consider + *ger.*	**envisager**	**de**	*none*
consist in + *ger.*	**consister**	**à**	*none*
constrain someone to + *inf.*	**astreindre**	**à**	direct
constrain oneself to + *inf.*	**s'astreindre**	**à**	*none*

contribute to + *ger.*	**contribuer**	**à**	*none*
contrive to + *inf.*	**s'efforcer** **s'ingénier** **parvenir** **réussir**	**de** **à** **à** **à**	*none* *none* *none* *none*
convince someone to + *inf.*	**convaincre**	**de**	direct
count on + *ger.*	**compter** **espérer** **penser**		*none* *none* *none*
dare to + *inf.*	**oser** **se risquer**	 **à**	*none* *none*
dare someone to + *inf.*	**défier**	**de**	direct
decide to + *inf.*	**décider** **décider** **se décider** **résoudre** **se résoudre**	**de** **à** **à** **de** **à**	*none* direct *none* *none* *none*
declare that	**déclarer**		*none*
demand to + *inf.* demand that	**exiger**	**de**	*none*
deny + *ger.*	**nier**		*none*
deserve to + *inf.*	**mériter**	**de**	*none*
desire to + *inf.*	**désirer**		*none*
desire strongly, have one's heart set on + *ger.*	**tenir**	**à**	*none*
despair of + *ger.*	**désespérer**	**de**	*none*
destine to + *inf.*	**destiner**	**à**	*none*
detest + *ger.*	**détester** **ne pas aimer** **avoir horreur**	 **de**	*none* *none* *none*
devote money to + *ger.*	**employer de l'argent**	**à**	*none*
devote oneself to + *ger.*	**se dévouer** **s'employer** **s'attacher** **se consacrer**	**à** **à** **à** **à**	*none* *none* *none* *none*
disdain + *ger.*	**dédaigner**	**de**	*none*
dispose someone to + *ger.*	**disposer** **préparer**	**à** **à**	direct direct
dispose oneself to + *ger.*	**se disposer** **se préparer**	**à** **à**	*none* *none*
doubt that	**douter**	**de**	*none*
do without + *ger.*	**se dispenser** **se passer**	**de** **de**	*none* *none*
dream of + *ger.*	**rêver** **songer**	**de** **à**	*none* *none*

drive someone to + *ger.*	**pousser** **mener** **conduire**	**à** **à** **à**	direct direct direct
drive oneself + *adjective* + *ger.*	**se tuer** **se rendre** + *adjective*	**à** **à**	*none* *none*
dread + *ger.*	**craindre** **avoir peur** **appréhender** **redouter**	**de** **de** **de** **de**	*none* *none* *none* *none*
encourage someone to + *inf.*	**encourager** **exhorter** **engager**	**à** **à** **à**	direct direct direct
endeavor to + *inf.*	**tâcher** **s'efforcer**	**de** **de**	*none* *none*
end up + *ger.*	**aboutir** **finir**	**à** **par**	*none* *none*
enjoy + *ger.*	**se plaire** **avoir du plaisir** **trouver du plaisir** **prendre plaisir**	**à** **à** **à** **à**	*none* *none* *none* *none*
envy + *ger.*	**convoiter** **avoir envie** **désirer**	**de** **de**	*none* *none* *none*
excell + *ger.*	**exceller** **être le meilleur**	**à** **à**	*none* *none*
excite someone to + *inf.*	**exciter** **pousser** **engager** **encourager**	**à** **à** **à** **à**	direct direct direct direct
excuse someone for + *ger.*	**excuser**	**de**	direct
exhaust someone (by) + *ger.*	**fatiguer** **tuer**	**à** **à**	direct direct
exhaust oneself (by) + *ger.*	**se fatiguer** **se tuer**	**à** **à**	*none* *none*
expose oneself to + *ger.*	**s'exposer**	**à**	*none*
fail to + *inf.*	**ne pas réussir** (or merely a single negative verb: **je ne comprends pas)**	**à**	*none*
fear + *ger.*	**craindre** **avoir peur** **appréhender** **redouter**	**de** **de** **de** **de**	*none* *none* *none* *none*
feel (something) + *ger.* (See §89, notes 5 and 6.)	**sentir**		direct
feel (adj.) + *inf.*	**se sentir** (See Adjective Table, §278D.)		
feel like + *ger.* (want to)	**avoir envie**	**de**	*none*
feel like + *ger.* (believe that)	**avoir l'impression**	**de**	*none*

feel up to + *ger.* (ability)	**se sentir de taille**	**à**	*none*
	se sentir capable	**de**	*none*
feel up to + *ger.* (mood)	**se sentir d'humeur**	**à**	*none*
feel repulsion, disgust for + *ger.*	**avoir horreur** **répugner** (literary)	**de** **à**	*none* *none*
feign to + *inf.*	**feindre** **faire semblant**	**de** **de**	*none* *none*
find something to + *inf.*	**trouver**	**à**	direct
find it (adj.) to + *inf.*	Refer to Adjective Table (§278D) or to *it is*, below.		
find it surprising to + *inf.*	**trouver étonnant**	**de**	*none*
finish + *ger.*	**finir** **achever**	**de** **de**	*none* *none*
flatter oneself about + *ger.*	**se flatter**	**de**	*none*
forbid someone to + *inf.*	**interdire** **défendre**	**de** **de**	indirect indirect
force someone to + *inf.*	**forcer** **contraindre** **obliger**	**à** **à** **à**	direct direct direct
forget to + *inf.*	**oublier**	**de**	*none*
forgive someone for + *ger.*	**pardonner**	**de**	indirect
get	See below. See also *make, have*, below and in index. See also Adjective Table, §278D.		
get + *adjective* + *infinitive*	See Adjective Table, §278D.		
get to + *inf.* (obtain)	**obtenir**	**de**	*none*
get to + *inf.* (succeed)	**arriver**	**à**	*none*
get to + *inf.* (manage)	**parvenir**	**à**	*none*
get to + *inf.* (have to)	**devoir**		*none*
get to + *inf.* (have the opportunity)	**avoir l'occasion**	**de**	*none*
get around to + *ger.*	**se mettre (enfin)**	**à**	*none*
get down and (§278G)	**descendre**		*none*
get down to + *ger.*	**se mettre**	**à**	*none*
get it into one's mind to + *inf.*	**s'aviser**	**de**	*none*
get ready to + *inf.*	**se préparer** **s'apprêter**	**à** **à**	*none* *none*
get tired + *ger.*	**se fatiguer**	**à**	*none*
get tired of + *ger.*	**être fatigué**	**de**	*none*
get up and (§278G) (go up)	**monter**		*none*
get up to + *inf.* (stand)	**se lever pour**		*none*
get used to + *ger.*	**s'habituer**	**à**	*none*
get someone used to + *ger.*	**habituer** **accoutumer**	**à** **à**	direct direct
give up + *ger.*	**renoncer**	**à**	*none*

give up hope about + *ger.*	**désespérer**	**de**	*none*
go and (§278G) go to + *inf.*	**aller**		*none*
goad into + *ger.*	**pousser** **exciter**	**à** **à**	*none* *none*
go back and (§278G) go back and (start again)	**retourner** **se remettre**	 **à**	*none* *none*
go down and (§278G)	**descendre** **descendre**	 **pour**	*none* *none*
go home and (§278G)	**rentrer** **rentrer**	 **pour**	*none* *none*
go up and	**monter** **monter**	 **pour**	*none* *none*
(I, you, he, she, etc.) had better + *inf.*	**(je) ferais mieux** **(je) ferais aussi bien**	**de** **de**	*none* *none*
(I, you, he, she, etc.) had rather + *inf.*	**(j')aimerais mieux** **(je) préférerais** **(j')aimerais autant**		*none* *none* *none*
happen (you may happen) to + *inf.*	**il peut (vous) arriver**	**de**	indirect
hate + *ger.* hate to + *inf.*	**détester** **ne pas aimer** **avoir horreur**	 **de**	*none* *none* *none*
have (something) to + *inf.*	**avoir (quelque chose)**	**à**	direct
have someone + *inf.* have something done	**faire**		(§297)
have a good time + *ger.*	**s'amuser** **avoir du plaisir**	**à** **à**	*none* *none*
have a hard time + *ger.*	**avoir du mal**	**à**	*none*
have the honor of + *ger.*	**avoir l'honneur**	**de**	*none*
have just (+ past participle)	**venir**	**de**	*none*
have the nerve to + *inf.* have the gall to + *inf.*	**avoir le toupet** (coll.) **avoir le culot** (coll.) **oser** **se permettre**	**de** **de** **de**	*none* *none* *none* *none*
have the pleasure to + *inf.* have the pleasure of + *ger.*	**avoir le plaisir**	**de**	*none*
have the right to + *inf.*	**avoir le droit**	**de**	*none*
have to + *inf.*	**devoir** **être obligé** **avoir besoin**	 **de** **de**	*none* *none* *none*
See some additional ***avoir*** expressions in §3H.			
hear someone + *inf.* or + *ger.* hear something + *inf.* or + *ger.*	**entendre**		direct
help someone (to) + *inf.*	**aider**	**à**	direct
hesitate to + *inf.*	**hésiter**	**à**	*none*

hope to + *inf.*	**espérer**		*none*
hurry and (§278G) hurry to + *inf.*	**se dépêcher** **se presser** **se hâter**	**de** **de** **de**	*none* *none* *none*
imagine + *ger.* imagine that	**imaginer** **s'imaginer** **se figurer**	**de**	*none* *none* *none*
implore someone to + *inf.*	**implorer**	**de**	direct
impose on someone to + *inf.*	**imposer**	**de**	indirect
incite someone to + *inf.*	**inciter** **pousser**	**à** **à**	direct direct
insist on + *ger.*	**tenir** **insister**	**à** **pour**	*none* *none*
inspire someone to + *inf.*	**inspirer**	**de**	indirect
intend to + *inf.*	**avoir l'intention** **se proposer**	**de** **de**	*none* *none*
invite someone to + *inf.*	**inviter**	**à**	direct
it is as well to + *inf.*	**il vaut autant**		*none*
it is better to + *inf.*	**il vaut mieux**		*none*
it is enough to + *inf.*	**il suffit** **il est suffisant**	**de** **de**	*none* *none*
it is enough for you to (all you have to do is)	**il vous suffit** **vous n'avez qu'à (see §203)**	**de**	*none*
it is fitting to + *inf.*	**il convient**	**de**	*none*
it is fortunate that	**c'est une chance**	**de**	*none*
it is pointless to + *inf.*	**il ne sert à rien** **ça ne sert à rien**	**de** **de**	*none* *none*
it is proper to + *inf.*	**il convient**	**de**	*none*
it is a serious matter to + *inf.*	**c'est une affaire sérieuse**	**(que) de**	*none*
it is a shame to + *inf.*	**c'est une honte que**	**de**	*none*
it is suitable to + *inf.*	**il convient**	**de**	*none*
it is unfortunate to + *inf.*	**ce n'est pas de chance**	**(que) de**	*none*
it is useless to + *inf.* it is no use + *ger.*	**il ne sert à rien** **ça ne sert à rien**	**de** **de**	*none* *none*
keep from + *ger.*	**se garder** **s'empêcher**	**de** **de**	*none* *none*
keep someone from + *ger.*	**empêcher**	**de**	direct
keep it to oneself to + *inf.*	**se réserver**	**de**	*none*
know how to + *inf.*	**savoir**		*none*
laugh at + *ger.* learn to + *inf.*	**rire** **apprendre**	**de** **à**	*none* *none*
leave it to me to + *inf.*	**je me charge**	**de**	*none*
leave it to someone to + *inf.*	**laisser**		direct

Leave it to me!	**Je m'en charge!**		
Leave it to them!	**Laisse-les faire!**		
let someone + *inf.* let something + *inf.*	**laisser**		direct
like to + *inf.* like + *ger.*	**aimer** **aimer**	 **à** (formal)	*none* *none*
limit oneself to + *ger.*	**se limiter**	**à**	*none*
listen to someone + *ger.* listen to something + *ger.*	**écouter**		direct
loathe + *ger.*	**avoir horreur** **répugner** (literary) **détester**	**de** **à**	*none* *none* *none*
look (seem) to + *inf.*	**sembler** **paraître**		*none*
look (see, watch) + *inf.* look (see, watch) + *ger.*	**regarder**		direct
love to + *inf.* love + *ger.*	**aimer** **aimer** (formal)	 **à**	*none* *none*
make someone + *inf.*	**faire**		See §297.
make (an) effort to + *inf.*	**s'efforcer**	**de**	*none*
make ready to + *inf.*	**s'apprêter** **se préparer**	**à** **à**	*none* *none*
make sure, certain to + *inf.* make sure, certain that	**veiller** **s'assurer que** (indicative)	**à**	*none*
make up one's mind to + *inf.*	**se décider** **décider**	**à** **de**	*none* *none*
manage to + *inf.*	**réussir** **parvenir** **arriver**	**à** **à** **à**	*none* *none* *none*
meddle in + *ger.*	**se mêler**	**de**	*none*
must + *inf.*	**devoir** **avoir besoin** **être obligé** **il faut** **il me faut** **il est nécessaire**	 **de** **de** **de**	*none* *none* *none* *none* *none* *none*
need to + *inf.*	**avoir besoin**	**de**	*none*
neglect to + *inf.* neglect + *ger.*	**négliger** **omettre** **oublier**	**de** **de** **de**	*none* *none* *none*
offer to + *inf.*	**offrir** **s'offrir**	**de** **à**	*none* *none*
offer someone to + *inf.*	**offrir** **proposer**	**de** **de**	indirect indirect
order someone to + *inf.*	**ordonner** **commander** **sommer**	**de** **de** **de**	indirect indirect direct

order that	**exiger**	**de**	*none*
owe it to oneself to + *inf.*	**se devoir**	**de**	*none*
permit someone to + *inf.*	**permettre** **autoriser**	**de** **à**	indirect direct
persist (in) + *ger.*	**persister** **s'obstiner** **persévérer**	**à** **à** **à**	*none* *none* *none*
persuade someone to + *inf.*	**persuader** **se persuader**	**de** **de**	direct or indirect *none*
place something (in order) to + *inf.*	**mettre**	**à**	*none*
plan to + *inf.* plan on + *ger.*	**envisager** **projeter** **méditer**	**de** **de** **de**	*none* *none* *none*
plot to + *inf.*	**comploter**	**de**	*none*
prefer to + *inf.* prefer + *ger.*	**préférer** **aimer mieux**		*none* *none*
prepare to + *inf.*	**préparer** **se préparer** **s'apprêter**	**à** **à** **à**	*none* *none* *none*
pretend to + *inf.*	**prétendre** **faire semblant** **feindre** **affecter**	 **de** **de** **de**	*none* *none* *none* *none*
prevent someone from + *ger.*	**empêcher**	**de**	direct
proceed to + *inf.* proceed with + *ger.*	**se mettre** **se mettre en devoir**	**à** **de**	*none* *none*
promise someone to + *inf.*	**promettre**	**de**	indirect
promise to + *inf.*	**promettre** **s'engager**	**de** **à**	*none* *none*
promise oneself that	**se promettre** **se jurer**	**de** **de**	*none* *none*
prompt someone to + *inf.*	**pousser** **amener**	**à** **à**	direct direct
propose to + *inf.* propose + *ger.*	**se proposer** **proposer**	**de** **de**	*none* indirect
provoke someone into + *ger.*	**provoquer** **pousser**	**à** **à**	direct direct
push someone into + *ger.*	**pousser** **inciter** **encourager** **engager**	**à** **à** **à** **à**	direct direct direct direct
put (in order to) + *inf.*	**mettre**	**à**	*none*
quit + *ger.*	**cesser** **arrêter** **finir** **s'arrêter**	**de** **de** **de** **de**	*none* *none* *none* *none*

recognize that	**reconnaître** **admettre**		*none* *none*
recommend + *ger.*	**recommander**	**de**	*none*
recommend to someone to + *inf.*	**recommander**	**de**	indirect
reduce someone to + *ger.*	**réduire**	**à**	direct
refrain from + *ger.*	**se garder** **éviter** **se retenir** **s'empêcher** **essayer**	**de** **de** **de** **de** **de ne pas**	*none* *none* *none* *none* *none*
refuse to + *inf.* refuse + *ger.*	**refuser**	**de**	*none*
regret + *ger.*	**regretter** **se repentir**	**de** **de**	*none* *none*
remember to + *inf.*	**ne pas oublier** **se souvenir**	**de** **de**	*none* *none*
remember + *ger.*	**se rappeler** **se souvenir**	 **de**	*none* *none*
remind someone to + *inf.*	**rappeler**	**de**	indirect
renounce + *ger.*	**renoncer**	**à**	*none*
repent from + *ger.*	**se repentir** **regretter**	**de** **de**	*none* *none*
reproach someone for + *ger.*	**reprocher**	**de**	indirect
reproach oneself for + *ger.*	**se reprocher**	**de**	*none*
reserve the right to + *inf.*	**se réserver le droit** **se réserver**	**de** **de**	*none* *none*
resign oneself to + *ger.*	**se résigner**	**à**	*none*
resolve (decisive) to + *inf.*	**décider** **résoudre**	**de** **de**	*none* *none*
resolve (hesitant) to + *inf.*	**se résoudre** **se décider**	**à** **à**	*none* *none*
risk + *ger.*	**risquer** **faillir** (past tense only)	**de**	*none* *none*
run and (§278G) run to + *inf.*	**courir** **courir**	 **pour**	*none* *none*
run the risk of + *ger.*	**courir le risque** **risquer**	**de** **de**	*none* *none*
run the risk of + *ger.* (take a chance, dare)	**se risquer**	**à**	*none*
rush (in, out, etc.) to + *inf.*	**accourir** **accourir**	 **pour**	*none* *none*
say that (+ past tense)	**dire** (+ past infinitive)		*none*
see someone + *inf.* see something + *inf.* see someone + *ger.* see something + *ger.*	**voir**		direct

seek to + *inf.*	**chercher**	**à**	*none*
seem to + *inf.*	**sembler** **paraître** **avoir l'air**	 **de**	*none* *none* *none*
send someone to + *inf.*	**envoyer**		direct
serve to + *inf.*	**servir**	**à**	*none*
show someone how to + *inf.*	**montrer comment**		indirect
skip + *ger.*	**se dispenser**	**de**	*none*
spare someone the trouble of + *ger.*	**épargner** **épargner la peine** **éviter (la peine)**	**de** **de** **de**	indirect indirect indirect
stand (bear) to + *inf.*	**supporter**	**de**	*none*
start to + *inf.* start + *ger.*	**se mettre** **commencer**	**à** **à**	*none* *none*
stay on (in order) to + *inf.*	**rester**		*none*
stay on late + *ger.*	**s'attarder**	**à**	*none*
stay on a long time before + *ger.*	**tarder**	**à**	*none*
stop + *ger.*	**arrêter** **s'arrêter** **cesser** **s'interrompre**	**de** **de** **de** **de**	*none* *none* *none* *none*
strive to + *inf.*	**s'efforcer** **s'évertuer**	**de** **à**	*none* *none*
succeed in + *ger.* succeed to + *inf.*	**réussir** **parvenir** **arriver** **obtenir**	**à** **à** **à** **de**	*none* *none* *none* *none*
suggest + *ger.* to someone	**suggérer**	**de**	indirect
suspect someone of + *ger.*	**soupçonner**	**de**	direct
swear to + *inf.* swear that	**jurer** **se jurer**	**de** **de**	indirect *none*
take (someone somewhere) to + *inf.*	**emmener** **mener** **conduire**		direct direct direct
take care to + *inf.*	**veiller** **ne pas manquer**	**à** **de**	*none* *none*
take care not to + *inf.*	**veiller à ne pas** **prendre garde** **se garder** **éviter**	 **de** **de** **de**	 *none* *none* *none*
take a chance, a dare on + *ger.*	**se hasarder** **se risquer** **tenter** **oser**	**à** **à** **de** 	*none* *none* *none* *none*
take it on (upon) oneself to + *inf.*	**se charger** **s'aviser**	**de** **de**	*none* *none*

teach someone (how) to + *inf.* teach someone + *ger.*	**enseigner** **apprendre**	**à** **à**	indirect indirect
tell someone to + *inf.* (by telegraph) (by telephone) (by mail)	**dire** **télégraphier** **téléphoner** **écrire**	**de** **de** **de** **de**	indirect indirect indirect indirect
tend to + *inf.*	**tendre** **avoir tendance** **être enclin**	**à** **à** **à**	*none* *none* *none*
tire oneself (be, get tired) + *ger.*	**se fatiguer** **être fatigué** **se fatiguer**	**de** **de** **à**	*none* *none* *none*
think that	**penser** **croire** **estimer** **songer**	 **à**	*none* *none* *none* *none*
think one can + *inf.* get it into one's mind to + *inf.*	**s'aviser**	**de**	*none*
think over + *ger.*	**méditer**	**de**	*none*
threaten to + *inf.* threaten someone with + *ger.*	**menacer**	**de**	direct
train someone to + *inf.*	**entraîner** **exercer** **former**	**à** **à** **à**	direct direct direct
train (an animal) to + *inf.*	**dresser**	**à**	direct
tremble at the thought of + *ger.*	**trembler** **trembler à l'idée** **frémir** **frémir à l'idée**	**de** **de** **de** **de**	*none* *none* *none* *none*
try to + *inf.* try + *ger.*	**essayer** **tenter** **chercher**	**de** **de** **à**	*none* *none* *none*
try hard to + *inf.* (with little result) (with no result)	**tâcher** **s'efforcer** **s'évertuer** **avoir beau**	**de** **de** **à** 	*none* *none* *none* *none*
wait to + *inf.* can't wait	**attendre** See *can't wait* above.	**de**	*none*
want to + *inf.*	**vouloir** **désirer** **avoir envie**	 **de**	*none* *none* *none*
warn someone to + *inf.*	**avertir** **prévenir**	**de** **de**	direct direct
watch someone + *inf.* watch someone + *ger.* watch something + *inf.* watch something + *ger.*	**regarder**		direct
wish for someone to + *inf.*	**souhaiter**	**de**	indirect

wish to + *inf.*	**désirer** **souhaiter**		*none* *none*
work at + *ger.*	**travailler** **s'occuper**	**à** **à**	*none* *none*
worry about + *ger.*	**se soucier** **se tracasser**	**de** **de**	*none* *none*
write s.o. (to tell him/her) to + *inf.*	**écrire**	**de**	indirect

D. After many adjectives used with ***être*** or a similar verb (***sembler, paraître, devenir***), in both personal and impersonal constructions.

Personal construction:

Cette athlète est heureuse d'avoir gagné la médaille d'or.
This female athlete is happy to have won the gold medal.

Impersonal construction:

Il est impardonnable de laisser un pays dans cet état de misère.
It is unforgivable to leave a country in this state of misery.
Il est troublant de voir tant de victimes de la famine.
It is disturbing to see so many victims of famine.

It should be noted that in the impersonal construction the actual subject of the verb is the prepositional phrase beginning with ***de***. The use of ***c'est*** for ***il est*** in this impersonal construction should be restricted to very familiar speech.

The following tables provide lists of common adjectives likely to be used with dependent infinitives. The first of the following lists contains French adjectives normally followed by a preposition and an infinitive. The preposition is generally ***à*** or ***de***. A few adjectives want ***pour***, others take no preposition at all.

English has corresponding constructions in which the adjective is followed by *to* and an infinitive or a gerund, or by another preposition and a gerund, or by a gerund without any preposition. It is also common for the adjective to be followed by a conjunctive clause introduced by *that*. The following table gives only the most common constructions.

ADJECTIVE + INFINITIVE IN PERSONAL CONSTRUCTIONS

English Adjective	French Adjective	Prep.	Object
be + *adjective* + *infinitive* be + *adjective* (+ *prep.*) + *gerund*	**être** + *adjective* **être** + *adj.*	* *	*none* *none*
	See also *it is* under the letter *i* in the verb list, and the table following this one.		

able to + *inf.*	**être capable**	**de**	*none*
amazed to + *inf.* amazed at + *ger.*	**être étonné**	**de**	*none*
anxious to + *inf.* anxious about + *ger.*	**être désireux** **être pressé**	**de** **de**	*none* *none*
ashamed to + *inf.* ashamed of + *ger.*	**être gêné** **être honteux**	**de** **de**	*none* *none*
bound to + *inf.*	**être obligé**	**de**	*none*
busy + *ger.*	**être occupé**	**à**	*none*
charged with + *ger.*	**être chargé** (in charge of) **être accusé** (accused of)	**de** **de**	*none* *none*
charmed to + *inf.*	**être charmé**	**de**	*none*
compelled to + *inf.*	**être obligé** **être forcé**	**de** **de**	*none* *none*
delighted to + *inf.*	**être ravi**	**de**	*none*
destined to + *inf.*	**être destiné**	**à**	*none*
difficult to + *inf.*	**être difficile**	**à**	*none*
easy to + *inf.*	**être facile**	**à**	*none*
enough to + *inf.*	**être suffisant**	**pour**	*none*
equivalent to + *ger.*	**être équivalent**	**à**	*none*
forced to + *inf.*	**être forcé**	**de**	*none*
glad to + *inf.*	**être heureux** **être content**	**de** **de**	*none* *none*
good to + *inf.*	**être bon**	**à**	*none*
grateful to someone for + *ger.*	**être reconnaissant**	**de**	indirect
happy to + *inf.*	**être heureux**	**de**	*none*
heavy to + *inf.*	**être lourd**	**à**	*none*
humiliated to + *inf.*	**être humilié**	**de**	*none*
hurried/in a hurry to + *inf.*	**être pressé**	**de**	*none*
inclined to + *inf.*	**être enclin** **être prédisposé**	**à** **à**	*none* *none*
impossible to + *inf.*	**être impossible**	**à**	*none*
invited to + *inf.*	**être invité**	**à**	*none*
late to + *inf.* late + *ger.*	**être en retard** **ne pas être à l'heure**	**pour** **pour**	*none* *none*
likely to + *inf.*	**être susceptible**	**de**	*none*
take a long time to + *inf.*	**être long**	**à**	*none*
mad to + *inf.* mad for + *ger.*	**être fâché** **être en colère**	**de** **de**	*none* *none*
miserable to + *inf.*	**être malheureux**	**de**	*none*
obligated/obliged to + *inf.*	**être obligé** **être forcé** **être requis**	**de** **de** **de**	*none* *none* *none*

pleased to + *inf.*	**être satisfait** **être heureux** **être content**	**de** **de** **de**	*none* *none* *none*
prepared to + *inf.*	**être prêt** **être préparé**	**à** **à**	*none* *none*
prone + *ger.*	**être enclin**	**à**	*none*
proud to + *inf.*	**être fier**	**de**	*none*
quick to + *inf.*	**être rapide**	**à**	*none*
ready to + *inf.*	**être prêt**	**à**	*none*
reluctant to + *inf.*	**être réticent** **être peu disposé**	**à** **à**	*none* *none*
satisfied to + *inf.*	**être satisfait**	**de**	*none*
slow to + *inf.* slow (in) + *ger.*	**être lent**	**à**	*none*
sorry to + *inf.* sorry for + *ger.*	**être désolé** **être navré**	**de** **de**	*none* *none*
suitable to + *inf.*	**être bon**	**pour**	*none*
supposed to + *inf.*	**être supposé** **être censé**		*none* *none*
surprised to + *inf.* surprised at + *ger.*	**être surpris**	**de**	*none*
surprised + *ger.* (doing something)	**être surpris en train**	**de**	*none*
the best (most) at + *ger.*	**être le meilleur**	**à**	*none*
to + *inf.*	**être supposé** **être censé**		*none* *none*
touched + *ger.*	**être touché**	**de**	*none*
troubled to + *inf.*	**être troublé**	**de**	*none*
unlikely to + *inf.*	**ne pas être susceptible**	**de**	*none*
up to + *ger.*	**être assez** + *adj.*	**pour**	*none*
used to + *ger.*	**être habitué**	**à**	*none*
used to + *ger.*	**avoir l'habitude**	**de**	*none*

ADJECTIVE + INFINITIVE IN IMPERSONAL CONSTRUCTIONS			
English Adjective	**French Adjective**	**Prep.**	**Object**
it is abnormal to + *inf.*	**il est anormal**	**de**	*none*
it is acceptable to + *inf.*	**il est acceptable**	**de**	*none*
it is amazing to + *inf.*	**il est étonnant**	**de**	*none*
it is astonishing to + *inf.*	**il est étonnant**	**de**	*none*
it is bad to + *inf.*	**il est mal**	**de**	*none*
it is better to + *inf.*	**il vaut mieux**		*none*
it is charming to + *inf.*	**il est charmant**	**de**	*none*

it is comforting to + *inf.*	**il est rassurant**	**de**	*none*
it is common to + *inf.*	**il est commun** **il est courant**	**de** **de**	*none* *none*
it is conceivable to + *inf.*	**il est concevable**	**de**	*none*
it is current to + *inf.*	**il est courant**	**de**	*none*
it is desirable to + *inf.*	**il est désirable** **il est à souhaiter**	**de** **de**	*none* *none*
it is dangerous to + *inf.*	**il est dangereux**	**de**	*none*
it is delightful to + *inf.*	**il est charmant**	**de**	*none*
it is difficult to + *inf.*	**il est difficile**	**de**	*none*
it is disturbing to + *inf.*	**il est troublant**	**de**	*none*
it is easy to + *inf.*	**il est facile**	**de**	*none*
it is enough to + *inf.*	**il suffit** **il est suffisant**	**de** **de**	*none* *none*
it is enough for you to + *inf.* (all you have to do is)	**il vous suffit** **vous n'avez qu'**	**de** **à**	*none* *none*
it is extraordinary to + *inf.*	**il est extraordinaire**	**de**	*none*
it is fair to + *inf.*	**il est juste**	**de**	*none*
it is fitting to to + *inf.*	**il est juste** **il est normal**	**de** **de**	*none* *none*
it is fortunate that it is a fortunate thing to + *inf.*	**c'est une chance**	**de**	*none*
it is good to + *inf.*	**il est bon**	**de**	*none*
it is hopeless to + *inf.*	**il est inutile d'espérer**		*none*
it is imperative to + *inf.*	**il est impératif**	**de**	*none*
it is important to + *inf.*	**il est important**	**de**	*none*
it is impossible to + *inf.*	**il est impossible**	**de**	*none*
it is inadmissible to + *inf.*	**il est inadmissible**	**de**	*none*
it is inconceivable to + *inf.*	**il est inconcevable**	**de**	*none*
it is just to + *inf.*	**il est juste**	**de**	*none*
it is too late to + *inf.*	**il est trop tard**	**pour**	*none*
it is logical, illogical to + *inf.*	**il est logique, illogique**	**de**	*none*
it is natural to + *inf.*	**il est naturel**	**de**	*none*
it is necessary to + *inf.*	**il est nécessaire**	**de**	*none*
it is normal to + *inf.*	**il est normal**	**de**	*none*
it is polite to + *inf.*	**il est poli**	**de**	*none*
it is pointless to + *inf.*	**il est inutile**	**de**	*none*
it is possible to + *inf.*	**il est possible**	**de**	*none*
it is preferable to + *inf.*	**il est préférable**	**de**	*none*
it is proper to + *inf.*	**il est convenable**	**de**	*none*
it is reasonable to + *inf.*	**il est raisonnable**	**de**	*none*

it is reassuring to + *inf.*	**il est rassurant**	**de**	*none*
it is a serious matter to + *inf.*	**il est grave**	**de**	*none*
it is a shame to + *inf.*	**il est honteux**	**de**	*none*
it is strange to + *inf.*	**il est étrange**	**de**	*none*
it is suitable to + *inf.*	**il est convenable**	**de**	*none*
it is surprising to + *inf.*	**il est surprenant**	**de**	*none*
it is troubling to + *inf.*	**il est troublant**	**de**	*none*
it is unfortunate to + *inf.*	**il est dommage**	**de**	*none*
it is unthinkable to + *inf.*	**il est impensable**	**de**	*none*
it is useful to + *inf.*	**il est utile**	**de**	*none*
it is useless, it is no use to + *inf.*	**il est inutile**	**de**	*none*
it is worth the trouble to + *inf.*	**ça vaut la peine**	**de**	*none*

E. To replace French subordinate clauses in which the subject of the main verb and the subordinate verb are the same, whether the verbs are indicative or subjunctive.

Il croit avoir fini. (Il croit qu'il a fini.)
He thinks he has finished.

Elle pense arriver à l'heure. (Elle pense qu'elle arrivera à l'heure.)
She thinks she'll be on time.

Je croyais avoir raison.
I thought I was right.

Elle avait peur d'échouer.
She was scared she would fail.

F. Instead of the imperative on road signs, information desks, public warnings of all kinds, in footnotes, cooking recipes, etc.

Ralentir. Pousser. Tirer.
Slow down. Push. Pull.

S'adresser au guichet No. 13.
Inquire at Window 13.

Couper les cornichons en tranches et disposer celles-ci sur le pâté.
Cut baby pickles in slices and arrange on pâté.

G. After ***venir, aller***, etc., where the purpose is expressed in the second verb. Informal English frequently places *and* instead of *to* between the two verbs.

Viens t'asseoir près de moi. Elle est venue s'asseoir.
Come and (to) sit by me. She came and sat down (to sit).

Cours dire à maman qu'il va être l'heure.
Run and tell mother that it's going to be time.

Descends voir qui est là. Je cours chercher le journal.
Run down to see who is there. I'm running out to get the paper.

J'ai envoyé Michel faire les courses.
I sent Michel out to do the shopping.

Nous nous sommes attardés à regarder les derniers chars du défilé.
We stayed on a bit to watch the last floats in the parade.

Ils sont restés finir leurs devoirs.
They stayed (home) to finish their homework.

Il accourut nous annoncer son succès.
He rushed (home) to announce his success to us.

Monte me prendre un paquet de levure, s'il te plaît.
Go upstairs to get a pack of yeast for me, please.

Viens voir ça! Et vous, venez m'aider!
Come and see this! And you, come and help me!

H. As subject or as object of a verb. (English uses a gerund for this purpose.) See also §270C2.

Manger excessivement fait grossir.
Overeating causes people to grow fat.

Je déteste pêcher.
I hate fishing.

279. The subjunctive.

The subjunctive is the mood used to show a relation and dependence of meaning between two verbs. The verb dependent on the other is in the subjunctive.

This dependence is shown in one of three ways:

A. *Meaning* (§280). The main verb has a meaning obviously calling for completion by another verb. The conjunction ***que*** is all that is needed to show which verb completes the meaning of the main verb.

B. *Conjunction* (§281). The main verb does not obviously call for completion of its meaning by another verb: a more precise conjunction than ***que*** shows the specific character of the relation between the subordinate verb and the main one. The conjunction is generally a conjunctive expression (more than one word). All conjunctions and conjunctive expressions belong in two categories: some require subordinate verbs in the subjunctive, others accept verbs in the indicative (or the conditional): see §174 and §179.

C. *Relative* (§282). The connecting word is not a conjunction, but a relative pronoun. Normally, the verb of a relative clause is in the indicative mood, because the relation is only factual or explanatory (adjectival clause). The use of the subjunctive instead of the indicative creates a closer relation and implies that the speaker has personal feelings or opinions about the matter in question.

280. Meaning: the conjunction que.

If the main verb has a meaning that calls for completion by a subordinate clause, the connector is the conjunction ***que***. It is convenient to consider the main verbs in two categories: the impersonal verbs and those that are not impersonal.

A. The main verb is *not* impersonal.

1) The subordinate verb *must* be in the subjunctive if the main verb expresses:

a. A feeling or emotion (fear, eagerness, joy, sadness, pity, regret, pleasure, surprise, doubt, anger, desire, liking, dislike, preference, satisfaction, wish).

Je suis content qu'il fasse beau et qu'on puisse se baigner.
I am glad (that) the weather is fine and (that) we can go swimming.
Elle doute que son petit ami vienne la voir.
She doubts (that) her boyfriend will come to visit her.
Je crains qu'elle n'ait oublié.
I am afraid (that) she may have forgotten.

"Ne" is normally used before the subordinate verb when the main verb is one of fear (***craindre, avoir peur***), or one of the conjunctions ***de crainte que, de peur que***. It may also be used after the conjunctions ***avant que*** and ***à moins que*** when some impending or threatening circumstance is to be suggested.

b. An idea of will or volition (order, interdiction, expectation, request, wish, desire, asking, begging, refusal).

Le professeur attend que nous ayons fini l'exercice.
The professor is waiting for us to be through with the exercise.
Il s'attend à ce que nous lisions tout le chapitre.
He expects us to read the whole chapter.
Le colonel ordonne que les soldats fassent leur devoir.
The colonel orders the soldiers to do their duty.
The colonel orders that the soldiers do their duty.
Elle défend que je parte avant elle.
She forbids that I (should) leave before her.
She forbids me to leave before her.
Je demande qu'on fasse silence.
I request that everyone be silent.
La femme du patron veut que la secrétaire soit renvoyée.
The boss's wife wants the secretary to be fired.

2) The subordinate verb *may* be in the subjunctive if the main verb expresses:

a. A statement or a declaration in a way that is not meant merely to "indicate" a fact; particularly in the negative or interrogative form or if the verb is in the conditional; or if the speaker does not intend the statement or the declaration to be absolutely objective or matter-of-fact.

Je ne dis pas que cela soit facile, bien au contraire.
I am not saying that this is easy, quite the contrary.

Cela n'implique pas qu'il ait tout compris, si?
That does not imply that he has understood everything, does it?

b. A thought or opinion in a way that is not meant to merely "indicate" a fact; particularly in the negative form, in the negative-interrogative form, and in the interrogative form; also in certain tenses and moods that clearly add a subjective or affective note to the expression of the thought or opinion. In those forms, the following main verbs are generally followed by subordinate verbs in the subjunctive:

croire	to believe, think, guess
être assuré	to be assured, certain, positive
espérer	to hope, expect
être certain	to be certain, sure, positive
être sûr	to be sure, certain, positive
penser	to think, believe, guess, reckon
supposer	to suppose, guess, reckon
(s')imaginer	to imagine, fancy, figure, think

The affirmative forms of the imperative of ***supposer, imaginer, s'imaginer, espérer*** express more than a mere thought or opinion: they place the thought or the opinion in the domain of the unreal, the hypothetical, therefore requiring a completion in the subjunctive.

Supposez qu'on ait un segment AB . . .
Suppose we have a segment AB . . .

Imaginez qu'elle ne puisse pas venir! . . .
Just imagine that (or: if) she cannot come! . . .

Espérons qu'elle ait pu prendre le premier train!
Let's hope (that) she was able to catch the first train!

Note that the use of the subjunctive is not mandatory. It merely *may* be used—and should be used—when the meaning sought is not that of a plain fact, or thought, or opinion. However, one should be careful not to use indicative and subjunctive erratically. Most verbs of thought or opinion, as well as verbs of declaration and statement, are used in structures that have been more or less fixed by usage. The verb ***espérer***, for instance, is generally accepted as a verb that no longer means "hope for something abstract, distant, doubtful," but "expecting something concrete, positive," and its interrogative, negative, negative-interrogative, and conditional forms are generally followed by the indicative mood rather than by the subjunctive, when such is its meaning.

Nous espérons qu'il ne pleuvra pas.
We hope (that) it will not rain.

Nous n'espérons pas vraiment qu'il aura le premier prix.
We are not really hoping (that) he will get the first prize.

N'espérez-vous pas qu'il est devenu millionnaire?
Don't you hope (that) he has become a millionaire?

NOTES: 1) When the main verb and the subordinate verb have a common subject, the conjunction ***que*** should be replaced by the preposition ***de*** (or ***à***, or no preposition at all, depending on the main verb as listed in §278C), and the subordinate verb by an infinitive. See also §178B.

J'ai bien peur d'avoir oublié la clé.
I am afraid I forgot the key.
("J'ai bien peur que j'aie oublié la clé" is not acceptable.)

Elle voudrait pouvoir épouser un millionnaire.
She wishes she could marry a millionaire.
("Elle voudrait qu'elle puisse épouser un millionnaire" is acceptable only if the two pronouns "elle" represent two different persons.)

2) Occasionally the subordinate verb may be subjected to a condition (*if*) or may express an eventuality. When such is the case, the subordinate verb is in the conditional.

Je ne suis pas certain qu'il viendrait si on lui disait pourquoi nous avons besoin de lui.
I am not sure (that) he would come if we told him why we need him.

Croyez-vous qu'il nous aurait reconnus?
Do you think he would have recognized us?

but: Croyez-vous qu'il nous ait reconnus?
Do you think he has recognized us?

B. The main verb *is* impersonal.

1) The subordinate verb *must* be in the subjunctive if the main verb expresses:

a. Judgment, opinion, necessity, importance, possibility, impossibility, etc. Notice that the French subordinate construction follows a regular pattern and may correspond to various English ones.

Comment se fait-il que tu sois déjà là?
How come you've already arrived?

Il est inadmissible que ce rapport ne soit pas terminé.
It is inadmissible that this report is not yet finished.

Il est important que je voie ce dossier.
It is important for me to see that file.

Il se peut que je passe chez vous en rentrant.
I may happen to drop by on my way home.

Il tout à fait normal qu'il se mette en colère.
It is quite normal that he should get angry.

Il est important que vous réussissiez dans cette affaire.
Being successful in this deal is very important for you.

For practical purposes, it is safer to remember that the subjunctive mood is required in the subordinate clause after the following impersonal expressions in all their forms, tenses, and moods:

how come he is . . .	**comment se fait-il qu'il soit . . .**
how is it that you . . .	**comment se fait-il que tu . . .**
it happens that someone . . .	**il arrive que quelqu'un . . .**
someone may happen to . . .	**il arrive que quelqu'un . . .**
it is abnormal	**il est anormal que**
il is acceptable	**il est acceptable que**
it is astonishing	**il est étonnant que**
it is as well	**il vaut autant que**
it is better	**il vaut mieux que**
it is comforting (without "to know")	**il est rassurant que**
it is common	**il est commun que, il est courant que**
it is conceivable	**il est concevable que**
it is current (commonplace)	**il est courant que**
it is desirable	**il est désirable que, il est à souhaiter que**
it is disturbing	**il est troublant que**
it is extraordinary	**il est extraordinaire que**
it is fortunate	**il est heureux que, heureusement que** (with indicative)
it is good	**il est bon que**
it is hopeless	**il est inutile d'espérer que** See also A2b above.
it is imperative	**il est impératif que**
it is important	**il est important que**
it is impossible	**il est impossible que**
it is inadmissible	**il est inadmissible que**
it is inconceivable	**il est inconcevable que**
it is just	**il est juste que**
it is natural	**il est naturel que**
it is necessary	**il est nécessaire que**
it is normal	**il est normal que**
it is a pity	**il est dommage que**
it is possible	**il est possible que**
it is preferable	**il est préférable que**
it is proper	**il est convenable que**
it is reasonable	**il est raisonnable que**
it is reassuring	**il est rassurant que**
it is a shame	**il est honteux que, c'est une honte que**
it is suitable	**il est convenable que**
it is surprising	**il est surprenant que**
it is troubling	**il est troublant que**
it is unfortunate	**il est dommage que, il est malheureux que, il est fâcheux que**
it is unthinkable	**il est impensable que**
it is useful	**il est utile que**
it is useless	**il est inutile que, il (cela) ne sert à rien que**
it is worth the trouble	**il (cela) vaut la peine que**

it may be that	**il se peut que**
it may happen that	**il se peut que**
it might be (happen) that	**il se pourrait que**
must (it is necessary)	**il faut que**

NOTE: If the subordinate verb has no definite subject, the indefinite pronoun ***on*** may be used to serve as subject, or the conjunction ***que*** and the subjunctive may be replaced by the preposition ***de*** and an infinitive.

Il est préférable que vous partiez maintenant.
It is preferable that you leave now.

Il est préférable qu'on parte maintenant.
It is preferable to leave now.

Il est préférable de partir maintenant.
It is preferable to leave now.

(See §278D for the use of the infinitive after the impersonal expressions listed above.)

b. Uncertainty or improbability with all the forms of the following verbal expressions *except the affirmative form.*

it is agreed	**il est convenu**
it is apparent	**il est visible**
it is (almost) certain	**il est (presque) certain**
it is clear	**il est clair**
it is evident	**il est évident**
it is expected	**il est prévu**
it is (well) known	**il est (bien) connu**
it is a well-known fact	**c'est un fait bien connu**
it is likely	**il est vraisemblable, il est probable**
it is obvious	**il est évident**
it is plausible	**il est plausible**
it is probable	**il est probable**
it is projected	**il est projeté, il est prévu**
it is proven	**il est prouvé**
it is a proven fact	**il est prouvé**
it is (almost) sure	**il est (presque) sûr**
it is true	**il est vrai**

CAUTION: In the form given above, these expressions command *indicative* in the subordinate verb (or *conditional* where a condition is stated).

Il clair que tout le monde comprend ce problème.
It is clear that everyone understands that problem.

Il est évident qu'ils ne seraient pas venus si vous ne les aviez pas invités.
It is obvious that they wouldn't have come if you hadn't invited them.

Uncertainty or improbablity may be conveyed by some of the above expressions used with negative words and prefixes as well as by normal negations.

Il est peu probable qu'ils puissent s'entendre.
It is unlikely that they will manage to get along.

but: Il est probable qu'ils se disputeront.
It is likely that they will have a fight.

Il n'est pas certain qu'il y ait assez de jus de fruit pour tous.
It is not certain that there will be enough soft drinks for everybody.

but: Il est évident que cet arbre va tomber.
It is obvious that this tree is going to fall.

Il était imprévu qu'une telle chose arrive!
It wasn't expected that such a thing would happen!

As impersonal expressions, only ***il est convenu*** and ***il est prévu***, among those listed above, can be constructed with dependent infinitives.

Il est prévu de construire un pont à cet endroit.
A bridge is scheduled to be built on this spot. (It is projected that a bridge will be built . . .)

Il n'était pas convenu de passer par Bruxelles.
It had not been agreed that we would go through Brussels.

2) The speaker can choose moods for the subordinate verb used with the expressions in B1b above to signal his or her own (1) belief of a fact (indicative), (2) uncertainty (subjunctive), or (3) belief that the fact is improbable (subjunctive again). When a third clause sets up a condition under which the event would have taken place, the subordinate verb is in the conditional.

Est-il vrai que vous ayez eu un accident?
Is it true that you had an accident?
(The speaker is uncertain.)

Est-il vrai que vous avez eu un accident?
Is it true that you had an accident?
(The speaker believes that it is so, and merely wants confirmation, expecting a YES answer.)

Est-il vrai qu'il serait mort s'il n'y avait eu un médecin sur les lieux?
Is it true that he would have died if there hadn't been a doctor on the scene?

Est-il vrai que le réservoir d'essence aurait pu exploser?
Is it true that the gas tank could have exploded?

Oui, il est clair que le réservoir aurait pu exploser.
Yes, it is clear that the tank could have exploded.

281. Conjunctions.

If a conjunction longer than ***que*** alone is the connecting term between the main verb and the subordinate verb, the latter must be in the subjunctive only if the conjunction being used requires it. See the list of conjunctions requiring the subjunctive in §174, and those requiring the indicative (or the conditional) in §179. See also the note in §280A1a.

Il est reparti avant que j'aie pu lui parler.
He went back before I was able to speak to him.
Il a lavé la voiture pendant que tu tondais la pelouse.
He washed the car while you mowed the lawn.

282. Relative clauses in the subjunctive.

If the subordinate clause is a relative clause instead of a conjunctive one, the verb it contains is generally in the indicative or the conditional. But it must be in the subjunctive in the following cases:

A. If the antecedent of the relative pronoun is modified by a superlative or by one of the following equivalents:

le seul	the only
l'unique	the only, the sole, the one and only
le premier	the first
le dernier	the last
il n'y a que . . .	there is only . . .
ne . . . personne	no one, nobody
ne . . . aucun	no . . ., not any . . ., none
ne . . . rien	nothing, not anything
ne . . . pas un seul . . .	not a single . . .
ne . . . pas un seul	not a single one
ne . . . pas un (deux, etc.) . . .	not one (two, etc.) . . .
ne . . . pas de . . .	not any . . . (noun)
ne . . . jamais de . . .	never any . . . (noun)
ne . . . plus de . . .	no longer any, no more . . . (noun) no more . . . (noun)
ne . . . guère de . . .	scarcely any . . . (noun)
ne . . . point de . . .	not any . . . (noun)
ne . . . nul . . .	not any . . . (noun)

C'est le plus beau château que j'aie jamais vu.
It's the most beautiful castle (that) I have ever seen.
Je ne connais pas de château qui soit plus beau.
I don't know any castle that is (or: could be) more beautiful.

NOTE: Occasionally one may use the indicative in the subordinate clause, when the antecedent of the relative pronoun is modified by a superlative or by one of the equivalents listed (except the negatives), if one wants to state a purely objective fact. However, it is preferable in that case to use a different turn of phrase altogether.

Jean est le dernier qui est sorti.
John was the last to leave.

This statement of a fact would be better expressed in either of the following manners:

Jean est sorti le dernier.
John was the last to leave.

or, for emphasis:

C'est Jean qui est sorti le dernier.
John was the last to leave.

B. If the relative clause shows only a characteristic of the antecedent that is *desirable, required, uncertain to be found*, as opposed to a characteristic that is known to exist. This "desirability" is always conveyed through verbs like *to look for, to try to find, to wish there was*, and the like.

Je cherche deux étudiants qui sachent parler (le) japonais.
I am looking for two students who know how to speak Japanese.
(I am uncertain to find two students with that qualification. The subjunctive shows my doubts.)

Je cherche quelqu'un qui sait parler japonais.
I am looking for someone who knows how to speak Japanese.
(That person exists. I am only trying to locate him or her.)

283. Sequence of tenses in the subjunctive.

The use of the correct tense of the subjunctive for a subordinate clause depends on the relation between two factors: the tense of the main verb, and the time of the action of the subordinate verb.

A. If the tense of the verb of the main clause is the present indicative or future indicative, the subordinate verb should be in one of the following tenses:

1) *Present subjunctive*, if the action it expresses is present or future in relation to that of the main verb.

Je veux que vous restiez.
I want you to stay.
(I want now that you stay now or later.)

Je demanderai qu'on me laisse entrer.
I'll ask that they let me in.
(I'll ask that they let me in then , the moment I ask, or afterwards.)

2) *Past subjunctive*, (passé composé), if the action it expresses is past in relation to that of the main clause, or will have to be completed (in the future) before another action (not necessarily expressed by the main verb) or before a certain time.

Je suis navré qu'il n'ait pas pu venir.
I am sorry that he could not come.
(He was not able to come.)

Quand il sera sous mes ordres, j'exigerai qu'il ait fini son travail avant de quitter son bureau.
When he is under my command, I shall demand that he be through with his work before leaving his office.

Je veux que vous ayez rempli cette fiche avant mon retour.
I want you to have filled (be through filling) this form before my return.

B. If the tense of the verb of the main clause is present conditional or any past tense of any mood, the subordinate verb should be in one of the following tenses:

1) *Imperfect subjunctive*, if the action it expresses is present or future in relation to that of the main clause.

Le lieutenant exigea qu'ils se rendissent.
The lieutenant demanded that they surrender.
(that they surrender at that very moment or some time afterwards)

Que vouliez-vous qu'il fît?
What did you expect him to do?

J'aurais préféré qu'elle ne vous revît pas.
I would have preferred that she not see you again.

Ayant souhaité qu'elle se convertît, l'abbé . . .
Having wished that she would convert, the priest . . .

2) *Pluperfect subjunctive*, if the action it expresses is past in relation to that of the main verb or would have to be completed before another action (not necessarily expressed by the main verb) or by a certain time.

Je souffrais qu'elle m'eût oublié.
I grieved that she had forgotten me.

J'aurais préféré qu'elle m'eût oublié.
I would have preferred that she had forgotten me.
(I wished that she had forgotten me.)

Je voulais qu'il eût terminé avant sept heures.
I wanted him to have finished before seven.

The strict sequence of tenses in the subjunctive is observed only in formal writing. It is normal to avoid using the imperfect and the pluperfect subjunctive in informal writing, and those tenses are almost never used in conversation. In informal writing, and in conversation, the simplified sequence of tenses should be observed (see §284).

There are cases, however, in which the imperfect subjunctive, and occasionally the pluperfect subjunctive, cannot be avoided. Indeed, there is between the imperfect subjunctive on the one hand, and the past subjunctive on the other, the same difference as between the imperfect indicative and the passé composé (see §261 and §264). Therefore, if the subordinate verb in the subjunctive mood describes a state of mind, a physical condition, an attitude, a habit, an inherent quality, an eventuality, something continuous or not yet finished, instead of an action seen as a mere fact, then the past subjunctive cannot be used.

Il se plaignait que nous fussions en retard tous les jours.
He complained that we were being late every day.
(In this example, the present subjunctive (see §284) cannot be used, since part of the "action" (being late) has occurred in the past. The past subjunctive and the pluperfect subjunctive cannot be used either, since both would imply that the "act of being late" occurred in the past for a time and was over by the time considered, which is not the

case. The only possible tense is the imperfect subjunctive, which describes the "action" as having begun in the past, still not completed, and also habitual.)

To avoid difficulties in the sequence of tenses in the subjunctive, see §285.

284. Simplified sequence of tenses in the subjunctive.

Only two tenses are commonly used in the subjunctive mood: the present and the past. Whatever the tense of the main verb, the tense of the subordinate verb should be:

A. Present subjunctive if the action it expresses is present or future in relation to that of the main verb.

Je suis heureux qu'il vienne.
I am happy that he is coming.

J'étais content qu'il vienne.
I was glad he was coming.

Je serais content qu'il vienne.
I would be happy if he would come (if he came).

J'avais envie qu'il vienne.
I wanted him to come.

B. Past subjunctive if the action it expresses is past in relation to that of the main clause or has to be completed before another action or by a certain time.

Je suis heureux qu'il soit venu.
I am glad that he came.

J'étais content qu'il soit venu.
I was glad he had come.

J'aurais voulu qu'il soit déjà arrivé.
I wish he had already arrived.
I would have wanted him to be there already.

Je n'ai pas regretté qu'il soit venu.
I was not sorry that he came.

285. Avoiding the subjunctive.

The subjunctive may be avoided in the following ways:

A. When the main verb and the subordinate verb have the same subject, the conjunction should be replaced by a corresponding preposition (if the main verb requires one), and the subordinate verb by a dependent infinitive. To find the preposition required by the main verb or verbal expression, see § 278C. For prepositions corresponding to long conjunctions, see §177.

J'exige d'être entendu.
I demand to be heard.

Elle ne pense pas pouvoir le faire.
She does not think (that) she can do it.

Elle n'est pas sure de pouvoir venir.
She isn't sure (that) she'll be able to come.

Je pars tout de suite de peur d'être en retard.
I am leaving at once for fear (that) I might be late.

B. When the verb of the main clause and the verb of the subordinate clause have different subjects, the following constructions are possible:

1) The conjunction may be replaced by a preposition (if the main verb requires one), the subject of the subordinate verb by a possessive adjective, and the subordinate verb by a suitable noun. However, the meaning may not be as accurate as with a subordinate clause.

Ils s'opposent à ce que nous venions.
Ils s'opposent à notre venue.
They are opposed to our coming, to our visit.

Je doute qu'il soit honnête.
Je doute de son honnêteté.
I doubt that he is honest.

Je crains que vous ne vous mettiez en colère.
Je crains votre colère.
I am afraid you will get mad.

2) The conjunction may be replaced by a preposition (if one is required by the main verb), the subject of the subordinate verb may be changed into a personal pronoun (direct object) immediately preceding ***voir, faire, laisser, entendre,*** etc., and the subordinate verb may be changed into an infinitive.

Je m'attends à ce qu'il décide n'importe quoi.
Je m'attends à le voir décider n'importe quoi.
Je m'attends à l'entendre décider n'importe quoi.
I expect to see (or: hear) him decide anything (make a foolish decision).

The choice of the added infinitive (***voir, laisser, faire,*** etc.) is a matter of usage, meaning, and style.

3) The main clause and the subordinate clause may each be turned into an independent clause. The relation between the two independent clauses thus obtained may be expressed by means of pronouns, adverbs, etc.

Il est heureux que nous soyons venus le voir.
Nous sommes venus le voir, et il est très heureux.
Nous sommes venus le voir, et cela le rend très heureux.
Nous sommes venus le voir. Maintenant il est heureux.
Nous sommes venus le voir. Il en est très heureux.
Etc.

4) The subjunctive mood may also be avoided by replacing the conjunction ***que*** by the phrase ***de ce que***, which requires the indicative. Only a few verbs permit this substitution (see §192).

5) To avoid the subjunctive mood, it is also possible to restructure the sentence entirely, using independent clauses and subordinate clauses of a nature that does not require the use of that mood. Many conjunctions introduce verbs in the indicative (see §179). The present participle and the past participle may be used to form circumstantial clauses (see §270B and C, §271B).

PROBLEM WORDS

286. *It is, he is, she is, they are.*

There are three ways to translate the subjects in *it is, he is, she is, they are* into French.
The first is with the demonstrative pronoun ***ce***.
The second is with the impersonal pronoun ***il***.
The third is with the regular personal pronouns ***il, elle, ils, elles***.

A. When *it* refers to nothing specific or is used in an impersonal way, three possibilities exist:

1) *It* refers to something vague, and can be replaced by *that*: ***c'est*** (in any tense required).

C'est beau. C'est magnifique. C'est impossible.
It is beautiful. It is magnificent. It is impossible.

C'était facile à faire.
It (that) was easy to do.

Ce serait trop dangereux.
It (that) would be too dangerous.

Ce sera vite fait.
It will be done quickly.

Il faut que ce soit prêt dans cinq minutes.
It must be ready in five minutes.

See §58C1.

2) *It is* (in any tense) is used to give emphasis to a noun, pronoun, proper noun, superlative, or adverbial phrase (manner, time, place, etc.), generally modified by a relative or by a conjunctive clause: ***c'est***.

C'est toi que je connais le mieux.
It is you that I know best.
You are the one I know best.

C'est Paul qu'elle aime.
It is Paul that she loves.

C'est le plus gros morceau qu'il a pris, évidemment!
Of course, he took the biggest piece!

C'est en 1769 que Napoléon est né.
It was in 1769 that Napoleon was born.

C'est à Noël que nous irons en Floride.
It is at Christmas that we will go to Florida.

C'était en 1946.
It was in 1946.

C'est is generally in the present tense, but may occasionally be in the same tense as the subordinate verb that follows.

C'était elle qui faisait toujours les meilleures tartes.
She was the one that always baked the best pies. (*Her* pies were always the best.)

When *c'est* is part of a subordinate clause, it must be in the tense and mood required by the context.

Je serais étonné que ce soit Paul qu'elle aime*.
I would be surprised if Paul was the one she loves.

*When *it is* is in a subordinate clause that must be in the subjunctive, the relative or conjunctive clause that follows must also be in the subjunctive, by attraction.

J'ai peur que ce soit lui qui sorte le dernier.
I am afraid it will be he who will come out last.
Je doute que ce soit Paul qui le fasse.
I doubt that it will be Paul who will do it.
Je vous aide afin que ce soit vous qui ayez fini le premier.
I'm helping you so that it will be you who will have finished first.
Je veux que ce soit à Noël que nous allions en Floride.
It is at Christmas that I want us to go to Florida.
J'aimerais que ce soit à Paris que nous passions nos vacances.
It is in Paris that I would like us to spend our vacation.
but: Je pense que c'est lui qui conduira la voiture.
I think that it will be he who will drive the car.

NOTES: 1) In very informal style, and whenever the pronoun ***ce*** is separated from the verb ***être*** (as in a compound tense, with ***devoir*** or ***pouvoir***, in the negative form, when a personal pronoun object precedes), ***ce*** (or ***c'***) may be replaced by the familiar form ***ça***, which does not elide before a vowel.

Ça devrait être mon tour. Ça ne peut être qu'une erreur.
It should be my turn. It can only be a mistake.
Ça m'est bien égal. Tout ça, c'est la même chose.
It is all the same to me. It's all the same.
Ça n'est pas facile. Ça aurait été utile.
It is not easy. It would have been useful.

2) The expression ***c'est*** is used far more frequently in French than its counterpart *it is* in English. ***C'est*** is used to render a variety of English emphatic forms of expression.

C'est lui qui a gagné le premier prix.
He won the first prize.
He is the one who won the first prize.

C'est en Europe que vous devriez aller.
Europe is where you should go.

C'est ça! C'est ça qu'il me faut!
That's it! That's what I need.

C'est là que j'ai trouvé le portefeuille.
That's where I found the wallet.

C'est alors qu'il a tenté de s'évader.
That's when he tried to escape.

C'est en tombant de l'échelle qu'il s'est cassé la jambe.
It was in falling from the ladder that he broke his leg.

3) *It is* is followed by an adjective, and *it* is impersonal (i.e., cannot be replaced by *that*).

The French structure must be ***il est*** followed by an adjective. The adjective may be followed either by ***de*** and an infinitive (with its own complements and modifiers, if any) or by ***que*** and a subordinate clause. For the infinitive construction, see §278D, which contains a list of the impersonal expressions allowing this phrasing. For the construction with the subordinate clause, see §280B, which presents a list of the impersonal expressions requiring subordinate clauses in the subjunctive or in the indicative (or conditional).

Il est difficile de comprendre ce problème.
It is difficult to understand this problem.

Il est dangereux d'être soldat.
It is dangerous to be a soldier.

Il est important de leur obéir.
It is important to obey them.

Il est important que vous arriviez à l'heure.
It is important that you arrive on time.

Il est évident que vous êtes un étranger.
It is obvious that you are a foreigner.

B. *He is, she is, it is* and *they are* correspond to two structures in French. The choice depends on the nature of the predicate complement.

1) If the predicate complement is a noun (or an adjective used as a noun, see §8D), a pronoun of any kind, a proper noun, or a superlative, *he, she, it,* and *they* are rendered by ***ce*** (***c'***). Note that the verb ***être*** is in the plural with all plural predicate complements, except with ***nous*** and ***vous***. Note also that the verb ***être*** may be in any tense.

C'est un Américain. C'est un Anglais.
He is an American. He is an Englishman.

C'est un avare. C'est un vieillard.
He is a miser. He is an old man.

C'est une étudiante. C'est une actrice.
She is a student. She is an actress.

Ce sont des étrangers. C'étaient des paresseux.
They are foreigners. They were lazy people.

Ce sont des riches. Ce sont des pauvres.
They are rich people. They are poor people.

C'est moi. C'est la mienne. C'est celui-là.
It is I (me). It is mine. It is that one (that's the one).

C'est nous. C'est vous.
It is we (us). It's you.

Ce sont eux. Ce sont elles.
It is they (masc.). It is they (fem.). (They are the ones)

C'était Paul. Ce sera Martine.
It was Paul. It will be Martine.

C'était le plus intelligent. Ç'aurait été la meilleure.
He was the most intelligent. She would have been the best.

NOTE: With predicate nouns, superlatives and substantivated adjectives referring to people, it is possible to use a personal pronoun (***il, elle, ils, elles***) instead of ***ce*** when the statement requires precision, identity, or specificity as a form of emphasis. By choosing a personal pronoun instead of ***ce***, the speaker establishes a subjective, affective connection with the person being described.

Il ne croit pas qu'elle est la femme de son voisin!
He doesn't believe that she is his neighbor's wife!

Elles sont sans aucun doute les plus jolies du groupe.
They are without a doubt the prettiest girls in the group.

Parmi nos juges, il est le plus sévère.
Among our judges, he is the toughest.

Elle est la première.
She is the first one.

2) If the predicate is an adjective, regular personal pronouns are used to translate *he, she, it,* and *they.*

Il est grand. Elle est jolie. Ils étaient puissants.
He is tall. She is pretty. They were powerful.

Il est solide. (: le mur, masculin)
It is strong, sturdy. (the wall)

Elle était fermée. (: la porte, féminin)
It was shut. (the door)

Ils étaient riches.
They were rich. (*they* represents a masculine plural)

Elles étaient pauvres.
They were poor. (*they* represents a feminine plural)

Note that two ways are possible in French to express what can often be said in only one way in English:

Il est étudiant. Or: **C'est un étudiant.**
He is a student.

Elle est étrangère. Or: **C'est une étrangère.**
She is a foreigner.

In these examples, the construction with the predicate adjective merely qualifies, giving a characteristic of the subject. The construction with the predicate nominative is much stronger: it personalizes the subject, it individualizes it, it gives it an identity.

287. *This is, that is, these are, those are.*

A. Referring to something vague, *this is, that is, these are,* and *those are* should be translated as "it is" (see §286).

B. Pointing out, *this is* and *these are* and *that is* and *those are* should be translated ***voici*** and ***voilà***, respectively (see §288).

Voici ma maison. Comment la trouvez-vous?
This is my house. What do you think of it?

Voilà mes intentions.
Those are my intentions.

To point emphatically to the uniqueness of a case or situation, ***voici*** and ***voilà*** may be replaced by ***c'est là, ce sont là*** in any appropriate tense.

C'étaient là des circonstances inhabituelles.
These were unusual circumstances.

C. Emphasizing difference, contrast, or opposition between terms, *this is* should be translated ***ceci est***, and *that is* should be translated ***cela est*** or, in informal style, ***ça, c'est***.

Ceci est très bon, mais cela paraît meilleur.
This is very good, but that seems better.

Cela est excellent. (informal: **Ça, c'est excellent.**)
That is excellent.

288. *Here (is, are). There (is, are).*

A. Pointing out: ***Voici*** or ***voilà***

Voici un taxi! Voilà un taxi!
Here is a taxi! There is a taxi!

Voici l'autobus! Voilà l'autobus!
Here is the bus! There is the bus!

Voici mon autobus! Voilà mon autobus!
Here is my bus! There is my bus!

Le (la) voici! Le (la) voilà!
Here it is! There it is!

Les voici! Les voilà!
Here they are! There they are!

Vous (te) voici! Vous (te) voilà!
Here you are! There you are!

B. Not pointing out: ***Il y a*** in all tenses and in combination with helping verbs like ***pouvoir, devoir, sembler, savoir,*** etc.

Il y a un arrêt d'autobus de l'autre côté de la rue.
There is a bus stop across the street.

Il n'y a pas de taxis dans les rues après minuit.
There are no taxis on the streets after midnight.

Sans publicité, y aurait-il de la télévision?
Without advertising, would there be television?

Il semble qu'il y ait une erreur. Il semble y avoir une erreur.
There seems to be a mistake.

Il n'aurait pas dû y avoir d'hésitation de votre part.
There shouldn't have been any hesitation on your part.

Il se pourrait qu'il y ait un tremblement de terre bientôt.
There might be an earthquake soon.

C. Impersonal: ***Il*** when *there* introduces a verb other than *to be.* (See §305.)

Il vient un temps où . . .
There comes a time when . . .

Il pourrait exister un pays où . . .
Il se pourrait qu'il existe un pays où . . .
Il pourrait y avoir un pays où . . .
There could exist a land where . . .

Il s'étendit sur la terre une obscurité surprenante.
There spread over the earth a wondrous darkness.

Il apparaîtra dans le ciel une étoile très brillante.
There will appear in the sky a bright star.

289. One.

A. As a number, *one* is ***un*** (masculine), ***une*** (feminine). It is not expressed in French for *one hundred* (***cent***) nor for *one thousand* (***mille***).

B. Used in correlation with *other*, *one* is translated ***l'un*** (masculine), ***l'une*** (feminine). (See §63B)

C. *One*, added to an adjective to form a noun, is not translated in French. An article or other determiner, placed before the adjective, is sufficient to transform the adjective into a noun.

Tu vois ces deux livres? Donne-moi le petit.
Do you see those two books? Give me the small one.

Voici les bons champignons. J'ai jeté les mauvais.
Here are the good mushrooms. I threw the bad ones away.

D. *This one, that one* are turned into the French demonstrative pronouns ***celui, celle, ceux, celles*** in the appropriate constructions (see §§57-58).

E. Expressions containing *the one*:

The one (meaning "the only")	**le seul** (masculine) **la seule** (feminine)
The one and only	**le seul et unique** (masculine) **la seule et unique** (feminine)
On the one hand	**d'une part, d'un côté**
On the other	**de l'autre**
On the other hand	**d'un autre côté, en revanche, par contre**

F. *One's* is translated ***son, sa, ses*** (possessive adjectives—see §53).

G. *The one*, in predicative position after the verb *to be* with a personal pronoun for a subject, is expressed in French by a disjunctive personal pronoun.

But if the subject of the verb *to be* is *this, that, these, those*, the expression *the one* should be expressed by a demonstrative pronoun: ***celui, celle, ceux, celles*** (§§57-58). If *the one* is modified by a prepositional phrase or a relative clause, again the French expression will use a demonstrative pronoun.

C'est elle qui m'a parlé de vous.
She is the one that talked to me about you.

C'est celle-ci que je voulais acheter. (robe, féminin)
This is the one I wanted to buy. (dress)

C'est celle qui porte une robe bleue qui m'a parlé de vous. (la jeune fille)
It was the one with the blue dress that talked to me about you. (the girl)

C'est celle de mon voisin qui vient de se marier. (la fille)
It's my neighbor's that just got married. (my neighbor's daughter)

Note that ***voici*** or ***voilà*** may be substituted for ***c'est***, but only if the demonstrative pronoun has a prepositional or a relative clause modifier.

C'est celle-ci que je voulais acheter.
Voici celle que je voulais acheter.
This is (here is) the one I wanted to buy.

H. *The one*, and occasionally *the ones* or *those*, as subject or object of any verb (but not in predicative position after "to be" as described in G above), are expressed by the demonstrative pronouns ***celui, celle, ceux, celles.***

. . . celui qui te suit . . . (le chien)
. . . the one that is following you . . . (the dog)

. . . celle que je regarde . . . (la jeune fille)
. . . the one I am looking at . . . (the girl)

An English relative clause that follows *the one* should be rendered by a relative clause in French, after the demonstrative pronoun. An English prepositional phrase that follows *the one* should generally be changed into a relative clause in French, unless the French preposition is ***de*** (or occasionally ***à*** or ***en***).

. . . celles à qui je t'ai présenté . . . (les dames)
. . . the ones to whom I introduced you . . . (the ladies)

. . . ceux dont je t'ai parlé . . . (les livres)
. . . the ones I talked to you about . . . (the books)

. . . ceux de droite et ceux de gauche . . . (les partis)
. . . the ones on the right and the ones on the left . . . (the political parties)

. . . celui qui est sur la table . . . (le couteau)
. . . the one on the table . . . (the knife)

. . . celles en couleur ou celles en noir et blanc? (les cartes postales)
. . . the ones in color or the ones in black and white? (the postcards)

. . . celui qui est au fond . . . (le client)
. . . the one in the back . . . (the customer)

. . . celle au chapeau de paille . . . (la fillette)
. . . the one in a straw hat . . . (the little girl)

. . . ceux en maillots verts . . . (les joueurs)
. . . the ones in the green jerseys . . . (the players)

290. Ago, before, earlier.

A. *Ago* is translated ***il y a***, followed by a period of time. The verb of the sentence should be in the passé composé to indicate a completed fact or action, and in the imperfect to describe a state, condition, circumstance, etc. (For use of those two tenses, see in §261 and §264).

Il a plu il y a deux jours.
It rained two days ago.

Il pleuvait il y a deux jours. Il y a deux jours, il pleuvait.
It was raining two days ago. Two days ago, it was raining.

B. When the verb of the English sentence is in the pluperfect, *ago* is replaced by *before* or *earlier*, which are translated indifferently ***plus tôt, auparavant***, or ***avant***, preceded by a period of time. The verb of the French sentence should be in the pluperfect to indicate a completed fact or action (past anterior in literary style), and in the imperfect to describe a state of things, a condition, a circumstance, etc.

Il avait plu deux jours plus tôt.
It had rained two days before.

Deux jours plus tôt, il pleuvait.
Two days earlier, it was raining.

La date limite était le 12. Nous eûmes fini trois jours avant.
The deadline was the 12th. We had finished three days earlier.

291. How long, for, since.

A. To ask and answer a question about a fact or action that has been going on for some time and *is still going on now*, observe the following indications:

1) *Question. How long* with a verb in the present perfect (continuous or not) is translated ***depuis quand***, or ***depuis combien de temps***, or ***combien de temps y a-t-il que***, with a verb in the present indicative.

Depuis combien de temps êtes-vous ici?
How long have you been here?

Depuis quand habitez-vous ici?
How long have you been living here?

Combien de temps y a-t-il que vous habitez ici?
How long have you been living here?

2) *Answer.* Use the *same tense as in the question*, translating *for* or *since* as shown in any of the following structures:

verb + ***depuis*** (*for, since*) + time (date, period)
verb + ***depuis que*** (*since*) + subordinate verb (moment of reference)
il y a (or ***voilà*** or ***ça fait***) + time period + ***que*** + verb

Je suis ici depuis dix minutes.
Voilà (il y a, ça fait) dix minutes que je suis ici.
I have been here for ten minutes.

Je suis ici depuis que la secrétaire est sortie.
I have been here since the secretary went out.

J'habite ici depuis 1985.
I have been living here since 1985.

B. To ask and answer a question about a fact or action that had been going on for some time, and *was still going on* at the moment of the past chosen as a point of reference ("*then*"), observe the following indications:

1) *Question. How long* with a verb in the pluperfect (continuous or not) is translated ***depuis quand***, or ***depuis combien de temps***, or ***combien de temps y avait-t-il que***, with the French verb in the imperfect indicative.

Depuis quand étiez-vous vous là?
How long had you been there?

Depuis combien de temps habitiez-vous à Londres?
How long had you been living in London?

Combien de temps y avait-il que vous attendiez?
How long had you been waiting?

2) *Answer*. Use the same tense as in the question, translating *for* or *since* as shown in any of the following structures:

verb + ***depuis*** (*for, since*) + time (date, period)
verb + ***depuis que*** (*since*) + subordinate verb (moment of reference)
il y avait (or ***ça faisait***) + time period (*for*) + ***que*** + verb

J'étais là depuis dix minutes.
Il y avait dix minutes que j'étais là.
Ça faisait dix minutes que j'étais là.
I had been there for ten minutes.

J'habitais à Londres depuis deux ans.
Il y avait (or ça faisait) deux ans que j'habitais à Londres.
I had been living in London for two years.

J'attendais depuis que vous aviez téléphoné.
I had been waiting since you had called.

C. To ask or answer a question about the duration of a fact or action, observe the following indications:

1) *Questions*. *How long* with a verb in the past (preterit), pluperfect indicative, future, future perfect, present conditional, or past conditional is translated ***combien de temps***, with the French verb respectively in the passé composé, pluperfect indicative, future, future perfect, present conditional, or past conditional.

Combien de temps nous avez-vous attendus?
How long did you wait for us?

Combien de temps nous aviez-vous attendus?
How long had you waited for us?

Combien de temps passerez-vous en Floride?
How long will you spend in Florida?

Combien de temps passeriez-vous en Floride si . . .?
How long would you spend in Florida if . . .?

2) *Answer*. Use the same tenses, translating *for* (if used) by ***pendant***. In English, and in French as well, the preposition may be omitted before the expression of time.

Je vous ai attendus (pendant) une heure, ensuite je suis rentré chez moi.
I waited for you (for) one hour, then I went back home.

Je vous avais attendus (pendant) une heure, ensuite j'étais rentré chez moi.
I had waited for you (for) one hour, then I had gone back home.

Nous passerons un mois en Floride, et ensuite nous irons au Mexique.
We'll spend one month in Florida, and then we'll go to Mexico.

Si je le pouvais, je resterais (pendant) un mois au Mexique.
If I could, I would stay (for) one month in Mexico.

292. Tenses after depuis que.

When the time element is indicated by ***depuis que*** and a subordinate clause, the verb of that subordinate clause may be in the following tenses:

A. If the verb of the main clause is in the present indicative (§291A), the verb following ***depuis que*** may be:

1) In the present indicative if the two actions or facts began at the same time and if both are still going on now.

Je l'écoute depuis qu'il parle.
I have been listening to him for as long as he has been speaking.

Nous sommes sous le pont depuis qu'il pleut.
We have been under the bridge for as long as it has been raining.

2) In the passé composé to point to the moment when the main fact or action (the main verb) began.

Je l'écoute depuis qu'il a commencé à parler.
I have been listening to him since (the moment) he began to speak.

J'apprends le français depuis que j'ai décidé de faire un voyage en France.
I have been learning French since (the moment) I decided to take a trip to France.

Il est à l'hôpital depuis qu'il s'est cassé la jambe.
He has been in the hospital since (the moment, the day) he broke his leg.

Nous sommes sous le pont depuis qu'il s'est mis à pleuvoir.
We have been under the bridge since (the moment) the rain started to fall.

B. If the verb of the main clause is in the imperfect indicative (§291B), the verb following ***depuis que*** may be:

1) In the imperfect indicative if the two actions or facts began at the same time and if both were still going on at the moment considered (*then*).

Je l'écoutais depuis qu'il parlait.
I had been listening to him for as long as he had been speaking.

Nous étions sous le pont depuis qu'il pleuvait.
We had been under the bridge for as long as it had been raining.

2) In the pluperfect indicative to indicate the moment when the main fact or action (the main verb) had begun.

Je l'écoutais depuis qu'il avait commencé à parler.
I had been listening to him since (the moment) he had begun speaking.

J'apprenais le français depuis que j'avais décidé de visiter la France.
I had been learning French since (the moment) I had decided to visit France.

Il était à l'hôpital depuis qu'il s'était cassé la jambe.
He had been in the hospital since (the moment, the day) he had broken his leg.

Nous étions sous le pont depuis que la pluie s'était mise à tomber.
We had been under the bridge since (the moment) the rain had begun to fall.

293. During, while.

During is translated ***pendant***, followed by a period of time. *While* is translated ***pendant que***, followed by a verb in the indicative mood or in the conditional mood.

Sentences with ***pendant*** and ***pendant que*** emphasize action and duration in relation to one another. To give more emphasis to the action, the sentence should begin with the main clause. To give more emphasis to duration, the main clause should come after the expression of time.

Je travaille pendant qu'il s'amuse.
I work while he plays.

Pendant qu'il s'amusait, je travaillais.
While he played, I worked. While he was playing, I was working.

Je ne fais rien pendant les vacances.
I do nothing during the holidays.

Pendant les vacances, je ferai une ascension en ballon.
During the holidays, I'll take a ride in a hot-air balloon.

Pendant que may be followed by a verb in the present indicative, imperfect indicative, future, or conditional—rarely any other tense.

294. To do, to make, to take.

A. *To do* and *to make* are both translated ***faire*** in normal use and in most idiomatic expressions. The following are some exceptions:

to make a decision	**prendre une décision**
to make a fool of someone	**tourner quelqu'un en ridicule**
to make a fool of oneself	**se tourner en ridicule, se ridiculiser**
to make do with something	**faire avec les moyens du bord, faire ce qu'on peut avec les moyens du bord, s'arranger avec quelque chose, s'arranger avec les moyens du bord**
to make fun	**se moquer (de)**
to make haste	**se presser, se dépêcher**
to make it a point to	**s'assurer, ne pas manquer de**
it makes sense	**c'est logique, ça semble logique, ça paraît logique**
he makes sense	**il est logique, il est clair, ce qu'il dit est logique,**

	ce qu'il dit est raisonnable
it makes no sense	**ce n'est pas logique, ça n'a pas de sens, ça ne veut rien dire**
he makes no sense	**il n'est pas logique, il n'est pas clair, ce qu'il dit n'a pas de sens, ce qu'il dit n'est pas logique**
to make sure	**s'assurer**
to make the best of	**tirer le meilleur parti de**
to do away with	**se débarrasser de**
to do without	**se passer de**
it will do	**ça ira, ça fera l'affaire**
How do you do?	**Comment allez-vous? Comment vas-tu? Comment ça va?** (fam.)

B. A number of English verbs and verbal expressions not containing *to do* or *to make* correspond to French expressions with ***faire***. Many expressions about the weather (precipitation, temperature, light) are among these. The following is a short list of the most common ones:

it is daylight	**il fait jour**
it is night	**il fait nuit**
to be a fool, an idiot	**faire l'idiot(e), l'imbécile**
to be a . . ., behave as a . . .	**faire le . . ., la . . .**
to cook	**faire la cuisine**
to court	**faire la cour à**
to deliver a lecture	**faire une conférence**
to face someone, confront	**faire face à quelqu'un**
to fell, push, push down	**faire tomber**
to face, confront someone	**faire face à quelqu'un**
to frighten, scare someone	**faire peur à quelqu'un**
to go "boom, kaboom"	**faire "boum, badaboum"**
it went "splash" ("plunk")	**ça a fait "plouf"**
to grow something	**faire pousser quelque chose**
to harm, hurt someone	**faire (du) mal à quelqu'un**
to hit the bull's eye, the target, hit the spot, hit home	**faire mouche**
to hurt oneself	**se faire (du) mal**
to keep someone waiting	**faire attendre quelqu'un**
to pay attention	**faire attention**
to pretend	**faire semblant de**
to send for	**faire venir** (also: **envoyer chercher)**
to show	**faire voir** (also: **montrer)**
the weather is . . .	**il fait . . .**

Note also the following English expressions containing *take*:

take a hike (coll.)	**va te faire voir ailleurs** (coll.)
to take a stand (for)	**prendre position (pour); prendre parti (pour)**
to take a step	**faire un pas** (literally), **faire une démarche** (figuratively)
to take a trip	**faire un voyage**
to take a walk	**faire une promenade**
take advantage of	**profiter de, tirer profit de**

to take five	**faire une pause, s'arrêter un moment**
to take hold	**prendre pied, se fixer**
to take notice	**faire attention (à), remarquer**
to take place	**avoir lieu, arriver**

C. *To make someone happy, mad, sick, etc.*: The verb *to make* in this type of expression is expressed by the French verb ***rendre*** followed by the appropriate adjective form.

Elles ont mangé trop de bonbons, ça les a rendues malades.
They ate too much candy, it made them sick.

However, some expressions modeled on the pattern *to make someone . . . (adj.)* may exist under another form than the one recommended above. For example "to make someone fat" may be rendered as ***faire grossir quelqu'un*** rather than with the verb ***rendre***. *To make someone happy* may be expressed as ***contenter quelqu'un, satisfaire quelqu'un***. The choice of the expression depends on the context and the nuances of meaning to be conveyed.

295. Do, does, did.

A. *To do* as a regular verb is generally translated ***faire***, except in some idiomatic expressions (see §294).

Je fais mon devoir.
I am doing my duty.

Qu'est-ce que vous avez fait?
What have you done?

Nous ferons ce qu'il faut pour y arriver.
We will do what it takes to get there.

but: Comment allez-vous?
How are you doing?

Nous pourrons nous en passer.
We will be able to do without it.

B. *Do, does, did* in negative and interrogative constructions are not translated.

Il ne pleut pas. Comprenez-vous?
It does not rain. Do you understand?

Note that *do* and *does* indicate a present tense, whereas *did* indicates a past tense.

Does he understand? Did they understand?
Est-ce qu'il comprend? Ont-ils compris?

C. When *do, does, did* are used in answers as replacement of a verb, the full verb of the question must be expressed in the French answer. Otherwise, only ***oui, si***, or ***non*** constitutes the complete answer.

Comprenez-vous? —Oui, je comprends. (or: **—Oui.**)
Do you understand? —Yes, I do.

Avez-vous compris? —Non, je n'ai pas compris. (or: **—Non.)**
Did you understand? —No, I didn't.

Il ne comprend pas? —Si, il comprend. (or: **—Si.)**
Doesn't he understand? —Yes, he does.

D. In emphatic constructions, *do, does, did* are left untranslated. A French adverb may be added to render the emphasis. In many cases, idiomatic expressions are available to render the emphatic force of the English expression with *do, does,* or *did.*

J'y tiens. J'insiste.
I do insist.

Entrez-donc. Entrez, je vous en prie.
Do come in.

Je vous assure que je l'ai vu. Je l'ai vu, c'est un fait. Je l'ai bien vu. Je l'ai vu, il n'y a pas de doute.
I did see him.

296. Possession.

A. For possessive adjectives *my, your, his, her,* etc., see §§53-56. See also §86.

B. For possessive pronouns *mine, yours, his, hers,* etc., see §§93-94.

C. The possessive case *'s* is detailed in §94. The following are examples of the English possessive case and its rendering into French.

Le jouet de l'enfant.
The child's toy.

Le chien de Charles.
Charles' dog.

La voix du peuple.
The people's voice.

Une école de garçons.
A boys' school.

Le devoir d'un homme.
A man's duty.

La voiture de leur ami.
Their friend's car.

Mon livre et celui de mon frère.
My book and my brother's.

Un des chats de notre voisine.
One of our neighbor's cats.

Ce livre est à quelqu'un d'autre.
That book is someone else's.

À Saint-Patrick. À la cathédrale (de) Saint-Patrick.
At (or: to) Saint Patrick's.

Nous avons déjeuné chez Paul.
We had lunch at Paul's.

Nous avons trouvé des noix chez l'épicier.
We found walnuts at the grocer's.

Conduisez-la chez le médecin.
Take her to the doctor's.

À la surprise de tous. À la surprise de chacun. À la surprise générale. À l'étonnement général.
To everyone's surprise.

La faute de (or: **à**) **personne.**
Nobody's fault.

On doit prendre soin de sa santé.
One must take care of one's health.

Pour l'amour du ciel!
For heaven's sake!

Un préavis d'un mois.
A month's notice.

Le salaire d'une semaine. Une semaine de salaire.
One week's wages.

(Une vue) à vol d'oiseau.
From a bird's eye view. (As the crow flies; in a beeline.)

Dans ton imagination.
In your mind's eye.

Le jour de l'an.
New Year's Day.

À cœur joie.
To one's heart's content.

D. *Whose* has two natures. As a relative pronoun, it is translated ***dont***, ***de qui***, or ***duquel*** (§§98-99).

As an interrogative pronoun, *whose* is translated ***à qui***, followed by the verb ***être*** or ***appartenir*** (*to belong*).

À qui est ce livre? À qui appartient ce livre?
Whose book is this?

Ce livre est à Paul. Ce livre appartient à Paul.
That book is Paul's.

Il est à Paul. Il appartient à Paul.
It is Paul's. (It belongs to Paul.)

Ce n'est pas le mien, c'est celui de Paul.
It isn't mine, it is Paul's.

297. To make someone do something. To have something done.

The use of ***faire*** with an infinitive is called the causative construction. The structures depend on the presence of a subject or an object of the infinitive—or both at the same time.

A. With a subject or an object.

	SUBJECT	
Paul a fait	**déraper**	**sa voiture**

Paul caused his car to skid. (car is subject of skid)
Paul made his car skid.

	OBJECT	
Il fera	**réparer**	**sa voiture.**

He will have his car repaired. (car is object of repair)

B. With both a subject and an object expressed:

	BOTH SUBJECT AND OBJECT		
Le patron a fait	**taper**	**la lettre**	**à la secrétaire.** or: **par la secrétaire.**
Paul fera	**réparer**	**sa voiture**	**au mécanicien.** or: **par le mécanicien.**

The boss had the secretary type the letter. (or: The boss had the letter typed by the secretary.)

Paul will have the mechanic repair his car. (or: Paul will have his car repaired by the mechanic.)

When the nouns are replaced by personal pronouns, the structures become the following:

Le patron la lui a fait taper.
The boss had her type it.

Paul la lui fera réparer.
Paul will have him repair it.

For the relative position of two personal pronouns before the same verb, see §88A and B.

NOTES: 1) In compound tenses, the past participle ***fait*** remains invariable if it is followed by a dependent infinitive.

2) The object personal pronouns must precede ***faire***, not the infinitive that follows. The same rule applies to ***laisser*** and to the verbs of perception followed by an infinitive (see §89A, notes 5 and 6).

3) The actual subject of the action being performed is constructed as an indirect object only if the verb expressing the action also has a direct object. Otherwise, the subject should be placed after the infinitive, in an inverted position.

4) The constructions are the same if only the subject of the action or the object of the action is expressed.

5) The choice between the prepositions ***à*** and ***par*** is only a matter of context and clarity: ***à*** followed by a noun may be mistaken for a real indirect object, whereas ***par*** followed by a noun cannot. Both ***à*** and ***par*** and their nouns must be turned into indirect object personal pronouns when pronouns are to be used.

298. Can, may.

A. *Can* is generally translated ***pouvoir***, in a variety of tenses and contexts.

Je peux me débrouiller. (fam.)
J'y arriverai. Je pourrai y arriver. Ça ira.
I can manage.
Il ne peut pas sortir. Il n'a pas le droit de sortir.
He cannot (: may not) go out.
Il sait nager.
He can swim. He knows how to swim.
Il peut nager sous l'eau.
He can swim under water. (ability)

B. *May* is expressed in various ways to show nuances of meaning:

1) Meaning *to be allowed, to have permission*, it is translated ***pouvoir***.

Vous pouvez partir. Puis-je ouvrir la fenêtre?
You may leave. May I open the window?

2) To express *there is a chance, a possibility that . . .*, use the French impersonal expression ***il se peut que . . .*** followed by a verb in the subjunctive.

Il se peut qu'elle parte sans dire au revoir.
She may leave without saying goodbye.

Note that the eventuality considered is much more probable with *may* than with *might* (§301).

3) The negative of *may*:

Vous ne pouvez pas sortir. Vous n'avez pas le droit de sortir.
You may not leave. You aren't allowed to leave.

Il se peut qu'elle ne parte pas tout de suite!
She may not leave right away. (: it is a possibility)

4) *May* expressing a wish:

Puisse-t-elle ne jamais revenir! Qu'elle ne revienne jamais!
May she never come back!

Que Dieu vous bénisse! (or: **Dieu vous bénisse!)**
May God bless you! God bless you!

5) With a subordinate verb, *may* does not have to be translated. Its meaning is rendered by the French subjunctive mood.

N'avez-vous pas peur qu'elle revienne?
Aren't you afraid she may come back?

However, if *may* itself is considered to be the subordinate verb, it should be translated ***pouvoir***, in the tense and mood required by the structure of the French sentence (see §252).

Taisez-vous afin que je puisse entendre l'orateur.
Be silent so that I may hear the speaker.

Je suis certain que vous pouvez sortir.
I am certain that you may go out.

C. Idiomatic expressions containing *can, may*, or the French verb ***pouvoir***:

I cannot help it.	**Je n'y peux rien.** **Je ne peux (pas) m'en empêcher.**
It cannot be.	**Cela ne se peut pas.** **C'est impossible.**
I'm doing the best I can.	**Je fais de mon mieux.** **Je fais ce que je peux.**
Can you . . .?	**Pouvez-vous . . .?**
—Yes, I think I can.	**—Oui, je crois que je (le) peux.** **—Oui, je crois que j'en suis capable.** **—Je crois que oui.**
—No, I don't think I can.	**—Non, je ne crois pas.** **—Non, je ne crois pas que je (le) puisse.** **—Non, je ne crois pas que je (le) pourrai.** **—Non, je ne crois pas en être capable.** **—Je crois que non.**
I can't go on.	**Je n'en peux plus. Je n'en puis plus.**
What does this mean anyway (what on earth, in the world, etc.)?	**Qu'est-ce que cela peut bien vouloir dire?**
All I can. The best I can.	**Mon possible. De mon mieux. Le plus possible. Le mieux possible.**

If I may.	**Si je puis me permettre. Si vous me le permettez. S'il vous plaît**
He may as well . . .	**Il ferait aussi bien de . . .**

299. Shall, will.

The two auxiliaries *shall* and *will* serve to form the English future tense. The French ***futur*** of the verb following *shall* or *will* is sufficient to translate them. However, the use of the French ***futur*** is in some ways different from that of the English future (see §262). The differences also apply to the use of the French ***futur antérieur***, compared with the English future perfect (see §266).

When *shall* and *will* are used for emphasis, the emphasis may be rendered in French in the following ways:

A. An adverb may be added to the verb in the future tense.

Tu ne tueras point. (***point*** is more emphatic than ***pas***)
Thou shalt not kill.

Tu ne seras certainement pas récompensé!
You shall not be rewarded.

B. A helping verb may be introduced into the sentence: ***devoir*** or ***falloir*** in the case of *shall*, ***vouloir*** or ***vouloir bien*** in the case of *will*.

Le candidat devra (or: doit) se conduire honorablement.
The applicant shall behave in a honorable fashion.

Je ne veux pas le faire!
I will not do it!

Si vous (le) voulez.
If you will.

Si vous voulez bien attendre quelques minutes.
If you will just wait a few minutes.

Si nous passions à table?
Shall we (sit at the table)?
How about sitting down at the table?

300. Must, need, have to, be necessary, be to.

A. Affirmative.

1) Obligation or necessity, whether subjective or external, are expressed in French by the verbs ***devoir*** and ***falloir***.

Je dois partir. Il faut que je parte.
I must leave. I have to leave.

Vous devez attendre. Il faut que vous attendiez.
You must wait. You have to wait.

Je devais travailler. Il fallait que je travaille.
I had to work. I needed to work. It was necessary for me to work.

Est-ce que je dois faire ce travail maintenant?
Do I need to do this work now?

The French expressions ***avoir besoin de***, ***il est nécessaire***, and the verb ***falloir*** preceded by an indirect object personal pronoun also translate the meaning of *to need.*

J'ai besoin de vacances. Il me faut des vacances.
I need a vacation.

Il lui faut un docteur. Il a besoin d'un docteur.
He needs a doctor.

The verb ***falloir*** may be used in infinitive constructions with or without a preceding indirect object personal pronoun. The personal pronoun identifies the persons concerned by the statement. The absence of the pronoun makes the statement general and indefinite.

Il nous faut du temps et de l'argent pour finir ce projet.
We need time and money to finish this project.

Il leur fallait trouver un véhicule à cause des enfants.
They needed to find a vehicle because of the children.

Il fallait trouver un véhicule à cause des enfants.
A vehicle had to be found because of the children.

The verb ***falloir*** followed by ***que*** and a verb in the subjunctive indicates that the need or the necessity is external, objective, not affective.

Il fallait qu'ils trouvent un véhicule à cause des enfants.
It was necessary to find a vehicle because of the children.

2) Supposition or the meaning of "probably" is expressed in French by the verb ***devoir***.

Je dois être en retard.
I must be late.

Il doit être endormi.
He must be asleep.

J'ai dû laisser mon livre à la maison.
I must have left my book at home.

Il devait être très fatigué.
He must have been very tired.

Nous devons prendre l'avion demain matin.
We are (supposed, scheduled) to take the plane tomorrow morning.

B. Negative.

1) Obligation not to and lack of obligation, need, or necessity are expressed in French by the negative forms of ***devoir, falloir, être obligé, avoir besoin, être nécessaire***.

Vous ne devez pas mentir. Il ne faut pas mentir.
You must not lie. One must not lie.

On ne doit pas le laisser seul.
Il ne doit pas être laissé seul.
Il ne faut pas le laisser seul.
Il ne faut pas qu'on le laisse seul.
He must not be left alone.

Il ne faut pas donner à manger aux animaux du zoo.
The animals are not to be fed. One must not feed the animals.

Vous n'avez pas besoin de venir.
Vous n'êtes pas obligé de venir.
Il n'est pas nécessaire que vous veniez.
You need not come. You don't have to come.

Il n'est pas nécessaire d'ouvrir la fenêtre.
Vous n'avez pas besoin d'ouvrir la fenêtre.
You don't have to open the window.

Ils n'ont pas besoin de crier.
Il n'est pas nécessaire qu'ils crient.
They don't have to shout. They needn't shout.

2) Supposition, probability, etc., of something negative is expressed in French by the verb ***devoir***.

Il ne doit pas être très heureux.
He must not be very happy.

Vous n'avez pas dû comprendre.
You must not have understood. You probably didn't understand.

NOTE: The English expression *have got to* is to be translated in the same manner as *to have to*.

301. Could, could have, might, might have.

A. Could: ***pouvoir***.

1) *Could* followed by a single verb may be past or conditional, depending on the meaning of the context. If the tense is past, it is important in French to distinguish between the imperfect and the passé composé (see §261, §264).

S'il était ici, il pourrait nous aider.
If he were here, he could help us.

Quand il avait dix-huit ans, il pouvait sauter deux mètres.
When he was eighteen, he could jump six feet eight.

Je n'ai pas pu venir parce que je n'avais pas fini mon travail.
I couldn't come because I had not finished my work.

Note that the French verb ***pouvoir*** also translates the verbs *to be able to, to manage,* and *to succeed* when these are substituted for *could.*

2) *Could have*, followed by a past participle, can only be rendered by the past conditional of the verb ***pouvoir***, followed by an infinitive. Note the difference of pattern in the expression of the verb group between French and English.

Vous auriez pu répondre quand je vous ai appelé.
You could have answered when I called you.

B. Might: ***pouvoir***.

1) *Might*, followed by a single verb, can only be rendered in French by the present conditional of the verb ***pouvoir***, followed by an infinitive, or by the expression ***il se pourrait*** followed by ***que*** and a verb in the subjunctive.

Il pourrait arriver demain.
Il se pourrait qu'il arrive demain.
He might arrive tomorrow.

Vous pourriez y arriver.
Il se pourrait que vous y arriviez.
You might make it.

Nous pourrions ne pas y arriver.
Il se pourrait que nous n'y arrivions pas.
We might not make it.

2) *Might have*, followed by a past participle, is rendered in French by the past conditional of the verb ***pouvoir***, followed by an infinitive. Note the difference of pattern of the verb group between English and French.

Nous aurions pu manquer l'avion.
We might have missed the plane.

Ils auraient pu ne pas venir.
They might not have come.

C. Idiomatic expressions:

It might be.	**Cela se pourrait.**
You might as well . . .	**Vous feriez aussi bien de . . .** (infinitive)
You (I, he, etc.) might just as well!	**Cela vaudrait autant!**
I wish I could . . .	**J'aimerais pouvoir . . .** (with infinitive)
Don't you wish they . . .	**Ne voudriez-vous pas qu'ils . . .** **N'aimeriez vous pas qu'ils . . .** **Ne préféreriez-vous pas qu'ils . . .** **Cela ne vous plairait-il pas qu'ils . . .** (all with subjunctive)

302. Should, should have, would, would have.

A. *Should** and *would* serving as auxiliaries to form the conditional tenses are rendered as follows:

1) Followed by simple verb forms, *should**, *would* correspond to the French present conditional.

S'il pleuvait, je ne sortirais pas.
If it rained, I would not go out.

Si nous avions de l'argent, nous irions en Europe l'été prochain.
If we had money, we would go to Europe next summer.

Le garçon (la serveuse) nous a demandé si nous prendrions du vin.
The waiter (the waitress) asked us whether we would have wine.

2) *Should* have, would have*, followed by past participle, correspond to the French past conditional.

S'il n'avait pas plu, je serais sorti.
If it had not rained, I would have gone out.

Si nous avions eu de l'argent, nous serions allés en Europe.
If we had had money, we would have gone to Europe.

Je me demandais comment il aurait pu nous retrouver.
I was wondering how he would have been able to locate us.

*In modern American, the auxiliary *should* is no longer used to form the conditional of the first person. The auxiliary *would* is used for all persons, and *should* is used to convey other meanings, as described in the next paragraphs.

B. *Should* meaning "ought to," and *should have* meaning "ought to have," are rendered in French by the present conditional and by the past conditional, respectively, of the verb ***devoir*** followed by an infinitive.

Vous ne devriez pas fumer.
You should not smoke. You ought not to smoke.

Vous auriez dû venir plus tôt.
You should have come earlier. You ought to have come earlier.

C. *Would* meaning "used to" is always rendered in French by the imperfect indicative of the verb in question.

Toutes les semaines, nous leur rendions visite.
Every week, we would pay them a visit.

D. *Would* conveying an idea of "will" or "wish" is generally rendered in French by a form of the verb ***vouloir***. The case is particularly frequent in the negative.

Voulez-vous fermer la porte, s'il vous plaît.
Would you shut the door, please?

Je lui ai demandé de me donner un coup de main, mais il n'a pas voulu.
I asked him to give me a hand, but he wouldn't.

Ils ne voulaient pas venir. Ils n'ont pas voulu venir.
They wouldn't come.

E. *Should* expressing eventuality or a hypothetical event, action, or fact is rendered in French by the subjunctive of the verb following *should*, except after ***si*** (*if*). See §183.

Si vous étiez en retard, je ne vous attendrais pas.
If you should be late, I would not wait for you.
Should you be late, I would not wait for you.

Supposez qu'il pleuve . . .!
Suppose it should rain . . .!

Cachez-vous de peur qu'il ne vous voie.
Hide lest he should see you. (Hide or else he'll see you.)

Je ne suis pas surpris qu'il soit en colère.
I am not surprised that he should be angry.

F. *Should* following the interrogative words *how* and *why* is rendered in French by the regular conditional of the verb in question, or by the simple indicative of the same verb, or by a form of the verb ***devoir*** preceding the infinitive of the verb in question.

Comment le saurais-je? Comment voulez-vous que je le sache?
How should I know?

Pourquoi serait-ce (or: **est-ce**) **à moi de lui annoncer la nouvelle?**
Why should I be the one to break him the news?

Pourquoi devrais-je (or: **dois-je**) **me taire?**
Why should I keep quiet?

The conditional is preferable when the speaker sees the obligation as unacceptable.

G. Idiomatic expressions.

Je me demande si je puis me permettre de . . .(infinitive)
I wonder if I should . . . (: am allowed to . . .)

Je me demande si je devrais . . .(infinitive)
I wonder if I should . . .

Je me demande si je puis me le permettre.
I wonder if I should. (: if I am allowed)
I wonder if I can afford to.

Oui, je le ferais. Oui, je (le) veux bien. Oui, je veux bien le faire. Oui, bien sûr. Oui.
Yes, I would. (answering: "Would you . . .?")

Si, je le ferais. Si, je (le) veux bien. Si, je veux bien le faire. Si, bien sûr. Si.
Yes, I would. (answering: "Wouldn't you . . .?")

Oui, vous devriez le faire. Oui, bien sûr. Oui. Oui, il faudrait que vous le fassiez.
Yes, you should. (answering : "Should I . . .?")

Si, vous devriez le faire. Si, bien sûr. Si. Si, il faudrait que vous le fassiez.
Yes, you should. (answering : "Shouldn't I . . .?")

J'aimerais mieux . . . (infinitive)
I would rather . . .
I had rather . . ., I'd rather . . .

Je ferais mieux de . . . (infinitive)
I would better . . ., I'd better . . .
I had better . . .

J'aimerais (bien) . . . (infinitive)
I wish I would . . .
I would like to . . .

J'aimerais que . . . (subjunctive)
I wish (you, he, they, etc.) would . . . (still possible)

J'aurais aimé que . . . (subjunctive)
I wish (you, he, they, etc.) had . . . (unreal: no longer possible)

303. Say, tell, speak, talk.

To say and *to tell* are both translated ***dire*** except in the phrase *to tell a story*: ***raconter une histoire***. *To speak* and *to talk* are both translated ***parler*** except in the phrase *to speak the truth*: ***dire la vérité***.

"Venez," dit-il.
"Come," he said.

Il a dit qu'il viendrait tout de suite.
He said that he would come right away.

Il m'a dit qu'il viendrait au plus tôt.
He told me that he would come at the earliest.

Qu'est-ce qu'il vous a dit?
What did he say to you? What did he tell you?

Dire l'heure.
To tell the time.

Dire la vérité.
To tell the truth. To speak the truth.

On m'a dit que vous . . .
I am told that you . . .
I was told that you . . .

On dit qu'elle . . .
She is said to . . .

Je vous l'avais (bien) dit.
I (had) told you so.

Il parle trois langues. Nous parlions de choses et d'autres.
He speaks three languages. We were talking (chatting) about this, that, and the other.

Je veux vous parler.
I want to talk to you (with you).

Je veux vous dire deux mots.
I want to have a word with you.

Parlez plus fort, plus haut. Élevez la voix.
Speak up. Talk louder.

Il m'a persuadé de le faire.
He talked me into it.

Il m'a persuadé de ne pas le faire.
He talked me out of it.

Nous parlons de vous.
We are talking about you.

À propos de musique; à propos de ce morceau de musique . . .
Speaking of music; speaking of this piece of music . . .

En général, . . .
Generally speaking, . . .

À strictement parler, . . .
Strictly speaking, . . .

Pour ainsi dire.
So to speak.

C'est-à-dire . . .
That it to say . . .

Un entretien, une conversation.
A talk.

Des pourparlers.
Talks. (diplomatic, between governments, etc.)

The following expressions are used *after* or *within* quotations of spoken words to indicate the manner in which the words were pronounced. The inversion is required if these expressions come within or after the quotes, but there can be no inversion if they precede them.

These expressions are presented in the third person singular of the passé simple indicative because they are most likely to be used in written contexts of storytelling, novels, short stories, etc.

annonça-t-il	he announced
avança-t-il	he proposed
bégaya-t-il	he stuttered, he stammered
commanda-t-il	he ordered
cria-t-il	he shouted, he screamed
dit-il	he said
s'exclama-t-il	he exclaimed
fit-il	he said (with a motion, a gesture)
grogna-t-il	he grunted, he snarled
hurla-t-il	he roared, he yelled
insista-t-il	he insisted
jura-t-il	he swore
laissa-t-il tomber	he dropped, he hinted
lança-t-il	he threw, he hurled, he snapped
menaça-t-il	he threatened

murmura-t-il	he murmured, he whispered
ordonna-t-il	he ordered
remarqua-t-il	he remarked
répéta-t-il	he repeated
répliqua-t-il	he retorted
répondit-il	he replied, he responded
supplia-t-il	he begged, he implored
suggéra-t-il	he suggested

304. Active, passive, pronominal voices.

There are important differences of use for the active voice, the passive voice, and the pronominal voice, in English as well as in French. The following notes will show how to choose the correct French voice or construction for the various English voices or constructions to be translated.

A. English reflexive verbs (i.e., accompanied by *myself, yourself, himself,* etc. and reciprocal verbs (i.e., accompanied by *each other* or *one another*) are generally translated into French by pronominal verbs (i.e., verbs accompanied by ***me, te, se, nous, vous, se.*** See §87).

Il s'est coupé. Nous nous sommes coupés.
He cut himself. We cut ourselves.

Ils se regardent. Vous vous regardez.
They are watching one another. You are watching one another.

For some details on reciprocal verbs, see §63B.

B. English active constructions are generally rendered in French by similar active ones. However, a number of English active verbs require the use of pronominal verbs for their translation into French (see E, below).

Je bois du vin. Il a cassé sa montre.
I drink wine. He broke his watch.

Je me brosse les dents avant de m'habiller.
I brush my teeth before I get dressed.

C. English passive constructions in which the agent (object of *by*) is expressed should also be passive constructions in French.

Le contrebandier a été arrêté par le douanier.
The smuggler was arrested by the customs officer.

However, if the English verb has a direct object, the English passive must be turned into a French active construction. The subject of the English passive verb becomes an indirect object.

Le patron a donné une augmentation à Paul.
Paul was given a raise by the boss.

Le patron lui a donné une augmentation.
He was given a raise by the boss.

Un policier lui a dit qu'il ne pouvait pas garer sa voiture à cet endroit.
He was told by a policeman than he could not park in that space.

Notre service de publicité vous expédiera un exemplaire gratuit de cette brochure.
You will be sent (mailed) a free copy of this brochure by our advertising department.

D. English passive constructions in which the agent (following *by*) is *not* expressed should be turned into French active constructions with the subject ***on***, or into constructions with pronominal verbs in the case of general truths.

On (m')a volé ma voiture.
My car has been stolen.

On m'a demandé d'attendre.
I was asked to wait.

On m'apprend (or: **on me dit, j'apprends, il paraît) que vous êtes étranger.**
I am told (I hear) that you are a foreigner.

On vient de nous apprendre que . . . On vient de nous dire que . . .
We have just been told that . . .

On dit que vous . . . On raconte que vous . . .
You are said to . . . You are rumored to . . .

On parle anglais.
English is spoken.

Le pain se vend (s'achète) dans une boulangerie.
Bread is sold (bought) in a bakery.

Ce machin-là s'appelle un casse-noisette.
This what-d'you-call-it is called a nutcracker.

"Aïe" se prononce comme "aille".
"Aïe" is pronounced like "aille".

Le Camembert se fabrique en Normandie.
Camembert is made in Normandy.

Les maisons américaines se construisent en bois.
American houses are built with wood.

L'arabe se lit de droite à gauche.
Arabic is read from right to left.

E. Many English verbs expressing movement, as opposed to attitude, which is static, and verb phrases expressing progression or change *(to become, get, grow, turn,* followed by adjective) are rendered in French by reflexive verbs. The following list of examples contains the most common ones (the alphabetical order is that of the French reflexive verbs).

Il s'abaisse à leur parler.
He condescends (humbles himself) to speak to them.

Je vais m'abonner à cette revue. (s'abonner)
I am going to subscribe to that magazine. (act of subscribing)

Je suis abonné à cette revue. (être abonné)
I have a subscription to that magazine. (subscription in progress)

Nous nous sommes abrités sous un arbre.
We took shelter under a tree.

Vous vous absentez trop souvent.
You are being absent (cutting class) too frequently.

Il s'abstient de faire des remarques.
He abstains from making remarks.

On s'accoutume vite aux choses les plus étranges.
One gets quickly used to the strangest things.

La population mondiale s'accroît rapidement.
The world population increases very rapidly.

Accroupissez-vous.
Squat down.

Tu t'acharnes en vain à résoudre ce problème.
You persist (rage) in vain to solve that problem.

Nous nous acheminions tranquillement.
We were going our way quietly.

Cet article s'achète beaucoup cette saison.
This item is bought a lot this season.
Many people buy this item this season.

Je m'adresse à vous. C'est à vous que je m'adresse.
I am talking to *you*.

Je me suis adressé au guichet numéro 3.
I inquired (applied) at window number 3.

Le malade s'affaiblit de jour en jour.
The sick man is growing weaker day after day.

Le sol s'est affaissé au dessus de la mine.
The ground sank (collapsed, caved in) above the mine.

Le soldat blessé s'est affaissé sans un cri.
The wounded soldier collapsed without a sound.

Le garçon a trébuché et s'est affalé de tout son long.
The boy stumbled and fell flat on the ground.

Ils se sont affolés dès le premier coup de feu.
They panicked right from the first gunshot.

Il s'agenouille. Il est à genoux.
He kneels down (movement). He is kneeling (attitude).

Son état s'aggrave.
His (her) condition is getting worse.

De quoi s'agit-il?
What is it all about? What is the matter in question?

Il s'agira de ne pas se faire prendre.
It will be a question of not getting caught.

Ils s'en sont allés, et je m'en vais aussi.
They went away, and I am going (away) too.

Je me suis allongé dans l'herbe.
I lay down in the grass. (movement)

Je suis allongé sur l'herbe.
I am lying on the grass. (attitude)

Sa santé s'améliore.
His (her) health is getting better, is improving.

Je m'amuse à peindre.
I am having fun painting.

Amusez-vous bien.
Have fun. Enjoy yourselves.

Ils se sont aperçus de notre absence.
They noticed our absence.

Je m'aperçois que vous avez oublié votre livre.
I notice that you have forgotten your book.

Je m'appelle Paul.
My name is Paul.

Ce règlement s'applique à tous.
These regulations apply to everyone.

Ils s'apprêtent à partir.
They are getting ready to leave.

Ils sont prêts à partir.
They are ready to leave.

Il faut s'approcher pour bien voir.
It is necessary to get closer to have a good view.

Approchez-vous.
Get closer.

Il s'est appuyé au bord de la table.
He leaned against the table. (movement)

L'échelle est appuyée au mur.
The ladder is leaning against the wall. (state)

Les radis s'arrachent plus facilement que les pommes de terre.
Radishes are easier to dig up than potatoes.

Il était si désespéré qu'il voulait s'arracher les cheveux.
He was so desperate that he wanted to pull his hair out.

Cet été, on s'arrache les chapeaux de paille.
This summer, there is a rush on straw hats.

Elles se sont arrangées pour ne pas nous rencontrer.
They arranged (connived, schemed) so as not to meet us.

Je m'arrête pour reprendre mon souffle.
I am stopping to catch my breath.

Je me suis arrêté de travailler à six heures.
I stopped working at six o'clock.

La voiture est arrêtée.
The car is not moving (is stopped, at a stop, parked).

Je m'assieds. Je m'assois.
I am sitting down. (movement)

Je suis assis. Elle est assise.
I am sitting. She is seated. (attitude)

Le ciel s'assombrit.
The sky is getting darker.

Son visage s'assombrit.
Her face is turning (growing) serious, gloomy, somber, etc.

Assurez-vous que vous n'avez rien oublié.
Make certain that you have not forgotten anything.

Nous nous attaquerons d'abord aux problèmes importants.
We'll deal (cope) first with the important problems.

Ne vous attardez pas après le cinéma.
Don't stay late after the movie.

À quoi vous attendiez-vous?
What were you expecting?

Attendent-elles quelqu'un?
Are they expecting (waiting for) someone?

Avancez-vous.
Step forward. Come forward.

Ne t'avise pas de sortir sans permission!
Don't you try to go out without permission!

Je me suis baigné dans le lac.
I went for a swim in the lake. I swam in the lake.

La porte est basse, baissez-vous.
The door is low, bend down.

Un singe se balance au bout d'une branche.
A monkey is swinging from the end of a branch.

Les petits chats se blottissaient les uns contre les autres.
The kittens were cuddling against each other.

Ce vin doit se boire frais.
That wine must be served cool. (lit.: must be drunk cool)

Le vase s'est brisé dans mes mains.
The vase broke in my hands.

Son cheval s'est cabré.
His (her) horse reared.

Il est allé se cacher derrière la maison.
He went to hide behind the house.

Les noix se cassent à l'aide d'un casse-noix.
Nuts are to be cracked with a nutcracker.

Essaie de mieux te conduire.
Try to behave better.

Elle s'est confiée à moi.
She confided in me.

Je m'y connais en voitures européennes.
I know all about European cars.

Nous nous couchons tous les jours à dix heures.
We go to bed at ten every day.

Il se croit très malin, très intelligent.
He thinks he is very clever, very smart.

Je me suis enfin décidé à lui parler.
I finally made up my mind to speak to him (her).

Je me demande quelle sera sa réaction.
I wonder what his reaction will be.

Il faut qu'ils se dépêchent s'ils veulent être à l'heure.
They've got to hurry if they want to be on time.

Il est inutile que vous vous déplaciez.
You need not move from where you are. You need not change seats.
You need not make the trip.

Ils se disposent à partir.
They are getting ready to leave.

Paul s'est disputé avec sa sœur.
Paul had a fight (argument) with his sister.

Je me doutais qu'il allait refuser.
I suspected that he was going to refuse.

Un obélisque se dresse au milieu de la place.
An obelisk rises (stands) in the middle of the square.

Les enfants s'ébattent dans le bassin, dans la piscine.
The children are splashing around in the pool.

Un tigre s'est échappé du cirque.
A tiger escaped from the circus.

Il s'échauffe pour un rien.
He gets carried away (passionate, mad, hot) over nothing.

Le ciel s'éclaircit.
The sky is clearing up.

Je comprends! Tout s'éclaire!
I understand! Everything is getting clearer.

Le temps peut s'écouler vite ou lentement.
Time can pass (flow, go by, run, etc.) quickly or slowly.

"Hourra!" s'écria-t-il.
"Hurray!" he exclaimed.

Le mur s'est écroulé. L'ivrogne s'est écroulé.
The wall collapsed. The drunkard collapsed.

La maison s'est effondrée. Le plancher s'est effondré.
The house collapsed. The floor sank (caved in).

Efforce-toi d'être à l'heure.
Make a big effort to be on time.

Les flèches de la cathédrale s'élèvent dans le ciel.
The spires of the cathedral rise into the sky.

Les romantiques s'émouvaient facilement.
The romantics were easily moved.

Les soldats se sont emparés de la forteresse.
The soldiers seized (captured) the fortress.

Je ne peux pas m'empêcher de rire.
I cannot help but laugh. I cannot help laughing.

Il s'emporte pour un oui ou pour un non.
He gets angry for no reason at all (at the drop of a hat).

Les vendeurs s'empressent auprès des clients.
The sales clerks are eager (forward, pushy) with the customers.

Je me suis endormi tout de suite.
I fell asleep (went to sleep) immediately.

Ce bruit m'énerve, et pourtant je ne m'énerve pas facilement.
That noise irritates (unnerves) me, and I am not easily unnerved.

Il s'est engagé pour dix ans.
He enlisted for ten years.

Je m'ennuie. Cela ennuie mes voisins.
I am getting bored. That annoys (bothers) my neighbors.

. . . Il s'ensuit que chacun croit avoir raison.
. . . It follows that each thinks he (she) is right.

Les oiseaux s'envolent.
The birds are flying away.

Elle s'est éprise de lui. Il s'est épris d'elle.
She fell in love with him. He fell in love with her.

Il s'étend sur le sable.
He lies down on the sand. (movement)

Il est étendu. Il est allongé.
He is lying (stretched out).

Elle étend sa serviette sur le sable.
She spreads her towel down on the sand.

Le désert s'étend sur des kilomètres et des kilomètres.
The desert spreads for miles and miles.

Quand on se réveille, on s'étire.
When one wakes up, one stretches.

Je m'étonne qu'il ait refusé.
I am surprised that he refused.

Un prisonnier s'est évadé.
A prisoner has escaped.

Elle s'est évanouie.
She fainted.

L'éther s'évapore très vite.
Ether evaporates very quickly.

Chaque printemps, la nature s'éveille.
Every spring, nature comes to life. (awakens)

Elle s'évertue à paraître belle.
She exerts herself to look beautiful.

Il s'est excusé d'avoir été impoli.
He apologized for having been impolite.

On s'extasie devant les chutes du Niagara.
One is breathtaken (in ecstasies) before the falls of Niagara.

Je crois que je vais me fâcher.
I think I am going to get mad.

Ne vous en faites pas. Je ne m'en fais pas.
Don't worry. I am not worried (worrying).

Il s'en est fallu de peu qu'il (ne) tombe.
He came close to falling down.

Je ne me fie pas à eux.
I do not trust them.

Il se figure qu'il a tout compris.
He thinks (imagines, figures) that he understood everything.

Elle s'est habillée toute seule.
She got dressed all by herself.

Je me suis très vite habitué à ce climat.
I got used to this climate very quickly.

Il s'imagine qu'il sait tout.
He thinks (imagines) that he knows it all.

L'eau s'est infiltrée par le plafond.
The water seeped in through the ceiling.

Elle s'ingénie à trouver une solution.
She racks her brain trying to find a solution.

La populace s'est insurgée.
The mob (populace) rebelled.

Je m'intéresse à la photographie.
I am interested in photography.

La Seine se jette dans la Manche.
The Seine empties into the English Channel.

L'audacieux bandit se joue de la police.
The daring bandit makes fun of (baffles) the police.

Elle ne cesse de se lamenter.
She does not stop complaining.

On se lasse vite de ne rien faire.
One gets quickly bored from doing nothing.

Je me lave les dents.
I brush my teeth.

Il s'est levé de bonne heure. Le soleil se lève.
He got up early. The sun is rising.

Il est levé. Le soleil est levé.
He is up. The sun is up.

Le fromage se mange à la fin du repas.
Cheese is to be eaten at the end of the meal.

Je me méfie d'eux.
I mistrust them. I don't trust them.

Il s'est mépris sur mes intentions.
He misjudged (misunderstood) my intentions.

Les fleurs se mettent dans des vases.
Flowers are to be placed in vases.

Elle s'est mise à pleurer.
She started crying. She began to cry.

Je me moque de son opinion.
I don't care about his opinion. (I don't give a darn . . .)

Il se moque de nous.
He is making fun of us.

Les écureuils se nourrissent de noix et de glands.
Squirrels feed on nuts and acorns.

Le ciel s'obscurcit.
The sky is growing darker.

Elle s'obstine à vouloir vous parler.
She insists (keeps) on wanting to speak to you.
She persists obstinately in wanting to speak to you.

Je m'occupe de tout.
I'm taking care of everything.

Je m'oppose à sa nomination.
I oppose (I am opposed to) his nomination.

Ces choses-là s'oublient vite.
These things are quickly forgotten.

Qu'est-ce qui se passe?
What's going on? What is the matter?

Cela s'est passé la semaine dernière.
That happened last week.

Il ne peut se passer de voiture.
He cannot do without a car.

Je me peigne. Je me peigne les cheveux.
I comb my hair.

Vous vous plaignez tout le temps.
You are always complaining.

Elle se plaît à lire.
She likes reading. She enjoys reading.

Les mini-jupes ne se portent plus.
Mini-skirts are no longer worn.

Il se peut qu'il neige.
It may snow.

Il se prend pour l'empereur.
He thinks he is the emperor.

Ils s'en prennent toujours aux plus faibles.
They always blame (bully, attack) the weaker ones.

Il sait s'y prendre pour ouvrir les huîtres.
He has the knack for opening oysters.

Ne vous pressez pas.
Do not hurry.

Nous nous sommes promenés dans le parc.
We took a walk in the park.

Le temps se rafraîchit.
The weather is turning cooler.

Je me rappelle cette aventure.
I remember this adventure.

Je me rappelle que je vous dois de l'argent.
I remember that I owe you money.

Attendez que votre potage se refroidisse un peu.
Wait for your soup to cool down a little.

Nous nous sommes réfugiés dans un monastère.
We took refuge in a monastery.

Je me réjouis de votre succès.
I am delighted with your success.

Vous rendez-vous compte de ce que vous faites?
Do you realize what you are doing?

Je me suis bien renseigné.
I got good information.

Il se repentira de cette action.
He will regret this action.

Nous nous reposerons un peu dans une heure.
We'll rest in an hour.

Il ne peut se résoudre à accepter ce poste.
He cannot make up his mind to accept that position.

Je me suis retenu de crier après ces galopins.
I refrained from shouting at those rascals.

La voiture s'est retournée dans le fossé.
The car overturned in the ditch.

Je me suis retourné en entendant du bruit.
I turned around when I heard a noise.

Nous nous réunirons le 10 mars.
We shall meet on the 10th of March.

Je me suis réveillé deux fois au milieu de la nuit.
I woke up twice in the middle of the night.

Quand on ne se réveille pas à l'heure, on se sent coupable.
When one oversleeps, one feels guilty.

Le voleur s'est saisi de mon sac et s'est enfui.
The thief grabbed my bag and fled.

Les hommes ne se sauvent pas avant les femmes et les enfants.
Men don't save themselves before women and children.

Il faut que je me sauve.
I have got to go. I must be off.

Il s'est senti ému en voyant pleurer la vieille dame.
He felt moved when he saw the old lady cry.

Il s'est servi d'un bâton comme levier.
He used a stick for a lever.

Il aura du mal à s'en sortir.
He will have a hard time getting out of it.

Je ne me soucie pas de ce qui lui est arrivé.
I do not care (worry) about what happened to him.

Ne vous souvenez-vous pas de nous?
Don't you remember us?

Il s'est suicidé.
He committed suicide.

Je me tairai.
I'll keep quiet. I won't say a word.

Il ne se tient pas comme il faut.
He does not behave properly.
He does not sit (or: stand) properly.

La classe s'est terminée à l'heure.
The class ended on time.

Je crois que vous vous êtes trompé de route.
I think you went the wrong way (took the wrong road).

Si je me trompe, arrête-moi.
If I make a mistake, stop me.
If I am doing the wrong thing, stop me.

Ce n'est pas ça, vous vous trompez.
That's not it, you are wrong (you are making a mistake).

La Provence se trouve dans le sud de la France.
Provence is in the South of France.

Il se trouve que moi aussi, j'habite dans cette ville.
It so happens that I live in that city also.
I also happen to live in that city.

Il peut se vanter de l'avoir échappé belle.
He can boast of having had a narrow escape.

Cela se voit de plus en plus souvent.
That can be seen more and more often.

Il s'est vu refuser l'entrée.
He was turned away at the door.
They did not let him in.

305. Impersonal verbs.

A verb is called ***impersonal*** when it is used in the third person singular with no clearly defined subject. It generally corresponds in English to the use of *it* or *there* with a verb. The pronoun ***il*** is only the *apparent* subject of the verb, the real subject being what is stated in a sort of indirect way after the verb.

Il manque un joueur pour faire une équipe complète.
We (you, they) are short one player for a full team.
(One player is lacking for a complete team.)

but: Il manquait toujours la cible. Il manquait toujours de pot! (coll.)
Tu me manques terriblement! Et moi, est-ce que je te manque?
He always missed the target. He was always unlucky!
I miss you terribly! And you, do you miss me?

Il se trouve justement que je n'ai rien à faire; je peux donc vous accompagner chez vous.
It so happens that I have nothing to do; so, I can walk you home.

Il vient un temps où l'homme doit enfin céder au destin.
There comes a time when man must finally yield to fate. (A time comes . . .)

Nous ferons ce qu'il faut pour résoudre ce problème, qu'il s'agisse de temps ou d'argent.
We'll do what it takes to solve that problem, whether it be a question of time or a question of money.

Il ne s'agit pas de se tromper! Il ne s'agirait pas qu'il oublie notre anniversaire de mariage!
We (they, you, I, etc.) had better not make a mistake! He'd better not forget our (wedding) anniversary!

Il ne manquait plus que ça! Il ne manquerait plus que ça!
That tops it all! That would take the cake!

Impersonal verbs associated with the use of the subjunctive and indicative moods are listed in §280B. Most impersonal verbs or verbal expressions consist of the pronoun ***il*** followed by the verb ***être*** and an adjective. Among the rest are single verbs and verbal expressions that are either essentially impersonal or accidentally so.

A. Essentially impersonal verbs pertain to the description of atmospheric phenomena (except ***il faut***). These verbs exist only in the infinitive and in the third person singular of all tenses:

bruiner	**il bruine**	it drizzles, there is light rain
grêler	**il grêle**	it hails, there is hail
neiger	**il neige**	it snows
pleuvoir	**il pleut**	it rains
venter	**il vente**	the wind is blowing
falloir	**il faut**	(expresses necessity, obligation)

B. Accidentally impersonal verbs and expressions are those that exist first as personal verbs or expressions but are used on occasion in impersonal constructions.

PERSONAL	IMPERSONAL
Il agit en bon citoyen.	Il s'agit d'un roman d'amour.
Paul a une Rolls Royce.	Il y a une Rolls Royce devant la maison.
Il est riche.	Il est midi. Il est l'heure.
	Il est des vérités qui ne se disent pas.
Le bonheur n'existe pas.	Il existe des gens qui ne croient en rien.
Il fait ce qu'il peut.	Il fait noir dans cette cave.
Nous faisons la cuisine.	Il fait jour. Il fait nuit. Il fait du vent.
	Il fait du brouillard. Il fait du tonnerre.
	Il fait chaud, froid, bon, humide, etc.
Je manque de courage.	Il me manque deux dollars.
Pouvez-vous m'aider?	Il se peut qu'elle m'aide.
On trouve des taxis à la sortie.	Il se trouve que j'y vais aussi.
L'action vaut mieux que la parole.	Il vaut mieux partir.
Une pensée lui vint à l'esprit.	Il lui vint à l'esprit que . . .

C. The impersonal construction is one in which verbs normally personal are used accidentally in an impersonal way. Compare the following pairs.

Un accident est vite arrivé!
An accident can happen so easily!

Il nous est arrivé un malheur.
We were victims of a tragedy. A tragedy befell us.

Les ouvriers sortent tous les jours des centaines de voitures de cette usine.
Every day the workers bring hundreds of cars out of that plant.

Il sort tous les jours des centaines de voitures de cette usine.
Every day hundreds of cars come out of that plant.

Il est passé nous voir, mais il n'a pas pu rester longtemps.
He came by to see us, but he could not stay long.

Il est passé plusieurs hélicoptères au-dessus de la maison.
Several helicopters flew over the house.

Il est arrivé hier soir.
He arrived last night.

Il est arrivé un télégramme pour vous.
A telegram arrived for you.

Lorsque le roi parut, toutes les dames firent la révérence.
When the king appeared, all the ladies curtsied.

Il a paru ce jour-là dans le ciel une lumière inconnue.
There appeared in the sky on that day a strange light.

Ce journal paraît tous les soirs.
That newspaper comes out every evening.

Il paraît que ce journal est au bord de la faillite.
Rumor has it that this paper is near bankrupcy.

Nous resterons là-bas quelques jours.
We'll stay over there for a few days.

Il nous reste quelques heures avant le décollage.
We have a few hours left until takeoff.

Comment s'est-il fait prendre?
How did he get himself caught?

Comment se fait-il qu'il ait été pris?
How come he was caught?

Vous semblez avoir faim.
You seem to be hungry.

Il semble que nous soyons en retard.
It seems that we are late.

Vous me semblez avoir sommeil.
You seem to me to be sleepy. You look like you are tired. (Am.)

Il me semble que vous avez sommeil.
It seems to me that you are tired.

Elle ne vaut pas mieux que lui.
She isn't (worth) any better than he. She doesn't deserve any better than he.

Ne vaut-il pas mieux qu'elle rentre chez elle en taxi?
Wouldn't it be better for her to take a cab home?

Une idée géniale lui vint à l'esprit.
A brilliant idea occurred to him.

Il lui vint à l'esprit qu'il sortirait avant les autres.
Il lui vint à l'esprit de sortir avant les autres.
It occurred to him that he would leave before the others.

NOTE: The impersonal construction frequently combines verbs such as ***devoir, pouvoir,*** and ***savoir*** with the expressions listed above in the examples. These combinations can be used in any tense and thus offer a wide range of possibilities. Observe the following:

Il arrive:	**Il peut arriver un malheur.** **Il pourrait arriver un malheur.** **Il aurait pu arriver un malheur.**
Il y a:	**Il doit y avoir une raison.** **Il devrait y avoir une solution.** **Il aurait dû y avoir plus de monde.** **Il aurait pu y avoir plus de monde.** **Il vient d'y avoir un accident.** **Il va y avoir du nouveau.**
Il est:	**Il ne saurait en être question!** **Il n'en a jamais été question** **Il est l'heure.** **Il doit être minuit.**
Il est (il y a, il existe):	**Il est des pays lointains où la nature règne encore.** **Il fut un temps où le bonheur était encore possible.**
Il s'agit:	**Il pourrait s'agir d'un manque de savoir-faire.** **Il doit s'agir de son collègue.**
Il existe:	**Il devrait exister des lois contre ce genre d'abus.**
Il fait beau:	**Il doit faire beau.** **Il devrait faire beau.** **Il devait faire beau.** **Il aurait pu faire beau.**

306. Adverbial expressions.

The following list offers a variety of expressions for use as adverbial phrases. Only the phrases have been listed on the French side. The simple adverbs can be found in the chapter on adverbs (§§195-248).

Prudence should be exercised in using these adverbial phrases, since each of them may be suitable only in a given context.

For the listed adverbs (English) that may also be prepositions or conjunctions, see those two chapters: §§104-170 (prepositions) and §§171-194 (conjunctions).

A

abreast	**de front / sur le même rang**
accordingly	**c'est pourquoi / en conséquence / pour cette raison**
actually	**en fait / à vrai dire / en réalité**
again	**de nouveau / à nouveau**
against all odds	**envers et contre tout /contre toute attente**
ahead	**en tête / en avant**
all in all	**à tout prendre / tout bien considéré**
all of a sudden	**tout à coup / tout d'un coup**
all the same	**quand même / tout de même**
all the time	**tout le temps / à tout propos**
and so forth	**et ainsi de suite**
anew	**de nouveau / à nouveau**
anytime	**n'importe quand / quand vous voudrez (tu, il, elle, etc.) / à tout moment**
anyway	**quand même / tout de même / de toute façon**
anywhere	**n'importe où / où vous voudrez (tu, il, elle, etc.)**
apart	**à part / de côté**
approximately	**à peu près**
aside	**de côté / à part**
askew	**de travers / de biais**
as a rough estimate	**en gros / grosso modo / à vue de nez (fam.)**
as the crow flies	**à vol d'oiseau**
astray	**de travers / dans la mauvaise direction**
at a glance	**d'un coup d'œil / du premier coup d'œil**
at all events	**à tout hasard**
at any cost	**à tout prix**
at (the) best	**au mieux**
at first	**d'abord / en premier lieu / au premier abord**
at first sight	**à première vue / du premier coup d'œil**
at leisure	**à loisir**
at long last	**en fin de compte / à la fin**
at once	**tout de suite / sur le champ / tout à coup / de ce pas / d'un seul coup / en même temps / à la fois**
at one's heart's desire	**à souhait**
at one's (own) risk	**à ses risques et périls**
at pleasure, will	**à volonté**

at random	**au hasard / à tort et à travers** (erratically)
at the bottom	**au fond / dans le fond**
at (the) least	**au moins / pour le moins / tout au moins**
at (the) most	**au plus / tout au plus**
at the same time	**en même temps / à la fois**
at the top of one's lungs	**à tue-tête**
at will	**à volonté**
awry	**de travers**

B

backward(s)	**en arrière / à reculons / à la renverse**
bare	**à nu**
beforehand	**d'avance / à l'avance**
blindly	**à l'aveuglette / sans regarder / à tâtons**
brilliantly	**avec éclat / avec brio**

C

carelessly	**par dessous la jambe / par dessus l'épaule**
ceaselessly	**sans cesse / sans interruption**
cheap	**bon marché, à bon marché**
close	**de près / à ras**
close up	**de près**
completely	**tout à fait / en entier**
confess (I confess . . .)	**à la vérité**
confusedly	**pêle-mêle / en désordre**
consequently	**par conséquent**
crooked (askew)	**de travers**
crosswise	**de biais / en travers**

D

day by day	**jour après jour**
deeply	**à fond / en profondeur**
directly (right away)	**de ce pas**
disgustingly	**d'un air dégoûtant / d'une manière dégoûtante**

E

early	**de bonne heure / de bon matin / en avance**
edgewise	**de biais / par le côté**
ever and again	**bien des fois / sans cesse**
every time	**chaque fois / à chaque fois**
excessively	**outre mesure / à l'excès**
extremely	**très bien / à l'extrême**

F

face down	**à l'envers**
face up	**à l'endroit**
farther than the eye can see	**à perte de vue**
figuratively	**au figuré / au sens figuré**
finally	**en somme / à la fin**
firmly	**de pied ferme, avec fermeté**
first, firstly	**d'abord / en premier lieu**
for ever	**pour toujours / à jamais**
from a distance	**de loin**

G

gently	**en douceur** (coll.)
gladly	**avec plaisir / avec joie**

H

habitually	**d'habitude**
half	**à moitié / à demi**
hardly	**à peine**
hastily, hurriedly	**en hâte / à la hâte**

I

immediately	**tout de suite / sur le champ**
in a circle	**en rond**
in addition to the rest	**par dessus le marché**
in a heap	**en tas**
in a line	**à la file / en file / en file indienne**
in a literal sense	**à la lettre**
in all	**en tout**
in a pile	**en tas**
in a straight line	**à vol d'oiseau**
in a way	**en quelque sorte**
in bulk	**en gros**
indeed	**en effet / à la vérité / en vérité / de fait**
in depth	**en profondeur / à fond**
in detail	**en détail / au détail**
in earnest	**avec attention / avec sérieux**
inexpensively	**bon marché / à bas prix**
in fact	**en fait**
in fashion	**à la mode**
in front	**en face / en tête / à l'avant**
in line	**en ligne / à la file/ en file**
in no time at all, flat	**en moins de rien / en un rien de temps**
inopportunely	**mal à propos / hors de propos**
in person	**en personne / en chair et en os** (fam.)

in short	**en somme / en résumé**
inside out	**à l'envers** (opposite: **à l'endroit)**
in succession	**à tour de rôle / tout à tour**
in that manner, in that way	**de la sorte / de cette façon / de cette manière**
in the bargain	**par dessus le marché**
in the end	**en fin de compte / au bout du compte**
in the figurative sense	**au sens figuré**
in the long run	**à la longue / en fin de compte**
in the main	**en gros / à tout prendre**
in the meantime	**en attendant / pendant ce temps / dans l'intervalle**
in the nick of time	**à propos / à point nommé / à point / juste à temps / à pic** (coll.)
in the open	**à découvert / à l'air libre**
in the twinkling of an eye	**en un clin d'œil**
in time	**à temps / en mesure** (rhythm)
into the bargain	**par dessus le marché**
in turn	**à son tour / l'un après l'autre / à tour de rôle**
in vain	**en vain** (verb: **avoir beau . . .** with infinitive)
inward	**en dedans / vers l'intérieur**
in your place (if I were you)	**à votre place**
irreparably	**sans retour**
irrevocably	**sans retour**
it is true that . . .	**à la vérité / en effet**

J

just now	**à l'instant / tout à l'heure** (formal)

L

lastly	**en dernier lieu / pour terminer**
late	**en retard**
lately	**ces temps derniers / récemment**
leisurely	**à loisir / sans se presser**
lengthwise	**en longueur / dans le sens de la longueur**
likewise	**de même/ de la même façon**
literally	**au pied de la lettre / à la lettre**
little by little	**peu à peu / petit à petit**
live (TV)	**en direct** (opposite: **en différé)**

M

maybe	**peut-être / il se peut que** (with subjunctive)
madly	**à la folie**
more and more	**de plus en plus**
moreover	**de plus / en plus / en outre**
mostly	**dans l'ensemble / pour la plupart**

N

naked	**à nu / à poil** (coll.)
naturally!	**bien entendu! / cela s'entend!**
nearby	**tout près / à proximité**
none of that	**pas de ça**
none the better	**pas mieux**
none the less	**pas moins**
none the worse	**pas plus mal**
none too many	**pas trop**
none too soon	**pas trop tôt**
nonsensically	**en dépit du bon sens**
nowadays	**de nos jours / à présent**
now and then	**de temps en temps / de temps à autre**

O

of course	**bien entendu / cela s'entend**
off and on	**de temps en temps / par intermittence**
on all occasions	**en toute occasion / à tout propos**
on an empty stomach	**à jeun**
once	**une fois / jadis**
on foot	**à pied**
on horseback	**à cheval**
on the contrary	**au contraire**
on the other hand	**d'autre part / par contre / en revanche**
on the spot	**sur-le-champ / sur place**
on the whole	**à tout prendre / en tout / dans l'ensemble**
on time	**à l'heure**
openly	**sans détour**
opportunely	**à propos / au bon moment**
otherwise, . . .	**sans quoi, . . .**
outdoors	**à l'extérieur / en dehors**
out of sight	**hors de vue / à perte de vue**
outward(ly)	**vers l'extérieur**

P

pell-mell	**pêle-mêle / en vrac** (coll.)
perfectly	**à la perfection / à fond**
perhaps	**peut-être / il se peut que** (with subjunctive)
perpendicularly	**à la verticale / d'aplomb**
pertinently	**à propos / à bon escient**
presently	**de nos jours / à l'heure actuelle**
privately	**en tête à tête** (two persons) **/ en privé**

Q

quite	**tout à fait**
quietly	**en douce / sans bruit**

R

red-handed	**en flagrant délit / la main dans le sac**
reluctantly	**à contre-cœur / à regret**
retail	**en détail / au détail**
right away	**tout de suite / sur-le-champ**
rightly or wrongly	**à tort ou à raison**
right now	**tout de suite / de ce pas / sur-le-champ**
right side out	**à l'endroit**
right side up	**à l'endroit**

S

scarcely	**à peine**
secondhand	**d'occasion**
secretly	**en secret / en cachette / en sourdine / ni vu ni connu**
sideways	**de biais/ de côté / de travers**
slowly	**avec lenteur / à petit pas / à pas comptés**
so (in that way)	**de la sorte**
so far	**jusqu'ici / jusqu'à présent**
somewhat	**quelque peu**
so much the better	**tant mieux**
so much the worse	**tant pis**
strictly speaking	**à la rigueur**
suddenly	**tout à coup / tout d'un coup**

T

thoroughly	**en entier / d'un bout à l'autre / à la perfection**
till now	**jusqu'à présent / jusqu'à maintenant**
to and fro	**de long en large**
to distraction	**à la folie**
too bad	**tant pis / dommage**
to the bottom	**à fond**
twice	**deux fois**

U

uncomfortably	**mal à l'aise**
unconnected	**sans suite**
undoubtedly	**sans doute / sans aucun doute**
unreservedly	**sans réserve**
unwillingly	**à contre-cœur / à regret**
up and down	**de haut en bas / de long en large**

upon the whole	**à tout prendre / en tout / dans l'ensemble**
upside down	**à l'envers**

V

visibly	**à vue d'œil / à l'œil nu**

W

were it not for that	**sans cela**
wholesale	**en gros**
wildly	**à tort et à travers / sans rime ni raison**
willingly	**de bon cœur**
willy-nilly	**bon gré mal gré / de gré ou de force**
with all one's might	**à tue-tête** (voice) / **de toutes ses forces**
with great difficulty	**à grand-peine / avec peine / avec difficulté**
without a noise	**sans bruit / à pas de loup / à pas feutrés**
without any doubt	**sans doute / sans aucun doute**
without being seen	**en cachette / ni vu ni connu**
without ceremony	**sans façons / sans cérémonie**
without fail	**sans faute**
without hesitation	**sans hésiter / de pied ferme**
without hiding	**à découvert / sans détour**
without logic or order	**sans suite / sans rime ni raison**
without reserve	**sans réserve**
without stopping	**sans cesse / sans arrêt**
with that exception	**à cela près**

Note on the Index

The index combines grammatical entries (referring to explanations) with vocabulary entries (referring to examples).

Where several page references are given, the numbers appear in ascending order unless a reference of major importance is present: such a page number appears in first position.

The many lists and tables contained in the book can be found under the word LISTS.

Index

A

B

C

D

F

G

I

J

K

L

M

N

O

P

Q

R

S

T

U

V

W

Y

Z

EXERCISES

The following exercises are arranged in the same general order as the chapters of the reference grammar, but with adjectives and pronouns presented together rather than separately. Conjunctions, prepositions, and adverbs have been grouped into one single unit, but there is also a separate section on prepositions. Despite these differences, reference to the grammar sections should be easy. The numbering of the exercises is sequential to provide easy reference to the Answer Key, placed at the end.

It is hoped that the exercises presented here will help reinforce the grammatical concepts that students of French must learn and master.

Note: In the Answer Key, entries found in parentheses represent alternate correct responses.

Articles

1. Write the definite article ***le***, ***la***, or ***l'*** as needed before the initial ***h***.

1. _____ homme
2. _____ honte
3. _____ héros
4. _____ hâte
5. _____ hégémonie
6. _____ hôtel
7. _____ hussard
8. _____ héroïne
9. _____ hasard
10. _____ hiver

2. Write the definite article ***le***, ***la***, or ***l'*** as needed before the initial ***h*** or vowel.

1. _____ hexagone
2. _____ humidité
3. _____ hermitage
4. _____ hideur
5. _____ hôpital
6. _____ huit de carreau
7. _____ onze novembre
8. _____ un et le deux
9. _____ hache
10. _____ hauteur

3. Write the definite article ***le***, ***la***, ***l'***, ***les***, or the indefinite article ***un***, ***une***, ***des***, if an article is needed. Write the contracted form required when the preposition ***de*** or ***à*** is present, deleting ***de*** or ***à***. Use the elided form ***d'***, as needed.

1. Est-ce que ____ terre tourne autour de ____ soleil?
2. ____ lune tourne autour de ____ terre.
3. ____ Mars et ____ Vénus sont aussi ____ planètes.
4. Toutes ____ planètes tournent autour de ____ soleil.
5. ____ quatre éléments premiers sont ____ air, ____ terre, ____ feu et ____ eau.
6. ____ amour est ____ passion.
7. Romeo et Juliette sont victimes de ____ amour impossible et tragique.
8. Romeo et Juliette sont victimes de ____ amour.
9. ____ jeunes amants de Shakespeare meurent à cause de ____ haine de leurs deux familles.
10. Shakespeare a basé ses pièces sur ____ jalousie, ____ envie, ____ colère et ____ amour.

4. Write the definite article ***le***, ***la***, ***l'***, ***les***, or the indefinite article ***un***, ***une***, ***des***, if an article is needed. Write the contracted form required when the preposition ***de*** or ***à*** is present, deleting ***de*** or ***à***, or write the elided form ***d'***, as needed.

1. ____ or et ____ argent sont ____ métaux précieux.
2. ____ mercure est ____ métal à ____ état liquide.
3. ____ arsenic est____ poison.
4. ____ arsenic est____ poison avec lequel Madame Bovary s'est suicidée.
5. Ferme ____ porte, mais laisse ouverte ____ des deux fenêtres.
6. J'apprends ____ allemand et ____ espagnol.
7. Nous suivons des cours de ____ français, de ____ maths et de ____ histoire.
8. ____ physique et ____ chimie sont ____ matières difficiles.
9. ____ philosophie et ____ anatomie sont ____ seuls cours facultatifs de mon cursus.
10. ____ Manitoba et ____ Québec sont ____ provinces de ____ Canada.
11. ____ Ohio, ____ Utah, ____ Texas et ____ Idaho sont ____ états de ____ États-Unis.

5. Write the definite article ***le***, ***la***, ***l'***, ***les***; the indefinite article ***un***, ***une***, ***des*** (or ***de***, ***d'*** alone); or leave blank, as needed. Make the necessary elisions and contractions, deleting the extraneous prepositions.

1. Est-ce que vous avez ____ clef de ____ coffre de ____ voiture?
2. Comment ____ professeur de maths a-t-il pu sortir de ____ bâtiment?
3. Il a dû passer par ____ fenêtre de ____ toilettes.
4. Nous avons vu ____ belles cathédrales.
5. ____ nombreux châteaux de ____ Renaissance sont au bord de ____ Loire.
6. Il y a beaucoup ____ châteaux près de Paris.
7. On trouve ____ autres châteaux partout en ____ France.
8. ____ nouveaux immeubles se construisent partout à Paris.
9. ____ milliers de ____ voitures cherchent ____ places de ____ stationnement tous ____ jours.
10. ____ moitié de ____ gens prennent ____ métro ou ____ bus pour aller à ____ travail.

6. Write the definite article ***le***, ***la***, ***l'***, ***les***; the indefinite article ***un***, ***une***, ***des***; the partitive article ***du***, ***de la***, ***des*** (or ***de***, ***d'*** alone); or leave blank, as needed. Make the necessary elisions and contractions, deleting the extraneous prepositions.

1. Aimez-vous ____ vanille? Moi, j'adore ____ chocolat, mais je déteste ____ cannelle.
2. ____ sucre de ____ canne est plus parfumé que ____ sucre de ____ betterave.
3. Je ne prends pas ____ sucre dans mon café.
4. Je n'aime pas ____ sucre. Je préfère ____ miel.
5. Je bois mon café sans ____ sucre, mais j'y verse toujours ____ lait.
6. ____ crème est trop riche pour le café.
7. Je mets un peu ____ lait dans mon café, et une tranche ____ citron dans mon thé.
8. ____ café et ____ thé contiennent ____ caféine.
9. Je préfère ____ jus de ____ pomme à ____ jus de ____ orange.
10. Je bois ____ lait au petit déjeuner, un grand verre ____ lait.
11. Je ne bois jamais ____ lait quand je dîne.
12. Je ne bois pas ____ vin non plus, je ne bois que ____ eau minérale.
13. J'aime ____ viande rouge. Je mange souvent ____ bœuf.
14. Avec mon steak, je bois ____ vin, un ou deux verres ____ vin rouge.
15. Je vous recommande ce vin, qui est ____ vin d'appellation d'origine contrôlée.

7. Write the definite article ***le***, ***la***, ***l'***, ***les***, or leave blank. Add the preposition ***de*** or ***à*** if needed and make the necessary elisions and contractions, deleting the extraneous prepositions.

1. Mettons-nous à ____ table.
2. Que prendrez-vous comme ____ dessert?
3. Je les ai trouvés tous ____ deux à ____ cheval sur la barrière du passage à niveau!
4. En ____ 1715, le roi Louis XIV mourait. Il est mort en ____ an 1715.
5. C'est en ____ été qu'on part en ____ vacances au bord de ____ mer.
6. En ____ automne et en ____ hiver, on se souvient de ses vacances.
7. ____ printemps, on prévoit les vacances d'été.
8. ____ riches ne sont pas toujours généreux envers ____ pauvres.
9. À ____ école, ____ grands se moquent souvent de ____ petits.
10. ____ États-Unis sont bien plus grands que ____ France, ____ Espagne, ____ Allemagne et ____ Danemark mis ensemble.
11. Bien vivre, c'est cela ____ essentiel. ____ reste importe peu.
12. ____ vie est courte. ____ mort nous atteint tous.
13. Tous ____ humains sont mortels. Tout ____ homme est mortel.
14. Tous ____ jours se ressemblent, tout ____ monde se plaint!
15. ____ impôts sont désagréables.
16. En ____ 1998, ____ taxe à ____ valeur ajoutée était de 20,6%.

8. Write the definite article ***le***, ***la***, ***l'***, ***les***; the indefinite article ***un***, ***une***, ***des***; or leave blank. Add the preposition ***de*** or ***à*** if needed and make the necessary elisions and contractions.

1. Elle était belle comme ____ déesse, elle dansait comme ____ fée.
2. Il marchera ____ yeux fixés sur ses pensées.
3. Il passera par ____ plaine, à travers ____ forêt, par-dessus ____ montagne.

4. Il marchera ____ long ____ rivière.
5. Sa pensée volera au-dessus ____ nuages.
6. Malgré ____ pluie et en dépit ____ vent, il marchera sans ____ plainte.
7. ____ ciel gris le laissera aussi impassible que ____ ciel bleu.
8. Il restera impassible comme ____ philosophe oriental.

9. Write the definite article ***le***, ***la***, ***l'***, ***les***; the indefinite article ***un***, ***une***, ***des***; the possessive article ***son***, ***sa***, ***ses***; or leave blank. Add the preposition ***de*** or ***à*** if needed and make the necessary elisions and contractions.

1. Il avait ____ yeux bleus, ____ cheveux roux et ____ nez pointu.
2. ____ yeux étaient bleus, ____ cheveux roux et ____ nez pointu.
3. Elle a ____ oreilles décollées et ____ taches de rousseur.
4. ____ oreilles sont décollées et elle a ____ taches de rousseur.
5. Il est entré ____ chapeau sur ____ tête et ____ mains dans ____ poches.
6. ____ chapeau était de travers sur ____ tête.
7. ____ mains étaient sales et ____ poches étaient trouées.
8. Je me suis frotté ____ mains en voyant ce résultat.
9. Je me suis gratté ____ tête en voyant le problème.
10. Il s'est essuyé ____ visage pour enlever ____ sueur qui coulait sur ____ front.
11. ____ sueur coulait sur ____ visage.
12. ____ sang de sa blessure lui collait ____ cheveux et pénétrait dans ____ oreille.
13. Essuyez-vous ____ pieds avant d'entrer.
14. Essuyez ____ pieds avant d'entrer.

10. Write the definite article ***le***, ***la***, ***l'***, ***les***, or the possessive article ***vos***.

1. Enlevez ____ chaussures.
2. Gardez ____ deux mains sur la table.
3. ____ deux mains doivent rester sur la table.
4. Haut ____ mains! Bas ____ pattes!
5. Ouvrez ____ bouche! Tirez ____ langue!

11. Write the definite article ***le***, ***la***, ***l'***, ***les***; the indefinite article ***un***, ***une***, ***des***; the partitive article ***du***, ***de la***, ***des*** (or ***de***, ***d'*** alone); or leave blank, as needed. Add the preposition ***de*** or ***à*** if needed, making the necessary elisions and contractions.

1. Comme ____ dessert, je prendrai ____ glace à ____ vanille.
2. ____ vanille est mon parfum préféré.
3. Mon camarade déteste ____ vanille.
4. Mon camarade travaille comme ____ garçon de restaurant.
5. Il travaille comme ____ esclave: ____ matin, ____ après-midi, ____ soir, même ____ nuit parfois.
6. Il gagne 8 dollars 50 ____ heure.
7. L'essence coûte 2 dollars 25 ____ gallon.
8. Sa voiture est vieille et roule, au mieux, à 60 miles ____ heure.
9. ____ télévision, ____ radio et ____ ordinateur, est-ce que c'est ____ même chose?

12. Recipe for Breton crêpes. Write the definite article ***le***, ***la***, ***l'***, ***les***; the indefinite article ***un***, ***une***, ***des***; the partitive article ***du***, ***de la***, ***des*** (or ***de***, ***d'*** alone or with the indefinite article); or leave blank, as needed. Make the necessary elisions and contractions, deleting the extraneous prepositions.

1. Pesez 250g de ____ sucre en ____ poudre.
2. Mettez ____ sucre au fond de ____ grand bol.
3. Cassez deux œufs et séparez ____ blanc de ____ jaune.
4. Mettez ____ blancs dans un autre bol.
5. Ajoutez à ____ blancs une pincée de ____ sel.
6. Battez-les en ____ neige assez ferme.
7. Mettez ____ jaunes sur ____ sucre et mélangez.
8. Remuez à ____ cuiller de ____ bois jusqu'à obtenir ____ mélange jaune pâle.
9. Faites fondre 100g de ____ beurre.
10. Versez ____ beurre fondu dans ____ mélange de ____ jaunes de ____ œufs et de ____ sucre.
11. Pesez 450g de ____ farine de ____ froment et 50g de ____ farine de ____ blé noir.
12. Ajoutez les farines petit à petit dans ____ bol de ____ mixeur.
13. Ajoutez un litre et demi de ____ lait.
14. Incorporez ____ blanc battu en ____ neige dans ____ pâte.
15. Laissez reposer ____ tout environ une heure, avant de commencer à faire les crêpes.

Nouns

Gender

13. Write ***un*** or ***une*** to indicate whether the noun is masculine or feminine.

1. ____ parti politique
2. ____ partie d'échecs
3. ____ part de gâteau
4. ____ repos bien mérité
5. ____ repas de fête
6. ____ reste de poulet
7. ____ arrêt de travail
8. ____ départ
9. ____ arrivée
10. ____ bienvenue
11. ____ livre de pain
12. ____ livre de lecture
13. ____ poste de village
14. ____ poste de secrétaire
15. ____ voile de bateau
16. ____ voile de mariée
17. ____ critique défavorable
18. ____ critique employé au *Times*
19. ____ pratique de tous les jours

20. _____ enfant en robe rose
21. _____ enfant en tenue de chasseur
22. _____ page de la cour du roi
23. _____ page de l'histoire de France
24. _____ mari et son épouse
25. _____ marié et sa femme
26. _____ mariée et son époux

14. Write ***un*** or ***une*** to indicate whether the noun is masculine or feminine.

1. _____ souris
2. _____ fourmi
3. _____ génie
4. _____ accalmie
5. _____ manie
6. _____ ennui
7. _____ époque
8. _____ période
9. _____ menace
10. _____ problème
11. _____ chèque
12. _____ hexagone
13. _____ hémisphère
14. _____ photographe
15. _____ photographie
16. _____ épicier
17. _____ épicerie
18. _____ pharmacie
19. _____ remède
20. _____ pari
21. _____ mari
22. _____ parti
23. _____ partie
24. _____ système

Nouns used idiomatically

15. Complete with the appropriate noun from the list, changing the article as needed: ***un jour–une journée***, ***un matin–une matinée***, ***un soir–une soirée***, ***un an–une année***.

1. tous _____ (every day, morning, afternoon, evening, year)
   tous les jours, ____
   ____
2. toute _____ (all day long, morning, afternoon, evening, year)
   ____
   ____

3. toute ____ (a whole day, morning, afternoon, evening, year)

____

____

4. une ____ entière (a whole day, morning, afternoon, evening, year)

____

____

Singular or plural?

16. Complete with the following vocabulary using singular or plural forms as appropriate (where an article is required, do not omit the necessary contraction with the preceding preposition): ***poisson rouge***, ***meuble***, ***fruit***, ***affaire***, ***cheveu***, ***poil***, ***nouvelle***, ***physique***, ***millier***, ***frais***.

1. Il y a beaucoup de ____________ dans l'aquarium.
2. une corbeille de ____________
3. un magasin de ____________
4. se faire couper ____________ en (à la) brosse
5. ramasser ____________ du chien sur le tapis
6. étudier ____________
7. une foule de ____________ de personnes
8. payer ____________ d'inscription à l'université
9. Le PDG s'occupe (de) ____________ de la compagnie.
10. demander ____________ d'un malade

Plural words

17. Complete with the following vocabulary: ***funérailles***, ***fiançailles***, ***alentours***, ***mœurs***, ***menottes***, ***pourparlers***, ***dépens***, ***arrhes***, ***décombres***, ***vivres***.

1. On a fait à cet homme illustre des ________________ nationales.
2. Les archéologues ont découvert un nouveau squelette aux ________________ de Lascaux.
3. Ces deux jeunes gens ont annoncé leurs ________________.
4. Les policiers ont mis les ________________ aux poignets du suspect.
5. Les ________________ de la nouvelle génération sont différentes de celles de la précédente.
6. Les deux pays ont entamé des ________________ pour la paix.
7. Les pompiers pensent qu'il reste des victimes sous les ________________ de l'immeuble.
8. Il a fallu verser des ________________ avant d'obtenir un bail.
9. Le siège de la ville a duré si longtemps que la ville a capitulé, faute de ________________.
10. L'accusé n'a pas eu d'amende à payer, mais il a été condamné aux ________________.

Irregular plurals

18. Write in the plural.

1. notre aïeul ______________________
2. ce bonhomme ______________________
3. madame ______________________
4. mademoiselle ______________________
5. mon œil ______________________
6. votre cheval ______________________
7. le canal ______________________
8. le mal ______________________
9. un malheur ______________________
10. un ciseau ______________________

19. Write in the plural.

1. le carnaval ______________________
2. un récital ______________________
3. un émail ______________________
4. le genou ______________________
5. un travail ______________________
6. un caillou ______________________
7. le vitrail ______________________
8. un pneu ______________________
9. un chou ______________________
10. un bijou ______________________

20. Write in the plural.

1. mon grand-père ______________________
2. un chef-d'œuvre ______________________
3. un passeport ______________________
4. le gratte-ciel ______________________
5. un beau-fils ______________________
6. une belle-mère ______________________
7. un camion-citerne ______________________

Collective words: singular or plural?

21. Write the verbs in the passé composé or give the appropriate French equivalent, as the case may be.

1. La police (arriver) ______________________ très vite sur les lieux.
2. Deux (officers) ______________________ ont interrogé les témoins.
3. La SAMU (administrer) ______________________ les premiers soins aux blessés.
4. L'ambulance (conduire) ______________________ le blessé à l'hôpital.

5. Debout sur le trottoir, (some people) ____________________ regardaient ce qui se passait.
6. La foule (regarder) ____________________ ce qui se passait.
7. L'armée (s'établir) ____________________ le long de la frontière.
8. Le Clergé (affirmer) ____________________ sa solidarité avec la Noblesse.
9. Le Sénat (se voter) ____________________ une augmentation de salaire scandaleuse.
10. L'Assemblée (refuser) ____________________ d'accepter sa dissolution demandée par le gouvernement.
11. Les députés (quitter) ____________________ leur siège en signe de protestation.
12. Les représentants (venir) ____________________ déposer leur bulletin dans l'urne.
13. Ma famille (aller) ____________________ passer le week-end à la plage. Elle passera (its) ____________________ prochaines vacances à la montagne.

Preference of the singular in French

22. Complete the sentences with expressions from the list, making all necessary changes: ***lever la main***, ***fermer la bouche***, ***ouvrir l'œil***, ***serrer la main***, ***avoir le chapeau sur la tête***, ***être pris la main dans le sac***, ***ouvrir son livre***, ***prendre son stylo***, ***rendre son devoir***, ***déposer son bulletin de vote***.

1. Si vous voulez poser des questions, il faut lever ____________________.
2. Faisons bien attention, ouvrons ____________________.
3. Quand ils arriveront, il faudra leur serrer ____________________.
4. Ils sont entrés ____________________ chapeau sur ____________________ tête.
5. Les cambrioleurs ont été pris ____________________ dans le sac.
6. Le professeur a dit aux élèves d'ouvrir ____________________ (possessif + livre) à la page 80.
7. Paul et Michel, est-ce que vous avez rendu ____________________ (your homework)?
8. Les électeurs doivent déposer ____________________ (possessif + bulletin) de vote dans l'urne en présence d'un témoin.

Adjectives

Agreement

23. Write in the feminine.

1. heureux ____________________
2. favori ____________________
3. cher ____________________
4. moyen ____________________
5. nul ____________________
6. jaloux ____________________
7. doux ____________________
8. gentil ____________________
9. neuf ____________________
10. actif ____________________

11. final ____________________
12. public ____________________
13. net ____________________
14. blanc ____________________
15. frais ____________________
16. fameux ____________________
17. roux ____________________
18. grec ____________________
19. bref ____________________
20. joli ____________________

24. Write in the masculine.

1. sèche ____________________
2. vieille ____________________
3. légère ____________________
4. grosse ____________________
5. bleue ____________________
6. bénigne ____________________
7. italienne ____________________
8. tragique ____________________
9. molle ____________________
10. discrète ____________________
11. dernière ____________________
12. grise ____________________
13. longue ____________________
14. fausse ____________________
15. marocaine ____________________
16. muette ____________________

25. Write in the plural.

1. bleu ____________________
2. jaloux ____________________
3. final ____________________
4. nouveau ____________________
5. meilleur ____________________
6. marron ____________________
7. ci-joint ____________________
8. fou ____________________
9. fatal ____________________
10. blanc ____________________
11. neuf ____________________
12. seul ____________________
13. nu ____________________
14. bleu-ciel ____________________

Position and agreement

26. Write the adjective before or after the noun, with the appropriate agreement.

1. bas la ______________ marée ______________
2. haut une ______________ montagne ______________
3. grand la ______________ route ______________
4. mauvaisun ______________ conseil ______________
5. bon une ______________ idée ______________
6. nouveaule ______________ locataire ______________
7. nouveaule ______________ vin ______________
8. brave une ______________ dame ______________ (a good lady)
9. certainun ______________ temps ______________ (an indefinite time)
10. maigre un ______________ jour ______________ (a day of fasting)

27. Write the adjective before or after the noun, with the appropriate agreement.

1. pauvre ______________ type ______________! ("You jerk!")
2. public une ______________ école ______________
3. national le ______________ produit______________
4. neuf une ______________ maison ______________
5. sec un ______________ été ______________
6. joyeux un ______________ luron ______________
7. dernier la ______________ semaine ______________ (last week)
8. dernier le ______________ mois ______________ de l'année (décembre)
9. meilleur un ______________ résultat ______________
10. certain une ______________ mort ______________ (unavoidable)

Nouns used as adjectives in English

28. Express in French.

1. a physics class ______________________________
2. a brick wall ______________________________
3. a sports car ______________________________
4. a love story ______________________________
5. a pearl necklace ______________________________
6. an ID card ______________________________
7. an oak table ______________________________
8. a gold chain ______________________________
9. a leather belt ______________________________
10. a safety pin ______________________________

29. Express in French (* = idiomatic or expressing purpose).

1. a road map ______________________________
2. a race horse ______________________________
3. a horse (race) track ______________________________

4. a spring break ______
5. a postage stamp* ______
6. a bookworm* ______
7. a leap year* ______
8. a clothespin* ______
9. a wineglass* ______
10. a bread knife* ______
11. a bag of bread flour* ______

30. Write the adjective ***grand*** in the following compound nouns.

1. le ______ -père
2. les ______ -pères
3. la ______ -mère
4. les ______ -mères
5. les ______ -parents
6. la______ -route
7. les ______ -routes
8. Il ne voit pas ______ -chose.

Comparative

31. Compare the two terms, taking into account the symbols in parentheses.

1. L'or / le plomb / précieux (+)
   L'or est ______.
2. Un bateau / un avion / rapide (−)
   Un bateau est ______.
3. Un Cézanne / un Renoir / valable (=)
   Un Cézanne est ______.
4. Mr. Wilson / le père de Dennis / grincheux (+)
   Mr. Wilson est ______.
5. Hägar / Attila / horrible (−)
   Hägar est ______.
6. New York / Rome / vénérable (not =)
   New York n'est pas ______.
7. Un dromadaire / une voiture de course / rapide (not =)
   Un dromadaire n'est pas ______.

32. Express the superlative using the suggested words and making all necessary changes.

1. Le Mont Everest / montagne / élevée / monde (Mount Everest is the highest mountain in the world.)
   Le Mont Everest est ______
   ______.
2. bon / toutes (This brand name is the best of all.)
   Cette marque est ______
   ______.

3. (It is the best brand name of all.)
   C'est ____
   ____.

4. célèbre / toutes (This brand name is the most famous of all.)
   Cette marque est ____
   ____.

5. (It is the most famous brand name of all.)
   C'est ____
   ____.

6. cher / magasin (This brand name is the least expensive in the store.)
   Cette marque est ____
   ____.

7. (It is the least expensive brand name of all.)
   C'est ____
   ____.

Demonstrative adjectives and pronouns

33. Write the appropriate demonstrative adjective ***ce***, ***cet***, or ***cette***. As needed, add ***-là*** to emphasize *that*.

1. (this year) _____ année
2. (that year) _____ année _____
3. (tonight) _____ soir
4. (that evening) _____ soir _____
5. (this week) _____ semaine
6. (that week) _____ semaine _____
7. (this fall) _____ automne
8. (that fall) _____ automne _____
9. (this winter) _____ hiver
10. (that winter) _____ hiver _____

34. Add the appropriate demonstrative adjective ***ce***, ***cette***, or ***ces***. As needed, add ***-ci*** or ***-là*** to emphasize *this/these* or *that/those*.

1. (these days) _____ jours _____
2. (those days) _____ jours _____
3. (that month) _____ mois _____
4. (this month) _____ mois _____
5. (that day) _____ jour _____
6. (in those days) en _____ temps _____
7. (this, but with no special emphasis) _____ nuit
8. (that night) _____ nuit _____
9. (this, but with no special emphasis) _____ matin
10. (that morning) _____ matin _____

35. Add the appropriate demonstrative adjective ***ce***, ***cet***, ***cette***, or ***ces***.

1. _____ affaire
2. _____ unique affaire
3. _____ arrêt d'autobus
4. _____ acteur dans _____ rôle
5. _____ autre acteur dans _____ autre rôle
6. _____ actrice chantant _____ air connu
7. _____ horrible personnage
8. _____ héros
9. _____ voyou
10. _____ affreux voyou
11. _____ affreux voyous
12. _____ occasion
13. _____ enfants
14. _____ autres enfants
15. _____ enfant gâté
16. _____ détestable enfant gâté
17. _____ adorable enfant en robe rose

36. Complete the sentences with demonstrative pronouns ***celui***, ***celle***, ***ceux***, or ***celles***. As needed, add ***-ci*** or ***-là*** to emphasize *this/these* or *that/those*.

1. Donnez-moi un kilo de ces haricots-ci et une livre de (those) _______________.
2. Je prendrai cette botte de radis et aussi (that one) _______________.
3. Ces cerises-là me paraissent moins belles que (these) _______________.
4. Il me faut deux ananas. Je voudrais (this one) _______________ et (that one) _______________, (the one) _______________ qui est le plus près des pamplemousses.
5. J'aime les pamplemousses de Floride, mais je préfère encore (the ones from Texas) _______________ du Texas.
6. (Those) _______________ qui disent que les myrtilles ne sont pas bonnes n'ont sûrement jamais goûté (those from the Carolinas) _______________ qui viennent des Carolines.
7. Tu aurais dû acheter le club en graphite au lieu de prendre (the metal one) _______________ en métal.
8. Garde ma raquette mais prête-moi (your father's) _______________ de ton père, la tienne ne me plaît pas.

37. Complete the sentences, expressing what is suggested in parentheses.

1. La cuisine de sa femme est presque aussi bonne que (his mother's) ____.
2. Le score de ce joueur est moins bon que (Tiger Woods's) ____.
3. La population de l'Inde n'est pas aussi nombreuse que (China's) ____.
4. L'histoire de Tristan et Iseult n'est pas aussi connue que (Romeo and Juliette's) ____.

5. L'amant d'Iseult est Tristan, (Juliette's is Romeo)
 ______________________________.
6. Rolls Royce et Mercedes sont deux marques d'automobiles, (the one, the latter) ______________________ est allemande, (the other, the former) ______________________ est anglaise.

38. Complete the following sentences with the demonstrative pronouns ***ce***, ***ça***, or ***cela***.

1. __________ ne vous regarde pas!
2. __________ que je fais ne vous regarde pas!
3. Qu'est- __________ que ________ ___ peut vous faire?
4. __________ que je préfère, __________ est le commencement.
5. __________ qui vient après est moins intéressant.
6. __________ est __________! Vous avez trouvé la solution!
7. __________ y est! J'ai trouvé!
8. Vous croyez que __________ vaut le coup?
9. Dites-moi __________ que vous allez faire.

39. Complete the sentences with the demonstrative pronouns ***ce***, ***ça***, ***cela***, or ***celui-là***.

1. __________ est lui qui commande. (He is the boss.)
2. __________ doit être mon tour. (It must be my turn.)
3. __________ était moi qui faisais tout ce bruit. (I was making all that noise.)
4. Je crois que __________ est à toi de payer. (I believe that it is your turn to pay.)
5. __________ vaut le coup! (It's worth it!)
6. À quoi __________ sert-il? (What is it for?)
7. __________ sera très utile. (It will be very useful.)
8. __________ est très bon. (That is very good.)
9. __________ est __________ que je veux avoir. (This is the one I want.) (masculine)

Indefinite adjectives and pronouns

40. Answer using the negative indefinite word that matches the underlined expression. Choose from the list: ***personne***, ***ni . . . ni***, ***nul(le)***, ***rien***, ***aucun***, ***ne . . . que***.

1. Est-ce que Patrick fait quelque chose?
   Non, il ______________________________.
2. Est-ce que Marc va quelque part?
   Non, il ______________________________.
3. Tu invites du monde?
   Non, je ______________________________.
4. Elle a beaucoup d'amis
   Non, elle ______________________________.
5. Ton amie est riche et belle, n'est-ce pas?
   Non, elle ______________________________.

6. Mon père parle trois langues. Et le tien?
   Le mien ______________________________ une seule langue.
7. Qu'est-ce que tu fais?
   Je ______________________________.
8. Quelqu'un a téléphoné?
   Non, ______________________________.
9. Est-ce que tu as quelques projets pour tes vacances?
   Non, je ______________________________.
10. Est-ce que quelque chose pourra te faire changer d'avis?
   Non, ______________________________.

41. Write in the passé composé.

1. Je ne vois personne.
   ____
2. Je ne comprends rien.
   ____
3. Elle ne va nulle part.
   ____
4. Nous ne comprenons ni la langue ni l'accent.
   ____
5. Ils ne vont ni au Louvre ni à Notre-Dame.
   ____
6. Rien ne me surprend.
   ____
7. Personne ne nous comprend.
   ____
8. Nous ne comprenons personne.
   ____
9. Vous ne comprenez rien.
   ____
10. Elles n'ont aucune occasion de se distraire.
   ____

42. Choose the expression from the list (some expressions may be repeated) that best completes each sentence, making all necessary changes: ***quelqu'un***, ***quelque chose***, ***quelque part***, ***quelque***, ***quelconque***, ***personne***, ***rien***, ***aucun***, ***plusieurs***, ***certains***, ***l'un***, ***l'autre***, ***ailleurs***.

1. J'ai demandé à ______________ (someone [male]) s'il pouvait me prêter ______________ (a few) dollars pour acheter ______________ (some [sweets]) friandises.
2. Il y a ______________ (somewhere) en Dordogne une grotte célèbre qui servait d'habitation à nos ancêtres pendant la préhistoire. Ce n'est pas la seule grotte, il y en a aussi ______________ (elsewhere).
3. Ne dites ______________ (nothing) à ______________ (to anybody).
4. Ne prononcez ______________ (no . . . at all) parole ______________, (some) vertébrés sont en danger de disparaître.

5. Voulez-vous que je vous apporte ______________ (a few) fruits ou ______________ (a few) bonbons?
6. ______________ (Some) fruits sont juteux, ______________ (others) sont plutôt secs.
7. Je ne suis pas difficile, il me faut une voiture ______________ (some kind of, any kind of), seulement pour faire un petit trajet de la maison à mon travail tous les jours.

43. Complete with one of the following adjectives or adjective expressions, making all necessary changes and additions: ***moins cher***, ***si laid***, ***dangereux***, ***chaud***, ***grave***.

1. Il fait très froid dehors, mettez quelque chose ______________.
2. Il a été admis à l'hôpital, mais le médecin dit que ce n'est rien ______________.
3. Méfiez-vous de ce type, c'est quelqu'un ______________.
4. Je n'ai jamais vu personne ______________ que cet homme-là!
5. Ces modèles-ci sont hors de prix. En avez-vous d'autres ______________?

44. Complete with the appropriate indefinite expression, making all necessary changes and additions: ***l'un (l'une)*** or ***l'autre***, ***les uns***, ***les autres***, ***quelqu'un***, ***certains***, ***autres***, ***quelque chose***.

1. Avez-vous besoin de ______________? (Do you need anything?)
2. Connaissez-vous ______________ dans cet immeuble? (Do you know someone/anyone in the building?)
3. ______________ (some/certain) aliments sont bons pour le cœur, ______________ (others) sont bons pour la digestion.
4. Parmi les candidats qui se préparent à passer le bac, ______________ (some) sont appréhensifs, ______________ (others) sont très calmes.
5. Les candidats au bac s'encouragent ______________ (one another).
6. Avez-vous vérifié si______________ (anyone, someone) avait laissé un message pour moi?
7. Je ne suis pas difficile, ______________ (either one) de ces chambres me conviendra.
8. Est-ce que ______________ (one, someone) d'entre vous a lu le dernier roman de John Lafurie?

45. Complete with one of the following expressions, making all necessary changes: ***n'importe comment***, ***n'importe lequel***, ***n'importe où***, ***n'importe quand***, ***n'importe quel . . .***, ***n'importe qui***, ***n'importe quoi***.

1. Taisez-vous, vous dites ______________.
2. C'est un travail très facile, ______________ pourrait le faire.
3. Où allez-vous en vacances cette année? — ______________, mais pas à la plage.
4. Ce jardinier ne sait pas jardiner, il sème ses graines ______________.
5. Il fait son travail par dessous la jambe, ______________.
6. Si vous vous sentez mal, appelez-moi, je viendrai à ______________ heure du jour ou de la nuit.
7. Ces vieilles affiches ne me plaisent plus, servez-vous, prenez ______________ (singular or plural).

46. Complete with ***chacun***, ***aucun***, or ***quelqu'un***, making all necessary changes.

1. Tous les réfugiés ont été identifiés. ______________ d'eux recevra un paquet d'urgence.
2. On a vérifié les documents. ______________ est authentique.
3. ______________ des filles a reçu une poupée et un livre de coloriage.
4. Elles ont toutes accepté leur cadeau. ______________ ne l'a refusé.
5. Les villageois ont reçu la visite de ______________ d'important de la Croix Rouge.
6. ______________ des enfants sont tombés malades pendant le trajet.
7. ______________ des fillettes ont même dû être hospitalisées.
8. Je ne vois ______________ objection à ce que vous restiez au camp un jour de plus.
9. Parmi certains groupes de réfugiés, c'était toujours ______________ pour soi.
10. ______________ des réfugiés s'occupaient quand même des plus démunis.

47. Complete with ***tout***, ***toute***, ***tous***, or ***toutes***.

1. On dit qu'à San Francisco il y a de la brume presque ______________ les jours.
2. ______________ vérité n'est pas bonne à dire.
3. ______________ les efforts qu'ils ont faits n'ont servi à rien!
4. ______________ ma famille est en vacances au Brésil.
5. Il est resté au soleil ______________ la journée, ______________ son corps est couvert de cloques.
6. ______________ les joueurs ont bien joué. ______________ la population les admire.
7. ______________ les habitants sont sortis dans la rue pour voir le défilé du 14 juillet.
8. Dans un procès, ______________ les témoins doivent dire ______________ la vérité.
9. Est-ce que ______________ les états des États-Unis sont sur le continent américain?
10. Il fallait lire ______________ cette page, pas seulement la moitié.

48. Complete with ***tout***, ***toute***, ***tous***, or ***toutes*** (adverb or adjective).

1. Ils étaient ______________ (just ready) prêts à quitter le stade quand le but a été marqué.
2. Ils étaient ______________ (all of them) prêts à quitter le stade quand le but a été marqué.
3. Elles étaient ______________ (completely) heureuses d'avoir gagné la Coupe du Monde.
4. Ils étaient ______________ (completely) heureux d'avoir gagné la finale de la Coupe du Monde.
5. Beaucoup de gens étaient ______________ (totally) surpris que le Brésil ait été battu.
6. La foule semblait ______________ (totally, quite) fière mais ______________ étonnée de cette victoire.
7. Du haut des gradins, la coupe avait l'air ______________ (quite) petite.

Interrogative adjectives

49. Write the question corresponding to each response using the interrogative adjective ***quel*** and inversion.

1. Mon nom est Bond, James Bond.

   ____

2. J'ai 35 ans.

____

3. Je suis agent secret pour Scotland Yard.

____

4. Mon adresse ne peut pas être divulguée.

____

5. Mon numéro de téléphone est le 007!

____

50. Write the question corresponding to each response using the interrogative adjective ***quel*** and ***est-ce que***. Make all necessary changes.

1. Je n'ai pas de préférence en matière de femmes.

____

2. Ma boisson préférée est le Dom Pérignon.

____

3. Je conduis généralement une voiture de sport très spéciale.

____

4. Les missions qu'on me donne sont souvent de caractère politique et international.

____

5. Je ne cours aucun danger grâce à l'équipe exceptionnelle de Scotland Yard.

____

51. Write the question that corresponds to the underlined part of the response. Use (a) subject/verb inversion, and (b) ***est-ce que***.

1. Autrefois, l'Angélus sonnait *à sept heures du matin, à midi, et à sept heures du soir*.
   a. _______________
   b. _______________
2. On mange du couscous *dans les pays du Maghreb* et du Moyen-Orient.
   a. _______________
   b. _______________
3. Les grandes péniches circulent surtout sur *les fleuves lents, comme la Seine*.
   a. _______________
   b. _______________
4. On sert du vin rouge avec *les viandes rouges*.
   a. _______________
   b. _______________
5. On réserve le champagne *pour les grandes occasions familiales*.
   a. _______________
   b. _______________

Interrogative pronouns

52. Write the question that corresponds to the underlined part of the response, as in the model.
Modèle:
C'est Lance Armstrong *qui a gagné le Tour de France en 2004.*
Qui a gagné le Tour de France en 2004?
Qui est-ce qui a gagné le Tour de France en 2004?

1. C'est *Leonard Bernstein* qui a composé cette musique.
2. C'est *Mary Cassatt* qui a peint ce portrait.
3. C'est *Amedeo Modigliani* qui a peint ces longs cous.
4. C'est *Félix Tournachon, nommé Nadar*, qui a photographié tous ces grands hommes du XIXe siècle.
5. C'est *Émile Zola* qui a écrit l'essai "J'accuse".

53. Write the question that corresponds to the underlined part of the response.
Modèle:
Walt Disney a créé Mickey Mouse.
Qu'est-ce que Walt Disney a créé?

1. Pablo Picasso a peint *"Les demoiselles d'Avignon"*.
2. Léonard de Vinci a fait *"La Joconde"*.
3. Maurice Ravel a composé *"Boléro"*.
4. Michel-Ange a sculpté *"David"*.
5. Ieoh Ming Pei a construit *la pyramide du Louvre*.

54. Write the question that corresponds to the underlined part of the response.
Modèle:
Le président dit que tout va bien.
Que dit le président?

1. Les Beatles font *une tournée aux États-Unis*.

2. Le président fait *une conférence de presse.*

3. La météo dit *qu'il va pleuvoir.*

4. Le peuple veut *moins d'impôts.*

5. Les médecins *ne peuvent rien faire.*

55. Repeat, if you please! You did not hear all of what was said, so you ask the question that corresponds to the underlined part—the part that you missed. Use (a) subject/verb inversion, and (b) ***est-ce que***. Follow the model.

Modèle:
On a découvert un cadavre d'homme préhistorique dans un glacier.
Dans quoi a-t-on découvert un cadavre d'homme préhistorique?
(Dans quoi est-ce qu'on a découvert un cadavre d'homme préhistorique?)

1. J'ai fait ces sculptures avec une tronçonneuse. (Use *tu.*)
   a.
   b.
2. Nous plaçons les lingots sur des chariots roulants.
   a.
   b.
3. Les dossiers sont rangés dans des classeurs.
   a.
   b.
4. Ils cachent leur coffre-fort derrière un rideau.
   a.
   b.
5. Ma fille peut faire des études supérieures grâce à une bourse.
   a.
   b.

Interrogative adverbs

56. Using subject/verb inversion, write the question that corresponds to the underlined part of the response. Choose from the interrogative adverbs: ***comment***, ***quand***, ***où***, ***combien de***, ***pourquoi***, ***depuis quand***, ***depuis combien de temps***.

1. Il est né au Japon.

2. Il est né en 1986.

3. Il parle quatre langues.

4. Il est en Floride depuis trois ans.

5. Il est étudiant depuis août 2000.
____
6. Il travaille très bien.
____
7. Il est en Floride parce qu'il a reçu une bourse.
____
8. Il pense rester en Floride encore un an.
____

57. Write the question that corresponds to the underlined part of the response, (a) using subject/verb inversion, and (b) using ***est-ce que***. Choose from the interrogative adverbs: ***pourquoi***, ***combien de***, ***comment***, ***où***, ***quand***.

1. Napoléon est né en Corse.
   a. ______________________________
   b. ______________________________
2. La première croisade a eu lieu à la fin du XIe siècle.
   a. ______________________________
   b. ______________________________
3. Charlemagne est allé en Espagne pour repousser l'invasion des Arabes musulmans.
   a. ______________________________
   b. ______________________________
4. Les Anglais ont fait mourir Jeanne d'Arc en la faisant brûler vive.
   a. ______________________________
   b. ______________________________
5. Les employés français ne travaillent que 35 heures par semaine.
   a. ______________________________
   b. ______________________________

Possessive adjectives and pronouns

58. Complete with the appropriate possessive adjective: ***mon***, ***ma***, ***mes***; ***ton***, ***ta***, ***tes***; ***son***, ***sa***, ***ses***; ***notre***, ***nos***; ***votre***, ***vos***; ***leur***, ***leurs***.

1. (Her) ____________ père et ____________ mère sont morts.
2. (His, their) ____________ enfants vivent avec ____________ grands-parents.
3. (My) ____________ frères et ____________ sœur travaillent à l'usine de conserves.
4. (My) ____________ arrière-grand-père et ____________ arrière-grand-mère sont encore en vie.
5. (Her) ____________ oncle est en Amérique, et ____________ tante aussi.
6. (His) ____________ habitude est de se lever à 5h du matin.
7. (Her) ____________ habitude est de se lever à 7h du matin.
8. (His) ____________ famille est originaire de Pologne.
9. (Their, their) ____________ cousins sont venus les voir avec ____________ amis.
10. (Our, his) ____________ petit-fils est passé nous voir avec ____________ fiancée.
11. Visitez (our) ____________ ville avec (its) ____________ château, ____________ vieilles rues, ____________ rivière, ____________ fête folklorique, ____________ artisanat et ____________ unique tradition religieuse.

59. Complete with the appropriate form of the possessive adjective (first blank) and the possessive pronoun (second blank). Note: *2S* = second person singular; *2P* = second person plural.

Possessive adjectives: ***mon, ma, mes; ton, ta, tes; son, sa, ses; notre, nos; votre, vos; leur, leurs.***

Possessive pronouns: ***le mien, la mienne, les miens, les miennes; le tien, la tienne, les tiens, les tiennes; le sien, la sienne, les siens, les siennes; le nôtre, la nôtre, les nôtres; le vôtre, la vôtre, les vôtres; le leur, la leur, les leurs.***

1. (His) ____________ attitude est plus acceptable que (yours, 2S) ____________, Bernard!
2. (Her) ____________ imagination est plus folle que (mine) ____________.
3. (Her) ____________ intelligence est supérieure à (yours, 2S) ____________.
4. (Their) ____________ méchanceté n'a pas d'égale. (Theirs) ____________ n'a pas d'égale.
5. (Her) ____________ bonté est légendaire. (Hers) ____________ est légendaire.
6. (Your, 2S) ____________ paresse mérite un Oscar! (Yours, 2S) ____________ mérite un Oscar!
7. (Our) ____________ train est en retard. (Ours) ____________ est en retard.
8. (My) ____________ avion part à 11h15. (Mine) ____________ part à 11h15.
9. (Your, 2P) ____________ taxi attend. (Yours, 2P) ____________ attend.
10. J'ai encore (my) ____________ cheveux, alors que toi, tu as perdu (yours) ____________.
11. Si tu ne peux pas te servir de (your, 2S) ____________ voiture, prends (mine) ____________.
12. Si tu ne peux pas prendre (your, 2S) ____________ raquette, sers-toi de (mine) ____________.
13. Si tu ne peux pas utiliser (your, 2S) ____________ ordinateur, sers-toi de (mine) ____________.
14. Si tu ne peux pas utiliser (your, 2S) ____________ ciseaux, sers-toi de (mine) ____________.
15. En prenant (your, 2S) ____________ affaires, fais attention à (mine) ____________.

60. Write in French.

1. Do you mind my leaving early?
____
2. Your complaining will not be of any use.
____
3. French men shake hands when they greet one another.
____
4. French girls give one another one, two, or three kisses on their cheeks when they meet.
____
5. Each country has its own customs.
____
6. We each have our preferences.
____
7. Wash your hands before you eat your sandwich, Michael!
____
8. Open your mouth, stick out your tongue, and say "AAH"!
____

Personal pronouns

61. Answer with a complete sentence, replacing the direct object noun of the question with the personal pronoun ***le***, ***la***, or ***les***.

1. Attendez-vous vos amis?
   — Oui, ___________________.
2. Quand est-ce que tu regardes la télé?
   — Je ___________________ le soir.
3. Est-ce que tu connais ce roman?
   — Oui, ___________________.
4. Tu cherches tes clés?
   — Oui, ___________________.
5. Est-ce que tu aimes les épinards?
   — Non, je ___________________.

62. Answer with a complete sentence, replacing the direct object noun with the personal pronoun ***le***, ***la***, or ***les***.

1. Marc peut-il prêter ses disques?
   — Non, il ___________________.
2. Est-ce que tu vas voir ce nouveau film?
   — Oui, je ___________________ ce soir.
3. Quand est-ce que vous allez voir vos grands-parents?
   — Nous ___________________ presque tous les weekends.
4. Alors, veux-tu manger tes épinards?
   — Non, je ___________________.
5. À quelle heure est-ce qu'il faut réveiller les enfants?
   — Il ___________________ à six heures et demie.

63. Answer with a complete sentence, replacing the direct object noun with the personal pronoun ***me***, ***te***, ***le***, ***la***, ***nous***, ***vous*** or ***les***. Watch the agreement of the past participle.

1. Marc vous a-t-il invitée, Mademoiselle Lenoir?
   — Oui, il ___________________.
2. Est-ce que tu as expédié les cartes de Noël, Michel?
   — Oui, je ___________________ ce matin.
3. Où est-ce que vous avez mis les fleurs, Ernestine?
   — Je ___________________ dans un vase, Madame.
4. Qui a pris ces belles photos?
   — C'est moi qui ___________________.
5. Tu veux lire ces vieux magazines?
   — Non, merci, je (have already read them) ___________________.

64. Answer with a complete sentence, replacing the indirect object noun with the personal pronoun ***me***, ***te***, ***lui***, ***nous***, ***vous***, or ***leur***.

1. Est-ce que tu téléphones parfois à Suzanne?
   — Oui, je ____________________ de temps en temps.
2. Tu demandes quoi à tes parents?
   — Je ____________________ de l'argent.
3. Qu'est-ce que tes parents te répondent?
   — Ils ____________________ que je dépense trop.
4. Tu écris souvent à ta grand-mère?
   — Je ____________________ une ou deux fois par an.
5. Est-ce que tu rends à tes amis les choses qu'ils te prêtent?
   — Bien sûr, je ____________________ toujours les choses qu'ils ____________________ prêtent.

65. Answer with a complete sentence, replacing the indirect object noun with the personal pronoun ***me***, ***te***, ***lui***, ***nous***, ***vous***, or ***leur***.

1. Qui est-ce qui va donner à manger au chien?
   — C'est Michel qui ____.
2. Est-ce que tu veux bien donner un coup de main à nos voisins?
   — Oui, ____.
3. Est-ce que vous avez besoin de parler au directeur tout de suite?
   — Oui, ____ tout de suite.
4. Quand est-ce que je devrai rendre la bicyclette à Cédric?
   — Tu ____ ce soir.
5. Il faudrait peut-être téléphoner à tes parents?
   — Oui, ____.

66. Answer with a complete sentence, replacing the indirect object noun with the personal pronoun ***me***, ***te***, ***lui***, ***nous***, ***vous***, or ***leur***.

1. Est-ce que la secrétaire a envoyé un message aux deux candidats? (Non)
   ____
2. A-t-elle parlé à sa collègue? (Oui)
   ____
3. Quand a-t-elle écrit au président? (hier)
   ____
4. Est-ce que vous avez donné votre dossier à la secrétaire? (Oui, . . . il y a cinq minutes)
   ____
5. Qui a répondu aux candidats? (C'est la secrétaire qui)
   ____

67. Answer with a complete sentence, replacing the underlined object with the personal pronoun ***en***.

1. Combien de fois par jour est-ce que vous buvez du soda?
____
2. Et des fruits, vous mangez souvent des fruits? (Oui . . . régulièrement)
____
3. Normalement, combien de repas prenez-vous par jour?
____
4. Est-ce que vous consommez parfois des boissons alcoolisées? (Non, . . . jamais)
____
5. Est-ce que vous prenez des suppléments vitaminés? (Oui, . . . parfois)
____

68. Answer with a complete sentence, replacing the underlined object with the personal pronoun ***en***.

1. Est-ce que tu vas commander des moules?
Oui, je _______________.
2. Tu crois que je devrais prendre des frites avec ça?
Oui, je crois que _______________.
3. Est-ce qu'on peut boire un verre de vin blanc?
Oui, on _______________.
4. Je me demande s'il faudra laisser un pourboire?
Je crois qu'il _______________.
5. Est-ce que tu veux prendre un hors-d'œuvre?
Non, _______________.

69. Answer with a complete sentence, replacing the object with the personal pronoun ***en***.

1. Est-ce que tu as acheté du jambon? (Oui, . . . six tranches)
____
2. Combien de biftecks as-tu pris? (trois)
____
3. Et des laitues, tu as pris des laitues? (Oui, . . . deux)
____
4. Est-ce que tu as commandé des langoustines pour dimanche? (Oui, . . . trois kilos)
____
5. Où est le poisson? Tu as acheté du poisson? (Non, . . . parce qu'il n'y en avait plus)
____

70. Answer with a complete sentence, replacing the underlined complement with the personal pronoun ***y***.

1. À quelle heure allez-vous au cinéma ce soir? (21h)
____
2. Est-ce que vous pensez parfois à la mort? (Oui)
____
3. Est-ce que tu es dans la cuisine? (Oui)
____

4. Est-ce que votre fils s'intéresse à l'informatique? (Non, . . . pas du tout)
____

5. Comment se rendront-ils au concert? (en taxi)
____

71. Answer with a complete sentence, replacing the underlined complement with the personal pronoun ***y***.

1. Est-ce qu'il faut s'arrêter à la douane?
Bien sûr qu'il ____!
2. Est-ce que tu veux bien venir avec moi au match de foot demain? (Oui, . . . use *aller*)
____.
3. Jacques, tu veux bien aller au magasin m'acheter une douzaine d'œufs? (Ok, I'm going)
D'accord, ____.
4. Michel, tu acceptes de conduire les invités au banquet?
D'accord, ____.
5. Combien de temps peux-tu nous attendre devant l'hôtel? (pas plus de dix minutes)
____.

72. Answer with a complete sentence, replacing the underlined complement with the personal pronoun ***y***.

1. Quand êtes-vous allés en Europe? (il y a un an)
____
2. Par où êtes-vous arrivés en Europe? (par l'Espagne)
____
3. Est-ce que vous êtes restés longtemps en France? (deux semaines)
____
4. Qu'est-ce que vous avez visité en Italie? (ne . . . que Venise)
____
5. Est-ce que vous avez aimé la Suisse? (We did not go there.)
____

73. Write the negative imperative of the verb in parentheses without omitting the personal pronoun complement if it is needed.

1. Il est très occupé, (déranger) ____________________.
2. Vous verrez. Tout ira très bien, (s'inquiéter) ____________________.
3. Cette chaise est cassée, (s'asseoir) ____________________ là.
4. (Rappeler) ____________________, Barbara, je ne décrocherai pas!
5. Les petits chats dorment, (ne pas réveiller) ____________________.

74. Write each sentence in the affirmative imperative, replacing the underlined object with a personal pronoun. Choose from the direct object pronouns ***me***, ***te***, ***le***, ***la***, ***nous***, ***vous***, ***les***; from the indirect object pronouns ***me***, ***te***, ***lui***, ***nous***, ***vous***, ***leur***; or choose from the adverbial pronouns ***y*** and ***en***.

1. Emballez bien mes achats, il me faut un paquet-cadeau.
   ____
2. Donnez le paquet à mon mari.
   ____
3. Donnez le paquet à mon mari.
   ____
4. Voici ma carte de crédit.
   ____
5. Montrez les chemises d'homme à mon mari.
   ____
6. Essayez celle-ci.
   ____
7. Prenez donc des petits-fours.
   ____
8. Allons au concert tout de suite pour avoir de bonnes places.
   ____
9. Je vous conseille de penser à vos obligations!
   ____
10. Dites à vos invités d'arriver assez tôt à la soirée.
   ____

75. Complete the sentences trying to express the meaning given in parentheses. Use the imperative form of the verb and choose the appropriate disjunctive pronoun: ***moi***, ***toi***, ***lui***, ***elle***, ***nous***, ***vous***, or ***eux***.

1. Je ne peux pas compter sur ce vieux réveil, s'il te plaît, (wake me up) ______________ demain matin!
2. Je n'ai pas envie de me lever si tôt moi-même, alors (fend for yourself = se débrouiller) ______________!
3. Faites comme chez vous, (sit down = s'asseoir) ______________!
4. (Listen [plural] to me = écouter) ______________, nous devons nous mettre d'accord là-dessus!
5. Je ne connais pas cette personne, s'il te plaît, (introduce me = présenter) ______________!

76. Complete with the suggested words using the appropriate direct or indirect object pronoun. In addition, use the adverbial pronoun ***en***, where appropriate.

1. Je voudrais du pâté de foie gras. — Combien (vouloir) ______________? (Give me) ______________ 500 grammes.
2. Je n'ai plus de piles pour mon portable. — Veux-tu que (I lend [= prêter] some to you) ______________?
3. Tu connais cette vieille tradition? — Non, je (don't remember it = se souvenir) ______________.

4. Je crois bien qu'il (doesn't give a hoot about it = se moquer) ______________.
5. Vous quittez notre immeuble? Vous avez de la chance! Mais est-ce que vous (realize it = se rendre compte) ______________?

77. Rewrite each sentence, replacing each underlined part with a personal pronoun. Use direct and indirect object pronouns. Where appropriate, use the adverbial pronouns ***y*** and ***en***.

1. Ils nous ont offert l'apéritif.
   ____
2. Je me souviendrai toujours de ce voyage.
   ____
3. Les voisins ont mis leur véhicule dans le garage.
   ____
4. Leur fils a sorti son vélo du garage.
   ____
5. J'ai vu le maire au supermarché ce matin.
   ____

78. Rewrite each sentence, replacing each underlined part with a personal pronoun. Use direct and indirect object pronouns, reflexive reciprocal pronouns, and the adverbial pronouns ***y*** and ***en***, where appropriate.

1. Le président va recevoir les délégations étrangères demain dans la galerie des glaces.
   ____
2. Nous voudrions offrir des cadeaux aux enfants pour Noël.
   ____
3. Il faut donner quelques renseignements à cette jeune touriste.
   ____
4. Les sénateurs pourraient peut-être se passer d'augmentation de salaire cette année!
   ____
5. Les Dupont ont envie de nous emprunter nos nouveaux films.
   ____

79. Rewrite each sentence, replacing each underlined part with a personal pronoun. Use direct and indirect object pronouns in addition to the adverbial pronoun ***en***, where appropriate.

1. Nous vous avons réservé deux places à l'orchestre pour *Rigoletto*.
   ____
2. Quand je suis revenu d'Europe, le douanier m'a fouillé tous mes bagages.
   ____
3. En arrivant, les invités ont offert des fleurs à leurs hôtes.
   ____
4. Les visiteurs ont demandé le numéro de l'appartement au concierge.
   ____
5. Mais qui donc a donné cet os au chien?
   ____

80. Write the following sentences in the negative. Use ***ne . . . pas*** and undo the subject/verb inversion.

1. Allez-vous-en!
2. Donnez-lui-en!
3. Apportez-les-leur!
4. Achetez-les-nous!
5. Expliquez-la-moi!

81. Write the verbs in parentheses in the imperative, in order to give the command or advice that corresponds to each question. Replace the underlined elements with direct and indirect object pronouns, or with the adverbial pronouns ***y*** and ***en***, where appropriate.

1. Est-ce que je donne le dessert aux enfants?
   Oui, (donner) ________________.
2. Maman, est-ce que je peux servir de la crème fouettée à mon petit frère?
   Oui, (servir) ________________.
3. Faut-il que nous emmenions les enfants à la piscine?
   Oui, (emmener) ________________.
4. Veux-tu que je te montre la photo de notre groupe?
   Oui, (montrer = show) ________________.
5. Est-ce que je dois prêter mon GI-Joe à Mike?
   Oui, (prêter) ________________.

82. Rewrite each sentence replacing the underlined elements with ***y*** or with an indirect object pronoun.

1. J'arriverai bien à découvrir la cause de ce problème.
2. Nous enverrons aussi des invitations à nos amis de New York.
3. Je renonce à comprendre!
4. J'ai envoyé un faire-part aux Dupont.
5. Je tiens à ce livre, ne le perds pas!

83. Rewrite each sentence replacing the underlined part with ***y*** or with the preposition ***à*** followed by a stress pronoun: ***lui***, ***elle***, ***eux***, or ***elles***.

1. Je me suis enfin adapté à ma nouvelle vie.

2. Mais j'ai eu du mal à m'habituer à mes nouveaux camarades de chambre.
____
3. Et toi, est-ce que tu as réussi à t'habituer à tes nouveaux camarades de chambre?
____
4. Nous pensons souvent à ces années de jeunesse insouciante.
____
5. Est-ce qu'il vous arrive de penser à vos grands-parents défunts?
____
6. Dis, chérie, on dirait que notre voisine s'intéresse beaucoup au jardinage.
____
7. Moi, je crois que tu t'intéresses un peu trop à la voisine!
____

84. Rewrite the questions, keeping the inversion, but replacing a portion of the sentence with the pronoun ***en***. Next, answer as directed on the second line, still using the pronoun ***en***.

1. Vous rendez-vous compte que nous devons rendre ce rapport demain matin?
____
Oui, je _______________.
2. Êtes-vous certain que nous devons payer mille euros pour le voyage aller-retour?
____
Non, je _______________.
3. N'avez-vous pas peur que le patron vous renvoie tous si le budget est déficitaire?
____
Si, nous _______________.
4. Se souviennent-ils que bientôt il leur faudra déménager?
____
Oui, _______________.
5. Ne se soucie-t-elle pas un peu du fait qu'elle prépare son avenir?
_______________.
Non, _______________ pas le moins du monde.

85. Answer the question using a neuter pronoun to replace the underlined elements.
Modèle:
Madeleine, es-tu prête à prendre ce risque*?*
Oui, je le suis.

1. Est-ce que tu regrettes d'avoir commis cette erreur?
____
2. Vous savez qu'il a eu un accident?
____
3. Croient-ils que l'argent pousse sur les arbres?
____
4. Tu te demandes si le jeu en vaut la chandelle?
____
5. Est-il vraiment fâché?
____

86. Complete the sentences with a personal pronoun and ***voici*** or ***voilà***.

1. Tu cherches des trombones? Tiens, ____________________.
2. Vous cherchez le dictionnaire? Eh bien, ____________________.
3. S'ils veulent du fromage, ____________________.
4. Vous attendez les coureurs du Tour de France? Eh bien, ____________________.
5. Vous vouliez me voir? ____________________.

Relative pronouns

87. Combine the two sentences using a relative clause beginning with ***qui*** or ***que***, which gives information about the underlined antecedent. Remember that ***qui*** replaces a subject, while ***que*** replaces an object.

Modèle:
Marie lit un livre. Ce livre l'intéresse.
Marie lit un livre qui l'intéresse.

1. Marie lit un roman. Elle a acheté ce roman hier.
   ____
2. Marie est en train de lire un roman. Ce roman a reçu le prix Goncourt.
   ____
3. Je préparerai un dessert. Tout le monde aimera ce dessert.
   ____
4. Le Languedoc est une région. Elle produit beaucoup de vin.
   ____
5. La Mustang était une belle voiture décapotable. Tout le monde voulait conduire une Mustang.
   ____
6. Neil Armstrong est un astronaute. Il a marché sur la lune.
   ____
7. Rends-moi le livre. Je t'ai prêté ce livre.
   ____
8. Je suis arrivé dans un village tranquille. Ce village avait l'air abandonné.
   ____

88. Combine the two sentences using a relative clause beginning with ***qui*** (for a subject) or ***que*** (for an object), which gives information about the underlined antecedent. Note the placement of the relative clause.

1. Cette photo est en réalité très vieille. Cette photo paraît récente.
   ____
2. L'acteur vient de mourir. Il jouait le rôle du capitaine dans ce film.
   ____
3. Le café n'est pas chaud. Vous m'avez servi ce café.
   ____

4. Le dernier film est un succès. Robert Redford a mis en scène ce film.
____

5. Ce personnage détruit tout autour de lui. Il a l'air inoffensif.
____

6. Le livre m'intéresse. Marie est en train de lire le livre.
____

Indefinite or neuter antecedent

89. Combine the two sentences using ***ce*** and a relative pronoun ***qui*** (for an antecedent that is a subject) or ***que*** (for an antecedent that is an object).

Modèle:
J'ai éteint le four et la température continue à monter. Je ne comprends pas cela!
J'ai éteint le four et la température continue à monter, CE QUE je ne comprends pas!

1. Marie est en train de lire. Cela me surprend.
____
2. Vous avez raison. Je dois l'admettre.
____
3. Ils ont encore oublié d'apporter l'addition. Cela commence à m'énerver.
____
4. Vous avez pris deux boissons. Cela vous coûtera 26,50 euros.
____
5. Elle n'a pas apporté sa carte de crédit. Elle le regrette vivement.
____
6. Les autres sont partis après nous et sont arrivés avant. Cela m'étonne.
____

90. Add the relative pronoun ***qui*** (to replace the subject of the clause) ou ***que*** (to replace the object of the clause).

1. J'ai choisi un film _____ n'est pas très connu.
2. Connaissez-vous l'acteur _____ nous venons de voir à la télé?
3. J'aime surtout les films étrangers _____ sont en version originale.
4. Gérard Depardieu est l'acteur _____ joue le rôle de Cyrano de Bergerac.
5. Le film _____ nous venons de voir a gagné la Palme d'Or au festival de Cannes.
6. L'actrice _____ je préfère est anglaise.
7. Quelle est l'actrice française _____ vous préférez?
8. Quelles sont les vedettes _____ ont servi de modèle pour le buste de Marianne?
9. La première vedette _____ on a choisie pour faire le buste de Marianne est Brigitte Bardot.
10. Celle _____ a été choisie ensuite est Catherine Deneuve.
11. Je ne connais pas la dernière vedette _____ on a prise comme modèle.
12. Est-ce que vous aimez les films _____ sont présentés en numérique?

91. Combine the two sentences using the relative pronoun ***dont*** to represent the underlined antecedent.

1. C'est un célèbre metteur en scène. Les films de ce metteur en scène ont toujours du succès.
   ____
2. L'actrice est une jeune femme. Le cousin de cette jeune femme est Cyrano.
   ____
3. Le colonel commande un régiment. Tous les soldats de ce régiment sont gascons.
   ____
4. L'actrice est une jeune "précieuse". Cyrano est amoureux de cette actrice.
   ____
5. La "précieuse" s'appelle Roxane. Christian tombe amoureux de cette précieuse.
   ____

92. Combine the two sentences using the preposition that is given and the relative pronoun ***lequel***, ***laquelle***, or ***lesquel(le)s*** to replace the underlined elements. Make the necessary changes to the relative pronouns so that they agree with an antecedent and combine with a preposition if they must.

1. On leur apporte du pâté et du poulet. Ils boivent du vin de Bordeaux avec ce pâté et ce poulet.
   ____
   ____
2. Les Gascons ont construit des barricades. Ils se sont défendus derrière ces barricades.
   ____
   ____
3. Le colonel portait une écharpe. L'ennemi aurait pu le reconnaître à cause d'elle.
   ____
   ____
4. Cyrano est passé sous un échafaudage. Une poutre est tombée du haut de cet échafaudage.
   ____
   ____

Prepositions

93. Add the appropriate prepositions, with an article if necessary.

1. Pour la dernière étape du Tour de France, les coureurs partaient ____ Chartres, et l'arrivée était ____ Paris, sur les Champs-Élysées.
2. Il y avait des coureurs de partout: ____ Espagne, ____ Portugal, ____ Pays-Bas, ____ Italie, ____ Allemagne, ____ Danemark et même ____ États-Unis.
3. Les coureurs se sont arrêtés ____ Reims, ____ Strasbourg, ____ Lyon et ailleurs.
4. Le Tour de France a lieu ____ été.
5. Les coureurs s'entraînent (pendant) toute l'année: ____ automne, ____ hiver et ____ printemps.
6. Le gagnant du Tour porte le maillot jaune. Depuis six ans (en 2004), le maillot jaune (= le coureur qui porte le maillot jaune) est un Américain ____ Texas: Lance Armstrong.

7. Est-ce qu'il y a des coureurs du Tour qui viennent ____ Japon ou ____ Corée?
8. Il en vient peut-être aussi ____ Canada, ____ Mexique, ____ Kenya ou ____ Maroc?
9. Certaines années, le tracé du Tour conduit les coureurs ____ Belgique, ____ Luxembourg, ____ Suisse, ____ Italie, ____ Monaco et ____ Espagne.
10. Il y a aussi des courses cyclistes ____ Arizona, ____ Caroline du Nord et du Sud, ____ Floride, ____ Québec et ____ Ontario ainsi que ____ New York.

94. Add ***à*** or ***de***, or nothing, as needed. Make all necessary elisions and contractions.

1. Nous commençons ____ comprendre.
2. Quel jour avez-vous décidé ____ partir?
3. Quelqu'un a encore oublié ____ fermer la fenêtre!
4. Je ne pouvais pas ____ me décider.
5. Maman a demandé à Pauline ____ faire la vaisselle.
6. Permettez-moi ____ vous aider, Madame!
7. Ils ont essayé ____ entrer sans payer.
8. Tu pourras ____ sortir quand tu auras fini ____ faire tes devoirs.
9. Est-ce qu'elle a réussi ____ trouver l'adresse de son oncle?
10. Elle déteste ____ écrire, elle préfère ____ téléphoner.

95. Add ***à*** or ***de***, or nothing, as needed. Make all necessary elisions and contractions.

1. Ils ont demandé à Jacques ____ suivre des cours de droit.
2. Où iriez-vous si vous pouviez ____ faire une croisière d'une semaine?
3. Et maintenant, qu'est-ce que je dois ____ faire?
4. Mes amis veulent ____ aller ____ faire une randonnée en montagne.
5. Attention au chat, ne le laisse pas ____ sortir!
6. Dites-leur ____ fermer la porte à clef quand ils partiront.
7. Est-ce qu'elle sait ____ nager?
8. Elle a commencé ____ suivre des cours d'auto-école.
9. Tout le monde cherche ____ éviter ____ faire des corvées, non?
10. Il a oublié ____ venir ____ passer son examen.

96. Add ***à*** or ***de***, or nothing, as needed. Make all necessary elisions and contractions.

1. Nous sommes heureux ____ être enfin rentrés chez nous.
2. Êtes-vous contents ____ avoir fait la connaissance de nombreux étrangers?
3. Je suis satisfait ____ avoir appris tant de choses sur ce pays.
4. Elle est étonnée ____ être la première de sa catégorie.
5. Nous sommes prêts ____ vous aider si cela devient nécessaire.
6. Nos voisins n'ont pas de chance, ils en sont réduits ____ demander l'aide de leur communauté après l'incendie de leur maison.
7. Ce fardeau va être lourd ____ porter!
8. Cette enfant est destinée ____ devenir une grande pianiste!
9. Quant à moi, je suis ravi ____ savoir que vous avez gagné le gros lot à la loterie nationale.
10. Le directeur ne peut pas vous recevoir, il est occupé ____ préparer un discours important.

97. Is a preposition necessary? Complete as appropriate.

1. ____ matin il fait plus frais que ____ après-midi.
2. C'est presque toujours ____ soir qu'on remarque la lune.
3. ____ lundi est généralement moins agréable que ____ samedi pour ceux qui travaillent.
4. ____ lundi prochain est un jour férié, c'est ____ lundi de la Pentecôte.
5. La semaine de travail va ____ lundi ____ vendredi. Ce sont les jours ouvrables.
6. ____ jeudis étaient autrefois les jours préférés des écoliers. Ils rêvaient de la "semaine ____ quatre jeudis". De nos jours, ils préfèrent ____ mercredis.
7. ____ week-end en France n'a pas les mêmes jours pour tout le monde. Certains travaillent ____ samedi. D'autres ont congé ____ samedi et ____ dimanche. D'autres encore ne travaillent ni ____ dimanche ni ____ lundi.
8. Lorsqu'un jour férié tombe ____ jeudi, il est courant que les salariés prennent congé aussi ____ vendredi pour faire "le pont" avec le week-end, ce qui leur donne quatre jours de congé.
9. ____ matin et ____ soir, la circulation est intense. Ce sont les heures de pointe.
10. ____ mardi qui commence le Carême s'appelle le Mardi gras. ____ mercredi qui suit est ____ mercredi des Cendres.

For, since, ago, during, in, how long? (*pour*, *depuis*, *il y a*, *pendant*, *en*, *dans*, *depuis quand? depuis combien de temps?* . . .)

98. Complete the following sentences as appropriate.

1. Il est absent ____________ la semaine dernière, on ne le voit plus.
2. Nous partons ____________ l'Europe ____________ deux jours.
3. ____________ une semaine qu'il est absent. Où est-il donc?
4. Le TGV fait-il Paris-Marseille ____________ trois heures et demie?
5. ____________ habitez-vous dans ce pays?
6. ____________ le Ramadan, les Musulmans jeûnent du lever au coucher du soleil.
7. Où est-elle? ____________ cinq minutes, elle était assise à son bureau.
8. Ils sont partis hier ____________ deux semaines de vacances.
9. Quand JFK a été assassiné, ____________ étiez-vous aux États-Unis?
10. ____________ bien longtemps qu'on ne voyage plus en carrosse.

The preposition *in*

99. Complete with the appropriate preposition as needed.

1. ____ Europe, toutes les maisons sont construites ____ brique ou ____ pierre. Très peu de maisons sont ____ bois.
2. Beaucoup de maisons sont crépies ____ ciment et peintes ____ blanc.
3. Il est rare qu'on achète une maison en payant ____ comptant.
4. ____ effet, une maison coûte généralement ____ -dessus de cinquante mille euros.
5. En France, les toits ____ ardoise sont abondants ____ la moitié nord du pays.
6. ____ sud, on trouve surtout des toits ____ tuiles.
7. La tuile et l'ardoise sont des matériaux ____ usage depuis des siècles.

8. Quel est le matériau de couverture le plus ____ la mode ____ États-Unis? C'est probablement la couverture ____ métal, qui se voit de plus en plus fréquemment.
9. L'isolation thermique est importante ____ le Midi, où il fait souvent plus de 30 degrés ____ l'ombre.
10. ____ quoi consiste le travail du couvreur? Est-ce qu'on peut faire confiance ____ n'importe quel ouvrier?

100. Complete with ***à*** or ***de***. Make all necessary elisions and contractions.

1. Cet exercice est difficile ____ faire.
2. Il sera difficile ____ trouver une solution à ce problème.
3. Il est impossible ____ leur garder rancune, ils sont si gentils!
4. Leur gentillesse est facile ____ voir.
5. Il est plus facile ____ dire que ____ faire!
6. Je suis heureux ____ avoir fait votre connaissance.
7. Il est toujours utile ____ avoir une carte de crédit.
8. Certains sont peu disposés ____ rendre service aux autres.
9. Nous sommes satisfaits ____ avoir accompli cette tâche dans les délais prévus.
10. Il est normal ____ éprouver du chagrin lorsqu'un être cher quitte ce monde.

101. Complete with ***à***, ***de***, or ***pour*** or leave blank. Make all necessary elisions and contractions.

1. Il est inutile ____ courir quand on est parti trop tard, il faut ____ partir à temps.
2. Je suis lent ____ comprendre ce genre de choses.
3. Êtes-vous prêt ____ assumer vos responsabilités?
4. Il est important ____ prévoir tous les détails avant d'entreprendre une ascension en montagne.
5. Vous n'aviez que ____ vous présenter à l'heure!
6. Il est trop tard ____ revenir sur nos pas! Nous devons ____ continuer!
7. Une carte d'identité n'est pas suffisante ____ permettre à quelqu'un ____ passer la frontière.
8. Le directeur ne peut pas ____ vous recevoir, il est occupé ____ régler un grave problème.
9. Madame X serait charmée ____ faire votre connaissance.
10. Il est dommage ____ n'avoir pas réussi ____ nous retrouver dans la foule à l'aéroport.

102. Complete with the appropriate preposition (if one is needed) choosing from the following list and making all necessary elisions and contractions: ***parler à***, ***téléphoner à***, ***jouer à***, ***jouer de + article***, ***penser à***, ***penser de***, ***penser ____***, ***décider de***, ***se décider à***, ***chercher ____***, ***chercher à + infinitif***, ***regarder ____***, ***attendre ____***, ***payer ____***, ***entrer dans***, ***se souvenir de***, ***se rappeler ____***, ***dire à***, ***dire de + infinitif***, ***demander à***, ***demander de + infinitif***.

1. Elle joue ____ la trompette dans le groupe de jazz de l'université.
2. Par contre elle ne joue jamais ____ le volley-ball ni ____ le basket.
3. Qu'est-ce que vous pensez ____ cette nouvelle actrice qui vient d'avoir un Oscar?
4. Je ne pense pas toujours ____ ce que je dois faire d'un jour à l'autre.
5. Est-ce que tu as décidé ____ téléphoner ____ tes parents ce soir?
6. Non, je ne suis pas décidé ____ leur téléphoner aujourd'hui.

7. Nous nous sommes enfin décidés ____ acheter un téléphone portable.
8. L'institutrice va téléphoner ____ les parents de l'élève indiscipliné.
9. Est-ce que vous cherchez ____ le directeur?
10. Je crois qu'ils regardent ____ un film policier.
11. Est-ce que ce n'est pas Annie, là-bas, qui attend ____ l'autobus?
12. Moi, je paie ____ les boissons, et vous, vous payez ____ le repas.
13. Quand vous entrerez ____ le musée, vous verrez une belle statue de Vénus.
14. Vous souvenez-vous ____ votre première journée à l'école?
15. Je me rappelle avec horreur ____ l'attaque des tours jumelles du W.T.C.
16. L'étudiant a demandé ____ la secrétaire ce qu'il fallait faire pour son transfert.
17. La secrétaire a dit ____ l'étudiant ____ remplir un formulaire.

103. Complete the sentences using the following prepositions and conjunctions: ***pendant / pendant que*, *à cause de / parce que*, *sans / sans que*, *pour / pour que*, *avant de / avant que*.**

1. J'ai fait du tennis ____________________ mon week-end.
2. Le soir, je jouais du piano ____________________ mon père lisait son journal.
3. Elle veut qu'il aille voir le médecin ____________________ il est malade.
4. Elle est très inquiète ____________________ la possibilité du cancer.
5. Ne partez pas ____________________ moi!
6. Il est parti ____________________ je puisse lui dire au revoir.
7. Ils se sont levés à 6h ____________________ faire de l'entraînement.
8. Nos grands-parents se sont levés tôt ____________________ nous puissions les voir une dernière fois avant le départ de l'avion.
9. Téléphone-leur ____________________ arriver!
10. Cache-toi vite ____________________ il (ne) te voie!

104. Complete with prepositions, adding articles where necessary.

1. aller quelque part ____ pied, ____ cheval, ____ voiture, ____ taxi, ____ avion, ____ bateau, ____ bicyclette, ____ moto. (= to walk, ride, drive, fly, etc., someplace)
2. mener quelqu'un ____ le bout du nez. (to lead someone by the nose)
3. Il nous a menés ____ bateau (He took us for a ride!). Vous entendez le moteur? Le moteur est ____ marche, nous ne sommes pas ____ panne. Ce n'est pas une blague!
4. conduire quelqu'un (to take someone home) ______________, (to the restaurant) ______________. Emmener quelqu'un (to take someone to the movies) ______________.
5. ____ gauche vous voyez la Tour Eiffel, et ____ droite le Sacré-Cœur. ____ centre il y a l'Arc de Triomphe de l'Étoile, et tout ____ fond, ____ arrière, c'est L'Arche de la Défense.
6. ____ quelle heure part le train? ____ 10h37? Il n'est que 10h30, donc nous sommes (on time) ____ heure.
7. J'ai entendu dire que les employés étaient ____ grève. ____ moyenne, il y a deux grèves de métro ____ an.
8. ______________________________ (You are out of luck), le train vient de partir.
9. Parfois des jeunes sautent ______________ (over) la barrière ______________ ne pas attendre la rame (de métro) suivante.
10. ____ lundi ______________ vendredi (Monday through Friday), il y a plus de trains de banlieue que ______________ week-end.

105. Complete with a preposition, if one is needed.

1. La plage est ____ deux heures d'ici, ____ 100 km ____ chez nous.
2. ____ quel âge avez-vous commencé ____ conduire une voiture?
3. C'est ____ faisant du ski qu'il s'est fait mal ____ genou et ____ la cheville.
4. Le petit garçon s'amuse ____ poursuivre le chien. Il tire le chien ____ la queue ____ toutes ses forces.
5. Le chien a mordu le garçon ____ la main gauche.
6. La voiture est passée devant la station d'essence ____ toute vitesse.
7. Appuyez ____ fond sur l'accélérateur et allez ____ tout droit, sans virer ni ____ droite ni ____ gauche.
8. Les aristocrates regardaient ____ la rue ____ les fenêtres (were looking at the street out/through the windows). Les révolutionnaires ont lancé des pierres ____ travers les carreaux des fenêtres.
9. Elle jouait un nocturne de Chopin ____ mémoire et ____ la perfection, sans jouer une seule note ____ travers.
10. ____ moyenne, trois mariages ____ cinq (3/5) se terminent ____ divorce.

106. Complete with prepositions and prepositional phrases.

1. Imaginez que vous êtes ____ la place de la Concorde, ____ Paris.
2. Vous vous tenez debout (at the foot of) ____________ l'Obélisque de Louxor, face ____ l'ouest, c'est-à-dire que vous regardez (toward) ____________ l'avenue des Champs-Élysées.
3. (In front of) ____________ vous, (at the end of) ____________ l'avenue des Champs-Élysées, il y a l'Arc de Triomphe, et (beyond) ____________ l'Arc de Triomphe, très loin, vous apercevez l'ensemble de La Défense.
4. (Behind) ____________ vous, il y a le Jardin des Tuileries. (In the middle of) ____________ ce jardin se trouvent l'Arc de Triomphe du Carrousel et la pyramide du Louvre.
5. ____ votre gauche se trouve le Palais Bourbon, siège de la Chambre des Députés, (on the other side of) ____________________ la Seine.
6. ____ votre droite, tout près, vous voyez deux bâtiments symétriques qui datent ____ dix-huitième siècle.
7. (Between) ____________ ces deux bâtiments, (at the end of) ____________ une courte rue, vous voyez les colonnes et le fronton triangulaire de ce qui ressemble ____ un temple romain, l'église de la Madeleine.
8. (Under) ____________ la place de la Concorde, il y a des tunnels pour le métro ainsi que des égouts.
9. ____ été, (above) ____________ tout cela il y a un ciel bleu et un soleil brillant.
10. Et ____________ les rues étroites comme ____________ les grandes avenues, ____________ la place de la Concorde, et surtout (around) ____________ l'Arc de Triomphe, une circulation incessante rend la vie des automobilistes et des piétons pénible et dangereuse.

107. Write the French equivalent, expressing motion from one place to another.

1. I usually walk to class.
2. Sometimes I ride my bike to class.
3. I drive home on weekends.
4. On occasion, I fly home.
5. People rarely cross the Atlantic by boat nowadays.
6. Two years ago, I traveled to Belgium, Germany, Switzerland, and Italy.
7. Last year I traveled to Europe.
8. I flew to Charles de Gaulle.
9. There I boarded a bus for downtown Paris.
10. Then I took a taxi to my hotel.

Conjunctions/prepositions/adverbs

108. Transformation. Replace the underlined part with a conjunctive clause, making all necessary changes.

1. Il pleut sans arrêt depuis notre arrivée.
2. Dès le retour du printemps, les hirondelles s'activent.
3. Pendant la remise des diplômes, les assistants avaient l'air impatients.
4. Il y a souvent de la brume avant le lever du soleil.
5. Vous n'arriverez jamais à temps, à moins de prendre le train de 11h15.

109. Transformation. Replace the underlined part with a prepositional group (preposition + noun + complements), making all necessary changes.

1. Après que les clients furent partis, les serveurs débarrassèrent les tables.
2. Avant que le facteur soit passé, j'avais mis trois lettres dans la boîte.

3. Dès que l'été était venu, on voyait des foules de gens sur le sable de la plage.
___

4. Lorsqu'il y avait des cérémonies religieuses, les femmes entraient à l'église la tête couverte d'un châle ou d'une écharpe.
___

5. Depuis que la petite école était fermée, un autocar conduisait les enfants au collège du canton.
___

110. Combine the two sentences using one of the following conjunctions (some conjunctions may be used more than once): ***alors que***, ***après que***, ***aussitôt que***, ***depuis que***, ***de sorte que***, ***lorsque***, ***parce que***, ***pendant que***, ***tandis que***.

1. Nous ne sommes pas arrivés chez eux à l'heure. Nous avions raté le premier train. (cause)
___
2. Nous avons raté le premier train. Nous ne sommes pas arrivés à l'heure chez eux. (conséquence)
___
3. Mes parents attendaient au café. Le mécanicien réparait le pneu crevé. (simultanéité)
___
4. Les perdants se taisaient. Les vainqueurs chantaient. (simultanéité et contraste)
___
5. Nous, nous avons attendu longtemps. Vous, vous avez été servis tout de suite. (contraste)
___
6. Les assistants se lèvent. Le juge fait son entrée. (temps—simultanéité)
___
7. La veuve porte des vêtements noirs. Son mari est décédé. (temps—séquence)
___
8. Certains sont attristés. D'autres restent indifférents. (simultanéité et contraste)
___
9. Les assistants s'assoient. Le juge s'est assis. (temps—séquence)
___
10. Les enfants sortent en courant. La classe est finie. (temps—immédiateté)
___

111. Combine the two sentences using one of the following conjunctions (each conjunction may be used only once): ***bien que***, ***afin que***, ***avant que***, ***pourvu que***, ***jusqu'à ce que***, ***sans que***, ***de peur que***, ***en attendant que***, ***de façon que***, ***puisque***.

1. Il a encore voulu manger des huîtres. Cependant celles-ci le rendent malade.
___
2. Vous vous lèverez à l'heure. Mais il faut mettre votre réveil en marche.
___
3. Il faudra rester près de votre voiture. La dépanneuse arrivera.
___
4. Essaie d'entrer discrètement. Le concierge ne doit pas t'entendre.
___

5. Téléphone-leur. Ils n'ont peut-être pas reçu le message.
____
6. Allumons une bougie. Ainsi les secouristes auront un repère.
____
7. Si nous nous asseyions à la terrasse? (attendre / le train / arriver)
____
8. Gardez l'œil sur vos bagages. Ainsi personne ne les volera.
____
9. Va vite composter ton billet! Le train va arriver!
____
10. Le contrôleur lui donnera sûrement une amende. Elle n'a pas composté son billet.
____

112. Complete the sentences using ***depuis*** or ***il y a***.

1. Nous sommes ici ____________ dix minutes.
2. ____________ dix minutes que nous sommes ici.
3. Je me suis levé ____________ une demi-heure.
4. Je suis debout ____________ une demi-heure.
5. Ils ont eu un accident ____________ juste cinq minutes.
6. J'étudie ____________ un quart d'heure.
7. ____________ combien de temps êtes-vous là?
8. ____________ deux ans que nous sommes inscrits à la fac.
9. ____________ quand y a-t-il une banque au centre-ville?
10. ____________ trois mois que le semestre est commencé.

113. Give the French equivalent of the following expressions containing the conjunction *as*.

1. As you please! As you will!
____
2. As I was saying . . .
____
3. She works as a waitress.
____
4. As far as I know . . .
____
5. As far as she is concerned . . .
____
6. As the temperature rises, the metal expands.
____
7. As soon as you arrive, we'll begin.
____
8. Stay as long as you want.
____
9. Take as much money as you need.
____

114. Write the adverb that corresponds to the adjective listed.

1. récent ______________
2. sérieux ______________
3. normal ______________
4. franc ______________
5. public ______________
6. constant ______________
7. malheureux ______________
8. premier ______________
9. définitif ______________
10. vrai ______________

115. Write the adverb that corresponds to the adjective listed.

1. complet ______________
2. gentil ______________
3. profond ______________
4. commun ______________
5. puissant ______________
6. poli ______________
7. régulier ______________
8. bref ______________
9. ultérieur ______________
10. abusif ______________

Synonymous expressions

116. In the first blank, write the adjective based on the noun in the expression on the left. Then write the corresponding adverb in the second blank.

Modèle:

avec politesse / d'une manière polie poliment

1. avec profusion / d'une manière ______________ ______________
2. avec audace / d'une manière ______________ ______________
3. avec courage / d'une manière ______________ ______________
4. avec patience / d'une manière ______________ ______________
5. avec fermeté / d'une manière ______________ ______________
6. avec douceur / d'une manière ______________ ______________
7. avec assurance / d'une manière ______________ ______________
8. avec vivacité / d'une manière ______________ ______________
9. avec finesse / d'une manière ______________ ______________
10. avec mollesse / d'une manière ______________ ______________

117. Write the noun that corresponds to each adverb to obtain a synonymous prepositional expression.

Modèle:
doucement avec ____ douceur ____

1. certainement avec ____________
2. lentement avec ____________
3. intelligemment avec ____________
4. souplement avec ____________
5. poliment avec ____________
6. fièrement avec ____________
7. franchement avec ____________
8. fréquemment avec ____________
9. élégamment avec ____________
10. joyeusement avec ____________

118. Complete the following sentences choosing the appropriate adjective to be used as an adverb: ***dur***, ***net***, ***haut***, ***fort***, ***bas***, ***juste***, ***faux***, ***droit***, ***ferme***, ***clair***, ***cher***, ***bon***, ***mauvais***, ***gros***, ***lourd***.

1. Pour réussir, il faut travailler ____________.
2. Cela vous coûtera très ____________.
3. Tout le monde n'a pas la même oreille, certains chantent ____________, d'autres chantent ____________.
4. Ne lâchez pas prise, tenez ____________, même si vous ne voyez pas ____________ dans cet endroit obscur!
5. Surtout ne tournez ni à droite ni à gauche! Si vous n'allez pas tout ____________, vous risquez ____________. Si vous voyez un trou, arrêtez-vous ____________!
6. Je trouve que cette nouvelle eau de toilette ne sent pas ____________, elle sent ____________, même si elle coûte très ____________!
7. Dans une cathédrale immense et sombre, les visiteurs, en général, parlent ____________.
8. Certains qui ne respectent pas le caractère sacré des lieux, parlent ____________, sans vergogne.

119. Complete with ***tout***, ***toute***, ***tous***, or ***toutes***, used as an adverb.

1. Il a plu à verse, Michel et Jacques ont été ____________ mouillés.
2. Il y a eu une averse soudaine, Janine et Françoise ont été ____________ mouillées.
3. Janine et Françoise étaient ____________ heureuses de partir en pique-nique.
4. Elles étaient ____________ impatientes de partir.
5. Elles étaient ____________ joyeuses et chantonnaient ____________ bas.
6. Ces photos sont ____________ autres, ____________ différentes des premières que tu nous avais montrées.

120. Write the adverb or adverbial expression giving the best opposite of the underlined word. If needed, change the affirmative sentence into a negative one.

1. Cet élève arrive toujours en retard.
   ____
2. Mon cousin a peu d'ambition.
   ____
3. Sa sœur va rarement au théâtre.
   ____
4. Certains conducteurs conduisent trop vite.
   ____
5. La préfecture n'est pas loin d'ici.
   ____
6. Suite au scandale de la compagnie, ces actionnaires sont presque ruinés.
   ____
7. Son fils est encore à l'école primaire.
   ____
8. Votre fille s'est très bien conduite en classe de philosophie.
   ____
9. C'est tant mieux pour elle.
   ____
10. Cet article-ci coûte plus cher que celui-là.
    ____
11. Ils nous ont fait garer la voiture devant.
    ____
12. On nous a servi le repas dedans.
    ____
13. Ma fille n'a pas encore son bac.
    ____

Verbs

Verbs in *-ger*, *-cer*, *-yer*

121. Write all the verbs in the present indicative.

1. En général, nous (voyager) ______________ pendant la belle saison.
2. Si nous (commencer) ______________ ce travail maintenant, nous le finirons avant ce soir.
3. Elle (essayer) ______________ toujours de passer la première!
4. Quand ils font la vaisselle ensemble, elle, elle lave, et lui, il (essuyer) ______________.
5. Prenez vos imperméables, l'orage (menacer) ______________.
6. Nous (manger) ______________ au restaurant le week-end.
7. Quand le feu passe au rouge, les voitures s'arrêtent et les piétons (s'avancer) ______________ dans le passage clouté.
8. Est-ce que vous (déménager) ______________?
9. Nous (emménager) ______________ demain dans notre nouvel appartement.
10. Les enfants (s'ennuyer) ______________ s'ils ne regardent pas la télévision.

Verbs in *-er* with stem in *e* or *é* (*appeler, acheter, préférer*)

122. Write all the verbs in the present indicative.

1. Il s' (appeler) ______________ Bond, James Bond.
2. Nous (acheter) ______________ surtout du porc ou du poisson, vous comprenez, à cause de la maladie de la vache folle!
3. Certains automobilistes (jeter) ______________ leurs mégots par la fenêtre.
4. Il (geler) ______________ au-dessous de 32 degrés Farenheit.
5. Est-ce que vous (emmener) ______________ vos petits-enfants à Disney World?
6. Je (préférer) ______________ le café au thé.
7. Nous (espérer) ______________ que vous viendrez nous voir bientôt.
8. Vous êtes bien sûrs que vous n' (exagérer) ______________ pas?
9. L'automobiliste qui arrive à un rond-point (céder) ______________ le passage à ceux qui y sont déjà.
10. Dans un grand restaurant, je (régler) ______________ toujours l'addition par carte bancaire plutôt que par chèque.

Verbs of the second group (*finir*)

123. Write all the verbs in the present indicative.

1. À quelle heure (finir) ______________ -vous de travailler?
2. Nous (choisir) ______________ généralement les marques bien connues.
3. Je (remplir) ______________ mon réservoir d'essence environ une fois par semaine.
4. Est-ce que les hôtels européens (fournir) ______________ aussi du shampooing à leurs clients?
5. À mesure que nous (vieillir) ______________ . . .
6. . . . nos cheveux (blanchir) ______________.
7. Les adolescents timides (rougir) ______________ facilement.
8. Quand on dessine au fusain, on se (noircir) ______________ les doigts.
9. Je (ralentir) ______________ toujours à l'approche d'un carrefour.
10. Les coups de feu (retentir) ______________ violemment dans le secteur de l'offensive.

Verbs of the third group (*répondre*)

124. Write all the verbs in the present indicative.

1. Je ne (répondre) ______________ pas des conséquences!
2. (Entendre) ______________ -vous les cloches de la cathédrale?
3. Nous (attendre) ______________ le départ de notre vol.
4. Elle (descendre) ______________ toujours au même hôtel quand elle vient à Paris.
5. "Cela (dépendre) ______________ des circonstances", répondit-il.
6. Les imprévus me (rendre) ______________ la vie difficile.
7. Beaucoup d'étudiants (vendre) ______________ leurs livres à la fin de l'année.
8. Si tu lui (tendre) ______________ les bras, elle viendra vers toi.
9. La télévision (répandre) ______________ les nouvelles plus vite que le journal.
10. On s'(étendre) ______________ au soleil pour se bronzer.

125. Write the answer using the present imperative (***vous***) and the personal object or indirect object pronouns needed to replace the underlined objects.

1. Monsieur le directeur, est-ce que je téléphone à ce client? (answer: Yes, call him.)
   Oui, ________________________________.
2. Est-ce que nous commençons les expéditions la semaine prochaine?
   Oui, ________________________________.
3. Faut-il que j'écrive à nos fournisseurs?
   Non, ________________________________.
4. Dois-je envoyer ce paquet au président du Comité des Fêtes?
   Non, ________________ ________________.
5. Est-ce que je dois vous rendre ce dossier?
   Oui, ________________________________.

126. Complete with a preposition, if one is needed.

1. Nous étions en train ____________ lire lorsqu'une explosion nous a fait ____________ sursauter.
2. Est-ce que vous allez ____________ vous mettre au travail ou faut-il que je vienne ____________ vous encourager de plus près?
3. Je n'ai plus envie ____________ manger parce que je viens ____________ déjeuner il y a tout juste un quart d'heure.
4. Nous commençons ____________ parler français presque aussi bien que des Français!
5. Est-ce que vous avez décidé ____________ partir en croisière? Est-ce que vous n'aimeriez pas ____________ aller aux Antilles ou au Mexique?
6. Je crois que j'ai oublié ____________ fermer la porte du garage. Peux-tu ____________ vérifier, s'il te plaît?
7. Le professeur s'est mis ____________ parler de géographie. Moi, je déteste entendre ____________ parler de géographie!
8. Je regrette ____________ avoir oublié ____________ vous inviter à la dernière réunion du club.
9. Les membres de la société ont demandé ____________ président ____________ démissionner!
10. Le Président a refusé ____________ capituler. Il a même exigé ____________ être nommé président à vie!

127. Complete the following sentences writing the suggested verbs in the imparfait or the passé composé, as appropriate.

1. Quand nous (vivre) ____________ en Europe, mes parents et moi, nous (aller) ____________ souvent dans des brasseries.
2. À l'âge de dix ans, je (être blessé) ____________ dans un accident de voiture.
3. Si je (être) ____________ libre, j'irais passer un mois à Hawaii.
4. Pendant que nous (attendre) ____________ l'autobus, nous (voir) ____________ un accident de voiture juste devant nous.
5. Je (être) ____________ en train de lire quand je (entendre) ____________ l'annonce de cette catastrophe à la radio.

6. Ils (aller) ______________ embarquer pour une croisière aux Antilles lorsqu'ils (recevoir) ______________ l'annonce de l'annulation du voyage.
7. Nous (venir) ______________ à peine d'arriver à la plage que les enfants (s'amuser) ______________ déjà dans les vagues.
8. Quand vous (faire) ______________ votre voyage à Paris l'été dernier, est-ce que vous (visiter) ______________ le Louvre?
9. Regarde ce type là-bas! Est-ce que ce n'est pas lui qui (gagner) ______________ le Tour de France? Il (faire) ______________ partie de l'équipe qui (représenter) ______________ la Poste des États-Unis.
10. Je (vouloir) ______________ passer mes vacances de printemps aux Bahamas, mais quand je (vouloir) ______________ acheter mon billet d'avion, l'agent de voyage me (dire) ______________ que je (ne pas pouvoir) ______________ y aller sans passeport.

128. Complete the following sentences writing the suggested verbs in the present indicative, future, or future perfect, as appropriate.

1. Demain matin, dès que le réveil (sonner) ______________, il faudra te lever.
2. Si le temps est beau samedi prochain, nous (aller) ______________ à la plage.
3. Quand tu (voir) ______________ le résultat de nos efforts, tu seras satisfait.
4. Vous n'aurez pas votre voiture tant que vous (ne pas payer) ______________ l'amende et les frais de dépannage.
5. Aussitôt que Michel (entrer) ______________, allumez la lumière et chantez "Bon anniversaire"!
6. Après que nous (faire) ______________ la visite du Musée d'Orsay, nous rentrerons à l'hôtel.
7. Ils iront faire du ski dans les Alpes pendant qu'ils (être) ______________ en stage à Lyon.
8. Je me demande si je pourrai parler couramment le français lorsque je (passer) ______________ une année entière à l'université d'Angers.
9. Si tu (faire) ______________ l'effort qu'il faut, tu pourras certainement parler français avec facilité au bout d'un an.
10. Est-ce que tu sauras conduire ta voiture dans Paris quand tu (aller) ______________ là-bas cet été?

129. Write all the verbs in the conditional present.

1. Si j'étais riche, je (acheter) ______________ une belle voiture décapotable.
2. À votre place, je (aller) ______________ en Grèce plutôt qu'en Norvège.
3. Garçon! Nous (vouloir) ______________ une bouteille de Margaux, s'il vous plaît.
4. Si nous étions quatre nous (pouvoir) ______________ jouer au bridge.
5. Moi, je n'ai pas de monnaie. Est-ce que tu en (avoir) ______________, toi, par hasard?
6. Vous n'êtes pas né en France, donc pour apprendre le français, vous (devoir) ______________ parler français tout le temps.
7. Si tu allais à Paris, est-ce que tu me (envoyer) ______________ une carte postale?
8. C'est le moment d'acheter une voiture, tu (faire) ______________ une bonne affaire.
9. Si les conditions étaient bonnes, nous (renouveler) ______________ notre abonnement à votre journal.
10. Est-ce qu'ils (savoir) ______________ se débrouiller tout seuls s'il arrivait une catastrophe?

130. Write all the verbs in the conditional past.

1. Nous (aimer) ______________ passer vous voir!
2. S'il avait pu, il nous (accompagner) ______________.
3. Quelle imprudence! Vous (devoir) ______________ vous renseigner sur les prévisions météorologiques avant de partir en randonnée!
4. Si nous avions eu une carte routière, nous (prendre) ______________ une route plus directe.
5. Mon mari (pouvoir) ______________ vous aider si vous nous aviez appelés.
6. Ils (vouloir) ______________ partir d'Atlanta, mais il n'y avait pas de vol pour Paris ce jour-là.
7. Qu'est-ce que vous (faire) ______________ à notre place?
8. Moi, je (demander) ______________ le remboursement des frais de déménagement.
9. Et toi, est-ce que tu (avoir) ______________ l'audace de faire une réclamation?
10. Je crois que le client (aller) ______________ tout droit dans le bureau du président si on ne lui avait pas donné satisfaction.

131. Write all the verbs in either the imperfect or pluperfect, as appropriate.

1. L'autre jour, le jour de son anniversaire, Columbo n'a pas pu faire démarrer sa voiture parce qu'il (perdre) ______________ sa clé.
2. S'il (pouvoir) ______________ prévoir cela, il aurait pris une clé de rechange.
3. Avant de partir de chez lui ce matin-là, il (avoir) ______________ la mauvaise idée de mettre un imperméable tout neuf.
4. En y réfléchissant, Columbo s'est dit qu'il (devoir) ______________ laisser sa clé dans la poche de son vieil imperméable.
5. L'imperméable neuf était celui que sa femme lui (offrir) ______________ pour son anniversaire.
6. Bien sûr, c'était le vieux qu'il (préférer) ______________.
7. Columbo (sentir) ______________ qu'il aurait fait de la peine à sa femme s'il (ne pas mettre) ______________ le neuf le jour de son anniversaire.
8. Columbo (savoir) ______________ qu'il (devoir) ______________ faire plaisir à sa femme sur ce chapitre ce jour-là.
9. Elle (être) ______________ bien contente que son mari soit si compréhensif, mais elle (se douter) ______________ que l'imperméable ne resterait pas neuf bien longtemps.
10. En effet, le soir même l'imperméable (sentir) ______________ mauvais parce que Columbo (mettre) ______________ les mégots de ses cigares dans ses poches.

132. Write all the verbs in the present subjunctive, present indicative, or future, as appropriate.

1. Nous savons tous que le printemps (venir) ______________ après l'hiver.
2. Il ne faut pas que vous (ouvrir) ______________ vos cadeaux avant que toute la famille (être) ______________ là.
3. Son père veut qu'elle (finir) ______________ ses études avant de se marier.
4. Je crois que le bébé (aller) ______________ déjà mieux. Il a moins de fièvre ce soir que ce matin.
5. J'espère que vous (avoir) ______________ vos passeports et vos billets!

6. Il vaut mieux que je (prendre) ______________ un cachet d'aspirine pour mon mal de tête.
7. Je doute que votre belle-mère (pouvoir) ______________ nous venir en aide.
8. Il est essentiel que tu (remplir) ______________ cette demande de bourse avant la date limite.
9. Nous sommes très heureux que vous (faire) ______________ cette croisière en même temps que nous le mois prochain.
10. Ses parents souhaitent que leur fille (devenir) ______________ avocate.

133. Write all the verbs in the present subjunctive or in the present indicative, as appropriate.

1. Mettez les enfants au lit avant que nous (revenir) ______________ de la réception chez l'ambassadeur.
2. Après que tous les invités (être) ______________ partis, les Dupont vont généralement se coucher sans penser à faire le ménage.
3. Il faut que le chauffeur se repose parce qu'il (être) ______________ trop fatigué pour continuer.
4. Est-ce que vous ne comprenez pas mieux le français depuis que vous (regarder) ______________ des films en version originale?
5. Donnez-lui donc un coup de téléphone de peur qu'il (avoir) ______________ des inquiétudes.
6. Nous prévoyons d'arriver chez vous à 18h à moins que vous (préférer) ______________ que nous arrivions plus tard.
7. Va donc lire le journal pendant que je (faire) ______________ le café.
8. Bien que la vitesse (être) ______________ limitée à 55 miles à l'heure, presque tous les automobilistes font au moins du 70 à l'heure.
9. Avertissez-les afin qu'ils (savoir) ______________ à quoi s'attendre.
10. Même si le vol a du retard, je veux que tu nous attendes à l'aéroport jusqu'à ce que nous (être) ______________ arrivés.

134. Write all the verbs in the subjunctive or in the present or past indicative, as appropriate.

1. Je connais quelqu'un qui (savoir) ______________ distinguer un vin de Bordeaux d'un vin de Bourgogne dès la première gorgée.
2. Il nous faudrait embaucher quelqu'un qui (pouvoir) ______________ s'occuper des commandes et de l'inventaire.
3. Je ne connais personne dont nous (devoir) ______________ nous méfier.
4. Personne ne vous (entendre) ______________. Rien ne (pouvoir) ______________ vous arriver.
5. Le magicien de la tour est le seul qui (pouvoir) ______________ sauver Frodo. Lui seul (pouvoir) ______________ le sauver.
6. Le jambon que nous avons goûté en Espagne est le meilleur que nous (manger) ______________ jamais ______________.
7. Des deux plans présentés, c'est le moins cher que nous (choisir) ______________.
8. C'est la première équipe qui (avoir) ______________ le plus grand nombre de points. C'est donc elle l'équipe gagnante.
9. Ce type est vraiment le dernier auquel je (vouloir) ______________ faire confiance.
10. C'est vraiment le plus grand artiste que je (connaître) ______________.

Histoire de Cunégonde

135. Passé simple. Write the infinitive of the underlined verbs.

. . . Elle reprit (1) ainsi le fil de son histoire. . . . "Le grand inquisiteur m'aperçut (2) un jour à la messe; il me lorgna (3) beaucoup, et me fit (4) dire qu'il avait à me parler pour des affaires secrètes. Je fus (5) conduite à son palais; je lui appris (6) ma naissance; il me représenta combien il était au-dessous de mon rang d'appartenir à un israélite. On proposa de sa part à don Issachar de me céder à Monseigneur. Don Issachar, qui est banquier de la cour, et homme de crédit, n'en voulut (7) rien faire. L'inquisiteur le menaça (8) d'un auto-da-fé. Enfin mon juif, intimidé, conclut (9) un marché par lequel la maison et moi leur appartiendraient (10) à tous deux en commun; . . ."

1. ______________
2. ______________
3. ______________
4. ______________
5. ______________
6. ______________
7. ______________
8. ______________
9. ______________
10. ______________

136. Transformation. Replace the underlined conjunctive clause with ***en*** and the present participle of its verb.

1. Il s'est cassé le bras quand il est tombé dans l'escalier.
   ____
2. Si tu réfléchis un moment, tu trouveras la solution du problème.
   ____
3. Nous nous sommes trompés de métro parce que nous avons essayé d'aller trop vite.
   ____
4. Il s'est senti soulagé quand il a avoué sa faute.
   ____
5. J'ai fait un faux pas au moment où j'ai sauté de l'escalier roulant.
   ____
6. S'ils refusent de payer le supplément, ils vont s'attirer de gros ennuis.
   ____
7. Lorsque nous sommes arrivés, nous avons trouvé l'appartement vide et sale.
   ____
8. Souvent les étudiants revisent leurs notes de cours et regardent la télévision en même temps.
   ____
9. Aussitôt qu'elle est entrée, elle s'est trouvée devant un groupe d'employés mécontents.
   ____
10. C'est parce qu'ils ont refusé de céder que les employés ont obtenu leurs revendications.
    ____

Answer Key

Note: Underscore lines indicate that no entry is to be made. Letters or words in parentheses indicate optional correct answers (by choice of alternate gender, number, article, and so forth).

1. 1. l'homme 2. la honte 3. le héros 4. la hâte 5. l'hégémonie 6. l'hôtel 7. le hussard 8. l'héroïne 9. le hasard 10. l'hiver

2. 1. l'hexagone 2. l'humidité 3. l'hermitage 4. la hideur 5. l'hôpital 6. le huit de carreau 7. le onze novembre 8. le un et le deux 9. la hache 10. la hauteur

3. 1. la, du 2. La, la 3. ___, ___, des 4. les, du 5. Les, l', la, le, l' 6. L', une 7. d'un 8. l' 9. Les, la 10. la, l', la, l'

4. 1. L', l', des 2. Le, un, l' 3. L', un 4. L', le 5. la (une), une 6. l', l' 7. ___, ___, d' 8. La, la, des 9. La, l', les 10. Le, le, des, du 11. L', l', le, l', des, des

5. 1. la, du, la 2. le, du 3. la, des 4. de 5. De (Les), la, la 6. de 7. d', ___ 8. De 9. Des, de, des, ___, les 10. La, des, le, le, au

6. 1. la, le, la 2. Le, ___, le, ___ 3. de 4. le, le 5. ___, du 6. La 7. de, de 8. Le, le, de la 9. le, ___, au, d' 10. du, de 11. de 12. de, de l' 13. la, du 14. du, de 15. un

7. 1. ___ 2. ___ 3. les, ___ 4. ___, l' 5. ___, ___, la 6. ___, ___ 7. Au 8. Les, les 9. l', les, des 10. Les, la, l', l', le 11. l', Le 12. La, La 13. les, ___ 14. les, le 15. Les 16. ___, la, la

8. 1. une, une 2. les 3. la (une), la (une), la (une) 4. le, de la (d'une) 5. des 6. la, du, ___ 7. Le (Un), le (un) 8. un

9. 1. les, les, le 2. Ses, ses, son 3. les, des 4. Ses, des 5. le (un), la, les, les. 6. Son, sa 7. Ses, ses 8. les 9. la 10. le, la, son 11. La (Sa), son 12. Le, aux, son 13. les 14. vos

10. 1. vos 2. les (vos) 3. Vos 4. les, les 5. la, la

11. 1. ___, une (de la), la 2. La 3. la 4. ___ 5. un, le, l', le, la 6. de l' 7. le 8. à l' 9. La, la, l', la

12. 1. ___, ___ 2. le, d'un 3. le, du 4. les 5. aux, ___ 6. ___ 7. les, le 8. la, ___, un 9. ___ 10. le, le, ___, d', ___ 11. ___, ___, ___, ___ 12. le, du 13. ___ 14. le, ___, la 15. le

13. 1. un 2. une 3. une 4. un 5. un 6. un 7. un 8. un 9. une 10. une 11. une 12. un 13. une 14. un 15. une 16. un 17. une 18. un 19. une 20. une 21. un 22. un 23. une 24. un 25. un 26. une

14. 1. une 2. une 3. un 4. une 5. une 6. un 7. une 8. une 9. une 10. un 11. un 12. un 13. un 14. un(e) 15. une 16. un 17. une 18. une 19. un 20. un 21. un 22. un 23. une 24. un

15. 1. tous les jours, tous les matins, tous les après-midi, tous les soirs, tous les ans 2. toute la journée, toute la matinée, tout(e) l'après-midi, toute la soirée, toute l'année 3. toute une journée, toute une matinée, toute un(e) après-midi, toute une soirée, toute une année 4. une journée entière, une matinée entière, un(e) après-midi entier(entière), une soirée entière, une année entière

16. 1. poissons rouges 2. fruits 3. meubles 4. les cheveux 5. les poils 6. la physique 7. milliers 8. les frais 9. des affaires 10. des nouvelles

17. 1. funérailles 2. alentours 3. fiançailles 4. menottes 5. mœurs 6. pourparlers 7. décombres 8. arrhes 9. vivres 10. dépens

18. 1. nos aïeux 2. ces bonshommes 3. mesdames 4. mesdemoiselles 5. mes yeux 6. vos chevaux 7. les canaux 8. les maux 9. des malheurs 10. des ciseaux

19. 1. les carnavals 2. des récitals 3. des émaux 4. les genoux 5. des travaux 6. des cailloux 7. les vitraux 8. des pneus 9. des choux 10. des bijoux

20. 1. mes grands-pères 2. des chefs-d'œuvre 3. des passeports 4. les gratte-ciel 5. des beaux-fils 6. des belles-mères 7. des camions-citernes

21. 1. est arrivée 2. agents/policiers 3. a administré 4. a conduit 5. des gens 6. a regardé 7. s'est établie 8. a affirmé 9. s'est voté 10. a refusé 11. ont quitté 12. sont venus 13. est allée, ses

22. 1. la main 2. l'œil 3. la main 4. le, la 5. la main 6. leur livre 7. votre devoir 8. leur bulletin

23. 1. heureuse 2. favorite 3. chère 4. moyenne 5. nulle 6. jalouse 7. douce 8. gentille 9. neuve 10. active 11. finale 12. publique 13. nette 14. blanche 15. fraîche 16. fameuse 17. rousse 18. grecque 19. brève 20. jolie

24. 1. sec 2. vieux 3. léger 4. gros 5. bleu 6. bénin 7. italien 8. tragique 9. mou 10. discret 11. dernier 12. gris 13. long 14. faux 15. marocain 16. muet

25. 1. bleus 2. jaloux 3. finals 4. nouveaux 5. meilleurs 6. marron 7. ci-joints* 8. fous 9. fatals 10. blancs 11. neufs 12. seuls 13. nus 14. bleu-ciel

26. 1. la marée basse 2. une haute montagne 3. la grande route 4. un mauvais conseil 5. une bonne idée 6. le nouveau locataire 7. le vin nouveau 8. une brave dame 9. un certain temps 10. un jour maigre

27. 1. Pauvre type! 2. une école publique 3. le produit national 4. une maison neuve 5. un été sec 6. un joyeux luron 7. la semaine dernière 8. le dernier mois de l'année 9. un meilleur résultat 10. une mort certaine

28. 1. une classe (un cours) de physique 2. un mur de (en) brique 3. une voiture de sport 4. une histoire d'amour 5. un collier de perles 6. une carte d'identité 7. une table de (en) chêne 8. une chaîne d'or (en or) 9. une ceinture de (en) cuir 10. une épingle de sûreté

29. 1. une carte routière 2. un cheval de course 3. un hippodrome 4. un congé (les vacances) de printemps 5. un timbre-poste 6. un rat de bibliothèque 7. une année bissextile 8. une épingle à linge 9. un verre à vin 10. un couteau à pain 11. un sac de farine à pain

30. 1. le grand-père 2. les grands-pères 3. la grand-mère 4. les grands-mères 5. les grands-parents 6. la grand-route 7. les grand-routes 8. grand-chose

31. 1. plus précieux que le plomb 2. moins rapide qu'un avion 3. aussi valable qu'un Renoir 4. plus grincheux que le père de Dennis 5. moins horrible qu'Attila 6. aussi vénérable que Rome 7. aussi rapide qu'une voiture de course

32. 1. la montagne la plus élevée du monde 2. la meilleure de toutes 3. la meilleure marque de toutes 4. la plus célèbre de toutes 5. la marque la plus célèbre de toutes 6. la moins chère du magasin 7. la marque la moins chère du magasin

33. 1. cette 2. cette année-là 3. ce 4. ce soir-là 5. cette 6. cette semaine-là 7. cet 8. cet automne-là 9. cet 10. cet hiver-là

34. 1. ces jours-ci 2. ces jours-là 3. ce mois-là 4. ce mois-ci 5. ce jour-là 6. en ce temps-là 7. cette nuit 8. cette nuit-là 9. ce matin 10. ce matin-là

35. 1. cette 2. cette 3. cet 4. cet, ce 5. cet, cet 6. cette, cet 7. cet 8. ce 9. ce 10. cet 11. ces 12. cette 13. ces 14. ces 15. cet 16. ce 17. cette

36. 1. ceux-là 2. celle-là 3. celles-ci 4. celui-ci, celui-là, celui 5. ceux 6. Ceux, celles 7. celui 8. celle

37. 1. celle de sa mère 2. celui de Tiger Woods 3. celle de la Chine 4. celle de Roméo et Juliette 5. celui de Juliette est Roméo 6. celle-ci, celle-là

38. 1. Ça (Cela) 2. Ce 3. ce, ça (cela) 4. Ce, c' 5. Ce 6. C', ça (cela) 7. Ça 8. ça (cela) 9. ce

39. 1. C' 2. Ce (Ça) 3. C' 4. c' 5. Ça 6. cela 7. Cela (Ça) (Ce) 8. Ça, c' 9. C', celui-là

*only if noun precedes

40. 1. ne fait rien 2. ne va nulle part 3. n'invite personne 4. n'a aucun ami 5. n'est ni riche ni belle 6. ne parle qu' 7. ne fais rien 8. personne n'a téléphoné 9. n'ai aucun projet pour les vacances 10. rien ne pourra me faire changer d'avis

41. 1. Je n'ai vu personne. 2. Je n'ai rien compris. 3. Elle n'est allée nulle part. 4. Nous n'avons compris ni la langue ni l'accent. 5. Ils ne sont allés ni au Louvre ni à Notre-Dame. 6. Rien ne m'a surpris(e). 7. Personne ne nous a compris. 8. Nous n'avons compris personne. 9. Vous n'avez rien compris. 10. Elles n'ont eu aucune occasion de se distraire.

42. 1. quelqu'un, quelques, des (quelques) 2. quelque part, ailleurs 3. rien, personne 4. aucune, certains (quelques) 5. quelques, quelques 6. Certains, d'autres 7. quelconque

43. 1. de chaud 2. de grave 3. de dangereux 4. de si laid 5. de moins chers

44. 1. quelque chose 2. quelqu'un 3. Certains, d'autres 4. les uns, les autres 5. les uns les autres 6. quelqu'un (on) 7. l'une ou l'autre 8. quelqu'un (l'un)

45. 1. n'importe quoi 2. n'importe qui 3. n'importe où 4. n'importe où (n'importe comment) (n'importe quand) 5. n'importe comment 6. n'importe quelle 7. n'importe laquelle (lesquelles)

46. 1.Chacun 2. Chacun 3. Chacune 4. Aucune 5. quelqu'un 6. Quelques-uns 7. Quelques-unes 8. aucune 9. chacun 10. Quelques-uns

47. 1. tous 2. Toute 3. Tous 4. Toute 5. toute, tout 6. Tous, Toute 7. Tous 8. tous, toute 9. tous 10. toute

48. 1. tout 2. tous 3. tout 4. tout 5. tout 6. toute, tout 7. toute

49. 1. Quel est votre nom? 2. Quel âge avez-vous? 3. Quelle est votre profession (occupation)? (Quel est votre métier?) 4. Quelle est votre adresse? 5. Quel est votre numéro de téléphone?

50. 1. Quelles femmes est-ce que vous préférez? 2. Quelle boisson est-ce que vous préférez? 3. Quelle voiture est-ce que vous conduisez? 4. Quelles missions est-ce qu'on vous donne? 5. Quel(s) danger(s) est-ce que vous courez?

51. 1a. (inversion) À quelle(s) heure(s) l'Angélus sonnait-il autrefois? 1b. À quelle(s) heure(s) est-ce que l'Angélus sonnait autrefois? 2a. (inversion) Dans quels pays mange-t-on du couscous? 2b. Dans quels pays est-ce qu'on mange du couscous? 3a. (inversion) Sur quels fleuves les grandes péniches circulent-elles? 3b. Sur quels fleuves est-ce que les grandes péniches circulent? 4a. (inversion) Avec quelles viandes sert-on du vin rouge? 4b. Avec quelles viandes est-ce qu'on sert du vin rouge? 5a. (inversion) Pour quelles occasions réserve-t-on le champagne? 5b. Pour quelles occasions est-ce qu'on réserve le champagne?

52. 1. Qui a composé cette musique? (Qui est-ce qui a composé cette musique?) 2. Qui a peint ce portrait? (Qui est-ce qui a peint ce portrait?) 3. Qui a peint ces longs cous? (Qui est-ce qui a peint ces longs cous?) 4. Qui a photographié tous ces grands hommes? (Qui est-ce qui a photographié tous ces grands hommes?) 5. Qui a écrit l'essai "J'accuse"? (Qui est-ce qui a écrit l'essai "J'accuse"?)

53. 1. Qu'est-ce que Picasso a peint? 2. Qu'est-ce que Léonard de Vinci a fait? 3. Qu'est-ce que Ravel a composé? 4. Qu'est-ce que Michel-Ange a sculpté? 5. Qu'est-ce que Ieoh Ming Pei a construit?

54. 1. Que font les Beatles? 2. Que fait le président? 3. Que dit la météo? 4. Que veut le peuple? 5. Que peuvent les médecins?

55. 1a. Avec quoi as-tu fait ces sculptures? b. Avec quoi est-ce que tu as fait ces sculptures? 2a. Sur quoi placez-vous les lingots? b. Sur quoi est-ce que vous placez les lingots? 3a. Dans quoi sont rangés les dossiers? (Dans quoi les dossiers sont-ils rangés?) b. Dans quoi est-ce que les dossiers sont rangés? 4a. Derrière quoi cachent-ils leur coffre-fort? b. Derrière quoi est-ce qu'ils cachent leur coffre-fort? 5a. Grâce à quoi votre fille peut-elle faire des études supérieures? b. Grâce à quoi est-ce que votre fille peut faire des études supérieures?

56. 1. Où est-il né? 2. Quand est-il né? 3. Combien de langues parle-t-il? 4. Depuis combien de temps (Depuis quand) est-il en Floride? 5. Depuis quand (Depuis combien de temps) est-il étudiant? 6. Comment travaille-t-il? 7. Pourquoi est-il en Floride? 8. Combien de temps pense-t-il rester en Floride?

57. 1a. Où Napoléon est-il né? b. Où est-ce que Napoléon est né? 2a. Quand la première croisade a-t-elle eu lieu? b. Quand est-ce que la première croisade a eu lieu? 3a. Pourquoi Charlemagne est-il allé en Espagne? b. Pourquoi est-ce que Charlemagne est allé en Espagne? 4a. Comment les Anglais ont-ils fait mourir Jeanne d'Arc? Comment est-ce que les Anglais ont fait mourir Jeanne d'Arc? 5a. Combien d'heures par semaine les employés français travaillent-ils? b. Combien d'heures par semaine est-ce que les employés français travaillent?

58. 1. Son, sa 2. Ses, leurs 3. Mes, ma 4. Mon, mon 5. Son, sa 6. Son 7. Son 8. Sa 9. Leurs, leurs 10. Notre, sa 11. notre, son, ses, sa, sa, son, son

59. 1. Son, la tienne 2. Son, la mienne 3. Son, la tienne 4. Leur, La leur 5. Sa, La sienne 6. Ta, La tienne 7. Notre, Le nôtre 8. Mon, Le mien 9. Votre, le vôtre 10. mes, les tiens 11. ta, la mienne 12. ta, la mienne 13. ton, du mien 14. tes, des miens 15. tes, aux miennes

60. 1. Est-ce que cela vous dérange que je parte de bonne heure? (Ça vous dérange que je parte tôt?) 2. Ça ne sert (servira) à rien que tu te plaignes (vous vous plaigniez). 3. Les Français se serrent la main quand ils se saluent. 4. Les Françaises se donnent un, deux ou trois baisers sur la joue (les joues). (Les Françaises s'embrassent une, deux ou trois fois sur les joues.) 5. Chaque pays a ses coutumes. 6. Nous avons chacun(e) nos préférences. 7. Lave-toi les mains avant de manger ton sandwich, Michel! 8. Ouvrez la bouche, tirez la langue, dites "AAH"!

61. 1. Oui, je les attends (nous les attendons). 2. Je la regarde le soir. 3. Oui, je le connais. 4. Oui, je les cherche. 5. Non, je ne les aime pas (je les déteste).

62. 1. Non, il ne peut pas les prêter. 2. Oui, je vais le voir ce soir. 3. Nous allons les voir presque tous les week-ends. 4. Non, je ne veux pas les manger. 5. Il faut les réveiller à six heures et demie.

63. 1. Oui, il m'a invitée. 2. Oui, je les ai expédiées ce matin. 3. Je les ai mises dans un vase, Madame. 4. C'est moi qui les ai prises. 5. Non, merci, je les ai déjà lus.

64. 1. Oui, je lui téléphone de temps en temps. 2. Je leur demande de l'argent. 3. Ils me répondent que je dépense trop. 4. Je lui écris une ou deux fois par an. 5. Bien sûr, je leur rends toujours les choses qu'ils me prêtent.

65. 1. C'est Michel qui va lui donner à manger. 2. Oui, je veux bien leur donner un coup de main. 3. Oui, j'ai besoin de lui parler tout de suite. 4. Tu devras lui rendre la bicyclette ce soir. 5. Oui, il faudrait peut-être leur téléphoner.

66. 1. Non, elle ne leur a pas envoyé de message. 2. Oui, elle lui a parlé. 3. Elle lui a écrit hier. 4. Oui, je lui ai donné mon dossier il y a cinq minutes. 5. C'est la secrétaire qui leur a répondu.

67. 1. J'en bois (une, deux, trois . . .) fois par jour. 2. Oui, j'en mange régulièrement. 3. Normalement, j'en prends trois (deux, quatre, etc.). 4. Non, je n'en consomme jamais. 5. Oui, j'en prends parfois.

68. 1. Oui, je vais en commander. 2. Oui, je crois que tu devrais en prendre. 3. Oui, on peut en boire un verre. 4. Je crois qu'il faudra en laisser un. 5. Non, je ne veux pas en prendre.

69. 1. Oui, j'en ai acheté six tranches. 2. J'en ai pris trois. 3. Oui, j'en ai pris deux. 4. Oui, j'en ai commandé trois kilos. 5. Non, je n'en ai pas acheté parce qu'il n'y en avait plus.

70. 1. J'y vais à 21h. 2. Oui, j'y pense parfois. 3. Oui, j'y suis. 4. Non, il ne s'y intéresse pas du tout. 5. Ils s'y rendront en taxi.

71. 1. Bien sûr qu'il faut s'y arrêter! 2. Oui, je veux bien y aller avec toi. 3. D'accord, je veux bien y aller. (D'accord, j'y vais.) 4. D'accord, j'accepte de les y conduire. (D'accord, j'accepte d'y conduire les invités.) 5. Je ne peux pas vous y attendre plus de dix minutes.

72. 1. Nous y sommes allés il y a un an. 2. Nous y sommes arrivés par l'Espagne. 3. Nous y sommes restés deux semaines. 4. Nous n'y avons visité que Venise. 5. Nous n'y sommes pas allés.

73. 1. ne le dérangez pas (ne le dérange pas) 2. ne vous inquiétez pas (ne t'inquiète pas) 3. ne vous asseyez pas (ne t'assieds pas) (ne t'assois pas) 4. Ne rappelez pas (ne rappelle pas) 5. ne les réveillez pas (ne les réveille pas)

74. 1. Emballez-les bien, il me faut un paquet-cadeau. 2. Donnez-le à mon mari. 3. Donnez-lui le paquet. 4. La voici. 5. Montrez-lui les chemises d'homme. 6. Essayez-la. 7. Prenez-en donc! 8. Allons-y tout de suite pour avoir de bonnes places. 9. Je vous conseille d'y penser! 10. Dites-leur d'arriver assez tôt à la soirée.

75. 1. . . . réveille-moi! 2. . . . débrouille-toi! 3. . . . asseyez-vous (assoyez-vous)! 4. Écoutez-moi . . . 5. . . . présente-moi!

76. 1. — Combien en voulez-vous? — Donnez-m'en 500 grammes. 2. — Veux-tu que je t'en prête? 3. — Non, je ne m'en souviens pas. 4. Je crois bien qu'il s'en moque. 5. Mais est-ce que vous vous en rendez compte?

77. 1. Ils nous l'ont offert. 2. Je m'en souviendrai toujours. 3. Les voisins l'y ont mis. 4. Leur fils l'en a sorti. 5. Je l'y ai vu ce matin.

78. 1. Le président va les y recevoir demain. 2. Nous voudrions leur en offrir pour Noël. 3. Il faut lui en donner quelques-uns. 4. Les sénateurs pourraient peut-être s'en passer cette année! 5. Les Dupont ont envie de nous les emprunter.

79. 1. Nous vous en avons réservé deux à l'orchestre pour *Rigoletto*. 2. Quand je suis revenu d'Europe, le douanier me les a tous fouillés. 3. En arrivant, les invités leur en ont offert. 4. Les visiteurs le lui ont demandé. 5. Mais qui donc le lui a donné?

80. 1. Ne vous en allez pas! 2. Ne lui en donnez pas! 3. Ne les leur apportez pas! 4. Ne nous les achetez pas! 5. Ne me l'expliquez pas.

81. 1. Oui, donne-le-leur. 2. Oui, sers-lui-en. 3. Oui, emmène-les-y. 4. Oui, montre-la-moi. 5. Oui, prête-le-lui.

82. 1. J'y arriverai bien. 2. Nous leur enverrons aussi des invitations. 3. J'y renonce. 4. Je leur ai envoyé un faire-part. 5. J'y tiens, ne le perds pas!

83. 1. Je m'y suis enfin adapté. 2. Mais j'ai eu du mal à m'habituer à eux. 3. Et toi, est-ce que tu y as réussi? 4. Nous y pensons souvent. 5. Est-ce qu'il vous arrive de penser à eux? 6. Dis chérie, on dirait que notre voisine s'y intéresse beaucoup. 7. Moi, je crois que tu t'intéresses un peu trop à elle!

84. 1.Vous en rendez-vous compte? — Oui, je m'en rends compte. 2. En êtes-vous certain? — Non, je n'en suis pas certain. 3. N'en avez-vous pas peur? — Si, nous en avons (bien) peur! 4. S'en souviennent-ils? — Oui, ils s'en souviennent. 5. Ne s'en soucie-t-elle pas un peu? — Non, elle ne s'en soucie pas le moins du monde.

85. 1. Oui, je le regrette. 2. Oui, je le sais. (Oui, nous le savons.) 3. Oui, ils le croient! 4. Oui, je me le demande! 5. Oui, il l'est (vraiment).

86. 1. en voici (en voilà) 2. le voici (le voilà) 3. en voici (en voilà) 4. les voici (les voilà) 5. Me voici. (Me voilà.)

87. 1. Marie lit un roman qu'elle a acheté hier. 2. Marie est en train de lire un roman qui a reçu le prix Goncourt. 3. Je préparerai un dessert que tout le monde aimera. 4. Le Languedoc est une région qui produit beaucoup de vin. 5. La Mustang était une belle voiture décapotable que tout le monde voulait conduire. 6. Neil Armstrong est un astronaute qui a marché sur la lune. 7. Rends-moi le livre que je t'ai prêté. 8. Je suis arrivé dans un village tranquille qui avait l'air abandonné.

88. 1. Cette photo, qui paraît récente, est en réalité très vieille. 2. L'acteur qui jouait le rôle du capitaine dans ce film vient de mourir. 3. Le café que vous m'avez servi n'est pas chaud. 4. Le dernier film que Robert Redford a mis en scène est un succès. 5. Ce personnage, qui a l'air inoffensif, détruit tout autour de lui. 6. Le livre que Marie est en train de lire m'intéresse.

89. 1. Marie est en train de lire, ce qui me surprend. 2. Vous avez raison, ce que je dois admettre. 3. Ils ont encore oublié d'apporter l'addition, ce qui commence à m'énerver. 4. Vous avez pris deux boissons, ce qui vous coûtera 26,50 Euros. 5. Elle n'a pas apporté sa carte de crédit, ce qu'elle regrette vivement. 6. Les autres sont partis après nous et sont arrivées avant, ce qui m'étonne.

90. 1. qui 2. que 3. qui 4. qui 5. que 6. que 7. que 8. qui 9. qu' 10. qui 11. qu' 12. qui

91. 1. C'est un célèbre metteur en scène dont les films ont toujours du succès. 2. L'actrice est une jeune femme dont le cousin est Cyrano. 3. Le colonel commande un régiment dont tous les soldats sont gascons. 4. L'actrice est une jeune "précieuse" dont Cyrano est amoureux. 5. La "précieuse" dont Christian tombe amoureux s'appelle Roxane.

92. 1. On leur apporte du pâté et du poulet, avec lesquels ils boivent du vin de Bordeaux. 2. Les Gascons ont construit des barricades derrière lesquelles ils se sont défendus. 3. Le colonel portait une écharpe à cause de laquelle l'ennemi aurait pu le reconnaître. 4. Cyrano est passé sous un échafaudage du haut duquel une poutre est tombée.

93. 1. de Chartres, à Paris 2. d'Espagne, du Portugal, des Pays-Bas, d'Italie, d'Allemagne, du Danemark, des États-Unis 3. à Reims, à Strasbourg, à Lyon 4. en été 5. en automne, en hiver, au printemps 6. du Texas 7. du Japon, de Corée 8. du Canada, du Mexique, du Kenya, du Maroc 9. en Belgique, au Luxembourg, en Suisse, en Italie, à Monaco, en Espagne 10. en Arizona (dans l'Arizona), en Caroline du Nord et du Sud, en Floride, au Québec (dans le Québec), dans l'Ontario (en Ontario), dans l'état de New-York

94. 1. à 2. de 3. de 4. __ 5. de 6. de 7. d' 8. __ , de 9. à 10. __, __

95. 1. de 2. __ 3. __ 4. __, __ 5. __ 6. de 7. __ 8. à 9. à, de 10. de, __

96. 1. d' 2. d' 3. d' 4. d' 5. à 6. à 7. à 8. à 9. de 10. à

97. 1. Le, l' 2. le 3. Le, le 4. __, le 5. du, au 6. Les, des, les 7. Le, le, le, le, le, le 8. le (un), le 9. le, le 10. Le, Le, le

98. 1. depuis 2. pour, dans 3. Il y a (Voilà), (Ça fait) 4. en 5. Depuis quand (Depuis combien de temps) 6. Pendant 7. Il y a (Voilà) 8. pour 9. depuis combien de temps (depuis quand) 10. Il y a (Voilà), (Ça fait) (fam.)

99. 1. En Europe, en brique, en pierre, en bois 2. en ciment, en blanc 3. __ (au) 4. En effet, au-dessus de 5. d'ardoise (en ardoise), dans la moitié nord 6. Dans le sud (Au sud), de tuiles (en tuiles) 7. en usage 8. à la mode, aux États-Unis, de métal (en métal) 9. dans le Midi, à l'ombre 10. En quoi, à n'importe quel

100. 1. à 2. de 3. de 4. à 5. de, de 6. d' 7. d' 8. à 9. d' 10. d'

101. 1. de, __ 2. à 3. à 4. de 5. qu'à 6. pour, __ 7. pour, de 8.__ , à 9. de 10. de, à

102. 1. de la 2. au volley-ball, au basket 3. de 4. à 5. de, à 6. à 7. à 8. aux 9. __ 10. __ 11. __ 12. __, __ 13. dans 14. de 15. __ 16. à 17. à, de

103. 1. pendant 2. pendant que 3. parce qu' 4. à cause de 5. sans 6. sans que 7. pour 8. pour que 9. avant d' 10. avant qu'

104. 1. aller quelque part à pied, à cheval, en voiture, en taxi, en avion (par avion), en bateau (par bateau), à bicyclette (coll: en bicyclette, en vélo), à moto (coll: en moto). 2. par 3. en, en, en 4. à la maison, au restaurant, au cinéma 5. À gauche, à droite, Au centre, au fond, à l'arrière (en arrière) 6. À, À, à l' 7. en grève, En moyenne, par an 8. Vous n'avez pas de chance 9. par dessus, pour 10. Du, au, le (pendant le)

105. 1. à, à, de 2. À, à 3. en, au, à 4. à, par, de 5. à 6. à 7. à, ___, à, à 8. dans, par, à 9. de, à, de 10. En, sur, en (par un) (par le)

106. 1. sur, à 2. au pied de, à, vers 3. Devant (En face de), au bout de, au-delà de 4. Derrière, Au milieu de 5. À (Sur), de l'autre côté de (sur l'autre rive de) 6. À (Sur), du 7. Entre, au bout d' (au fond d'), à 8. Sous (Au-dessous de) 9. En (Pendant l') (Durant l'), au-dessus de 10. dans, sur, sur, autour de

107. 1. D'habitude je vais en classe (au cours) à pied. 2. Parfois (Quelquefois) je vais au cours (en classe) à vélo (à bicyclette). 3. Le week-end je rentre (vais) chez moi (à la maison) en voiture. 4. De temps en temps, je prends l'avion pour rentrer chez moi (Je rentre chez moi en avion). 5. Peu de gens traversent l'Atlantique en bateau (par bateau) de nos jours. 6. Il y a deux ans, je suis allé (j'ai fait un voyage) en Belgique, en Allemagne, en Suisse et en Italie. 7. L'année dernière (L'an dernier, L'an passé, L'année passée), j'ai fait un voyage (je suis allé[e]) en Europe. 8. J'ai pris l'avion jusqu'à Roissy-Charles de Gaulle. 9. Là, je suis monté dans (j'ai pris) un autobus pour aller au centre de Paris. 10. Ensuite j'ai pris un taxi pour aller à mon hôtel.

108. 1. depuis que nous sommes arrivé(e)s. 2. Dès que le printemps est revenu (revient), 3. Pendant qu'on remettait les diplômes, 4. avant que le soleil se lève. 5. à moins que vous (ne) preniez le train de 11h15.

109. 1. Après le départ des clients . . . 2. Avant le passage du facteur . . . 3. Dès la venue de l'été . . . 4. Lors des cérémonies religieuses . . . 5. Depuis la fermeture de la petite école . . .

110. 1. Nous ne sommes pas arrivés chez eux à l'heure parce que nous avions raté le premier train. 2. Nous avons raté le premier train de sorte que nous ne sommes pas arrivés chez eux à l'heure. 3. Mes parents attendaient au café pendant que le mécanicien réparait le pneu crevé. 4. Les perdants se taisaient tandis que (alors que) les vainqueurs chantaient. 5. Nous, nous avons attendu longtemps alors que (tandis que) vous, vous avez été servis tout de suite. 6. Les assistants se lèvent lorsque le juge fait son entrée. 7. La veuve porte des vêtements noirs depuis que son mari est décédé. 8. Certains sont attristés alors que (tandis que) d'autres restent indifférents. 9. Les assistants s'assoient une fois que (après que) (lorsque) le juge s'est assis. 10. Les enfants sortent en courant aussitôt que la classe est finie.

111. 1. Il a encore voulu manger des huîtres bien que celles-ci le rendent malade. 2. Vous vous lèverez à l'heure pourvu que vous mettiez votre réveil en marche. 3. Il faudra rester près de votre voiture jusqu'à ce que la dépanneuse arrive. 4. Essaie d'entrer discrètement sans que le concierge t'entende. 5. Téléphone-leur de peur qu'ils n'aient pas reçu le message. 6. Allumons une bougie de façon que les secouristes aient un repère. 7. Si nous nous asseyions à la terrasse en attendant que le train arrive? 8. Gardez l'œil sur vos bagages afin que personne ne les vole. 9. Va vite composter ton billet avant que le train (n') arrive. 10. Le contrôleur lui donnera sûrement une amende puisqu'elle n'a pas composté son billet.

112. 1. depuis 2. Il y a 3. il y a 4. depuis 5. il y a 6. depuis 7. Depuis 8. Il y a 9. Depuis 10. Il y a

113. 1. Comme il vous plaira! Comme vous voudrez! 2. Comme je (le) disais . . . 3. Elle travaille comme serveuse. 4. Pour autant que je sache . . . 5. En ce qui la concerne . . . 6. À mesure que la température monte, le métal se dilate. 7. Aussitôt que (Dès que) vous arriverez, nous commencerons. 8. Restez aussi longtemps que vous (le) voudrez. 9. Prenez autant d'argent qu'il vous faut.

114. 1. récemment 2. sérieusement 3. normalement 4. franchement 5. publiquement 6. constamment 7. malheureusement 8. premièrement 9. définitivement 10. vraiment

115. 1. complètement 2. gentiment 3. profondément 4. communément 5. puissamment 6. poliment 7. régulièrement 8. brièvement 9. ultérieurement 10. abusivement

116. 1. profuse, profusément 2. audacieuse, audacieusement 3. courageuse, courageusement 4. patiente, patiemment 5. ferme, fermement 6. douce, doucement 7. assurée, assurément 8. vive (vivace), vivement 9. fine, finement 10. molle, mollement

117. 1. certitude 2. lenteur 3. intelligence 4. souplesse 5. politesse 6. fierté 7. franchise 8. fréquence 9. élégance 10. joie

118. 1. dur 2. cher 3. faux, juste 4. ferme, clair 5. droit, gros (lourd), net 6. bon, mauvais, cher 7. bas 8. haut (fort)

119. 1. tout 2. toutes 3. tout 4. tout 5. toutes, tout 6. tout, toutes

120. 1. Cet élève n'arrive jamais en retard. 2. Mon cousin a beaucoup d'ambition. 3. Sa sœur va souvent au théâtre. 4. Certains conducteurs conduisent trop lentement. 5. La préfecture est près d'ici. 6. Suite au scandale de la compagnie, ces actionnaires sont complètement (tout à fait, totalement) ruinés. 7. Son fils n'est plus à l'école primaire 8. Votre fille s'est très mal conduite en classe de philosophie. 9. C'est tant pis pour elle. 10. Cet article-ci coûte moins cher que celui-là. 11. Ils nous ont fait garer la voiture derrière. 12. On nous a servi le repas dehors. 13. Ma fille a déjà son bac.

121. 1. voyageons 2. commençons 3. essaie 4. essuie 5. menace 6. mangeons 7. s'avancent 8. déménagez 9. emménageons 10. s'ennuient

122. 1. s'appelle 2. achetons 3. jettent 4. gèle 5. emmenez 6. préfère 7. espérons 8. exagérez 9. cède 10. règle

123. 1. finissez 2. choisissons 3. remplis 4. fournissent 5. vieillissons 6. blanchissent 7. rougissent 8. noircit 9. ralentis 10. retentissent

124. 1. réponds 2. Entendez 3. attendons 4. descend 5. dépend 6. rendent 7. vendent 8. tends 9. répand 10. s'étend

125. 1. Oui, téléphonez-lui. 2. Oui, commencez-les la semaine prochaine. 3. Non, ne leur écrivez pas. 4. Non, ne le lui envoyez pas. 5. Oui, rendez-le-moi.

126. 1. de, ___ 2. ___, ___ 3. de, de 4. à 5. de, ___ 6. de, ___ 7. à, ___ 8. d', de 9. au, de 10. de, d'

127. 1. vivions, allions 2. j'ai été blessé 3. j'étais 4. attendions, avons vu 5. J'étais, j'ai entendu 6. allaient, ont reçu 7. venions, s'amusaient 8. avez fait, avez visité 9. a gagné, faisait, représentait 10. voulais, j'ai voulu, m'a dit, ne pouvais pas

128. 1. sonnera 2. irons 3. verras (auras vu) 4. n'aurez pas payé 5. entrera (sera entré) 6. aurons fait 7. seront 8. j'aurai passé 9. fais 10. iras

129. 1. j'achèterais 2. j'irais 3. voudrions 4. pourrions 5. aurais 6. devriez 7. m'enverrais 8. ferais 9. renouvellerions 10. sauraient

130. 1. aurions aimé 2. aurait accompagné(e)s 3. auriez dû 4. aurions pris 5. aurait pu 6. auraient voulu 7. auriez fait 8. j'aurais demandé 9. aurais eu 10. serait allé

131. 1. avait perdu 2. avait pu 3. avait eu 4. avait dû 5. avait offert 6. préférait 7. sentait, n'avait pas mis 8. savait, devait 9. était, se doutait 10. sentait, avait mis

132. 1. vient 2. ouvriez, soit 3. finisse 4. va 5. avez 6. prenne 7. puisse 8. remplisses 9. fassiez 10. devienne

133. 1. revenions 2. sont 3. est 4. regardez 5. ait 6. préfériez 7. fais 8. soit 9. sachent 10. soyons

134. 1. sait 2. puisse 3. devions 4. entend, peut 5. puisse, peut 6. ayons jamais mangé 7. choisissons (avons choisi) 8. a 9. veuille 10. connaisse (j'aie connu)

135. 1. reprendre 2. apercevoir 3. lorgner 4. faire 5. être 6. apprendre 7. vouloir 8. menacer 9. conclure 10. appartenir

136. 1. en tombant dans l'escalier 2. En réfléchissant 3. en essayant d'aller trop vite 4. en avouant sa faute 5. en sautant de l'escalier roulant 6. En refusant de payer le supplément 7. En arrivant 8. tout en regardant la télévision 9. En entrant 10. en refusant de céder